An Introduction to Unreal Engine 4

An Introduction to

Unreal Engine 4

Andrew Sanders

CRC Press is an imprint of the
Taylor & Francis Group, an **informa** business
AN A K PETERS BOOK

CRC Press
Taylor & Francis Group
6000 Broken Sound Parkway NW, Suite 300
Boca Raton, FL 33487-2742

Printed on acid-free paper
Version Date: 20160802

International Standard Book Number-13: 978-1-4987-6509-1 (Paperback)

Visit the Taylor & Francis Web site at
http://www.taylorandfrancis.com

and the CRC Press Web site at
http://www.crcpress.com

Printed and bound in the United States of America by Sheridan

Contents

Introduction ix

Who This Book Is For xi

Author xiii

1 Project Type Selection and Start-Up 1

Exploring the Unreal Launcher 1
Choosing a Project Type and Location 2
An Overview of the Unreal Engine 4's User Interface 4
A Look at the Tab System 4
Chapter Review 8

2 An Overview of the Level Design Process 9

Introduction 9
The Conceptual Design of Levels 9
The Suggested Work Flow of Level Design 10
The Process of Creating a Level in UE4 11
Chapter Review 13

3 Blocking Your First Level 15

Introduction 15
Exploring the Modes Panel Focusing on BSPs 16
Using BSPs to Build the Foundation 16
Chapter Challenge 20
Continuing to Block Out Your Level 20
Play-Testing the Level 22
Using Geometry Editing Mode 24
Chapter Challenge 31
Chapter Review 32

4 Finishing the Blocking of Your Level 33

Introduction 33
Extend the Blocking Done in the Previous Chapter 33
Continuing to Block the Level 38

Cleaning Up the Level 47
Importing Assets into Unreal 47
Creating Your First Blueprint 50
Exploring the Swapping Process 52
Chapter Challenge 56
Creating Your Initial Materials 56
Adding Your First Point Light 60
Chapter Challenge 62
Chapter Review 62

5 Exploring Blueprints 63

Introduction 63
Creating the Hallway Blueprints 63
Chapter Challenge 73
Adding Hallway Blueprints to the Level 73
Using Layers to Group Objects 78
Chapter Challenge 87
Error Checking through Play-Testing 88
Modifying Your Blueprints and Adding Doorframes 89
Correcting Collisions 92
Chapter Review 99

6 Materials 101

Introduction 101
Textures versus Materials 101
Material Types 102
Input Types 103
Adding Textures 104
Modifying Channels 109
Chapter Challenge 110
Chapter Review 115

7 Lighting Concepts 117

Introduction 117
Common Lighting Techniques 117
Lightmass Importance Volumes 118
Reflection Nodes 119
Toggleable Lighting 122
Chapter Challenge 131
Chapter Review 131

8 Blueprint Animation 133

Introduction 133
Creating Automatic Doors 133
Matinee 156
Chapter Challenge 164
Chapter Review 164

9 Populating Your Level 165

Introduction 165
Importing the Rest of Your Objects 165

Creating Time-Based Materials 169
Creating Layered Materials 172
Adding Actors 181
Chapter Challenge 184
Adding Physics to an Actor 189
Chapter Challenge 192
Chapter Review 192

10 Particle Systems 193

Introduction 193
Overview of Cascade 193
Emitters 196
Curve Editor 202
Chapter Review 203

11 Advanced Blueprint Techniques 205

Introduction 205
Using Blueprints to Create Custom Length Hallways 205
Chapter Challenge 224
Changing Colors during Runtime 224
Interacting with Blueprints 228
Chapter Review 232

12 Working with Landscapes 233

Introduction 233
Creating and Working with Landscapes 233
Importing Landscapes 235
Building a Landscape 235
Chapter Challenge 238
Painting on Landscapes 239
Adding Water 246
Adding Foliage 248
Chapter Challenge 250
Chapter Review 250

Index 251

Introduction

Unreal Engine was created in 1998 with the advent of the first-person shooter *Unreal*. This version of the Unreal Engine combined a number of systems, including rendering, collision detection, AI, visibility, networking, scripting, and file management. The Glide API at the core was specifically developed for 3dfx GPUs. Unreal Tournament followed Unreal and made great strides to improve rendering and network performance. The Unreal Engine became largely popular because of the modular design of the engine's architecture and the inclusion of a scripting language called UnrealScript. Based largely on C++, UnrealScript allowed users to create modifications easily.

In 2002, the second version of Unreal Engine debuted with the release of the America's Army video game. This version of the engine was largely a rewritten version, recreating the core code and rendering engines. This also marked the release of UnrealEd 2. The second version of Unreal Engine added support for the GameCube and Xbox.

Unreal Engine 3's first publicly released screenshots appeared in 2004. Even though this new version of the engine had only been in development for 18 months, it marked significant changes including a new lighting model that worked on a per-pixel basis rather than the prevertex method used in previous versions. This new lighting method allowed for the use of normal maps, along with high- and low-resolution textures. The previous versions of the engine required that the details be modeled directly; the use of maps allowed for a lower poly count while still maintaining a high level of detail. Unreal Engine 3 was also designed to use both DirectX and OpenGL, which expanded the available user base to include OS X, iOS, Android, Flash, Javascript, and HTML 5.

By 2009, the Unreal Development Kit (UDK) was released to the public. UDK marked the first freely available version of the engine. All previous versions of the engine were only available at significant costs. While games like Unreal Tournament and Gears of War had built-in editors, to create a new IP with Unreal, it would have to be purchased from Epic Games.

The most recent version of the engine, Unreal Engine 4, was released in 2014. This version marked some of the most significant changes to date. Key feature improvements include the removal of Kismet, a visual scripting system present in earlier versions, which was replaced by the much more user-friendly Blueprints system. The lighting system was again refreshed to use a new algorithm to reduce computational cost while improving overall quality. Unreal Engine 4's editor was reworked to improve the overall build time to help increase the speed at which game iterations could be processed. By reducing the amount of time needed to rebuild a game, the editor has drastically changed the speed at which modifications can be made.

Who This Book Is For

This book is designed to help introduce new users of the Unreal Engine to its many different built-in components, while giving users of previous engine versions a quick-access guide to the changes that have been made to this new version.

Author

Andrew Sanders is a technical artist. He graduated from Wayne Community College in 2012, focusing on 3D modeling and asset creation, level design, and texture art. After graduating, he returned to Wayne Community College as an adjunct instructor teaching 3D modeling and animation, along with level design using Unreal Engine. Mr. Sanders worked as a level designer at Figure 8 Technologies before moving on to work at Epic Games. Ultimately realizing the joy of teaching, he returned to teach the following year. He also went back to school to get a BS in computer information systems. This combination of courses gave him a perfect perspective to become a well-rounded technical artist. With the advent of Unreal Engine 4, an opportunity arose to create this book based on his method of teaching Unreal to his classes.

Project Type Selection and Start-Up

Exploring the Unreal Launcher

For the purposes of this book, we will be using Unreal Launcher, version 2.11, and Unreal Engine 4, version 4.11 (this should not be confused with version 4.1). When first opening Unreal, you will be presented with the Unreal Launcher. The Launcher is a quick-access hub to all of your projects, along with links to many other helpful tools. The launcher is broken into two sections. On the left is a navigation tab. The launch button is at the top and is highlighted in a light orange. On the right side of the launch button there is a down arrow that gives you access to all versions of Unreal currently installed. Below the launch button are some quick links to key elements in the launcher, which include community, learn, marketplace, and library. On the right-hand side, you have the info panel, which displays content based on the quick link you have selected. A quick glance at the following figure shows the current launcher version with the Learn link opened.

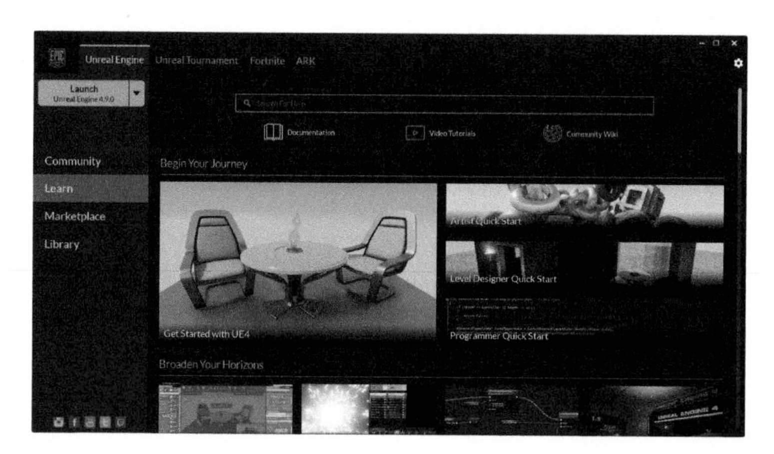

The community link has some of the most recent news regarding Unreal. This section frequently shows recent updates to the engine, any new events or programs, a spotlight section for recent projects, and a community blog. The learn link gives you access to a myriad of tutorials, videos, and examples—all to help further your education in Unreal Engine 4. The marketplace houses all created content that is currently available for download or purchase. Finally, the library link gives you access to all installed versions of the engine, along with access to any associated projects and downloaded content you may have.

Choosing a Project Type and Location

Once you have made your way through the different sections of the Launcher, it is time to begin. Using the dropdown arrow beside the Launch button, choose Unreal Engine 4.11 and click Launch. The Unreal Project Browser window will open, giving you access to two main tabs, Projects and New Project. The Projects tab allows you to access any projects currently associated with Unreal on your computer. It will also show you what version of the engine the project is currently associated with if it is not the currently open version, by displaying the version number in the lower right corner of the thumbnail image.

The New Project tab gives you access to two main types: Blueprint and C++. This book will focus on using the Blueprint versions. The C++ versions require a compiler like Visual Studios to create and build projects. With the Blueprint tab selected, you should have a view similar to the figure below.

There are a number of different types of projects available in Unreal Engine 4. The following is a list of each type along with a brief description.

- **Blank**—an empty project with no established player
- **First person**—a project that contains a first-person player, camera, and controller
- **Flying**—a project that contains a flying ship, camera, and controller
- **Puzzle**—a project that does not have a specific player, but has a fixed camera
- **Rolling**—a physics-based rolling ball template
- **Side scroller**—a typical side-scroller template represented in 2.5D fashion
- **2D side scroller**—a side-scroller template in 2D
- **Third person**—a project that has a player with a camera positioned slightly above and behind the player
- **Top down**—a project that has a player with a camera that is above the player
- **Twin stick shooter**—a project that has a player with a camera that is almost directly above the player with two virtual joysticks used to control the characters' aim and movements
- **Vehicle**—a physics-based vehicle project with two camera views
- **Vehicle advanced**—an extension of the vehicle template with the addition of advanced physics suspensions

Each project has a specific game type and provides assets for that type, such as a player, player controller (used to move the player), and starting assets. For example, the First Person project gives you a first-person player and controller, while the Vehicle project gives you a car and its associate controller. The Blank project type does not supply any form of player or player controller. I recommend you take some time exploring each to get a better idea of how they work so that you will be better prepared to choose a starting template when working on your own. While it is possible to change project types after creation, knowing which one you want to use ahead of time will save you time and energy later on.

Below the game type section are the primary configuration settings. The first of these three is used to determine the target platform and has options for desktop/console and mobile/tablet. The second determines the rendering quality for the project and has options for maximum quality and scalable 3D or 2D. The final option determines if the starter content will be added to your project. The starter content contains a few sample objects and materials that can be used in any project you choose; however, if you choose not to add the starter content, you will not have access to any initial content. The final area of the project browser shows the path to where your content will be saved along with the project name. It is important to note that the name used here will be used in all the created files and cannot be changed later without extra work.

For the purposes of this book we will most commonly work in Third Person, as this mode gives you a better feel for scale while play-testing your level. Click on Third Person and use the following options:

- Desktop/console
- Maximum quality
- With starter content

Note: A project with the default starter content requires approximately 1 GB of space.

It is also good to note the current path so that you can find your project later. You can direct the path to a removable media device like an external hard drive or USB drive; however, you will have much better performance by saving the project to the computer's hard drive and copying it to your storage device after you have stopped working on your project. You can have any number of different projects on your computer, so make sure to use a name that is easy to identify later. (For this book we use the name **Learning_Unreal**.) After you have added all the necessary information, click on **Create Project** in the bottom right corner.

An Overview of the Unreal Engine 4's User Interface

A Look at the Tab System

You will be presented with the default layout of the Unreal Editor. The Unreal Editor deploys a tab-based system to help organize the Editor windows. This has a large benefit in comparison to other methods because it allows the user to adjust the layout in a manner that best suits individual preferences. The default arrangement of the tabs should by the same as shown in the following figure.

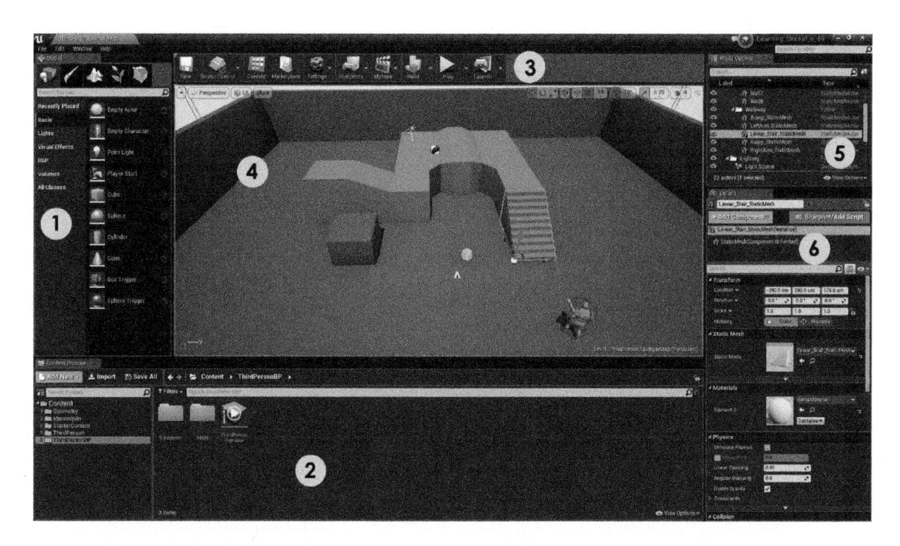

Looking at the figure above, you can see each section identified as follows:

- 1—Modes panel
- 2—Content browser
- 3—Toolbar
- 4—Viewport
- 5—World outliner
- 6—Details panel

Take a moment to explore the layout. Note that any tab here can be pulled away and placed in nearly any other section you choose. This allows the Editor to be tailored to the user's work flow needs. You may also notice that the toolbar and viewport 1 do not have a tab visible. If you click the triangle in the upper left corner, it will expose the tabs for those panels. Let us take a more in-depth look at the panels that are open when you first start Unreal.

Modes panel—This panel contains a number of useful features that you will constantly be working with. Starting at the top of this panel, there are five icons: Place, Paint, Landscape, Foliage, and Geometry Editing. You can cycle through using Shift + 1–5 or by clicking on the desired mode. Each mode contains a number of features and clicking on a mode will change the lower section of the panel.

Content browser—This panel contains a folder structure that reflects the folder structure of the current project. By default, Unreal creates a number of folders to help organize your project. You should have the following folders inside a content folder: Geometry, Mannequin, StarterContent, ThirdPerson, and ThirdPersonBP. Inside each folder you will find a series of folders and/or content. One thing I would like to point out now is that Unreal does not allow spaces in its naming conventions. If you look at the left-hand side of the content browser, you should notice that StarterContent is one word. If you were to attempt to create a new item using a space in the name, you will again see the red warning bar containing information about the error. Instead of attempting to use spaces, you can combine CamelCase (capitalizing the first letter of each word) and an underscore to separate the words—for example, Learning_Unreal.

Toolbar—The toolbar is a quick-access panel that has a short list of items that are commonly used throughout the level building process. We will cover each item more thoroughly as we progress through the book.

Viewport 1—This is the main window that will be used to work on a level. Within the viewport there are a number of different icons spread out across the top. On the left side, they are as follows:

- **Viewport options** contains the main option to control how content is displayed within the viewport. This menu contains an option for Realtime preview, Stats, and first person shooter, among others.
- **Camera options** contains available camera views, including perspective, top, bottom, left, right, front, and back.
- **View mode** contains the option to change how the viewport displays the scene. Options include Lit, Unlit, and Wireframe, along with additional visualization modes.
- **Show menu** contains a list of all types of objects that can be displayed.

On the right side are the following:

- **Manipulator** contains the three available manipulator types: move, rotate, and scale.
- **Space modifier** changes the manipulator between local and global.
- **Movement options** contains options for surface snapping, grid toggle, and snap size.
- **Rotate options** contains options for rotation snapping toggle and rotation snap size.
- **Scale options** contains options for scale snapping toggle and scale snap size.
- **Camera speed** adjusts how fast you can move through the level.
- **Maximize or restore viewport** toggles between different viewport setups.

The **Manipulator** is the gizmo used to adjust the position, rotation, and scale of an actor. The options for each gizmo allow you to adjust how and when an actor will snap to the grid. When using the Maximize or Restore Viewport button, the viewport will change from the single perspective view to a multiport view. When using multiport, the default views in a clockwise order are side, front, top, and perspective, as seen in the figure below. While in the multiport view, you will notice that each window has a single box in the upper right corner. Clicking on that box will maximize the selected viewport. Inside the Perspective window, click that box to restore it to full size.

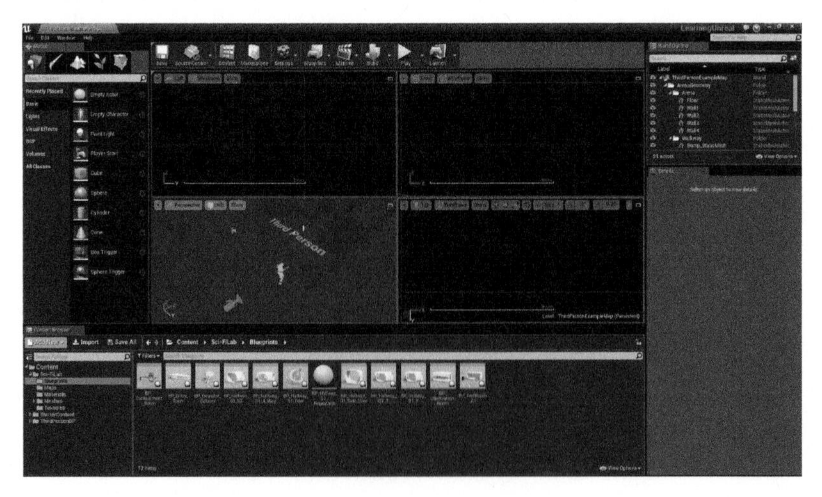

World outliner—The world outliner contains a list of all items in the current scene. You have the ability to toggle the visibility of each by clicking on the eye-shaped icon to the left of the name, as well as to create groups or folders to organize the outliner as needed. The world outliner also contains some limited information about the type of each object in the level, along with a total count of objects in the level.

Details tab—The details tab contains all the available properties of the selected object. It will also display any variables that have been added that are accessible to the public. A later chapter will discuss how to add new variables that you can then adjust using the details tab.

Another area of attention is the Editor Preferences window as seen in the figure below. The editor preferences can be accessed by selecting Edit→Editor Preferences.

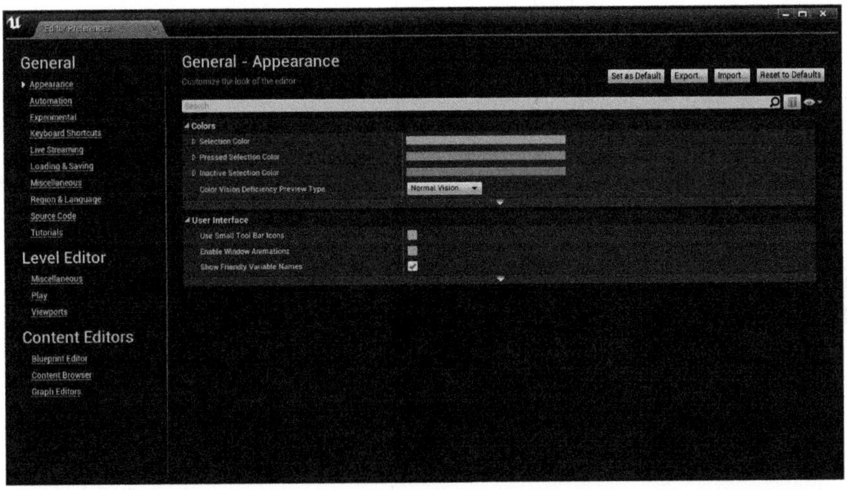

The Editor Preferences menu contains a number of options that will affect the overall view and experience of the Unreal Editor. The Editor Preferences menu has a number of options that I strongly suggest you look through. One of the most commonly sought options is the AutoSave option found under the Loading & Saving menu item.

Maneuvering the viewports—For those used to working in other 3D applications, the controls may seem a little odd. Using the left mouse button (LMB) and moving the mouse will turn the camera side to side or move forward and backward. Using the middle mouse button (MMB) and moving the mouse will pan the viewport in the direction the mouse is moving. The scroll wheel zooms in and out. And finally, using the right mouse button (RMB) and moving the mouse will turn the camera in the direction the mouse is moving. As you move through the level, you should notice that you can click on any object in the level and see its available properties displayed in the Details tab. Familiarize yourself with the layout of the Details tab, as it is a crucial part of the Editor. There are also three commonly used shortcuts as follows:

- W—move gizmo
- E—rotate gizmo
- R—scale gizmo

After you feel comfortable with the layout, you will run your very first play test. Make sure that you are in the Perspective window and it is maximized (click the square icon in the upper right if not). On the toolbar, click the Play button. This will launch the game in the currently selected viewport. The player will spawn in the middle of the level and you can now play. The movement keys are the standard WASD; the mouse controls the camera and the spacebar jumps. Run around in the level for a minute to get the feel of how the player reacts and moves. Since you will be spending a lot of time with this configuration, it is worth getting used to it now. Once you are done playing, you can hit Esc to exit and return to the edit mode.

Chapter Review

This chapter introduced the Unreal Launcher. You learned the basic method of creating a new project along with exploring the different project types. You were introduced to the editor and tabs system. You took a look at the viewport and some of the commonly used options. You learned some basic information about the other visible tabs and looked at changing the viewport view and maneuvering the viewports. You also played the default level and got more familiar with how to move around the level in a third-person Blueprint project. You also took a look at the Preferences window found under the Edit menu. You should be comfortable enough with the interface now to begin building your first level.

In the next chapter you will take an in-depth look at the recommended level design process. You will explore the recommended work flow for the entire level design process from conception through final creation and all the steps in between.

2

An Overview of the Level Design Process

Introduction

Since Unreal has been around for a quite a while now and has gone through a number of revisions, it is extremely well suited for both newcomers and experienced level designers. The team at *Epic Games* has worked long and hard to create an engine that is very flexible and lends itself to the design process.

The methods being used to create levels have also changed dramatically over the years. Here you will learn some recommended best practices to make level design both faster and more efficient. The techniques used here are by no means the only way to create levels, but they are methods that were developed throughout years of practice. Though the process has evolved along with tools over the years, there are still a few common rules that should be observed to help in the creation process.

The Conceptual Design of Levels

Most people have seen concept art associated with a game or movie. The conceptual design of a level can take many different forms. It can be a quick sketch, a brief description, or a complete set of blueprints. Some companies have been known to even create quick prototype versions in 3D programs like Google SketchUp to help get a better feel for the space of the level. The primary focus here is get a good idea of what you want to make and how you want it to look so that you are not guessing or just working blindly. A complete design is rarely necessary to begin working on a level, but planning ahead can certainly save you time later on.

In this book you will be building a futuristic sci-fi laboratory. For this book, all the conceptual designs have been done so that you can focus more on the creation aspect. You will be able to follow the measurements given, so you do not need to create drawings unless you wish to veer from the book. For this level, see the following two images for an idea of what you will be doing.

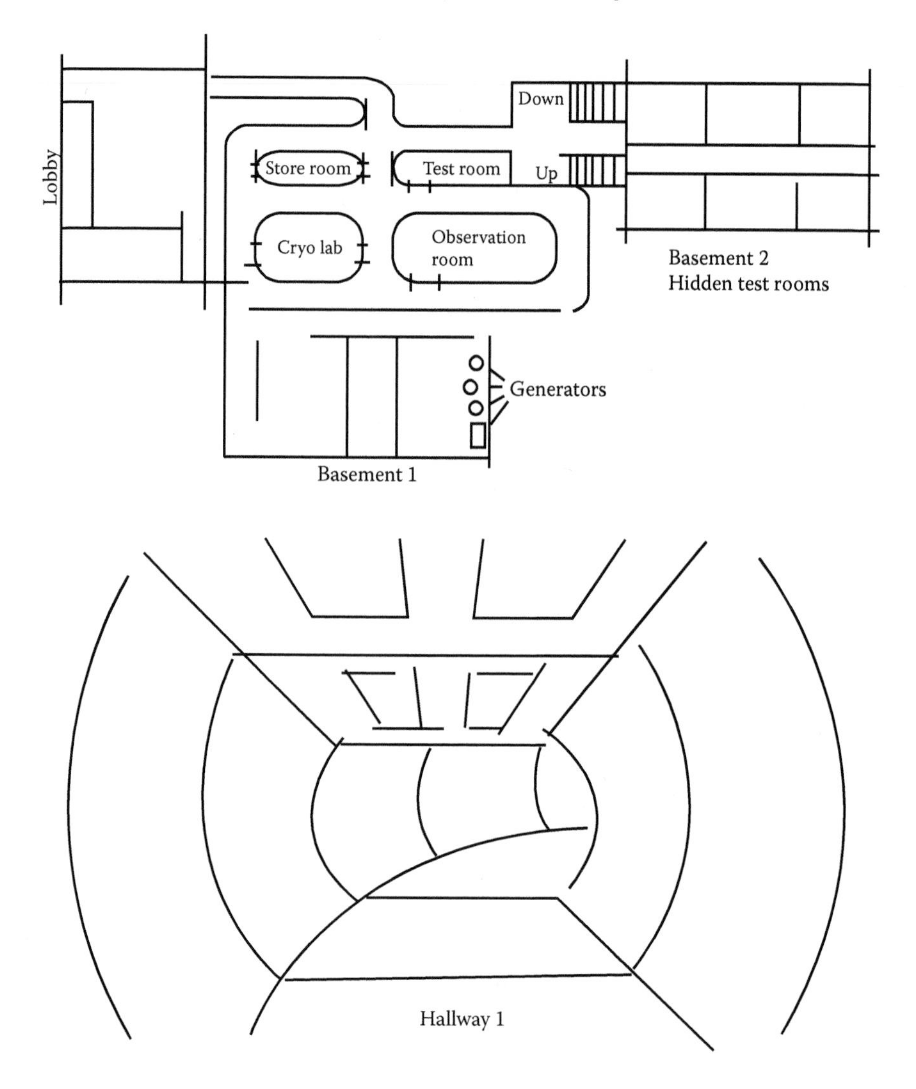

The Suggested Work Flow of Level Design

As mentioned earlier, there are some common rules that should be followed to help you be successful in creating levels on your own. While there are different reasons to stray from this path, for a beginner, the work flow you will use is a best practice designed to allow for play testing very early, which can be a very important key element in large or complex levels. Throughout this chapter, you will get an introduction to the tools used as you begin to build your first level.

Now that you have a basic idea of how the conceptual process works, let us talk about the process itself. Every level should start with some kind of conceptual design. As was discussed earlier, the concept can be in a number of different forms but the key element is always the same; to give you an idea of what you want the level to be. The second step in the process is called **blocking** and is the basic layout of the level using **binary space partitions** (BSPs) in place of assets. From this point your level is now testable and should be tested after each iteration. The third step is to add your assets into the level. This step allows you to replace BSPs with assets. Since the level has already been blocked out, you now know where the objects should go and what size they need to be. Again, your level should remain playable throughout this process. The fourth step in the process is to add lighting. Building the lighting requires both time and patience, so be prepared to spend a large amount of time tuning the lighting. The fifth step is to create atmosphere. This means adding things like fog and particles along with sounds and music. Finally, you will do some final detail iterations to help improve the game space. This means that you will do a final pass, adding or changing objects and lighting to fine-tune the level for final production along with a pass to fix bugs and address any feedback from testing.

One of the biggest issues facing a level designer in the past dealt with content creation. Oftentimes, level designers and 3D artists would be working on content at the same time. Since it was not always possible to stay in constant communication, issues would arise with the scale and placement of objects in the level. One way around this issue was for the level designer to wait for content to be created before starting on the level. Time is money, so having part of the team on hold can be a costly proposition.

This version of Unreal can allow the level designer to continually work on the level while the artist is creating the content, as well as allow them both to play-test constantly. Creating a level that is always playable is the primary focus here and should always be a key element when creating levels. By blocking out a level using BSP, the level designer can prototype a level to get scale and placement done very quickly. This serves two primary purposes. Having a playable level at all times limits much of the guess work involved and helps to eliminate the question of "if I do this, what will happen?" The second advantage here is that the content creators have specific dimensions they can use to create objects. Giving an artist the dimensions of an object before he or she starts can save a lot of time later on. Since the blocking of the level is already determined, many of these BSPs can stay in place by turning them into a **blocking volume**—an invisible cage that limits movement. You can think of this as a sort of bounds to sections of the level. You can place BSPs anywhere you want an object to be, using the scale you would like the object to be, and continue to play-test the level to ensure there are no conflicts. Once the object has been created, you can add it to the level in the location of the BSP and then change that BSP to a blocking volume, leaving only the object visible, while still maintaining the size and shape specified during blocking. As the shape and scope of a level increase, this fundamental change in the work flow of level creation becomes exponentially more important. When you add in the possible sheer size of levels that Unreal can create, knowing ahead of time that the spacing is correct can save many hours of testing and corrections later.

The Process of Creating a Level in UE4

Since you now have an understanding of what you should do, let us begin creating! The editor has opened a prebuilt level and you do not want to change that, so you should make a new level. In order to keep your project organized you need to create some folders first. In the content browser select Content. This should highlight the content folder on the left and show its contents on the right. On the right side, right-click and choose New Folder. Name the folder something appropriate to your project (in this example, the project is named Sci-FiLab, and that is the name I will use for my folder). Once you have named it, press enter. On the left side, click on your new folder. On the right side, again right-click, create a new folder, and name it Maps. This is where you save all your levels. The editor is designed to clean up on close, so any empty folders will be removed. Let us create the level now. Click on File and choose New Level. A new window will open with two options. You can choose default or empty level, as seen in the following figure.

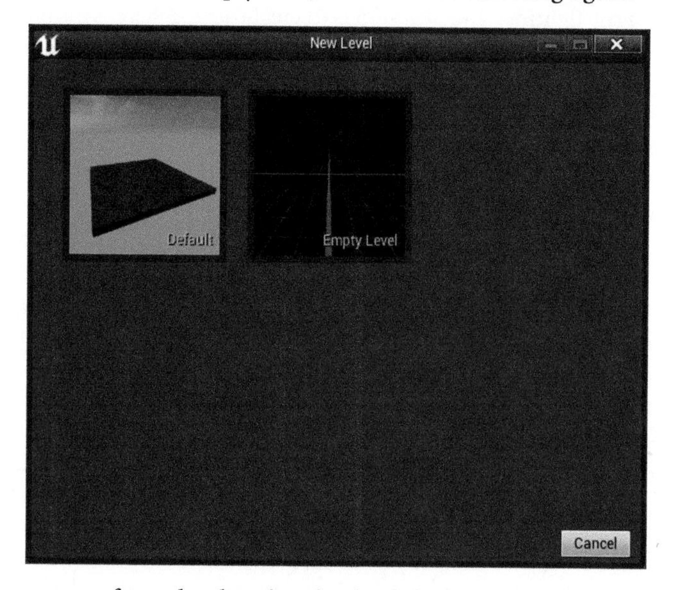

As you can see from the thumbnails, the default level has a few things like a sky and a starting point, while the empty level is empty. Choose default and the editor should open in a new level that looks like the thumbnail. Now you will name and save your level. Click on File and choose Save As. A new window like that in the figure below should open. Click on Maps inside your project folder. Give your level a name and then click Save.

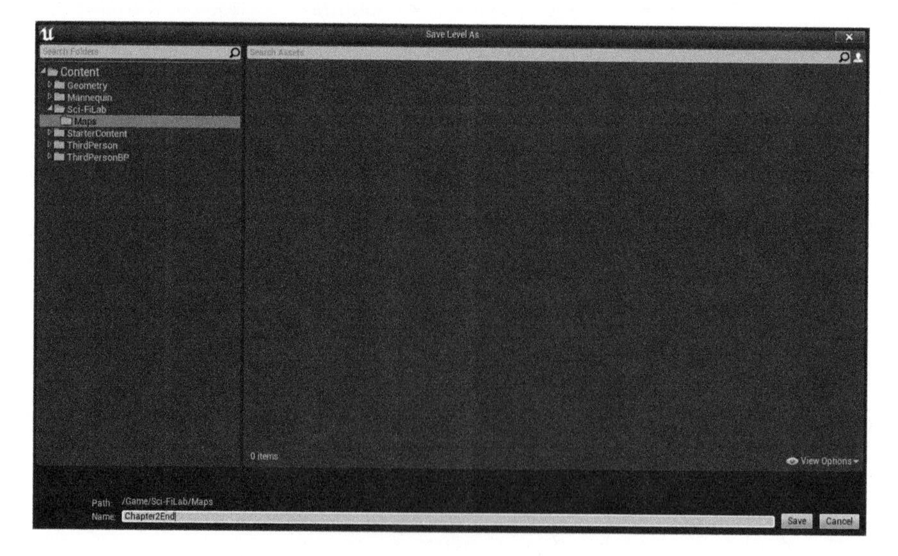

OK, so now you have a new project and a new level; however, if you were to close the editor and reopen it, you would go back to the original level rather than your level. You can change this in the Project Settings window located under the Edit menu. Select Maps & More in the left column and change the editor startup map to your level. See the figure below for the Project Settings window.

Note: If you are experimenting you may want to leave this as the default level instead of changing it in case there is an error in your map.

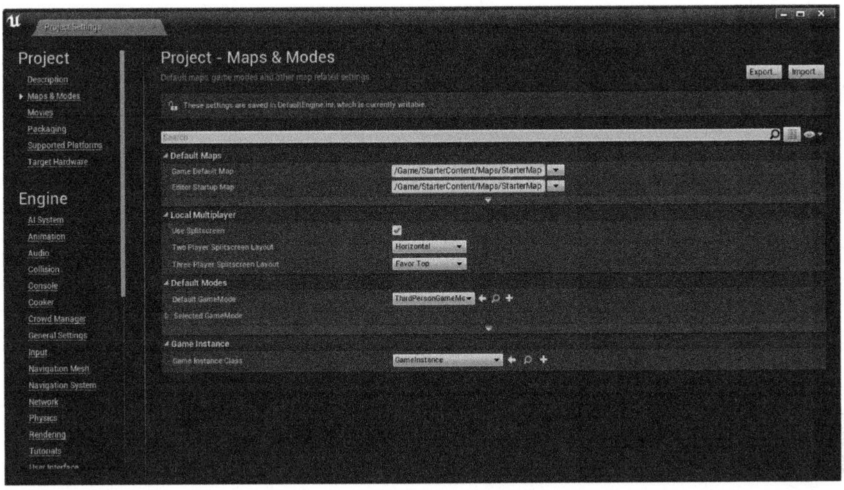

Note: While working on this level it is a good idea to save a copy with a new name. This will allow you to return to a previous version if any issues arise.

Chapter Review

In this chapter you took a look at the conceptual design elements used to generate an idea for a level. You looked at a suggested work flow design that will help to reduce the number of issues that could arise with spacing and scale of objects. You created a couple of new folders to help organize your project. You looked at the process of creating a new level. Finally, you looked at the Project Settings and explored how to change the default level for the editor.

3

Blocking Your First Level

Introduction

If you do not have a project open, follow the steps in the previous chapter to create a new project and level. Once you have your project open, be sure to open your newly created level before you continue. You should have your new level open as in the following figure.

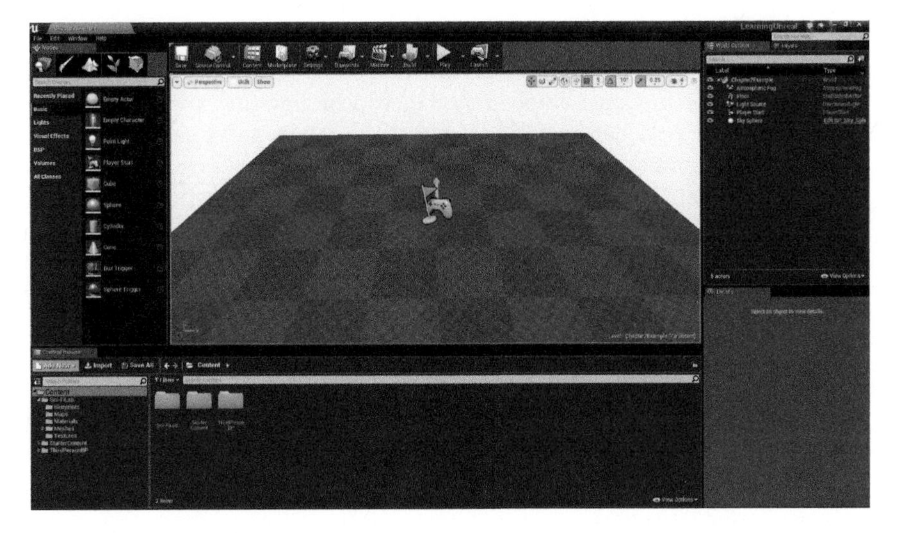

You can see a couple things going on here already. First, you have a **static mesh** for the ground. While this static mesh may appear similar to a BSP, it does not contain the same properties. You can use the Details tab to confirm the differences as you continue. You also have your sky and a player start (flag and controller). Right away, you can play this level if you would like, though there is not much to do aside from fall off the ground. Since we only want to work with BSPs right now, you need to remove the ground. You can select the ground in the viewport and then press the delete key to remove it.

Exploring the Modes Panel Focusing on BSPs

In the Modes tab, select the Place tab (the first icon). With Place selected, you have a number of different options available. A quick look at each of the sections will reveal a multitude of different options. Take a moment to familiarize yourself with the different sections. For now you will work with BSPs, so click on BSP on the left-hand side. See the figure below.

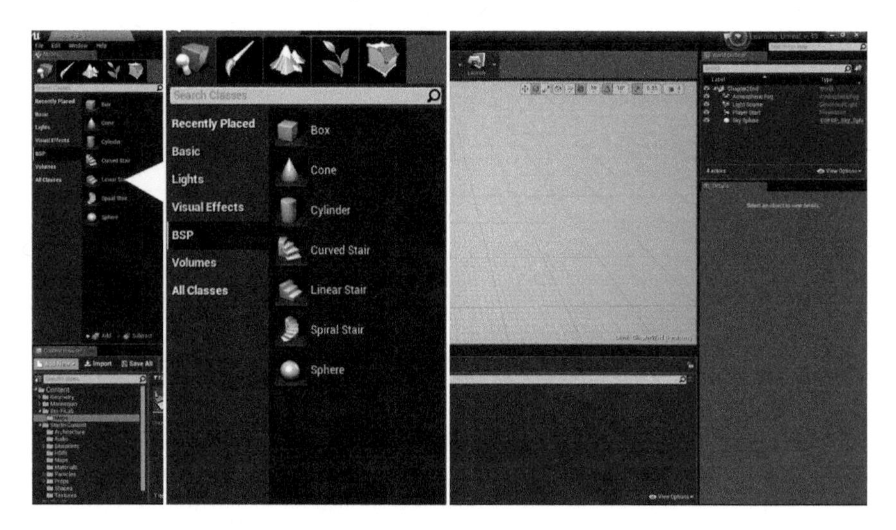

Using BSPs to Build the Foundation

Since you are going to be creating a ground and walls, you will start off with a box BSP. To place the first one, simply drag the box icon into the viewport. This will create the first block. You should notice that the details panel has changed and now there are a number of different options available. To set up your ground, you need to take a look at two different sections in the details panel. I would like to point out that you have two different ways to change the size of the box. First, you can adjust the size by using scale under the Transform section. Alternately, you can adjust the X, Y, and Z channels under the Brush Settings. While the overall effect is the same, using the Brush Settings will give a clearer picture of what is happening. Since you will want to convert many of the BSPs, you need to avoid using the scale options because they will always be reset to 1 when converting to blocking volumes, which will lead to alignment issues later on. This also makes it easier to keep track of modifications later. Modify the Brush Settings as follows:

- X—8000 (length)
- Y—3400 (width)
- Z—50 (height)

Change the location to

- X—44
- Y—(-2570)

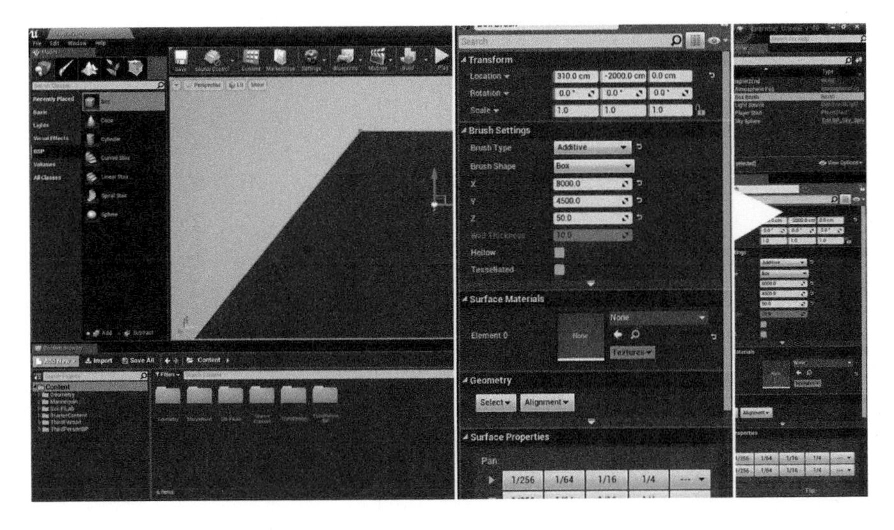

You should now have a rather large ground to start blocking out the level on. Now that you have a playable surface, you can take some time to adjust some of the default components to suit your needs. Let us start by taking a look at the Player Start. In the World Outliner, select the Player Start. Hover the mouse over the viewport and press the "F" key. This will "frame" the selected object in the Viewport.

As you can see in the figure above, the Player Start is partway through the floor. If you were to play-test now, the player would begin to fall indefinitely. You will need to move the Player Start upward so that it sits on top of the BSP. If you do not have the Move gizmo selected, press the "W" key. Click and drag the blue arrow of the Move gizmo upward to raise the location of the Player Start. If you should notice that, while dragging upward, the Player Start seems to skip, this is because of the snapping size currently being used. A quick look at the movement options indicates that snapping is on and is set to 10. This means that as you drag in any direction, you will snap to the next grid location that is 10 cm from the start location. You can change the snap size by clicking on the 10 to bring up a dropdown menu and selecting one of the options listed. If you move the Player Start up to approximately 90 cm in the Z (blue), a new label will appear on Player Start.

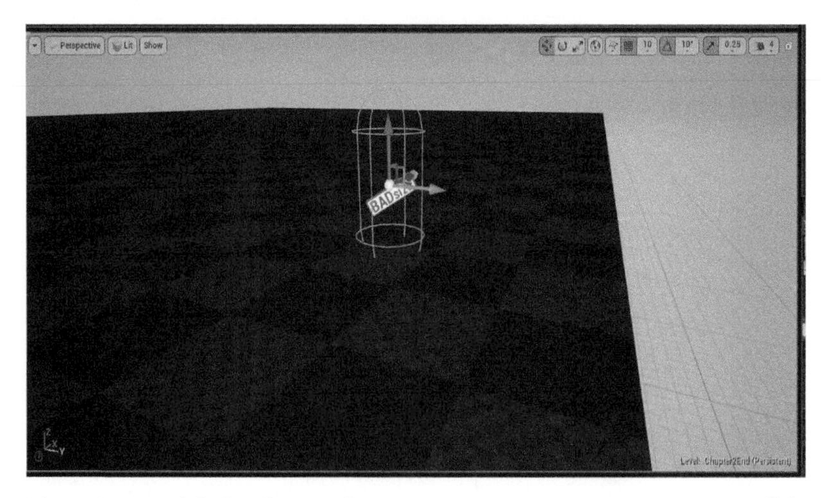

The BAD size label indicates that, at its current position, you may still have problems when starting. Continue to move the Player Start upward until the label disappears (120 cm).

Now that you have a valid starting point, you can take a look at the default lighting here. In the World Outliner, select Light Source and then frame in the viewport. While you can move the light around the scene, right now that will not have much of an effect on the level. This is because the light source is a directional light. A **directional light** is designed to project light in a set direction from a source that is infinitely far away. Because of this design, the light will affect all objects equally, casting all shadows in a parallel manner. This type of light is perfect for simulating a large light source like the sun. While moving the light does not exhibit any real change, rotating the light has a huge impact on the scene. See the following figure as a starting point.

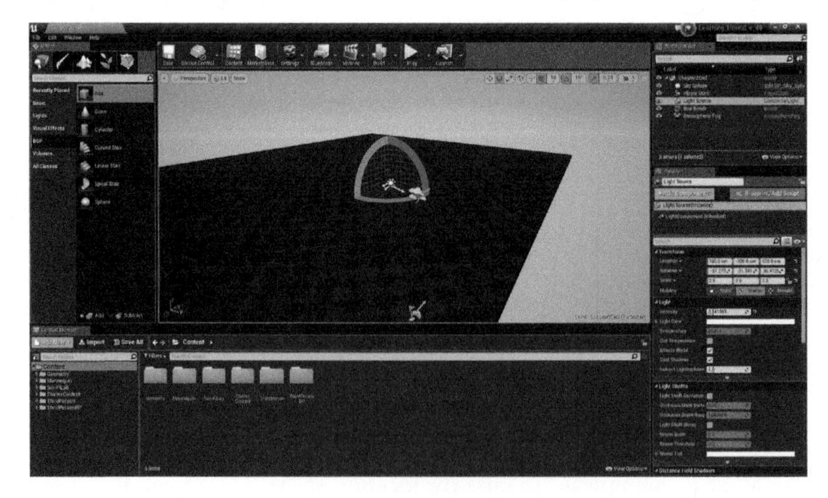

Now that you have an initial rotation, take some time to rotate the light around and see how it affects the scene. With the light selected, press "E" on the keyboard to select the Rotate gizmo. Similarly to the Move gizmo, the Rotate gizmo has three sections specified by the colors red (roll), green (pitch), and blue (yaw). Click and drag the red side upward, rotating the light to about –120 degrees. Notice that while rotating the light, you again have a snapping effect. Looking back at the rotation options, you can see that snapping is on, and the snap distance is 10 degrees. Once you reach the –120 degree rotation, release the gizmo and admire the new lighting, or lack thereof. Since the directional light's source is infinitely far away, and you have rotated the light to point upward, there is now very little light hitting the top of your platform. You should have a scene similar to that in the first figure below.

You may notice that even though you changed the direction of the light, the sky remained the same. The two are in fact linked, but require that a variable be changed in order to activate the connection. Select the Sky Sphere in World Outliner. In the Details tab, find the *Default* section. Under this section, the first entry is Refresh Material and has a checkbox to the right of it. Now you should have a scene similar to that in the second figure below.

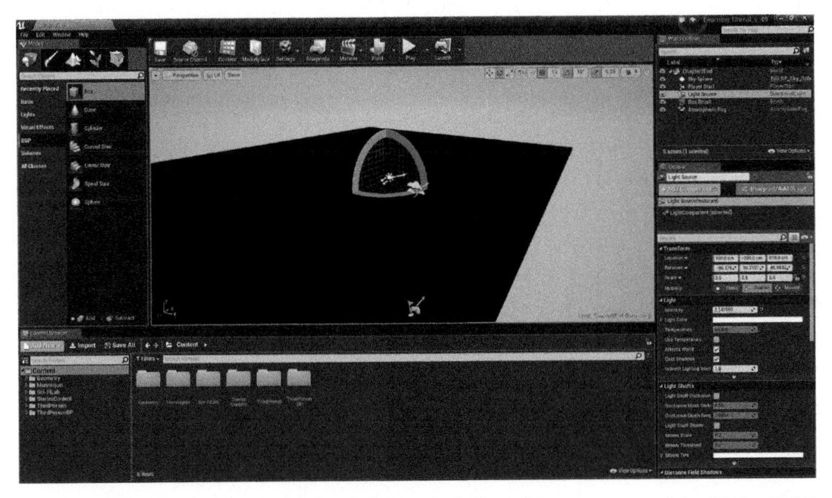

If you were to check the Refresh Material checkbox, you would tell the Editor to update the material on the Sky Sphere based on the light's direction.

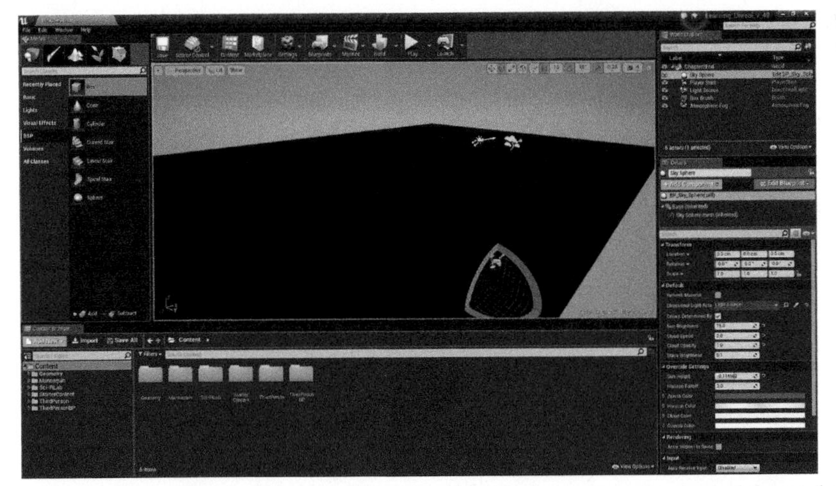

Since you now know how to update the Sky Sphere to the rotation of the Light Source, rotate the light again and update the Sky Sphere to see the changes.

Chapter Challenge

Using what you have learned, move the player to the center of the floor. Next rotate the light until the arrow points straight down, and then update the Sky Sphere. Play-test the level and explore your environment. This is what you will use as baseline. While you will cover assets in a later chapter, you do need something to show the changes in lighting. Browse to StarterContent→Props. Choose an object and add it to the level by clicking on it and then dragging it into the viewport. Add as many as you would like (keep in mind that they may need to be removed later). Adjust their size, rotation, and location as you desire. Once you feel good about the scene, play-test and look at the shadows and how the light affects the objects. Stop play-testing when satisfied, then rotate the light source, update the Sky Sphere, and then play-test again to see how the changes look. Once you have made some visual notes about the lighting, adjust the lighting so that everything appears well lit and easy to see.

Continuing to Block Out Your Level

Now you can block in a few walls. Sometimes, there will be instances where you want to copy objects in the viewport. This can be accomplished a few different ways. One of the more commonly known methods is to use the copy and paste commands. You can select the floor and press Ctrl + C to copy the object. Once an object has been copied, you can paste it by pressing Ctrl + V. This is a common method and works well; however, if you are like me, you want to do this in as few steps as possible. If the floor is not selected, do so now. Press the *Alt* key on the keyboard and drag your object in any direction. Now you have a copy of the floor. Adjust the dimensions of the copy to Brush Settings:

- X—50
- Y—1000
- Z—1000

Move the wall using the Transforms section to

- X—500
- Y—(-3750)
- Z—500

You should have something similar to the following image.

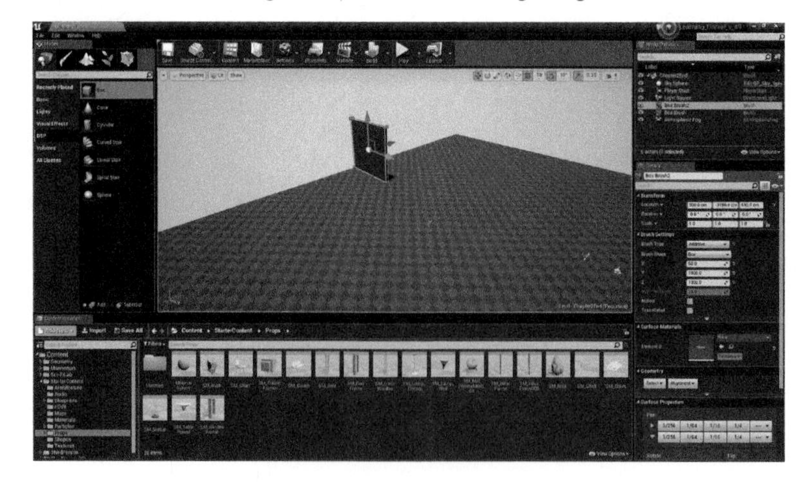

Duplicate this wall using the Alt drag method or the Ctrl + C, Ctrl + V method and move the new wall to

- X—(-300)

Repeat the process two more times, moving each one along the X, 800 cm at a time. You should end with something similar to what appears in the following figure.

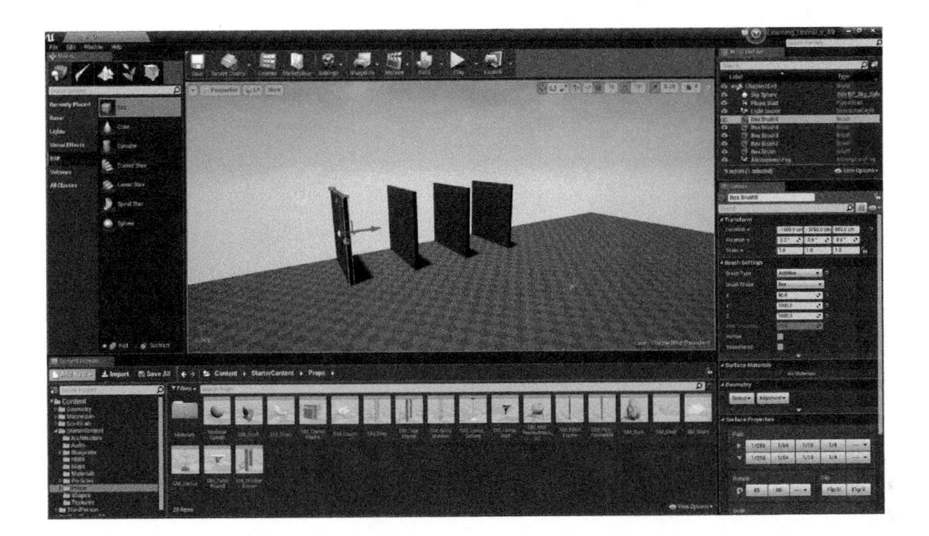

Next you need to add a wall to the back side of these walls. Duplicate one of the walls and set to the following dimensions:

- X—2400
- Y—50
- Z—1000

Position similarly to the way shown in the figure below.

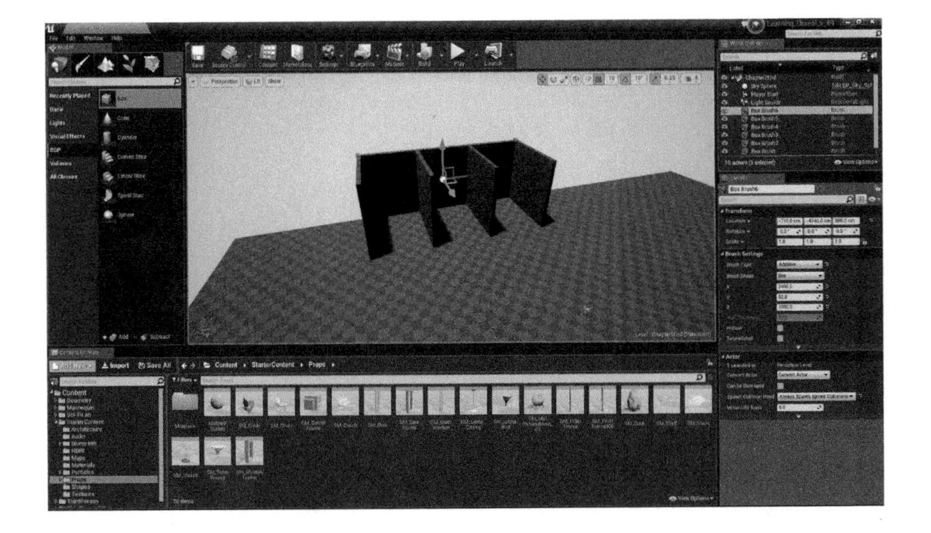

Play-Testing the Level

Play-testing the level now reveals that these walls are very tall in comparison to your player because you will be making a multistory structure here. In order for you to space out your second floor correctly, you will need to create a new type of BSP. In the Modes panel under the BSP menu, drag in Linear Stair. With the stairs selected, under the Brush Settings change Num Steps to 16. Use the Rotate gizmo by pressing the “E” key and rotate the stairs 180 degrees in the Z (blue).

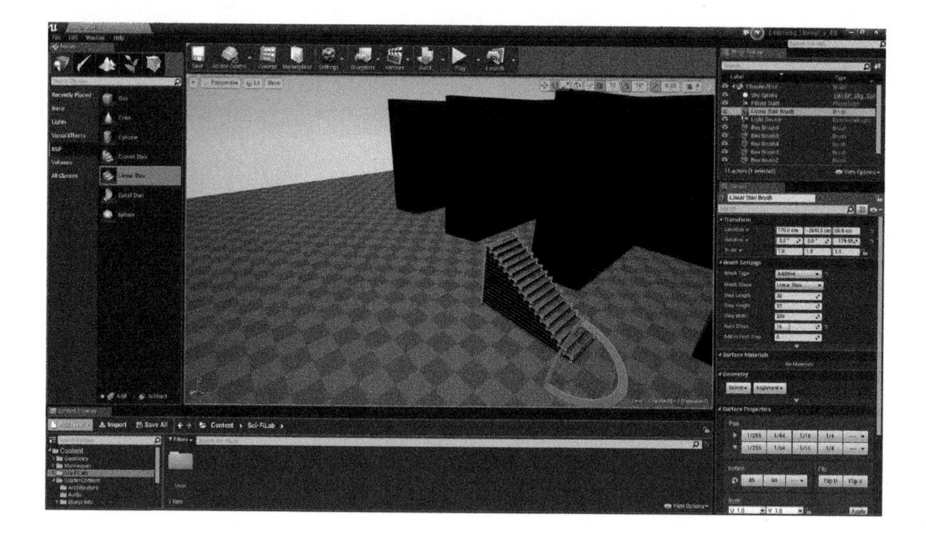

Once you have your stairs rotated correctly, you can move them into place using the following for location:

- X—300
- Y—(-2750)
- Z—45

If you are having an issue moving the stairs to the correct Z location, you can change the Movement Options snap size to 5 by clicking on the Movement Options snap grid size and selecting 5 from the dropdown menu.

Now that you have your stairs in place, you can add the second floor. Since the back wall is already the same length as your structure, it will be the easiest to modify. Create a copy of the wall and set to

- X—2400
- Y—1300
- Z—50

After you have the shape locked in, you can move the floor to align with the top of the stairs.

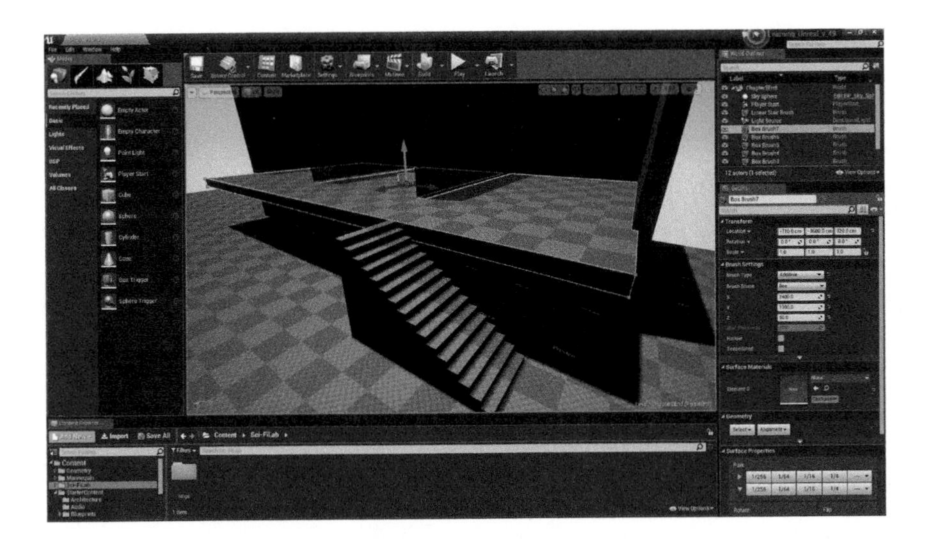

If you were to duplicate the stairs and move them up to give access to the third floor, you would run into a very interesting issue. As you can see in the figure below, you would have no way to use the lower set of stairs. There are a number of different solutions for this problem. You could build your own stairs by creating a single step and then duplicating and moving the step until you had created the whole set of stairs. You could also build a ramp out of a Box BSP. The first thing you need to do is add the BSP. Drag in a Box from the modes panel. You know that the step height was 20, so you can use this for the height of your new box by changing Z in the Brush settings to 20. Move the BSP down to the floor beside the stairs so that you have a good starting location.

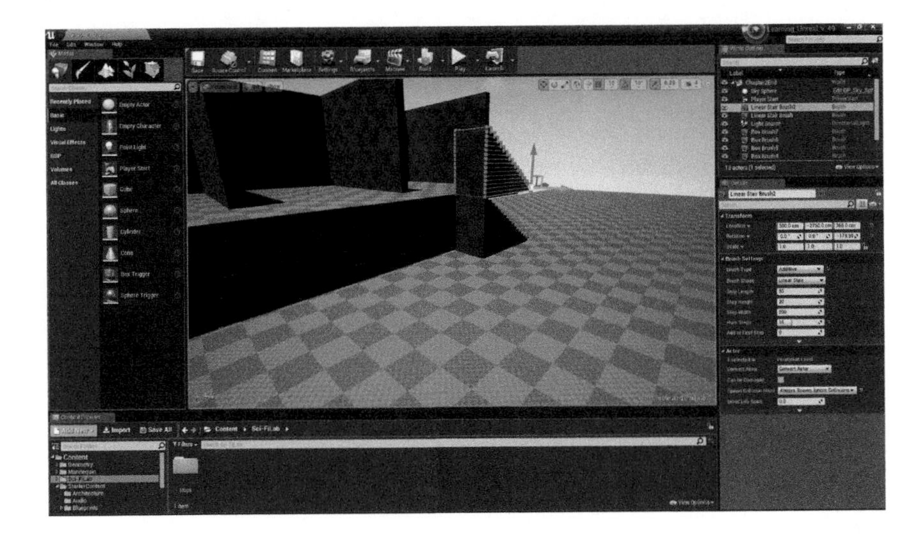

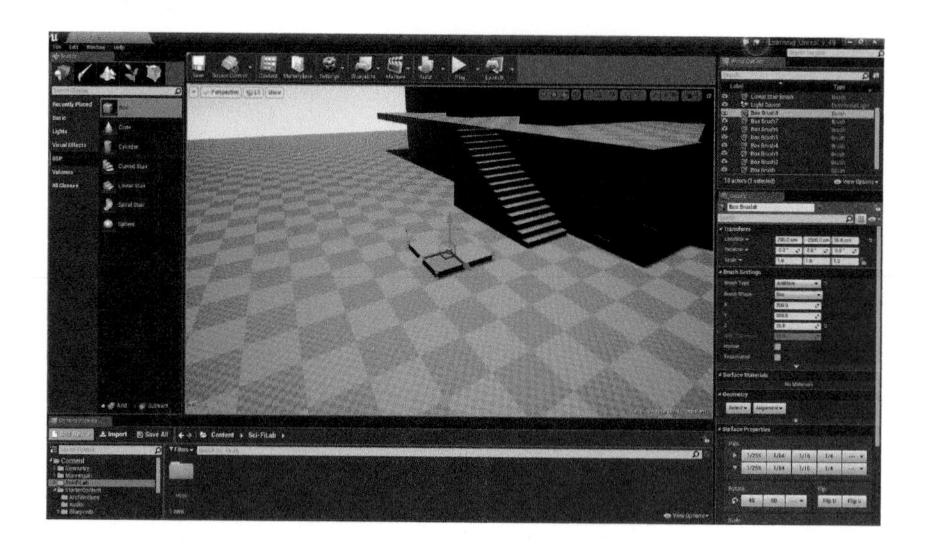

Using Geometry Editing Mode

In order to create a ramp, you can use the Geometry Editing mode. In the Modes panel, select the last icon to switch modes. **Geometry Editing** mode allows you to edit the shape of a BSP by moving edges, faces, or vertexes. You will start by selecting the back face of your box.

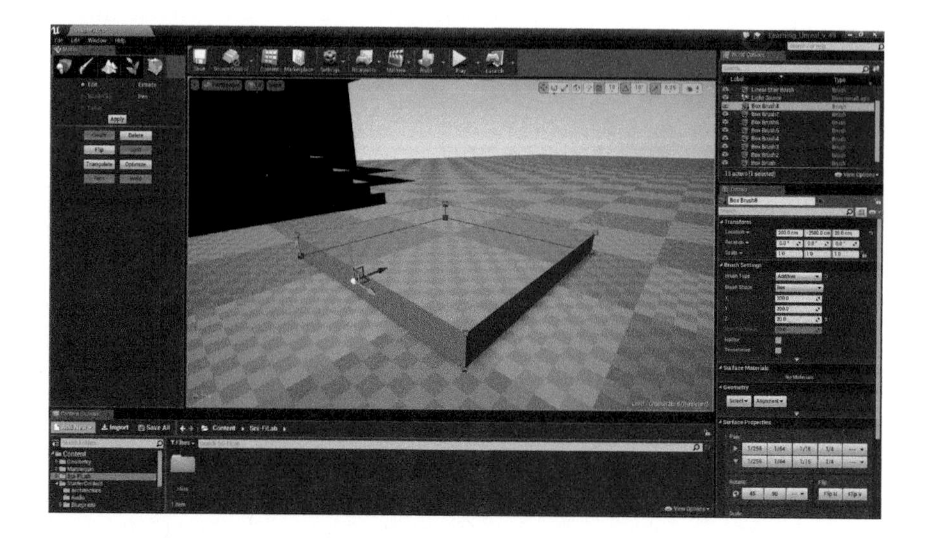

Once the face is selected, you can move it to adjust the shape of the box. You want to make sure that the ramp will be the same size as the stairs, so you will be switching views to make it easier to see where you need to move the face. Click on the Maximize or Restore button. You need to use the Front view here, so click on the Maximize or Restore button in the Front view.

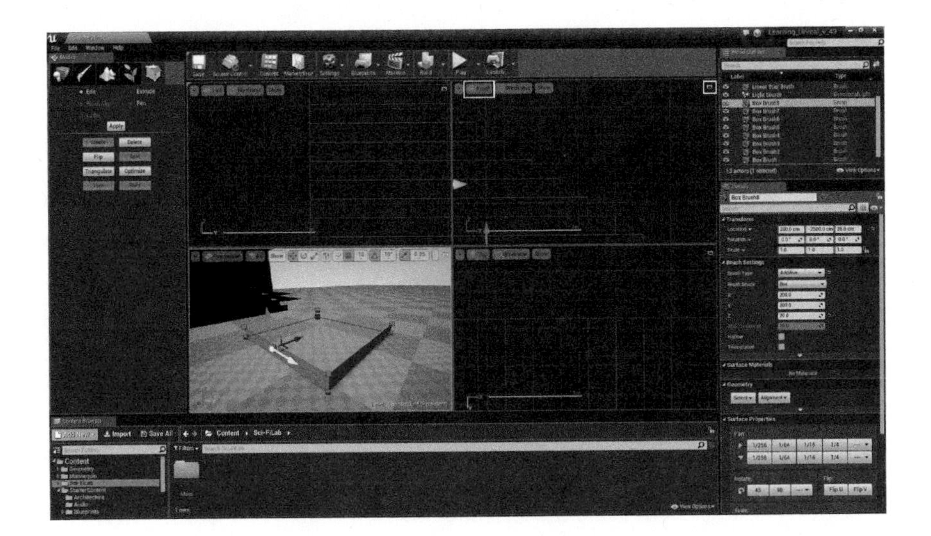

Now you can move the face up and to the left to align with the top step.

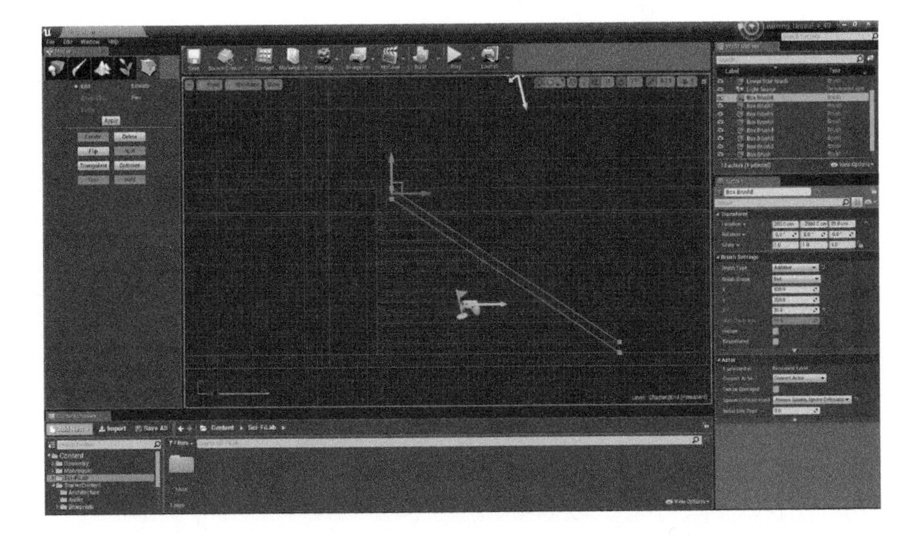

You can also use another function of the Geometry Editing mode here called **Extrude**, which will add a new section to the ramp based on what you have selected. With the face still selected, change the Geometry Editing mode to Extrude. You may receive a warning message that says Extrude only works with local coordinates systems. You can click the Close button and Unreal will automatically switch for you.

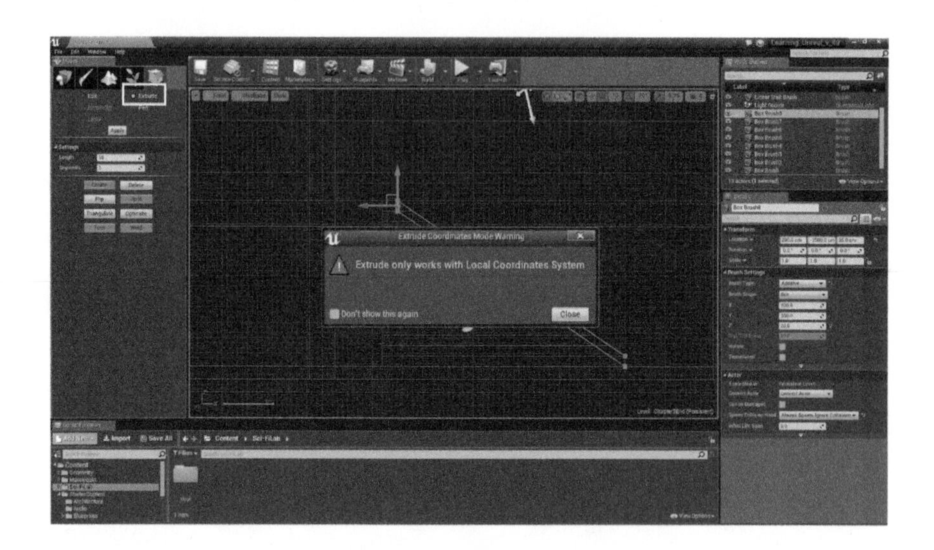

Drag the Movement gizmo to the left again to create a new section of the ramp. One thing to note about using the Extrude function is that, every time you release and then move the face again, it will extrude a new section—so be sure to switch back to Edit mode before making any other adjustments.

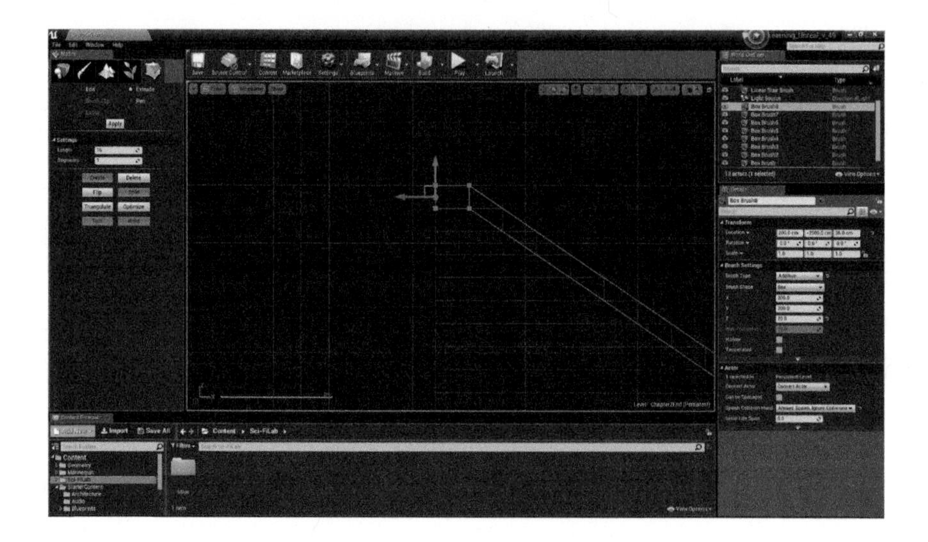

Switch back to the Perspective view to see your completed ramp. To exit Geometry Editing mode, click the Place mode icon. Be sure to return to World Coordinate System mode before continuing by clicking the icon seen in the following figure.

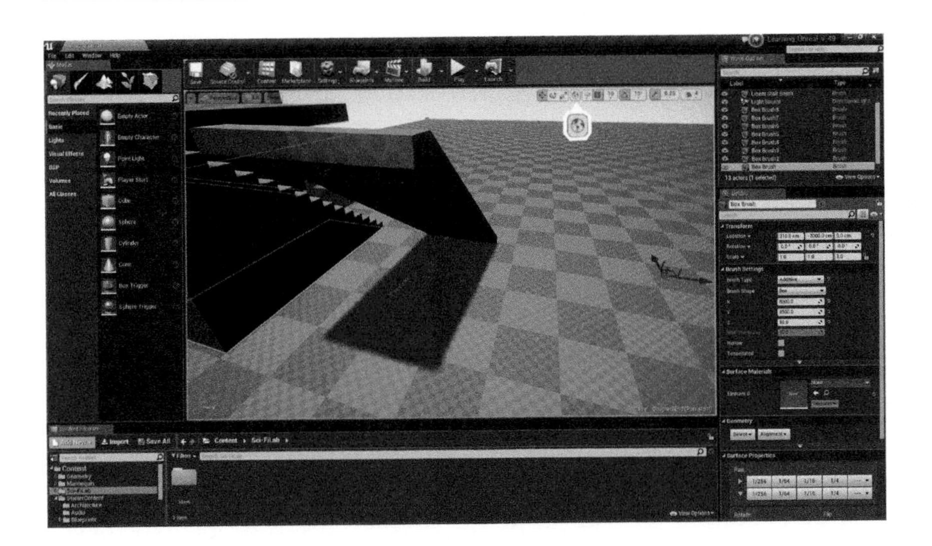

Now that you have your ramp completed, you can move it into place. Be sure that you have switched the Modes tab back to Place before trying to move your ramp. To place it in the same location as the stairs, you can use the Top view. Instead of using the Maximize or Restore button, you can use the Camera Options dropdown. Click on Perspective in the upper left and choose Top from the dropdown menu that appears.

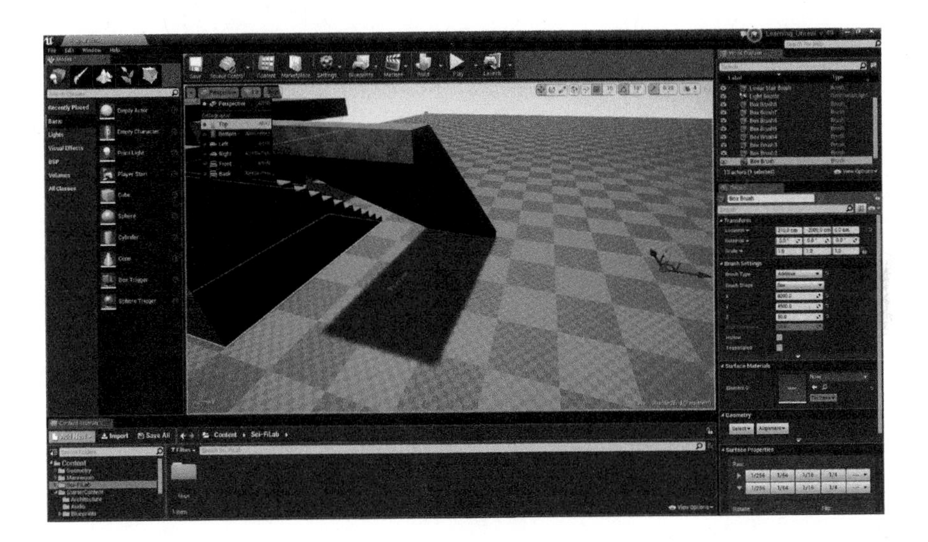

In the Top view, align the ramp with the stairs as seen in the following figure.

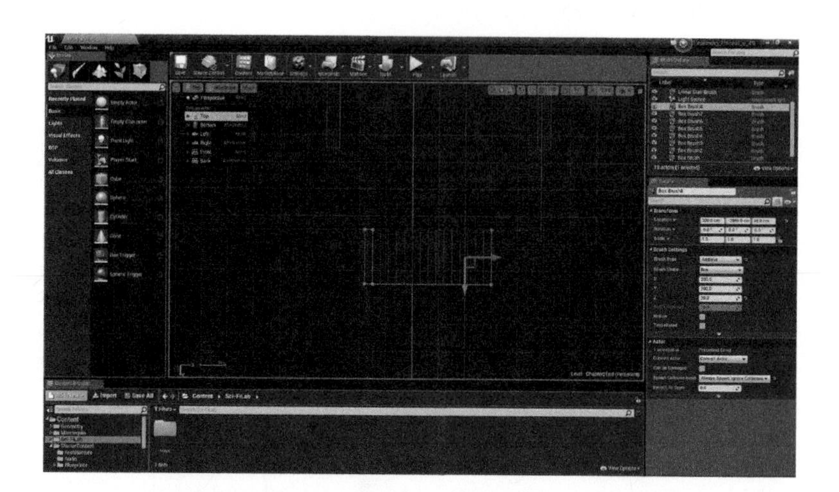

Now you can switch your view to Left and move the ramp upward. Align the bottom line of the ramp with the top of the stairs.

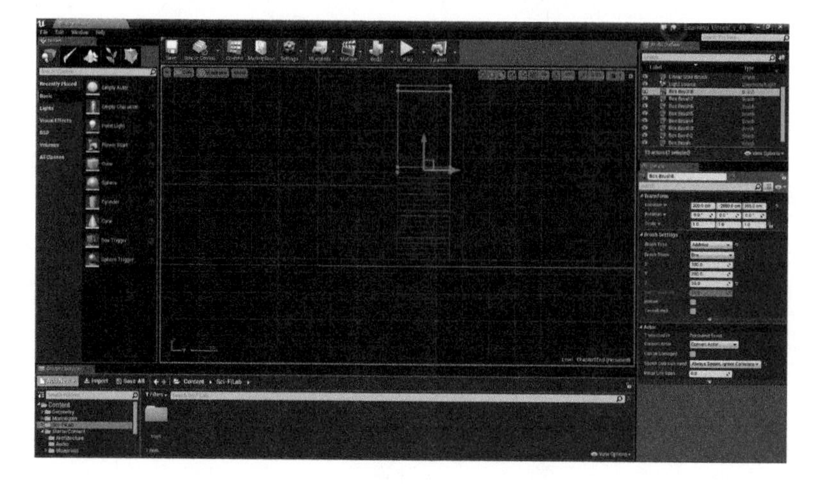

Once you are comfortable with the location, you can switch back to your Perspective view once again. You may need to adjust your lighting to see more clearly. When you are done, you should have something similar to the figure below.

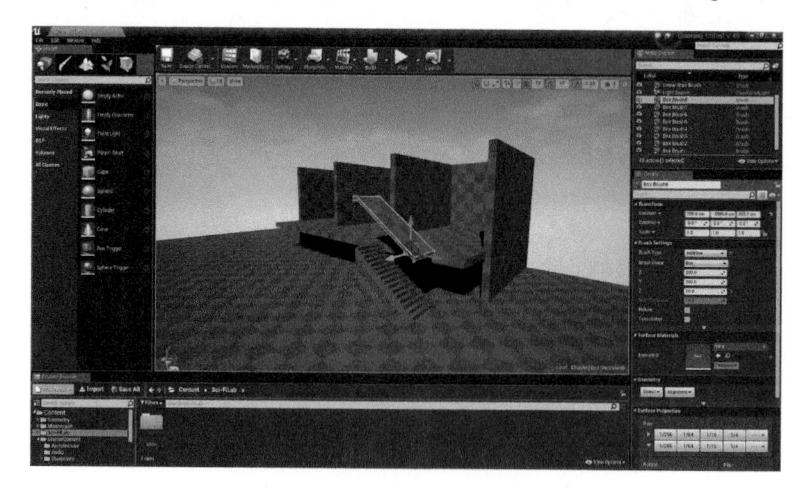

To add the third floor, you can duplicate the second floor and move it up to be even with the top of the ramp.

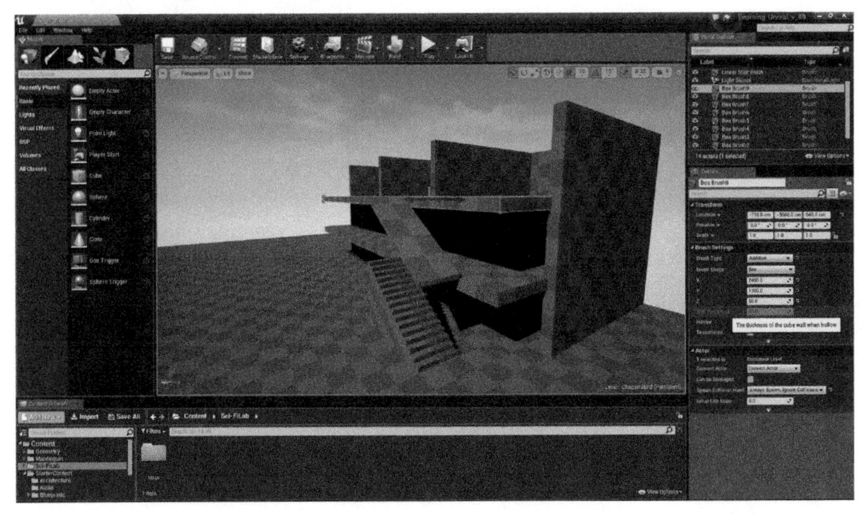

Before you add the roof, you can add a little more detail to the structure. Let us add some pillars at the end of each wall. The pillar dimensions I used are

- X—75
- Y—75
- Z—1000

By making the pillars slightly wider than the walls, you get a nice corner piece effect. Place the pillars similarly to those in the image below.

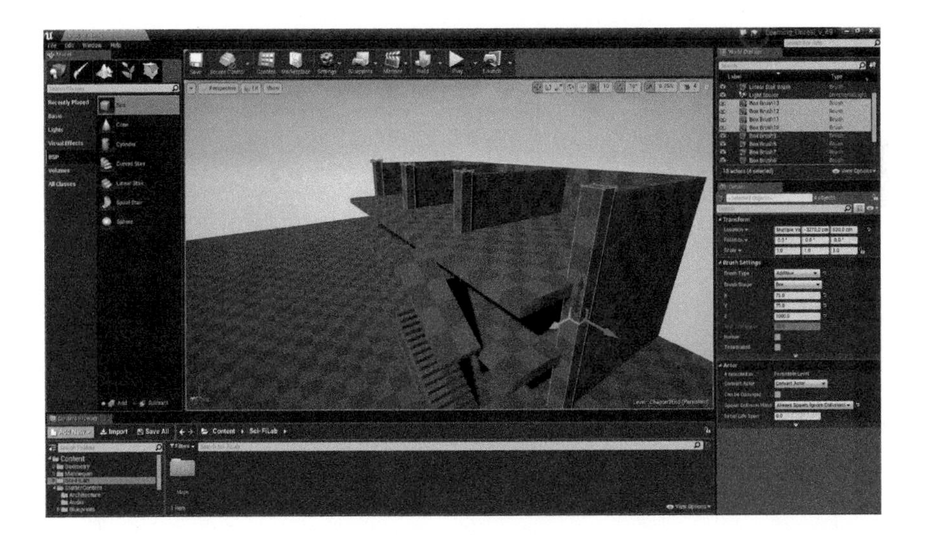

To add the front wall, you can duplicate the back wall and move to the front. To add the roof, you can duplicate the third floor and move up. Once you have added the front wall and roof, you should have a building similar to that seen in the following figure.

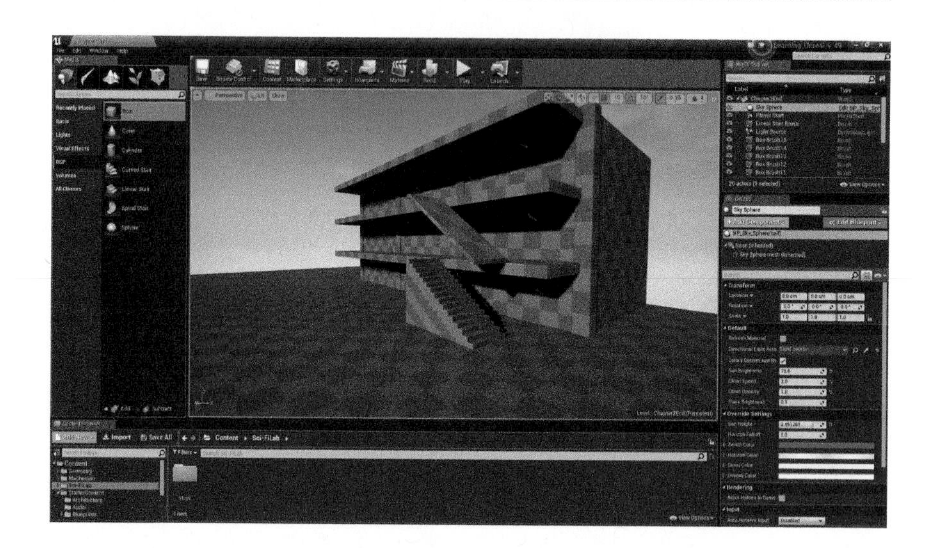

If you play-test now, you should notice the lack of access at the top of the stairs and the bottom and top of the ramp. You will build the balconies and base to clean up these access points. The balconies are made of three boxes and the base is made of one. Use the figure below to guide you. Create a new BSP with the following dimensions:

- X—500
- Y—300
- Z—50

Place this at the top of the stairs.

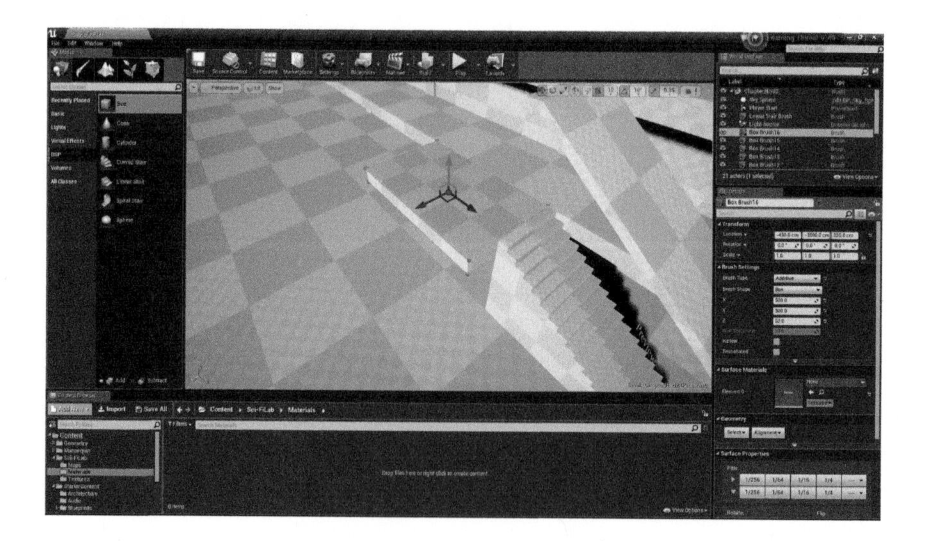

Duplicate the balcony floor and move to the end of the ramp, adjusting the size as needed.

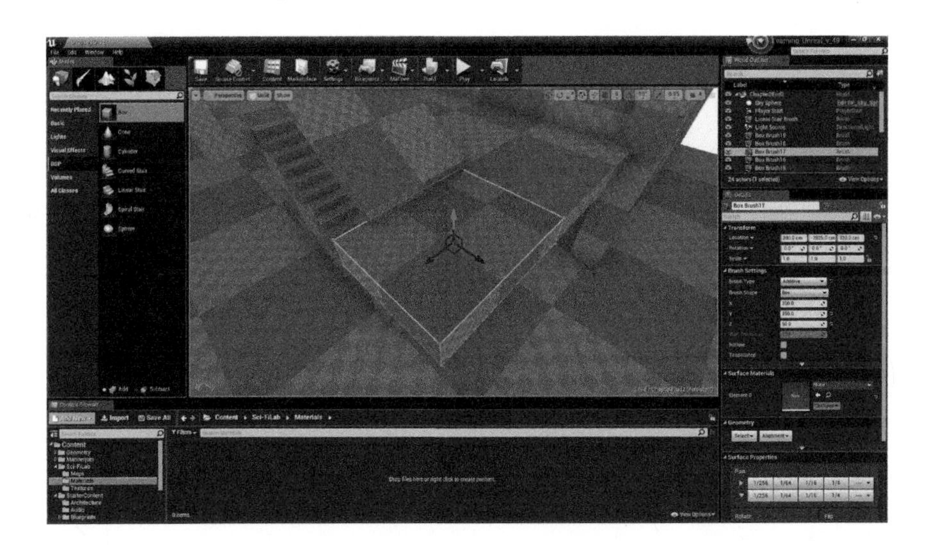

To finish out this section, create two small walls for the balcony. Once you have the balcony completed, you can select all three parts and copy them using either method mentioned earlier and then move them up to create the balcony for the third floor.

Chapter Challenge

Create a new level. Using all the steps you have learned so far, create a level that incorporates the following:

- At least two floors
- Stairs (linear and spiral)
- Cylinder (could be used as a center piece for the spiral stairs)

Using just these simple building blocks, create a fun level large enough to have at least one to two minutes of game play. Try creating a tower that has a staircase wrapping around it. You can use a cone for the point on the top of the tower. See how much of a castle you can build with what you have learned so far.

Chapter Review

In this chapter you learned how to add BSPs to your level. You used the Details tab to manipulate both the size and location of objects. You learned how to manipulate objects in the viewport and looked at switching views through two different methods. You used the Geometry Editing mode to change the shape of a box, creating a ramp. You learned how to adjust the default lighting to create different times of day and different angles of shadows. You also took a look at the player start and one issue that may arise when moving it.

Finishing the Blocking of Your Level

Introduction

In the previous chapter you started blocking out your level. In this chapter, you will finish blocking out your level and then explore how to add assets. After you have added some new assets to your game, you will begin looking at how you can add these new objects to your level while always keeping the level playable.

Extend the Blocking Done in the Previous Chapter

When you look back at your sketches, you can see a few more things that need to be added. First, in the area in which you made the first structure, you need to add some more walls along with a large block to encompass some detail pieces. After you have completed the lobby area, you will be free to create the hallways and basements that will house the remainder of the level.

In order to ensure that everyone is on the same page, if you have been following along so far, you can open your level. If you do not have this level, or if you wish to use the example map, you can open the Chapter4Start level found in the Chapter 4 Assets.

If you play-test your level now, everything should be easily accessed. However, there is one issue that remains: You cannot enter any of the rooms that you have created. In order to do this, you can add a BSP box and modify some settings to cut a hole in the wall where you would like the doors to be. Drag in a new box and set as follows:

- X—175
- Y—50
- Z—260

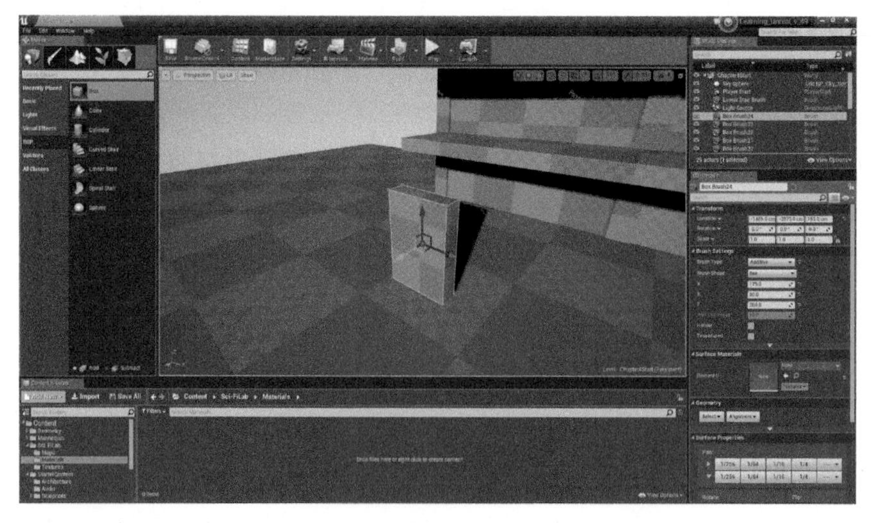

Now that you have the shape and size down, you can take a quick look at another option. In the Details tab under Brush Settings there is an option for Brush Type. There are two options for the Brush Type: **Additive** and **Subtractive**. Up to this point you have only used Additive. The additive type of brush adds to a level wherever it is placed. A subtractive brush works in the opposite way. Before you can subtract, you must have added something. To get a better handle on this, you can go ahead and switch the type.

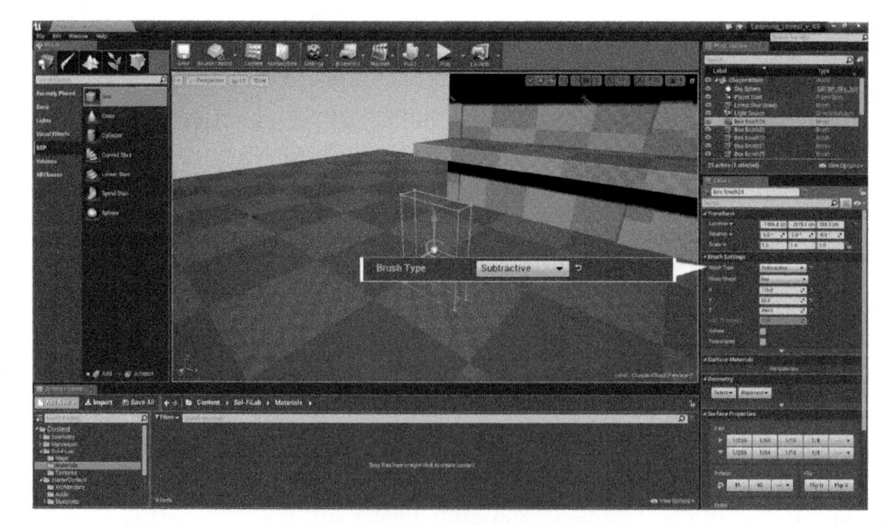

You should notice that the box is now transparent. If you were to click off the box, it would virtually disappear. This is because, at its present location, there is nothing to subtract from. Move the box over to the front wall of your structure and see what will happen.

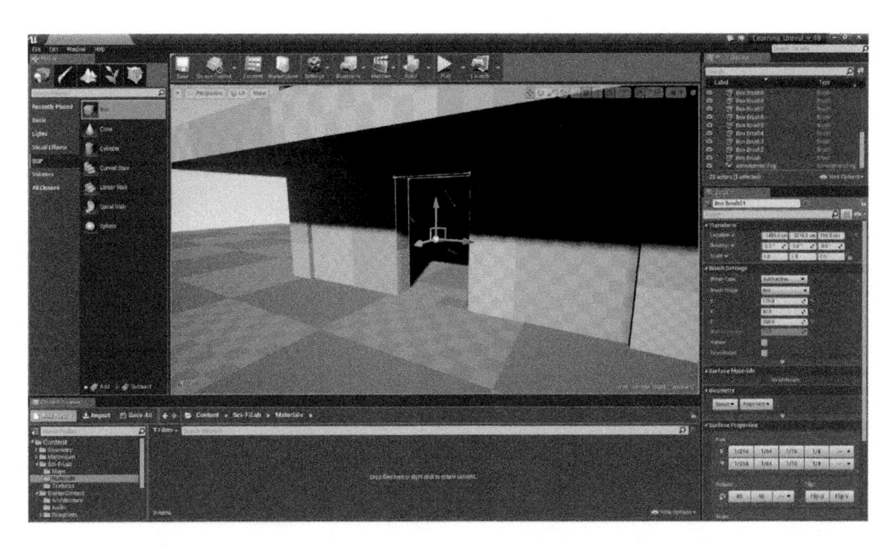

Now you have a doorway. When you overlap an additive BSP with the subtractive BSP, it cuts a hole in the wall, exposing the room behind. While you are looking at the subtractive brush you can view one more valuable option. **The BSP system works on a hierarchal system. The BSPs work based on the order they were added to the level.** This means that if you had added the subtractive BSP first, it would not have cut the doorway out of the additive BSP. The Order option allows you to change the order in which the brushes are built. The most recent one built will override any overlapping boxes. With the brush still selected, expand the arrow at the bottom of the Brush Settings and click on Order. There are two options here: To First and To Last. Choose To First and the hole will disappear, while choosing To Last will make it reappear. These options work by telling the engine that you want to move the BSP to either the first item placed or the last item placed. This will work on virtually any BSPs within the level.

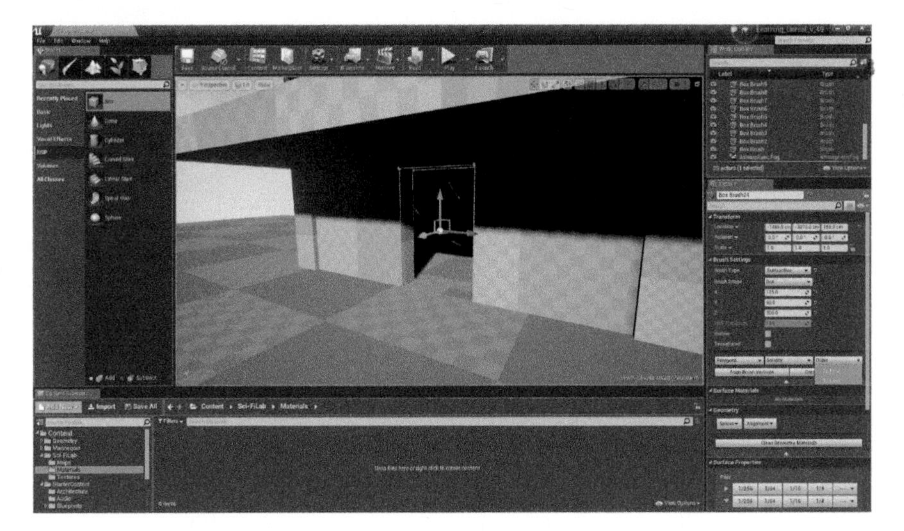

Duplicate the subtractive brush and move to the next room. Repeat the process, creating a doorway for each room. Use the following image as a guide.

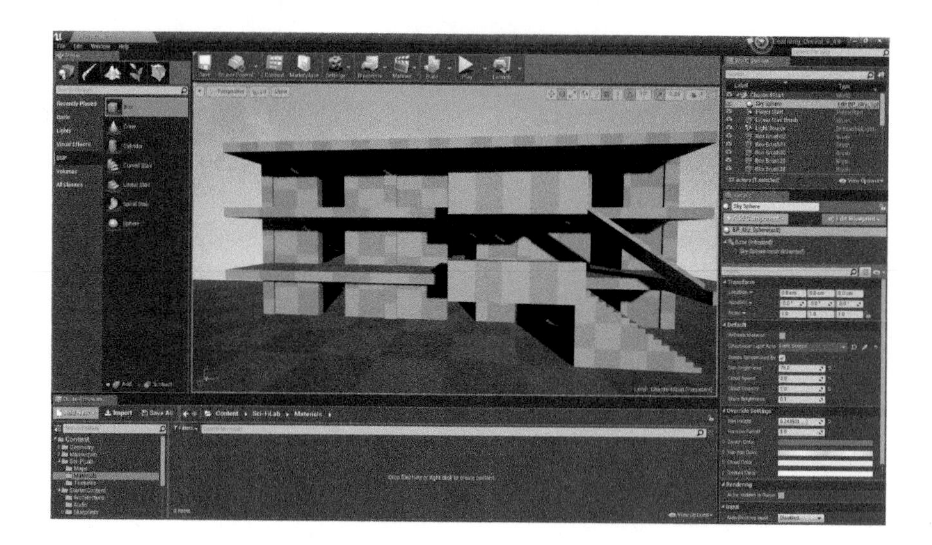

Play-test your level and be sure that you can enter each room without any issues. If an issue does arise, make the necessary corrections and test again.

Before you start creating the boundaries for the entryway, you have one more box to add. Create or copy a new box and set the following:

- X—750
- Y—2000
- Z—320

Place as seen in the figure below.

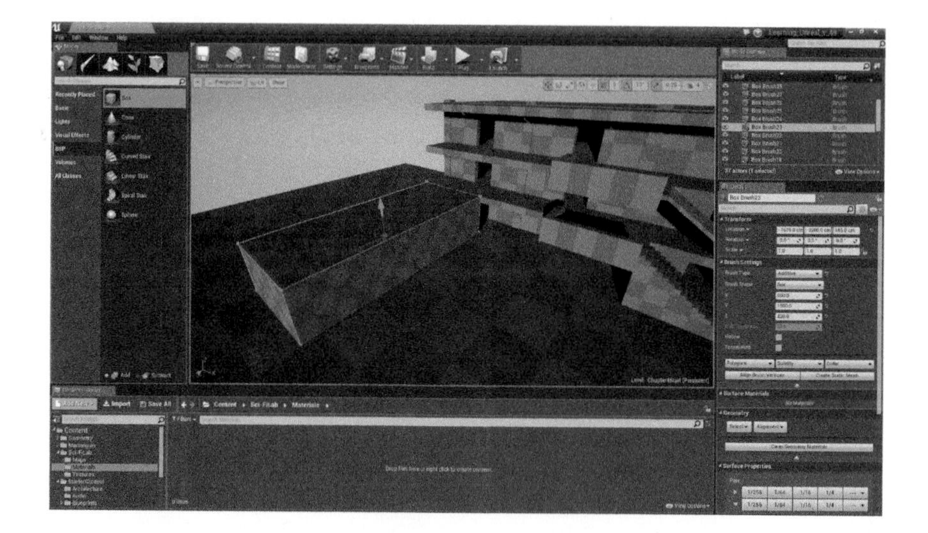

To finish out the entryway, you need to close off the open area surrounding the entryway. Use the figure below as a guide. The width and length of the room can be adjusted as you see fit; however, the height of these walls should remain at 1000 in the Z. This will guarantee that the player cannot jump off the third floor and out of the map.

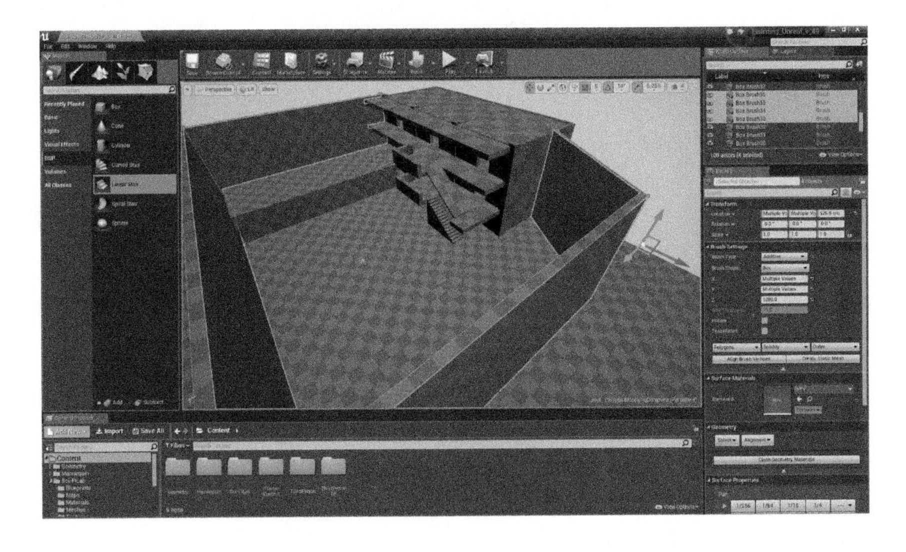

After you have completed the walls around the perimeter, you can explore another feature. You may start to notice a larger amount of shadows cropping up. Adjust your lighting to minimize these as much as possible. Once you are satisfied with the direction of your lighting, you can explore the **Build** button on the Toolbar, which gives you access to a number of different options. From the top these options are

- Build lighting only
- Lighting quality
- Lighting info
- Use error coloring
- Show lighting stats
- Update reflection captures
- Precompute static visibility
- Build geometry
- Build geometry (current level)
- Build paths
- Build level of details (LODs)
- Build and submit
- Map check

See the following figure.

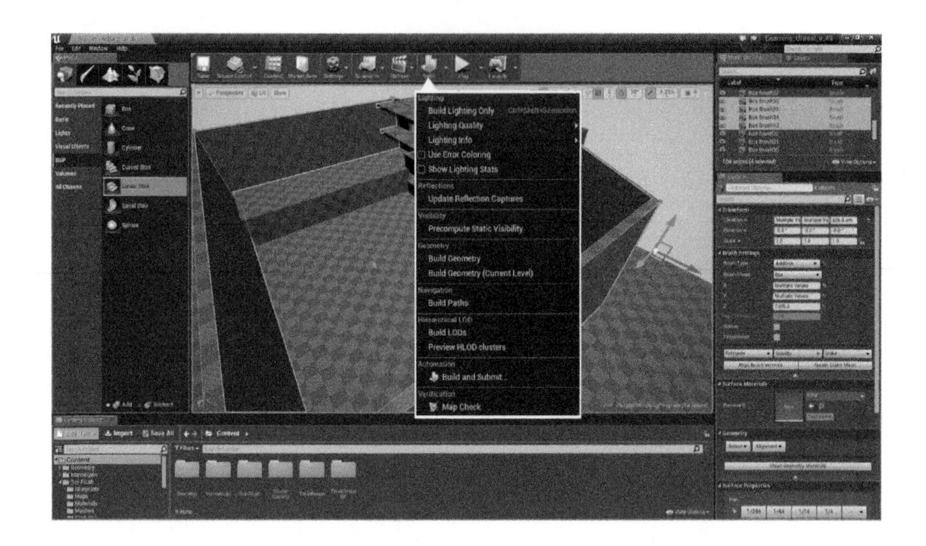

We will not be covering most of these options right now, but we do want to look at the first two. **Lighting Quality** has a dropdown menu giving you access to the different quality levels you can use. By default this is set to Preview. While there may not be a large difference currently in build time, it should be noted that, as you add more lighting and objects to your level, the build time increases exponentially based on the level of quality. Unless you are ready to review the final (or close to final) lighting, avoid using the Production quality level as it can drastically increase the amount of time needed to build lighting.

Now that you have a basic understanding of the build qualities, let us talk about the Build Lighting Only option. As it implies, this will build the lighting, and only the lighting, for your level. Since you do not have any geometry that needs to be built at this time, using this option can help to speed up the building time required. Take note of your current lighting and then choose Build Lighting Only to launch the build process. If this is your first time running a build, you may be prompted to allow access for the Swarm Agent. Simply put, the **Swarm Agent** can use any computers on a network that are currently running Swarm.

Continuing to Block the Level

If you remember in your level sketch, a series of hallways ran off the lobby. For the hallways, you will make all the walls 400 tall in the Z. You can block those out now using the dimensions seen in the following figure.

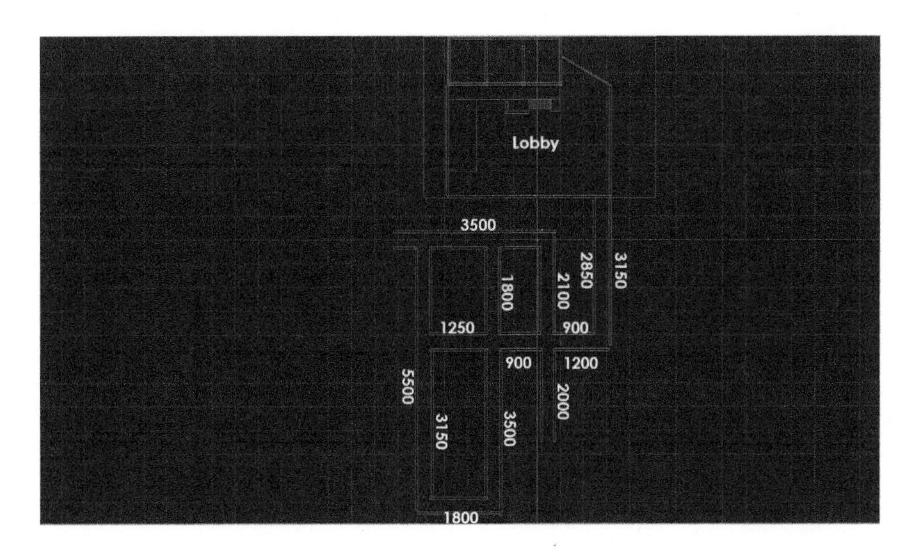

You may notice that the base floor under the lobby has been resized. Changing the Brush Shape X to 5000 will help to reduce the overall area you need to examine.

Once you have all the walls constructed, make sure to add the remaining floors. There are two sections of floor that need to be added. Use the figure below as a guide.

Note: We are using multiple sections of floor because we do not want to hide all of the floors. For example, the floor for the entryway will remain visible.

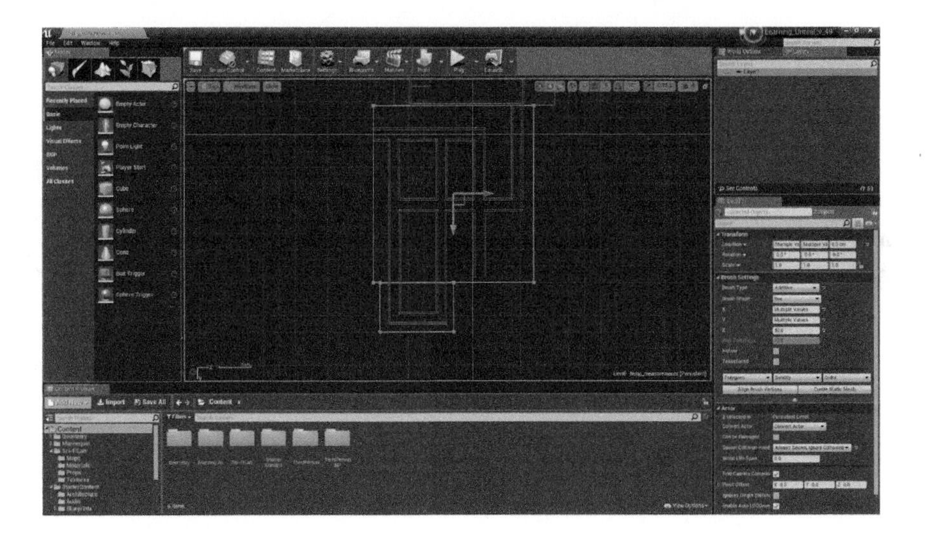

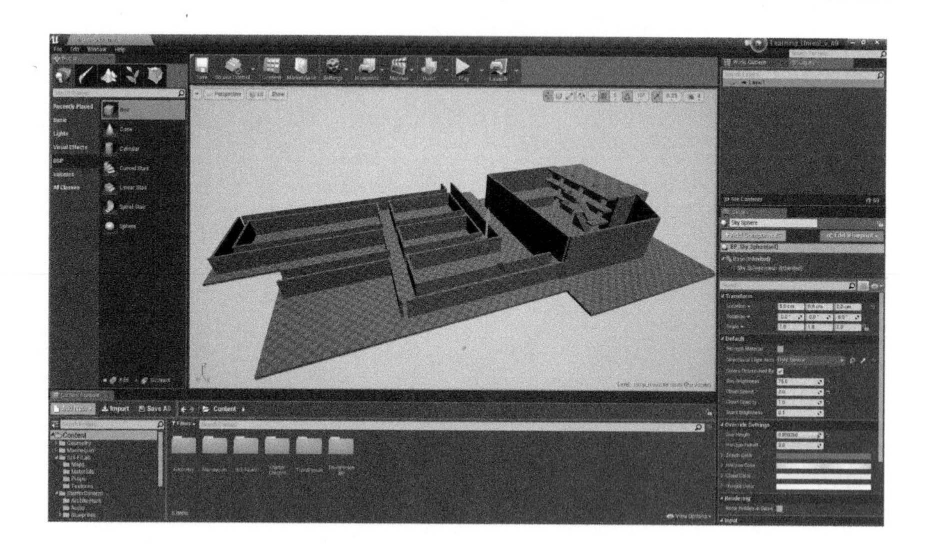

Before we move on to the swapping process, let us take some time to complete the rest of the blocking for the level. If you refer back to the concept art, there are two basements that need to be built. To create the stairs for the first basement section, you will use both an additive and subtractive BSP. This will allow you to have just the steps and remove the base that comes along with it. Start by bringing in a linear stair. Set the number of steps to 15.

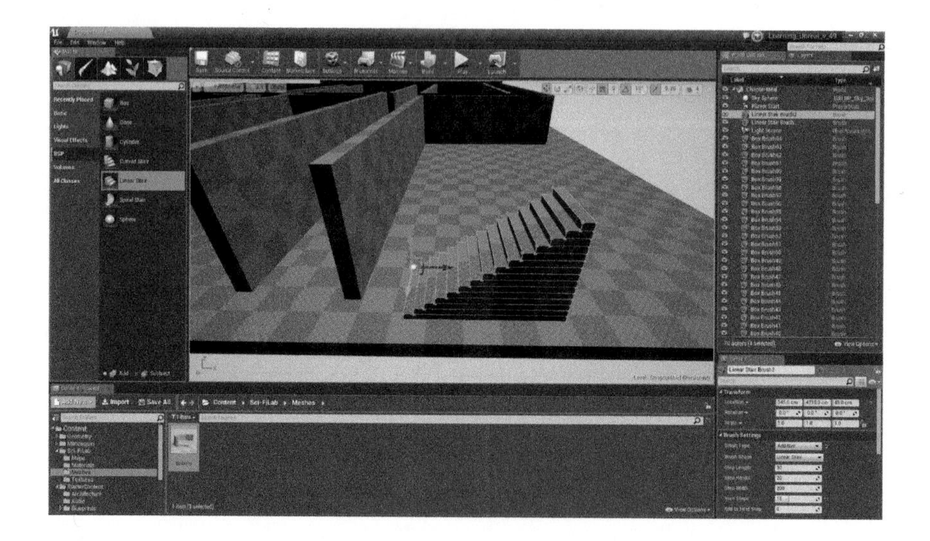

Duplicate the stairs using the Alt + drag method. With the new stairs selected, change the Brush Type to Subtractive. Adjust the subtractive stairs so that they overlap all but the actual steps. See the following figure.

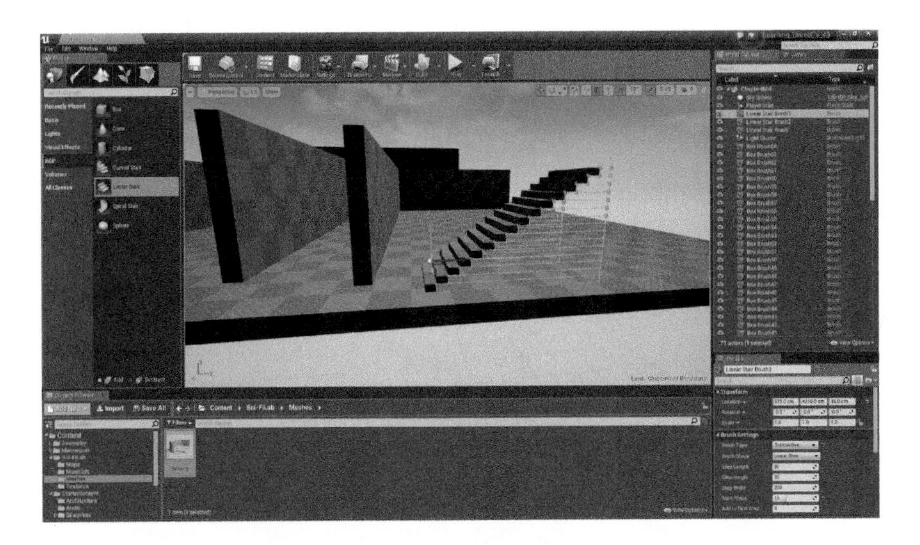

Once you have your stairs built, select both parts (Additive and Subtractive) and press Ctrl + G. By pressing Ctrl + G, you create a **group**, which is a collection of objects that can be moved as one. Since you created a group out of the two stairs, they will now act as a single object and you can move and adjust them as needed without being worried about having to align them again. Taking a look at the figure below, you can tell that objects have been grouped when you have the green lines at the corners.

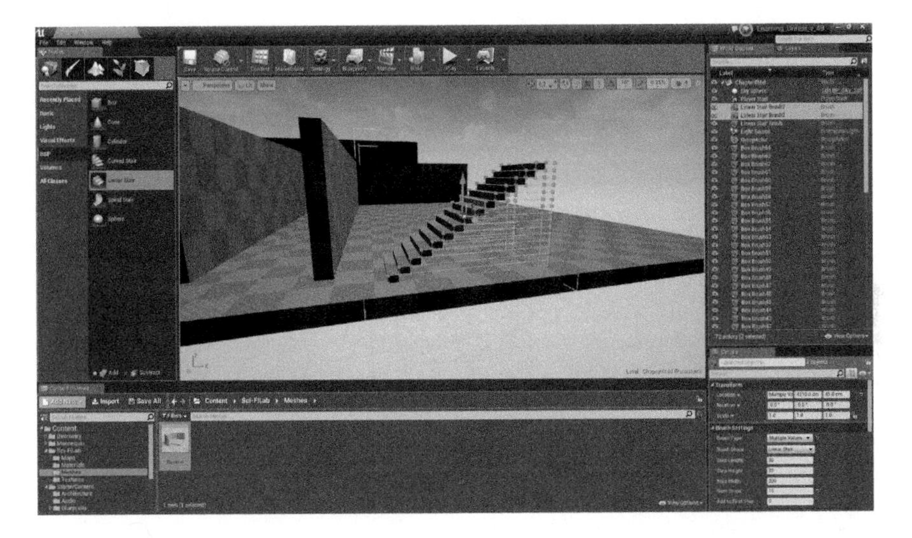

Now that you have your stairs built and grouped, you can begin to place them where you want them to be. For this section of the level, there are two stairwells that you will be building. Both sets of stairs start on the main floor. The right stairwell should go upward, while the left goes downward. Use the next two figures as guides to the placement of the stairs.

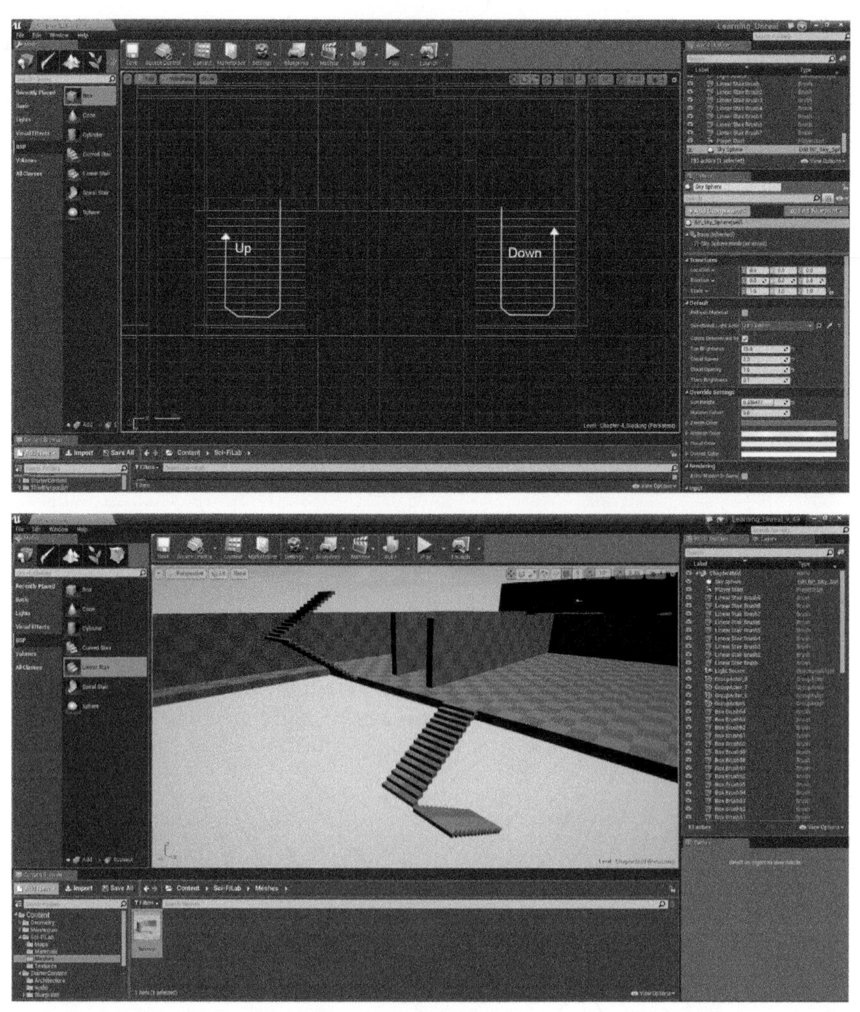

Since both sets of stairs have a turn in them, you need to add a platform in the middle. Use another BSP box to create a platform and place it at the interchange of the stairs.

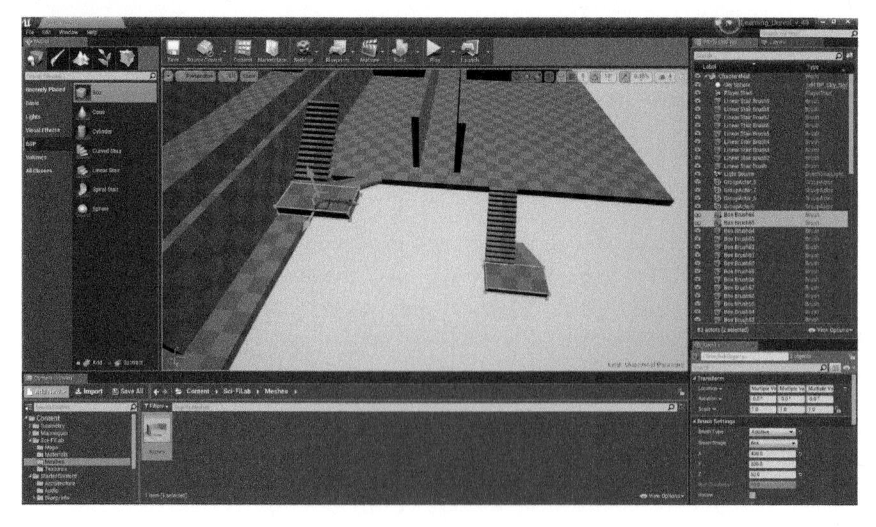

Now you need some walls for your stairwells. Take some time to create the walls surrounding the stairs seen in the following figure. Because one set of stairs goes up while the other goes down, the walls surrounding them will be offset.

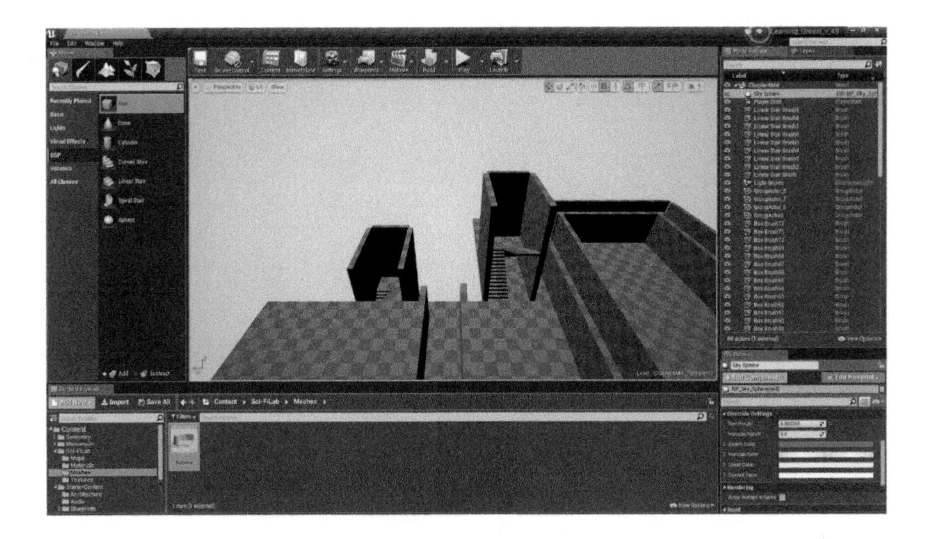

Next you need to create the floor for the basement. Duplicate another floor or bring in a new box BSP and set its shape to

- X—2500
- Y—4200
- Z—50

Move the floor down until it is even with the bottom of the lowest step. Now you need to create a few walls. All the walls should have a Z of 500 and should be placed as seen in the figure below.

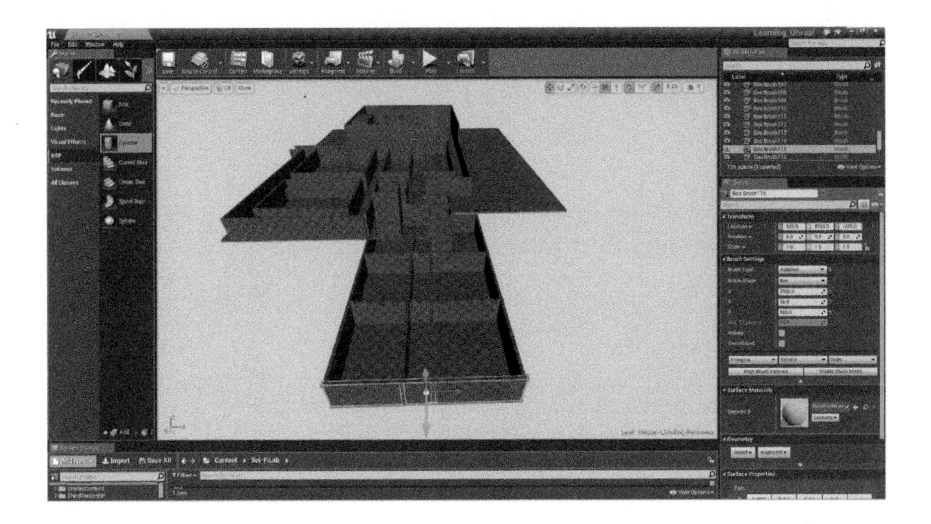

Now you can add doorways to the different rooms as desired.

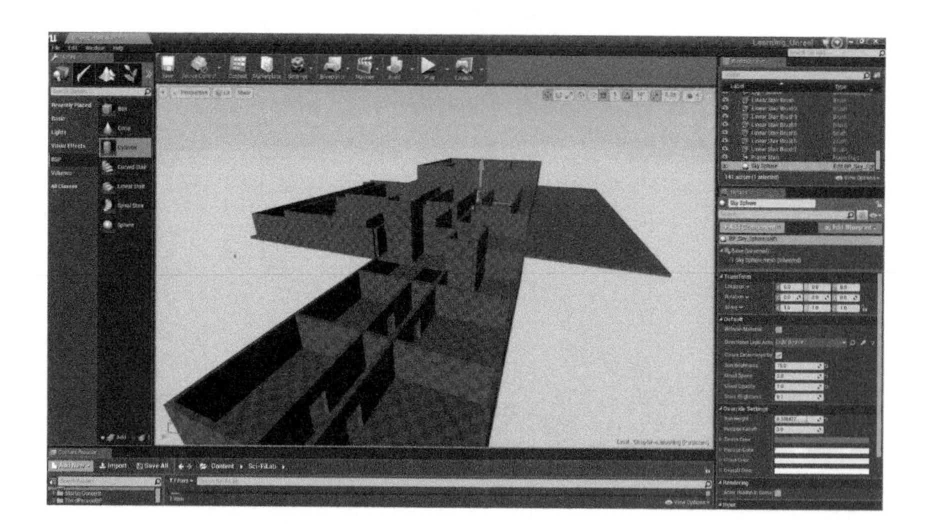

There is one final section of the blocking you need to address. By looking at the figure below, you can see where two walls stop at the border of your ground.

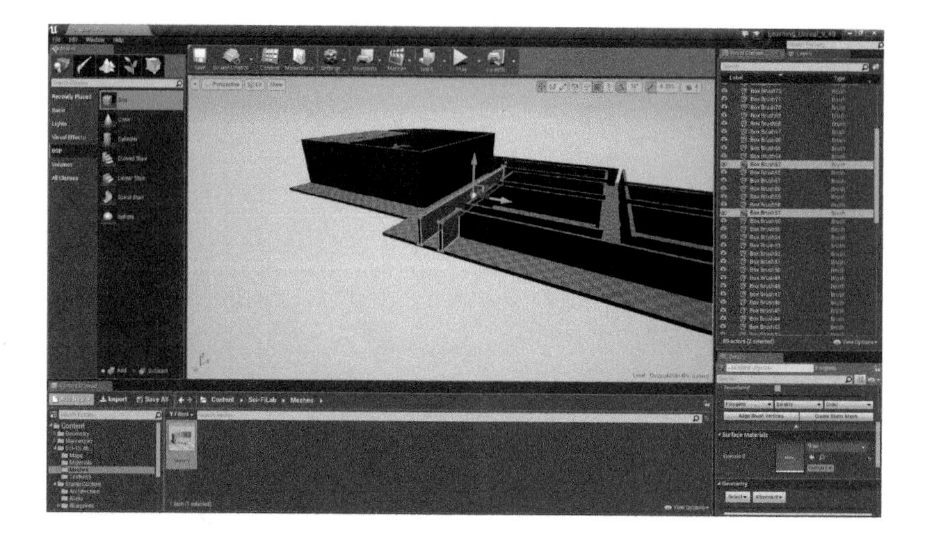

You will use this area to create your second sub-basement. Since this is sub-basement 2, it will be farther down than the last one, but you do not need to create a multilevel staircase. Create a new linear stair and set as follows:

- Num Steps—30

Place the steps at the edge of the ground. Create a wall and doorway at the top of the stairs as seen in the following figure.

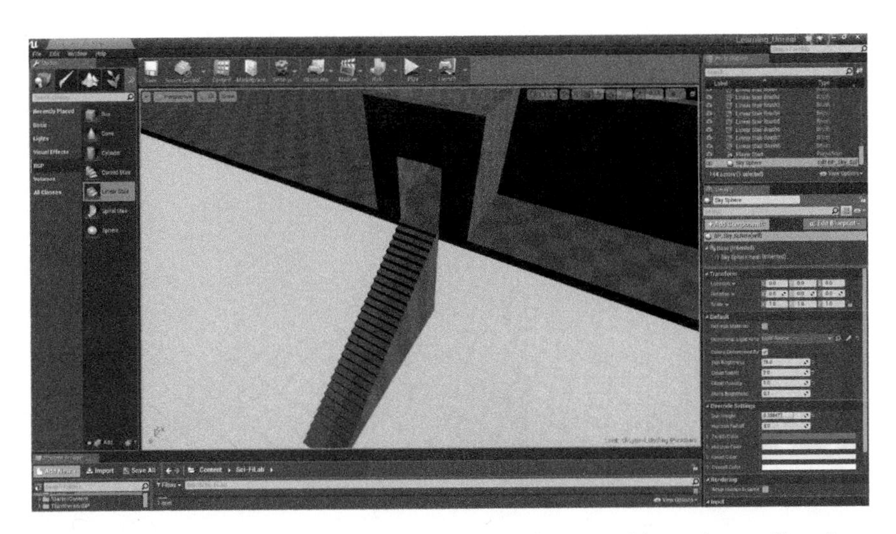

You need the walls for your basement; duplicate or add another wall and set the shape to

- X—2500
- Y—50
- Z—1000

Place this wall on the right side of the steps. Duplicate it and set its shape as follows:

- X—500
- Y—50
- Z—1000

Take the time to use your side or front view to align the bottom of the walls with the bottom of the steps.

Place this wall on the left side of the steps. Duplicate another wall and set to

- X—50
- Y—2500
- Z—1180

Move this wall to the end of the outer wall for the basement. Duplicate again and set to

- X—50
- Y—2250
- Z—1180

Finally, duplicate again and set to

- X—2000
- Y—50
- Z—1180

Move to the end of the room.

Note: If you are starting to have difficulty seeing due to shadows, you can increase the intensity of your light source and then build lighting.

You should have a room similar to that shown in the following figure.

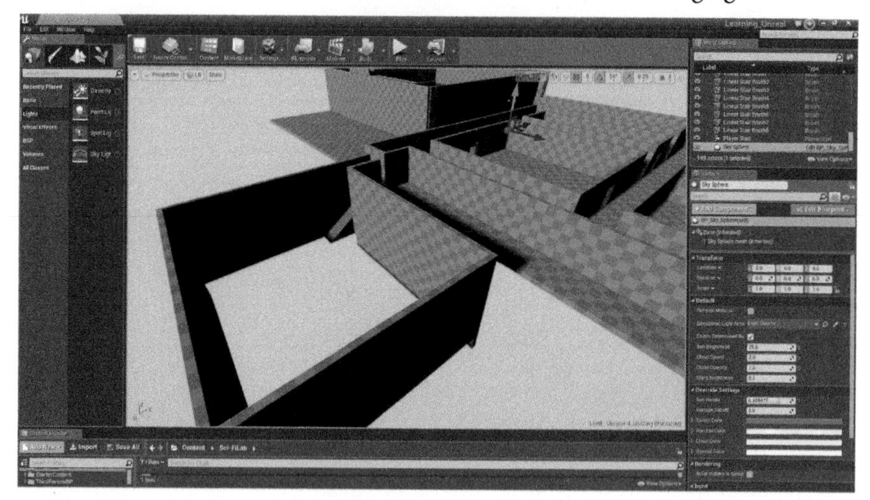

To finish off this room and your blocking, you need to create a floor for this room. You can make any floor you would like here or follow the example floor. To make the example floor, first duplicate a wall and set to

- X—2000
- Y—1000
- Z—50

Place this section of floor directly under the stairs. Duplicate and set as

- X—2000
- Y—500
- Z—50
- Rotate X—20

Duplicate a final time and set to

- X—2000
- Y—1000
- Z—50

Place the three sections of the floor similarly to the image shown below.

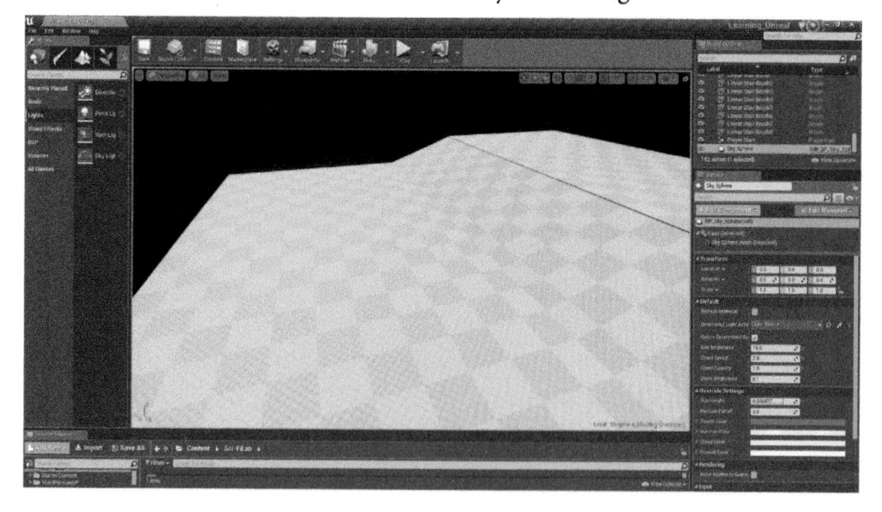

That completes the blocking of your level. Adjust lighting and build as needed and then save your level.

Cleaning Up the Level

Now that you have all your main blocking done, you can go through and do some cleanup. Play-test your level to look for any areas that need to be addressed. One area that was overlooked here was that there is no doorway leading into the hallways. After you have added a doorway, play-test again and look for any other areas that may need work. Take a look at the following figure and you should notice that the walls do not connect to the floor. While this may not cause an issue with game play, it certainly was not intentional either. This is an example of what to look for while play-testing.

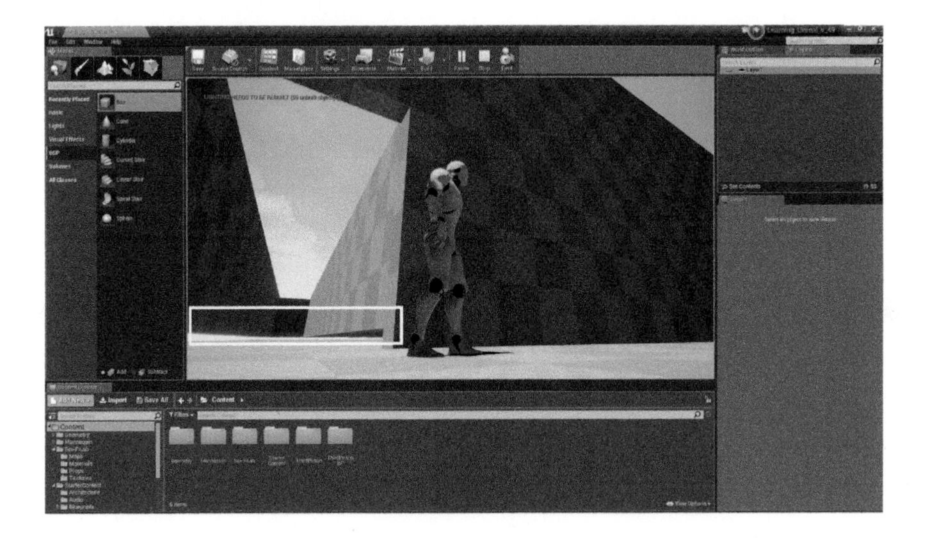

You may also notice in the figure above that there is a red warning in the upper left corner of the viewport. The warning reads: **LIGHTING NEEDS TO BE REBUILT (59 unbuilt object(s))**. This can be corrected by building the lighting using the method discussed earlier. Make sure to save your level after you have completed the cleanup. You will be adding some more doorways later, but until you add your mesh objects, you do not know exactly where they will end up. A **mesh** is any object that can be imported Unreal that is made up of polygons. This can be anything from a car to a person or a desk or a set of pipes. Meshes have their own editor, which we will explore later.

Importing Assets into Unreal

While this book does not cover the creation of assets, it is essential that you understand how to import objects into Unreal. This section has a large impact on how you proceed. If you have never **imported** assets into Unreal, be sure to take your time and read thoroughly. There are a lot of settings that can impact the process. We will cover the basics here and explain the more commonly used options.

Before you can begin importing, you need a place to put your objects. Within your project folder (mine is the Sci-FiLab folder) right-click and create a new folder. Name the folder Meshes. In the Meshes folder, right-click and choose Import to/. For now you will only import the balcony from the Chapter 4 assets folder. Once you have selected the balcony, you can click on Open. You will be presented with the FBX Import Options dialog box.

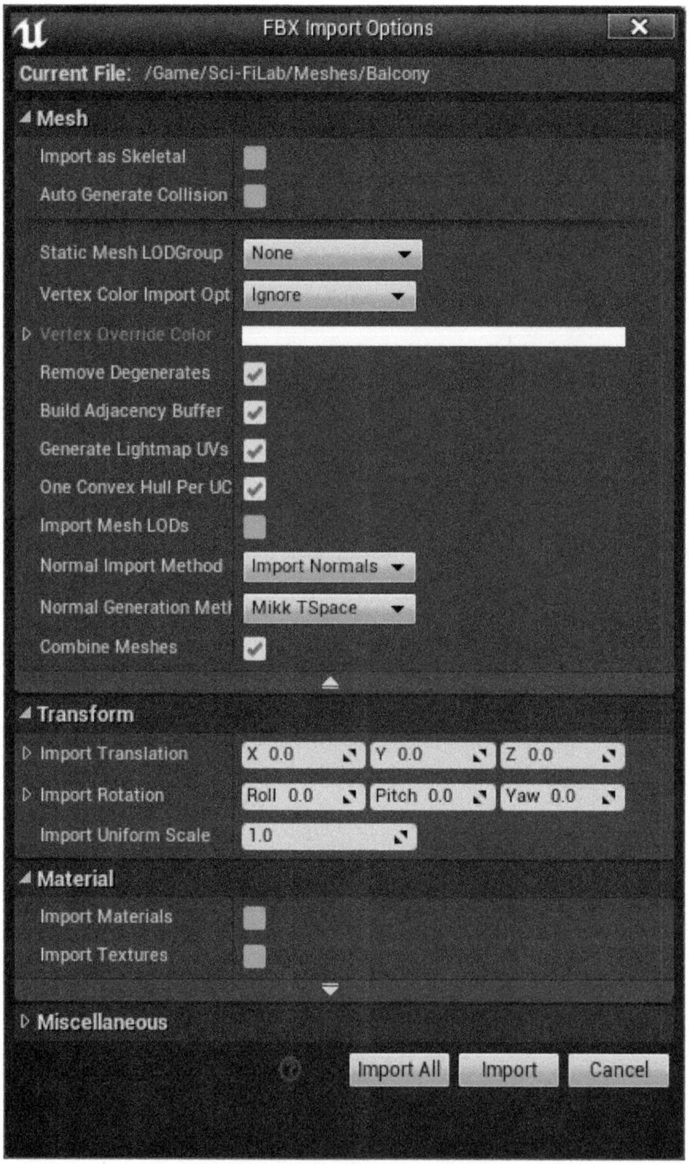

The first option we will look at is the **Auto Generate Collision** option under the Mesh section. When Auto Generate Collision is on, it will create a box or series of boxes around the object that will work as the invisible collision. Since you have been building your level up to this point with the plan to use your BSPs as your collisions, you do not need to generate any here, so you can uncheck that option. The next two options that will be changed are under the Material section. When **Import Materials** and **Import Textures** are checked, Unreal will attempt to load any associated files relating to the materials. Again, you will be creating new materials in a later chapter, so you will uncheck both these options. I would like to take the time to point out that if you do not uncheck these two options, you *will* end up with a lot of materials being added to your Meshes folder, which is undesirable. Make sure that both these options are unchecked before continuing. Finally, click on the *Import* button to finish the import.

Importing more than one asset at a time works in the exact same manner as importing a single asset. To finish importing the rest of the objects you need, right-click again within the Meshes folder and choose Import to/. From here we can select as many objects to import as we would like; however, the more items you have selected at once, the longer it will take to import them. This time we are going to add all the parts we need for the entryway and hallway type 1. The following list contains every mesh we need to import:

1. Entry_Roof
2. Entry_Wall
3. Escalator
4. Hallway_01_4_Way_Ceiling
5. Hallway_01_4_Way _Floor
6. Hallway_01_4_Way_Wall
7. Hallway_01_90_Ceiling
8. Hallway_01_90_Floor
9. Hallway_01_90_Inner_Wall
10. Hallway_01_90_Outer_Wall
11. Hallway_01_Straight_Ceiling
12. Hallway_01_Straight_Floor
13. Hallway_01_Straight_No_Door
14. Hallway_01_Straight_W_Door
15. Hallway_01_Y_Ceiling
16. Hallway_01_Y_Floor
17. Hallway_01__Y_Inner_Wall
18. Hallway_01_Y_Outer_Wall

This time in the FBX Import Options dialog box, click on **Import All** to see Unreal run through each one and add it to the project. If you choose Import rather than Import All, you will have to continually click Import for each item. You should now have all the different components you selected stored in the Meshes folder.

You will be working on the swapping process shortly; however, there are a few things to consider first. Up to this point, we have referred to meshes as either objects or assets. Unreal Engine 4 has what is called an Actor that we can use. An **actor** as seen in Unreal is any object that can be placed in a level. As such, there are many different classifications within the Actor class. Some examples of actors would be a static mesh (like the objects you imported), a camera, or a player start.

You now have to start considering how you want to control the placement of your actors. What do I mean by placement? To best answer this, you can look at your hallways. Looking at the concept image, you can see that there are a number of areas where there are long hallways with little change through the middle. You could simply add floors over and over, and then add the walls, ceiling, etc. or create a blueprint.

Creating Your First Blueprint

Blueprints are an extremely powerful tool in Unreal. By creating a blueprint, you can group objects, lights, triggers, collisions, and a number of other objects together and then use that blueprint repeatedly throughout the level. While that does not seem too different from simply grouping objects in the Editor, there are two major differences. First, when using a blueprint you can make modifications to it and it will be populated through all instances of the blueprint currently in the level. This means that if, for example, you did not like the color of the light you added in a blueprint, you could change the blueprint's light and it would change **all** instances of that blueprint. The second advantage to using blueprints is that you can add actions, variables, and scripting to a blueprint that cannot be added to a group.

You will begin by making a blueprint for the entryway. Before you can begin you need a place to store your blueprints. Create a new folder within your Sci-FiLab folder and name it Blueprints. Double-click the folder to open it. In the right-hand side of the content browser, right-click and choose **Blueprint Class**.

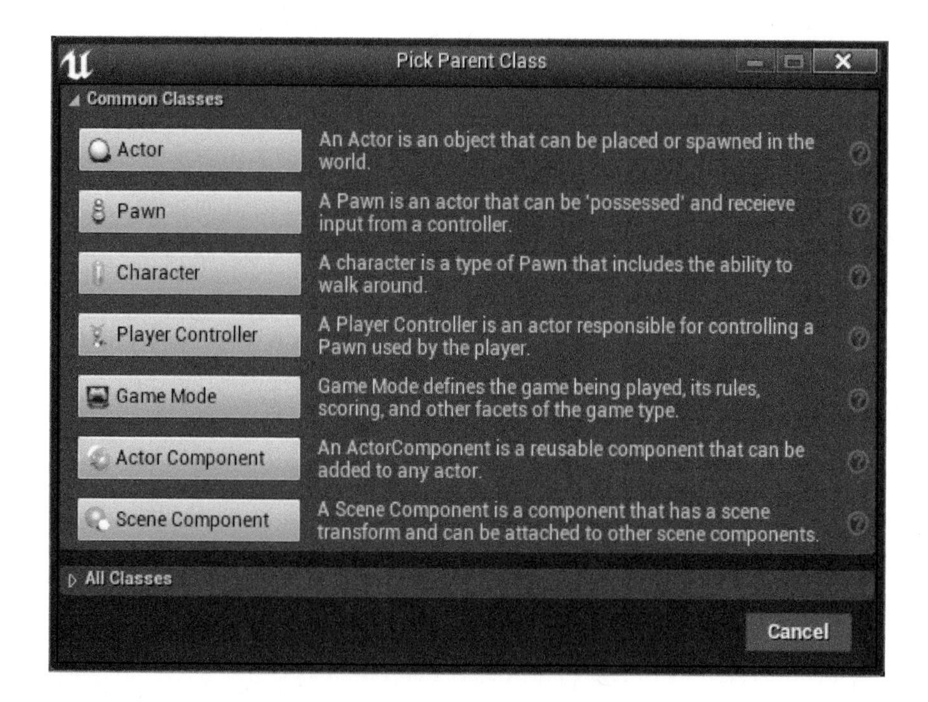

The Pick Parent Class window allows you to choose a multitude of different options. You can take some time to get acquainted with each type. When ready, choose Actor. Name the new blueprint *BP_Entrywall*. Double-click to open the blueprint in the **Blueprint Editor**. You should see something similar to what is shown in the figure above.

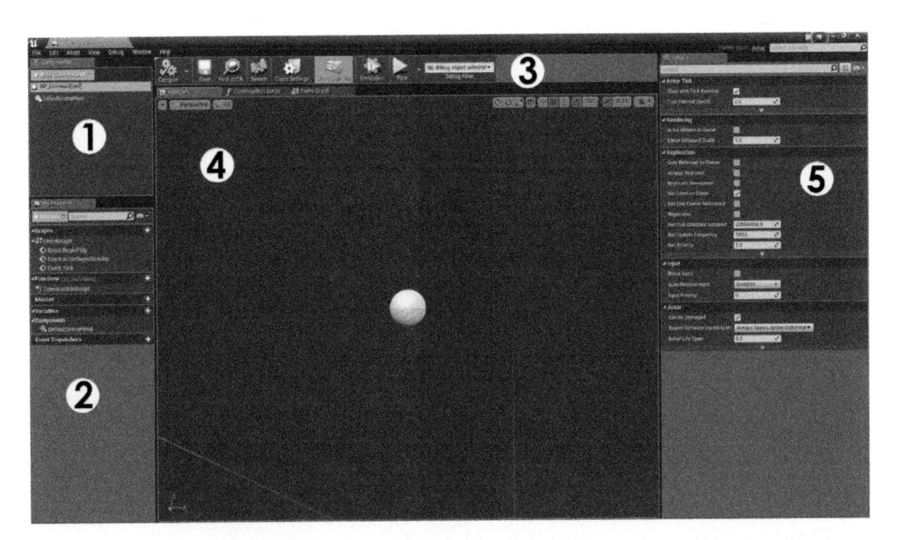

Before you start adding to your blueprint, you should examine the Blueprint Editor. There are a number of different sections in the Blueprint Editor, as follows:

1. **Components** shows a list of all components in the blueprint and allows you to add more.
2. **My Blueprint** contains a list of all Variables, Functions, Graphs, Macros, and the Event Dispatcher.
3. **Toolbar** holds the most commonly used tools including Compile and Save.
4. **Viewport** houses the 3D viewport and any graphs associated with the blueprint.
5. **Details** holds any changeable options for the selected portion of the blueprint.

In the content browser, select Entry_Wall in the Meshes folder by single-clicking on it. Back in the Blueprint Editor, in the upper left corner, click on *Add Component*. A dropdown menu will open (see the figure below). Halfway down the list you should see Static Mesh (Entry_Wall). Click on it to add it to the blueprint.

Note: If you see only Static Mesh, make sure you still have Entry_Wall selected in the content browser.

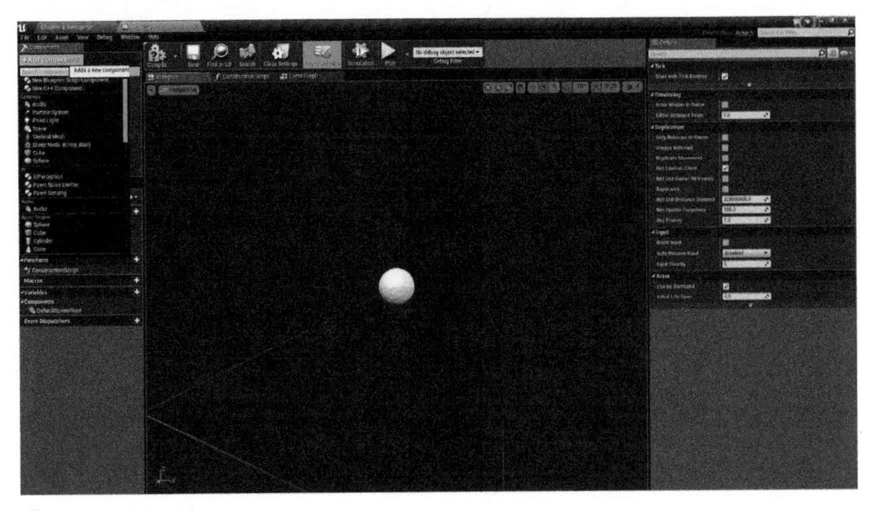

Return to the content browser and select Entry_Roof. Again go to the blueprint and choose Add Component. You should notice that Static Mesh has changed to Static Mesh (Entry_Roof). Select it to add it to the blueprint. You should now have something similar to the following image.

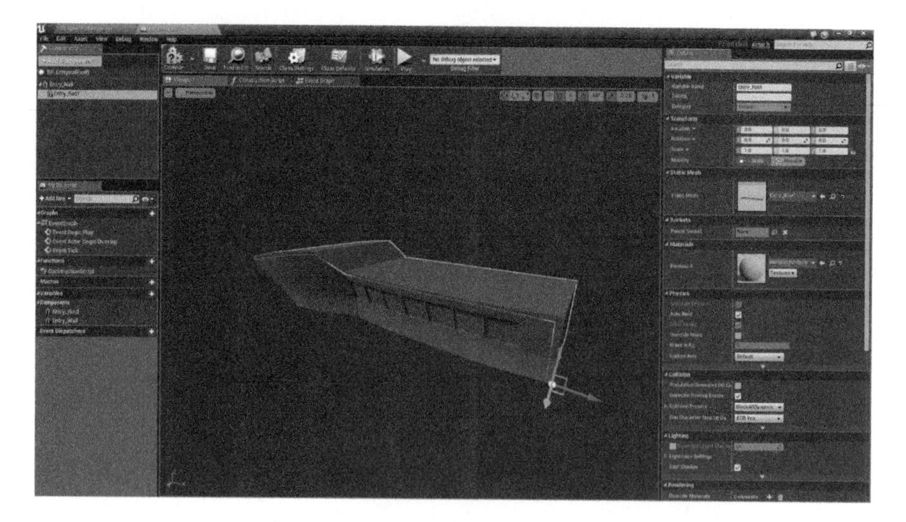

In the tools panel at the top of the blueprint, click the Compile icon. The icon should change to a green checkmark. While you do not actually have anything to compile currently, it is a good practice to use. Click Save and close the blueprint.

Exploring the Swapping Process

Now that you have a blueprint created, you can look at how the swapping process can be used to improve the appearance of your level. If you look back at your entryway, you added a rather large box at the back of the room.

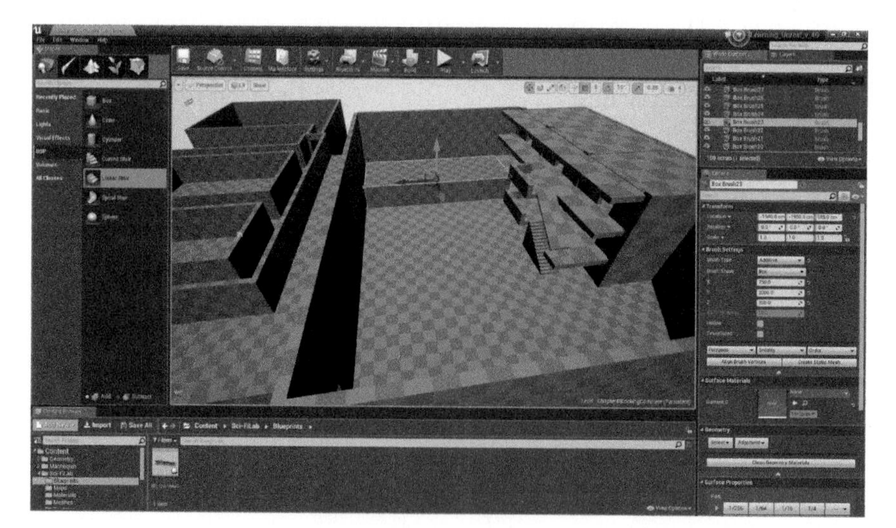

This will be the blocking volume for your entry wall blueprint. You can begin by dragging the blueprint into the scene from the content browser.

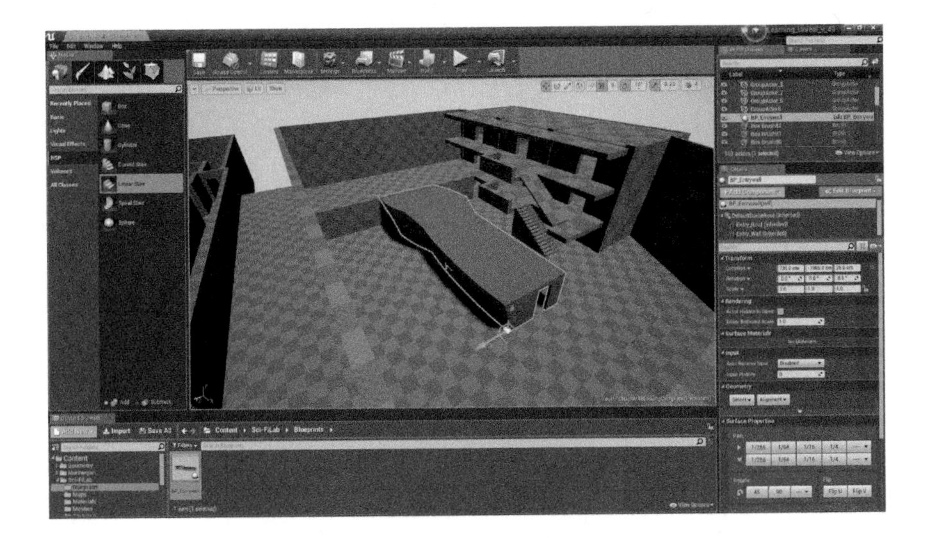

Take the time to position the *BP_Entrywall* blueprint so that it is *inside* the box.

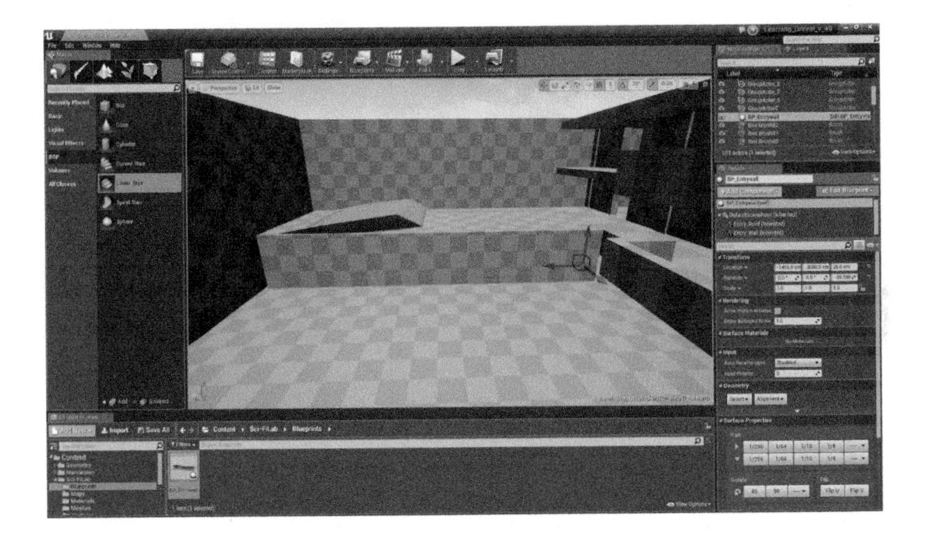

Now you can **convert** the BSP into a blocking volume. As discussed earlier, a blocking volume is an invisible barrier that blocks the player movement. Select the BSP and then in the Detail tab scroll down to find the section labeled Actor. Under the Actor section find the option for Convert Actor.

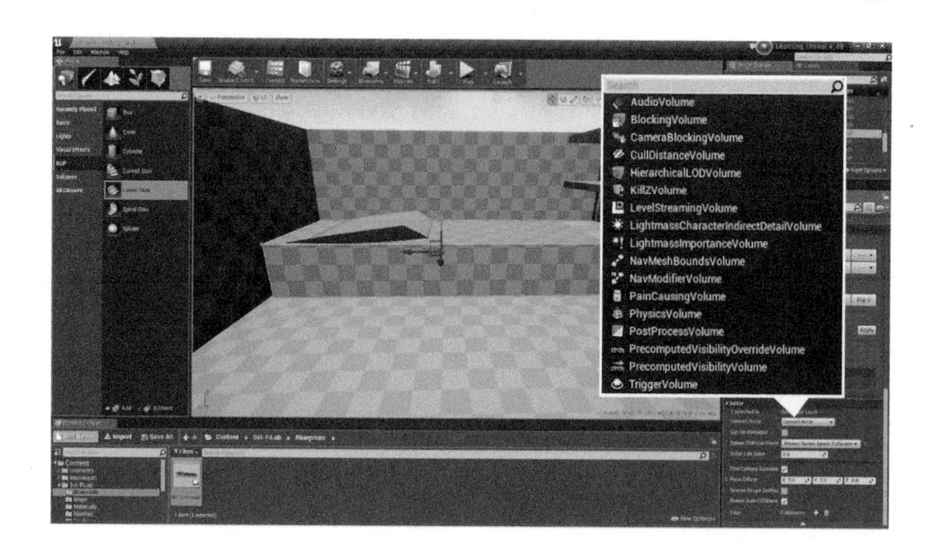

Click on the dropdown menu and find BlockingVolume. Once you click on BlockingVolume, the box will disappear.

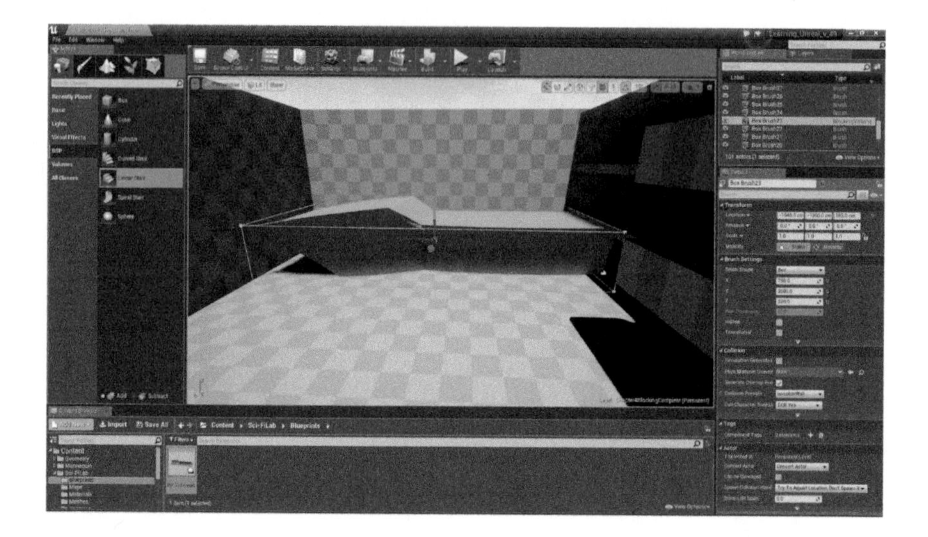

Note: If your box does not become invisible, click the Build button on the Toolbar.

You can play-test the level now to see how the blocking volume affects game play.

The next two parts you can swap out are the balconies. Change to the Meshes folder and locate the balcony static mesh. Drag the balcony into the scene. Align the second floor balcony first. Once you have the second floor balcony in place, you can convert the floor and two walls to blocking volumes. Duplicate the balcony mesh and move it to the third floor. Align and repeat the process of converting to blocking volumes.

If you are having issues seeing due to excessive shadows, you can change the lighting mode. Changing to Unlit will allow you to view your level without the shadows and lighting. Remember, though, if you do change to Unlit, this will not represent the in-game view and you should change back to Lit prior to adjusting the lighting any further.

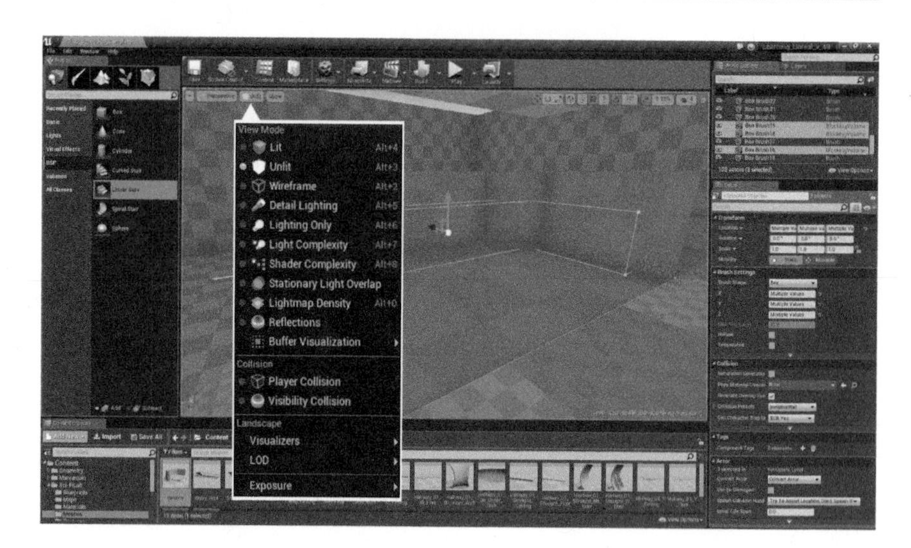

Before we move onto the next section, we have one more mesh we can swap out. Add the escalator to the scene. We will be swapping the stairs and ramp in the entryway with escalators.

Chapter Challenge

For the third-floor balcony and escalator, try creating a blueprint containing both objects and use that instead of copying the two meshes. You could also try using a group here if you do not wish to make a new blueprint.

Creating Your Initial Materials

Now that you have a few objects and a lot of area that needs some beautifying, you can create a basic material. **Materials** in Unreal are designed to be physically based. This means that the material is calculated based on how light reacts rather than how we think it reacts. Materials are applied to meshes and BSPs to change their appearance. Before you can start creating materials, you need a folder to save your materials in. Create a folder named Materials in the Sci-FiLab folder.

Open the new folder and then right-click and choose Material. Name the new material *M_Entry_Base*. Double-click the material to open the Material Editor:

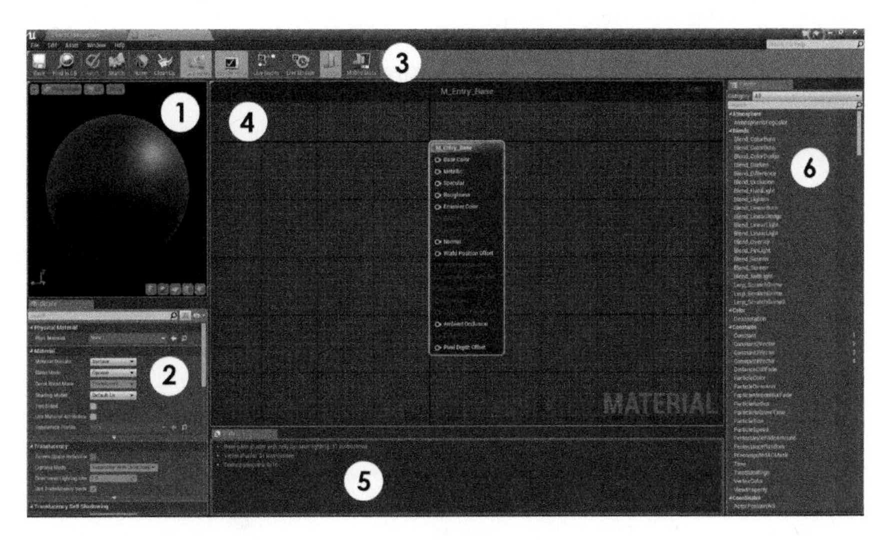

1. Viewport
2. Details panel
3. Toolbar
4. Material graph
5. Stats
6. Palette

Looking at the Material Editor, we can see a couple new items. The **Material Graph** is where you will create the different nodes used to define the material. The **Palette** is a complete list of available nodes that can be used on this material.

To create your material, you need to start by setting the *Metallic* and *Roughness* properties. You need to add a Constant node. A **constant** is a number that does not change during game play. To add a constant to the graph, hold the "1" key and then click anywhere in the graph.

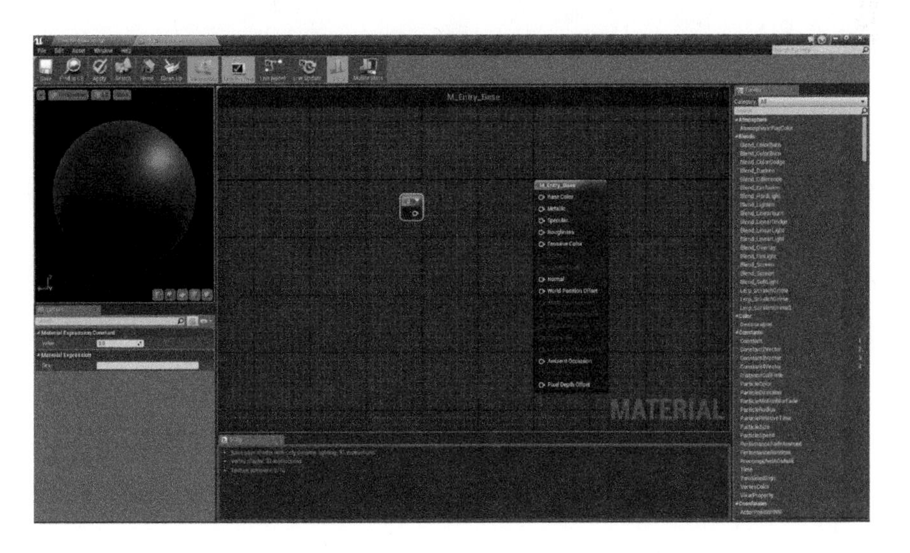

Connect this constant to the Metallic input of the material by dragging the out-pin from the constant to the in-pin for Metallic. Add a second constant and connect it to the Roughness input.

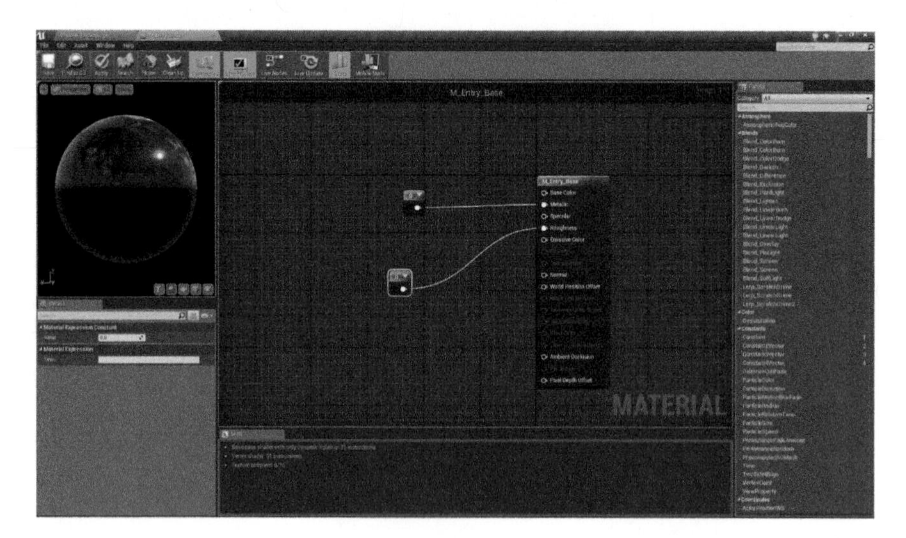

You should already notice a big change in the material. Looking at the viewport, you can see that now your material is shiny and smooth. The change is attributed to the constant node that is connected to Roughness. Because the Roughness is set to 0, you get the smooth material you now see.

The last thing you need to add to your material is a Vector node. A **vector** is made up of three numbers to create a certain color. Hold the "3" key and click in the graph to add the Vector node. Connect the new vector to the Base Color input of the material. You should have a material similar to the image below.

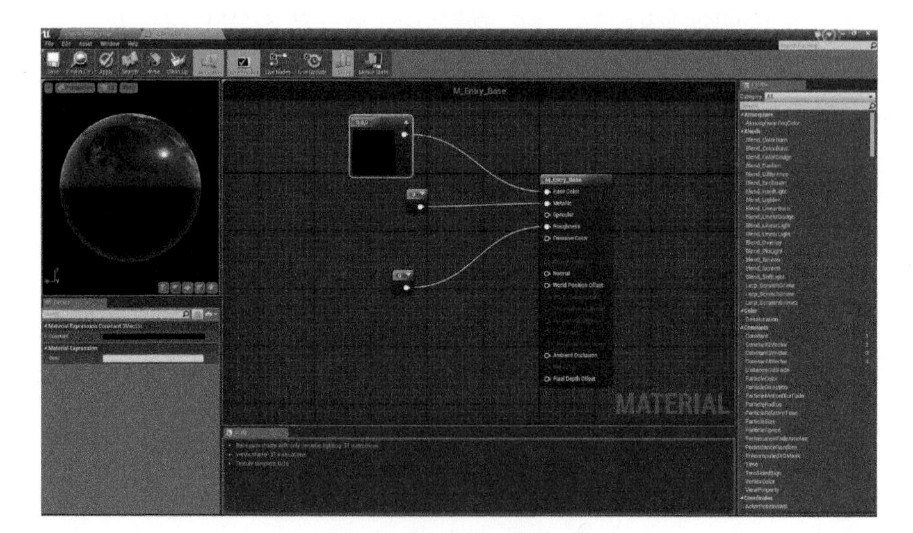

Now that you have all the components you need, you can begin to adjust the settings to create a material that you want to use. Let us adjust the color. Click on the Vector node and then, in the Details tab, click on the color block beside Constant to open the Color Picker window. Here you can select a color from the color wheel or type in the values you wish to use. Make the color an off-white similar to the color in the following figure.

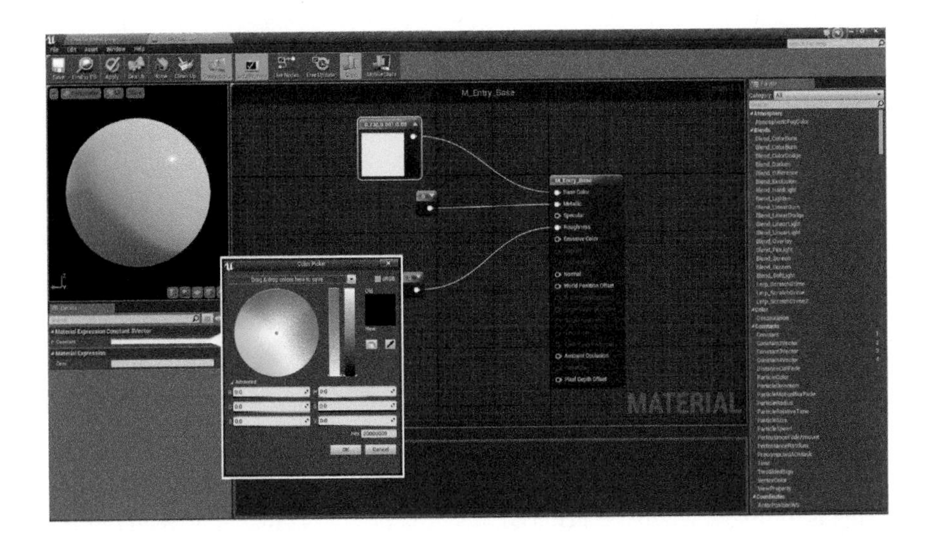

While we will cover material instances in depth in a later chapter, we will use one here. To create a material instance, right-click on the *M_Entry_Base* material and choose Create Material Instance.

Name the material instance *M_Entry_Inst01*. You can have multiple instances of one material. Material instances do not need to be recompiled, which can save on load times and precious processing power. You need to add your material instance to some surfaces in your entryway now. The easiest way to apply materials to your BSPs is to drag the material from the content browser directly onto the surface you want to change. Apply the Material Instance to the floors and walls in the entryway. For now you will avoid adding any materials to your meshes.

You should notice a rather significant change in the appearance of the level. This is an extremely basic material, but it is pretty obvious how material can improve the visuals of the level. Take a moment to play-test your level now. Once you are done play-testing, correct any issues and save your work.

Adding Your First Point Light

During your recent play-test you should have noticed that some of the rooms seem rather dark, while the outer areas are really bright.

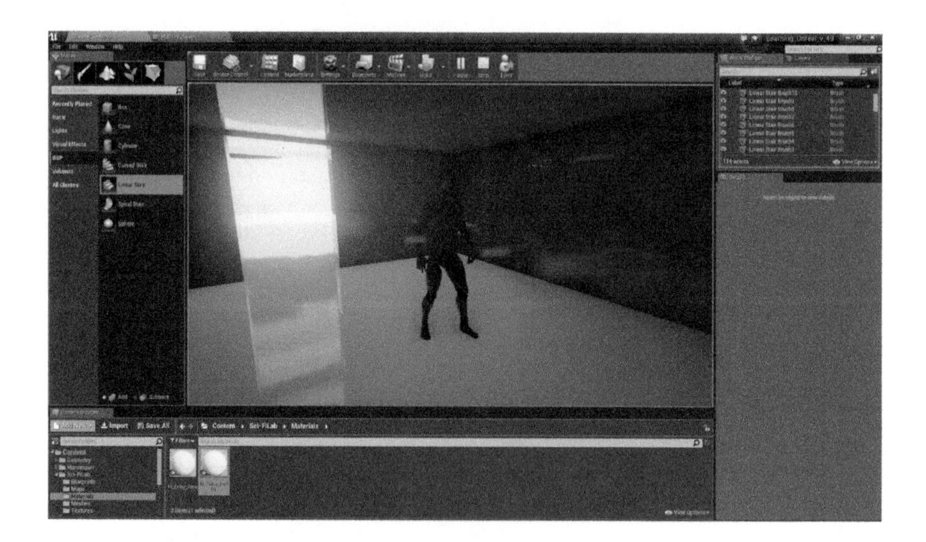

Since you want to be able to easily see all the different areas of the map, you can add a few lights and adjust the initial light source. Before you start adding more lights, decrease the intensity of the initial light source. Select Light Source in the World Outliner or find the light in the viewport and then adjust the intensity to

3.0. Now you can add a **point light** to the scene. A point light works differently from the light source we already have. Unlike the directional light that the light source is made of, a point light emits light in all directions from a single source. A point light is more closely similar to a light bulb, where the directional light is like the sun.

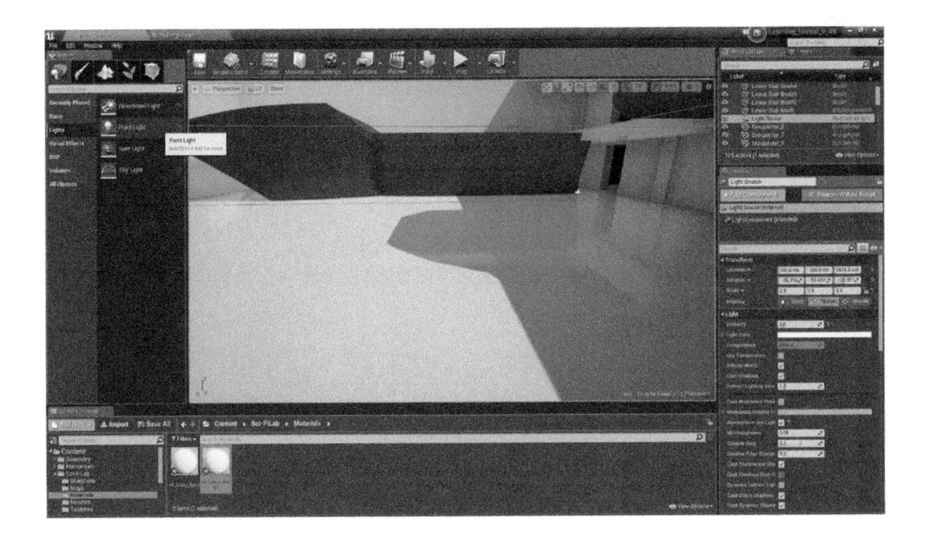

In the Modes panel, change the type to Lights. You can drag the Point Light into the level just like a BSP. Add one to your level now. With Point Light selected, find the Attenuation Radius under the Light settings in the Details panel. The **attenuation radius** controls the distance of the influence of the light. Adjust the radius to 300. Move the light inside one of the rooms to see how the point light affects its surroundings. The figure below shows the room without a point light, while the figure on the next page shows the room with a point light.

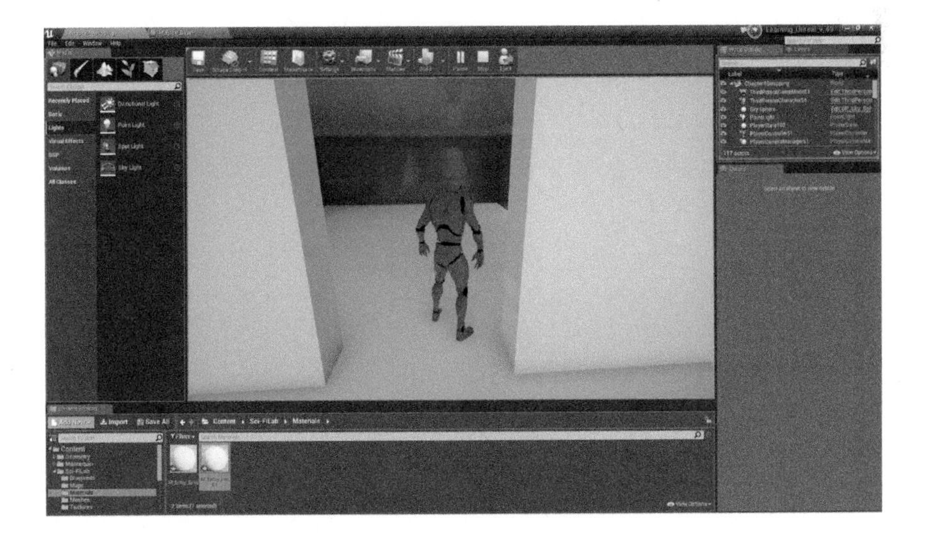

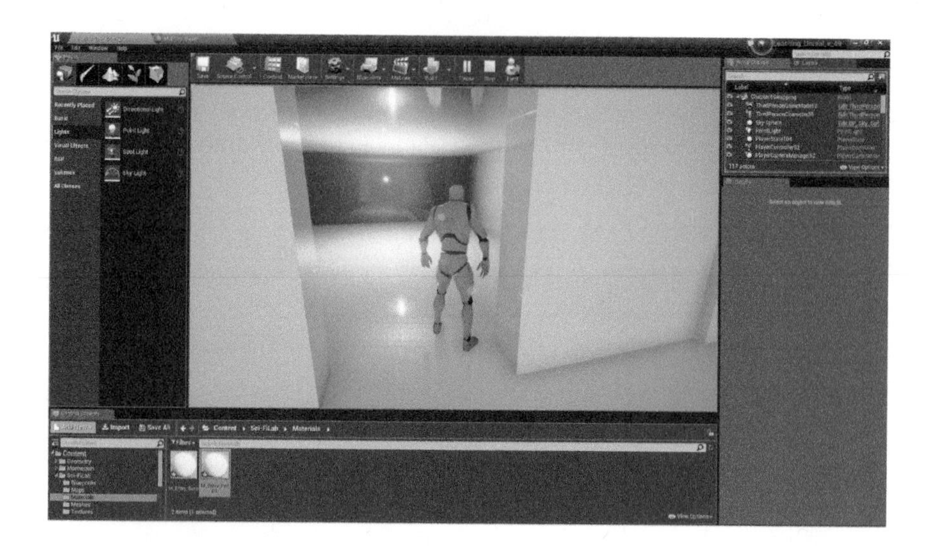

Chapter Challenge

Create a new level. Using what you have learned, build two materials of contrasting color. Create a structure that has multiple rooms and apply the materials to different walls. Add a few point lights and change the light color, intensity and attenuation radius to see how the changes affect their surroundings. Put lights in each room. Play-test your level to see how it feels during game time.

Chapter Review

In this chapter you learned a number of different things. You learned how to import objects and add them to your level, as well as how to create a basic blueprint. You also learned how to create a material and material instance. You learned how to add more lighting to your level and looked at how to add materials to the level and the impact that even a basic material can have on the level. Finally, you learned how to convert BSPs into blocking volumes to control player movement.

5

Exploring Blueprints

Introduction

In the previous chapter we took a quick look at blueprints and some of the powers they possess. In this chapter we will explore some of the finer points and see how truly powerful blueprints can be. We will look at adding more meshes to a single blueprint. We will also add lights to a blueprint. Let us get started.

Creating the Hallway Blueprints

The first blueprint you will be making is a four-way intersection. Browse to your Blueprints folder, right-click, choose Blueprint Class, and then choose Actor as the base class. Name the new blueprint *BP_Hallway_01_4_Way*. Now you are going to open a second content browser so that you can easily move back and forth. Under the Window menu, select content browser and choose **Content Browser 2**. A new content browser will open, allowing you to browse to the Meshes folder, while Content Browser 1 is still in the Blueprints folder.

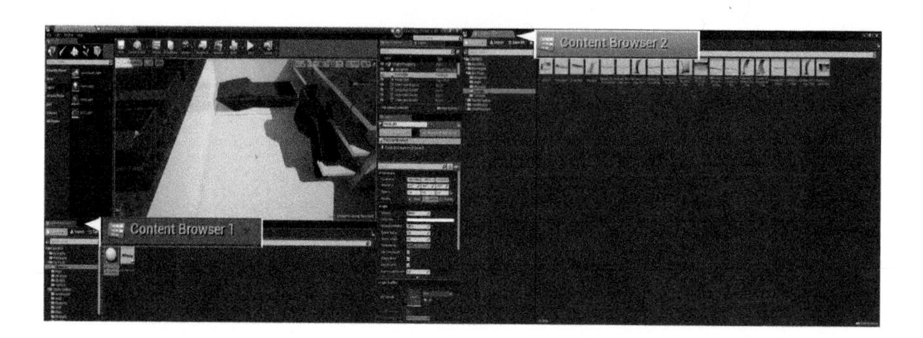

Double-click the new blueprint to open it. While working with BSPs you have been using a drag-and-drop type of method to add objects to the level. Blueprints will also allow you to use the same method to add meshes to an open blueprint.

In the Meshes folder, find *Hallway_01_4_Way_Floor* and drag it into the blueprint. You should notice that when you added the floor to the blueprint, it *nested* the floor under the DefaultSceneRoot node in the Components tab. The DefaultSceneRoot is displayed in the viewport as a small white sphere, which will be hidden during game play.

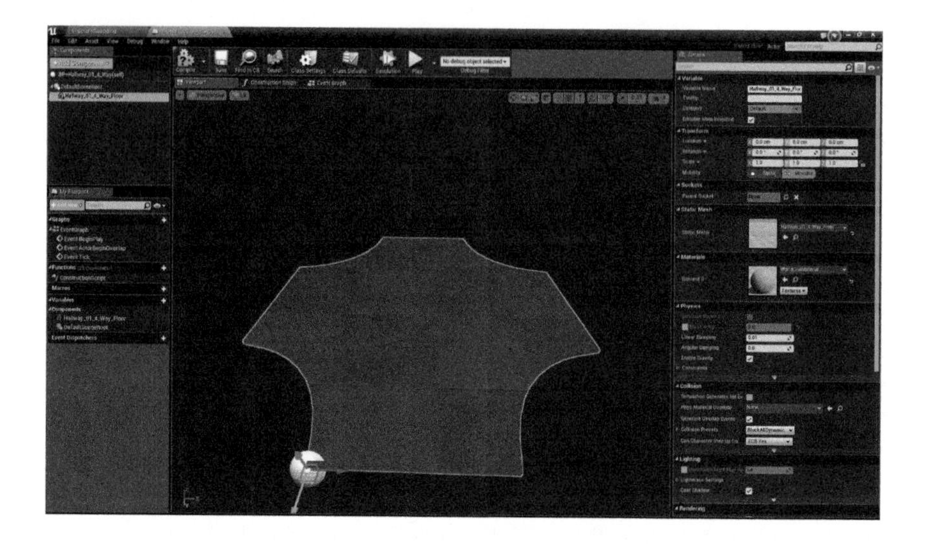

Next, find *Hallway_01_4_Way_Wall* and drag it into the blueprint.

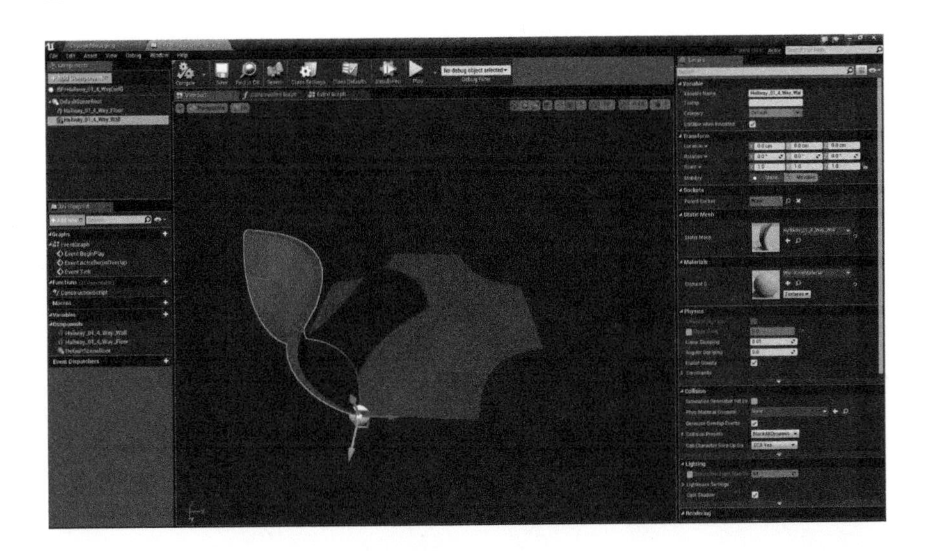

You should have something similar to the figure above. As you can probably tell, you need a few more walls. From Content Browser 2, drag in another *Hallway_01_4_Way_Wall*. As you drag in the additional wall, you may notice that the wall does not appear in the viewport. It is in fact there; however, it is in the exact same location as the previous wall. You can look at the Components tab to ensure the wall has been added. Before adjusting the second wall, let us make sure that the first wall is in its correct location. Select the first wall in the Components tab and set its location to

- X—10
- Y—15

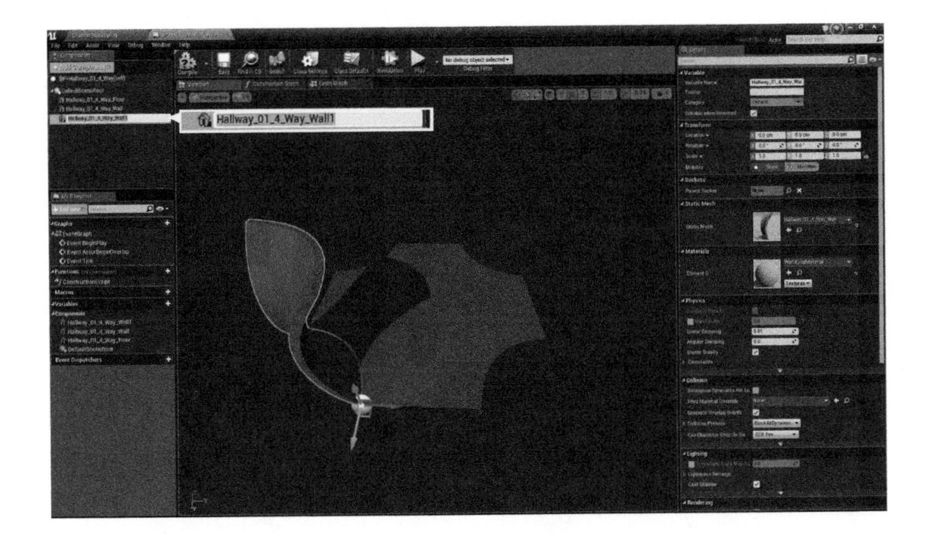

With the second wall still selected, adjust it as follows:

- Rotate Z—(-90)

Location:

- Z—600
- Y—(-260)
- Z—0

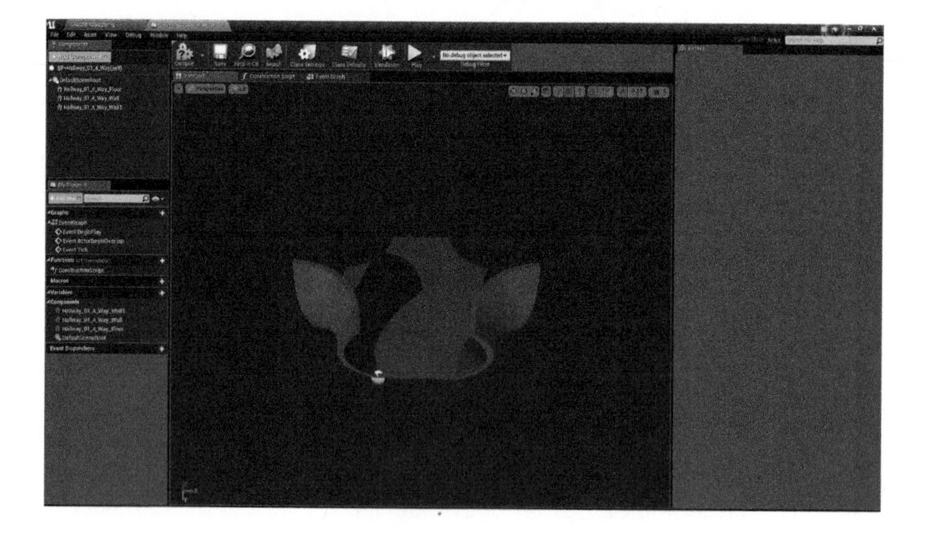

Add a third copy of the wall and move to

- Rotate Z—180

Location:

- X—325
- Y—(-850)
- Z—0

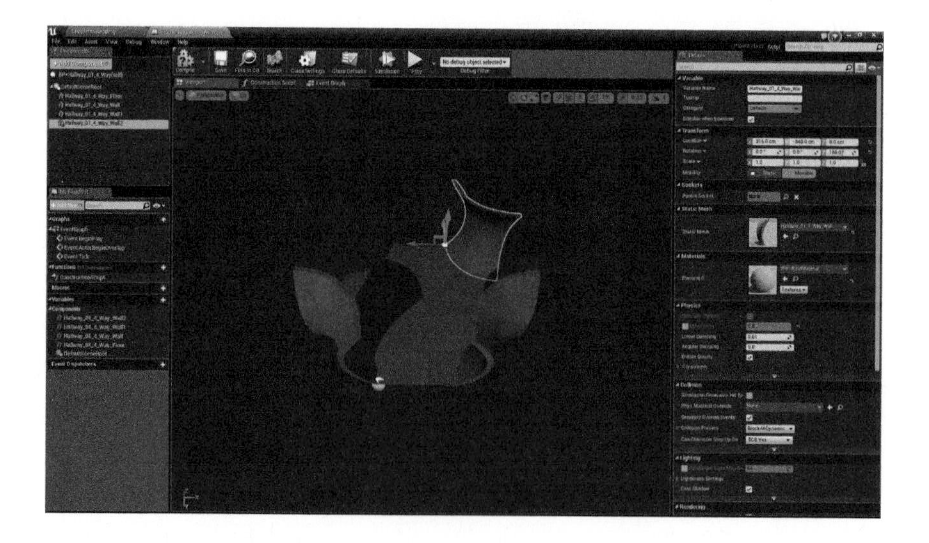

Add the final wall and set as follows:

- Rotate Z—90

Location:

- X—(-265)
- Y—(-575)
- Z—0

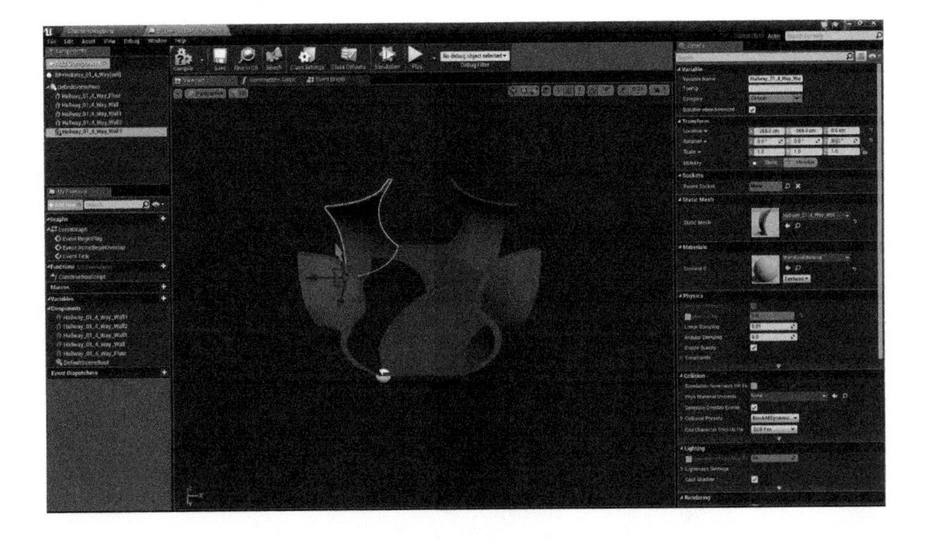

Now let us add the ceiling. In Content Browser 2 find *Hallway_01_4_Way_Ceiling* and drag it into the blueprint. Move the ceiling to location Z—400. Location:

- Z—400

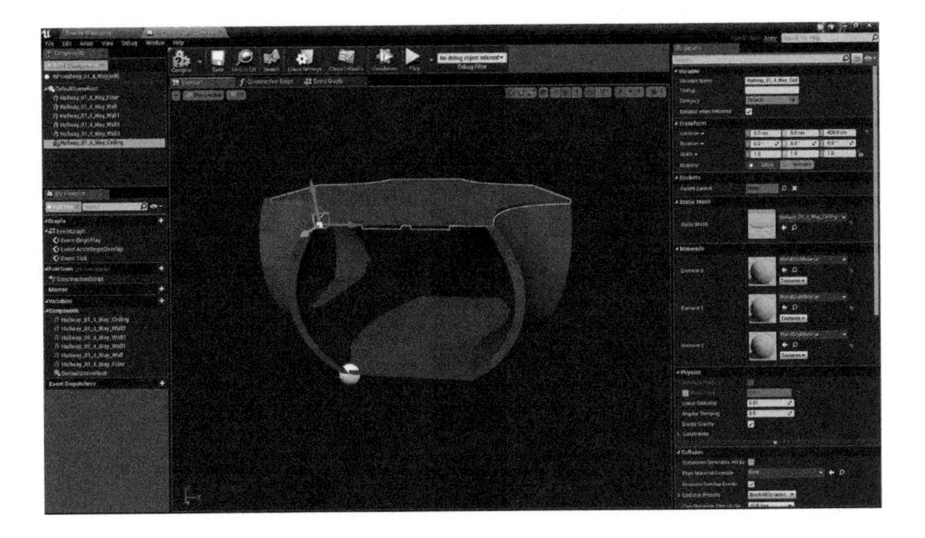

Now that you have all the parts added to the blueprint, you can add some lights. In the Components panel, click on the Add Components button and find Point Light. Click to add to the blueprint. Before you move the light to its final location, you can modify some of the properties to make it better suit the blueprint needs. Start by changing the intensity to 1000. Next, change the attenuation radius to 500. This reduces the overall brightness and range of the light. Since these hallway sections will all be connected, you want the lighting to remain the same throughout the entire hallway. To ensure that they all are similar, it may be a good idea to write down the settings used, including the color chosen. This will help add to the consistency of the level.

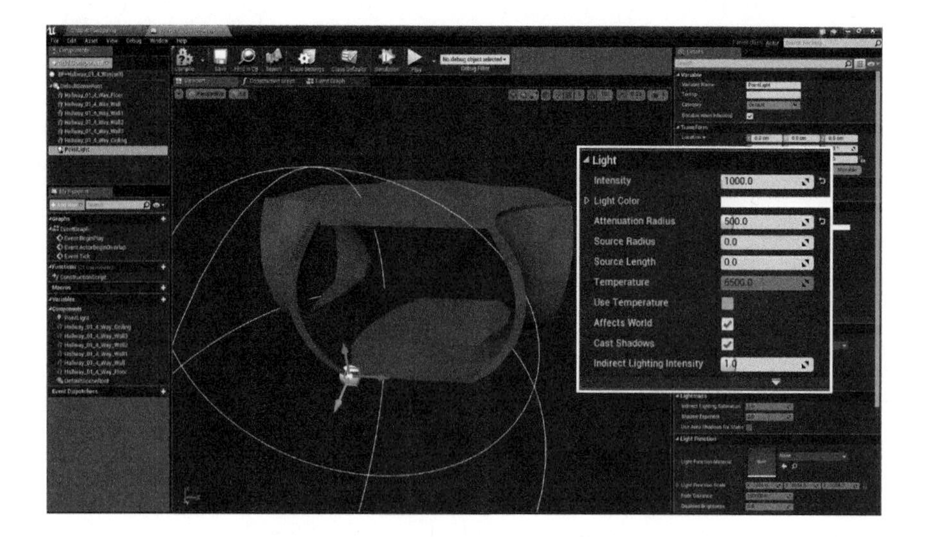

Looking at the ceiling section, you can see that there are four light fixtures. Position the point light so that it is directly below one of the fixtures. You should set the location Z to about 300.

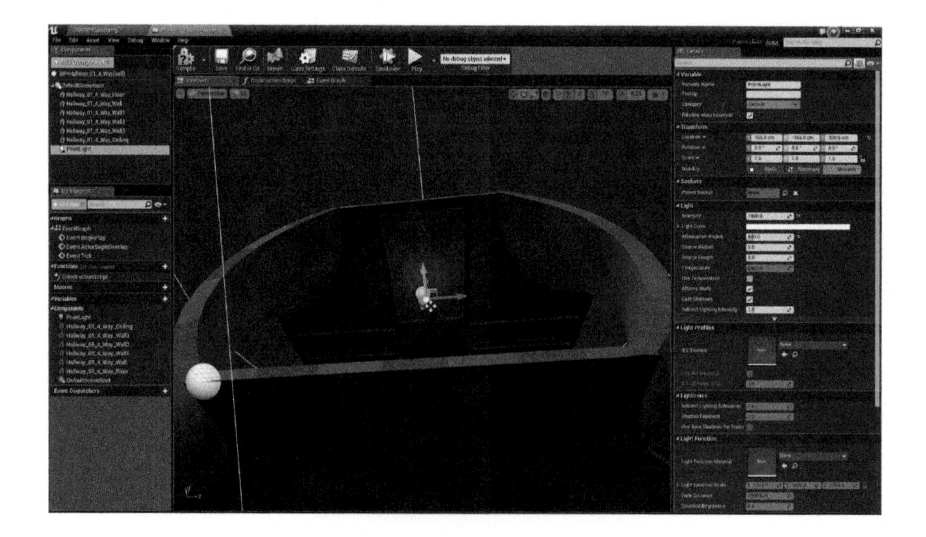

Repeat the process of adding a point light and then adjusting its properties. Finally, move the new light below one of the other three fixtures. Continue repeating the process for all four light fixtures.

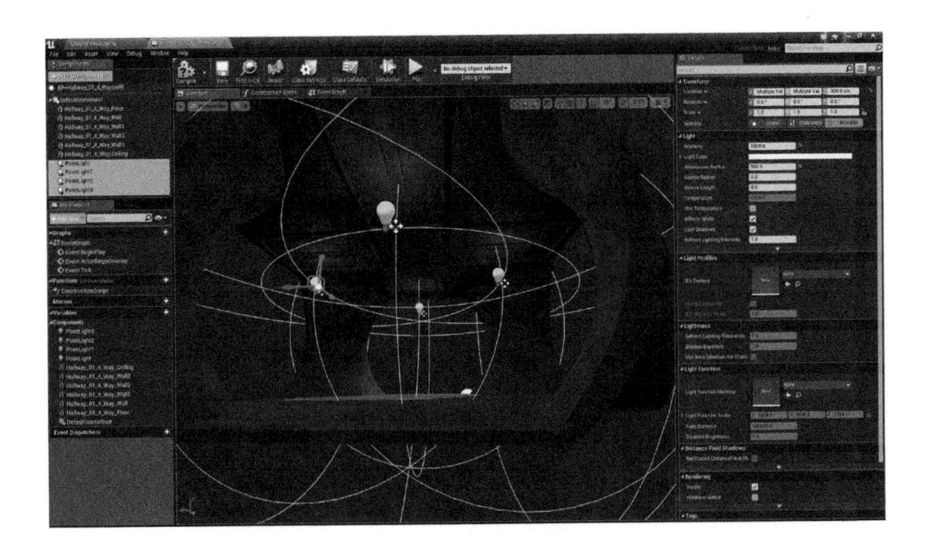

Before you close the blueprint, you need to compile it. Click on the Compile button on the toolbar and be sure that the green checkmark appears. You will cover the duties of the Compile button a little later. Save the blueprint and close it.

The next blueprint you will create is a straight section of the hallway that has a doorway in the side. Using the same steps as before, create a new blueprint, and name it *BP_Hallway_01_Straight_W_Door*. Double-click the new blueprint to open it. In the Content Browser 2 window, find the *Hallway_01_Straight_Floor* mesh and add it to the blueprint.

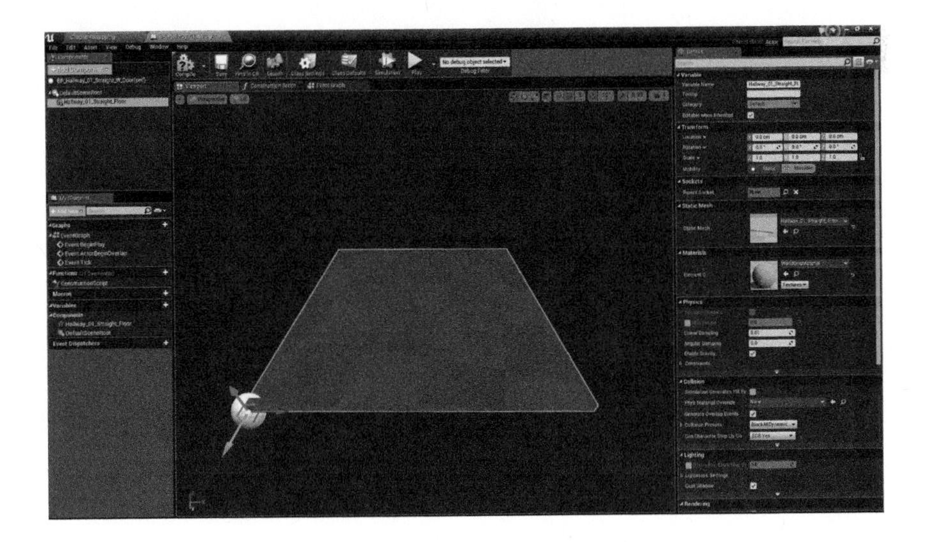

The next part you will add is the wall section with the doorway. In Content Browser 2 find *Hallway_01_Straight_W_Door* and add it to the blueprint. Set its location to X—10.

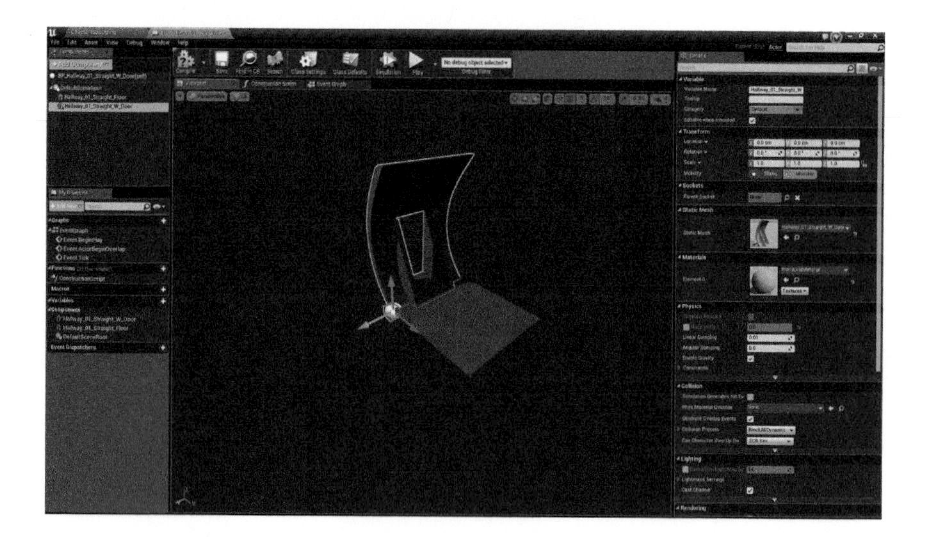

Add the *Hallway_01_Straight_No_Door* mesh next. Set the following:

- Rotate Z—180

Location:

- X—310
- Y—(-320)

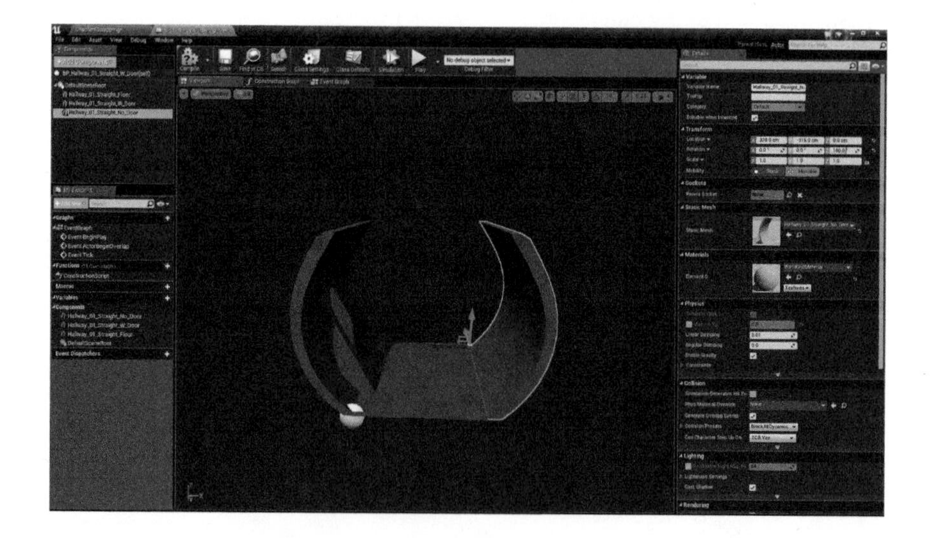

The final mesh you need to add is the ceiling. Find the mesh named *Hallway_01_Straight_Ceiling* and add it to the blueprint. Move the ceiling straight up on the Z axis to 400.

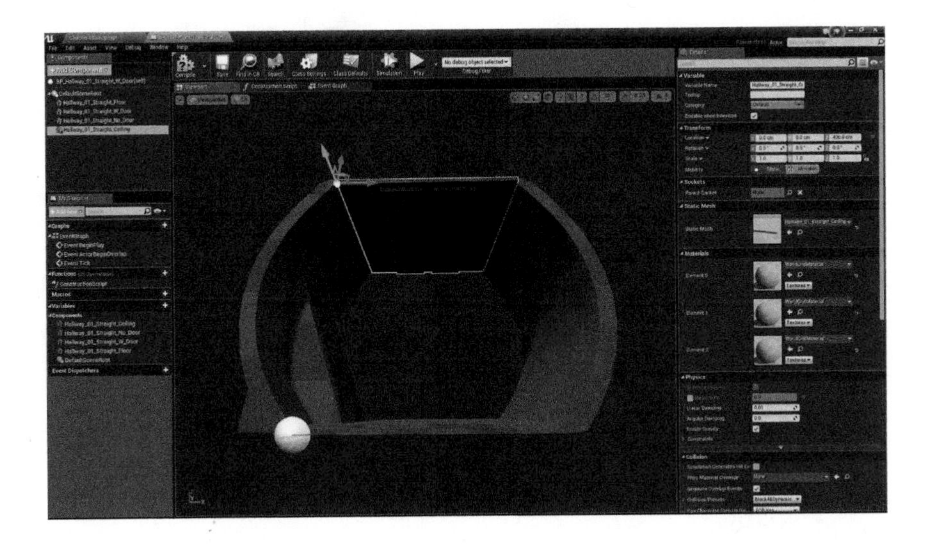

There is one light fixture on the ceiling, so you need to add a point light. Using the same steps and settings as before, add a point light and position it below the fixture. If you took my advice earlier and wrote down the settings of the lighting, you can use those same settings for the light here. Remember that you can change the view to top if you need some help aligning the light with the fixture.

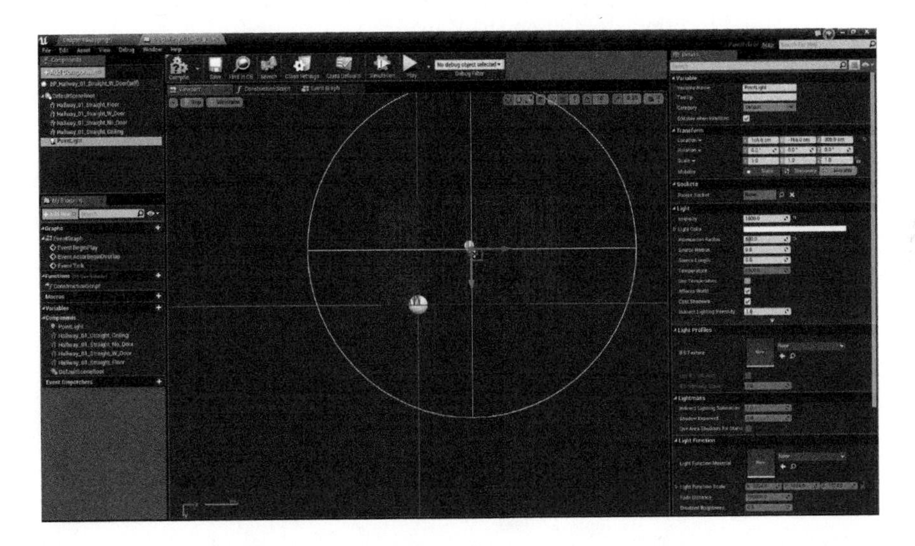

Compile and then save and close the blueprint. The next blueprint will have a 90 degree turn. Create a new blueprint and name it *BP_Hallway_01_90*. Again, add the floor first (*Hallway_01_90_Floor*).

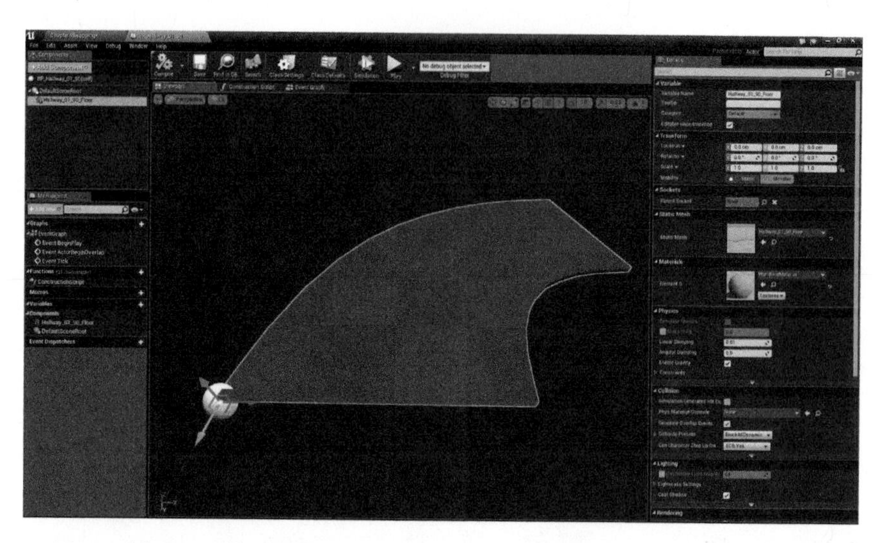

Next add the walls (*Hallway_01_90_Inner_Wall* and *Hallway_01_90_Outer_Wall*). Position the walls as follows:

Outer wall location:

- X—10

Inner wall location:

- X—315

Now you can add the ceiling. Find *Hallway_01_90_Ceiling* and add it to the blueprint. Adjust along Z to 400. By now you should be noticing a pattern. You are adding the floor first, then the walls, and then the ceiling. You are also setting all the ceiling locations to 400 on the Z, which will ensure that they all line up properly as you place these blueprints into the level.

Add any point lights needed. When finished, you have something similar to the following figure.

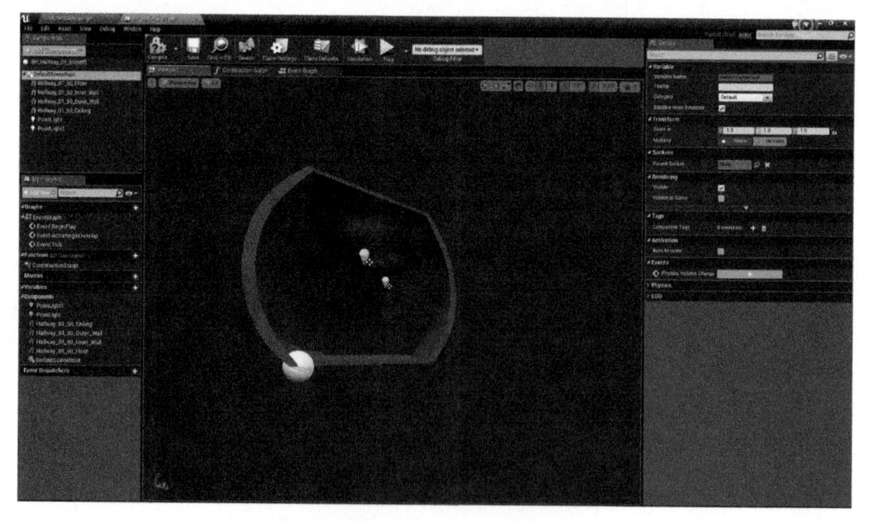

To finish out the rest of the Hallway 1 section blueprints, you have two more to build. Create a straight hallway blueprint similar to *BP_Hallway_01_Straight_W_Door* and name it *BP_Hallway_01_Straight_No_Door*. For the walls, you can use the wall that does not have a doorframe for both sides. You also need to create a blueprint for the Y section of the hallway. You can name the Y section blueprint *BP_Hallway_01_Y*. Use the following images and the previous steps as a guide. Remember that, for each light fixture on the ceiling, you should add one point light with the same settings as before.

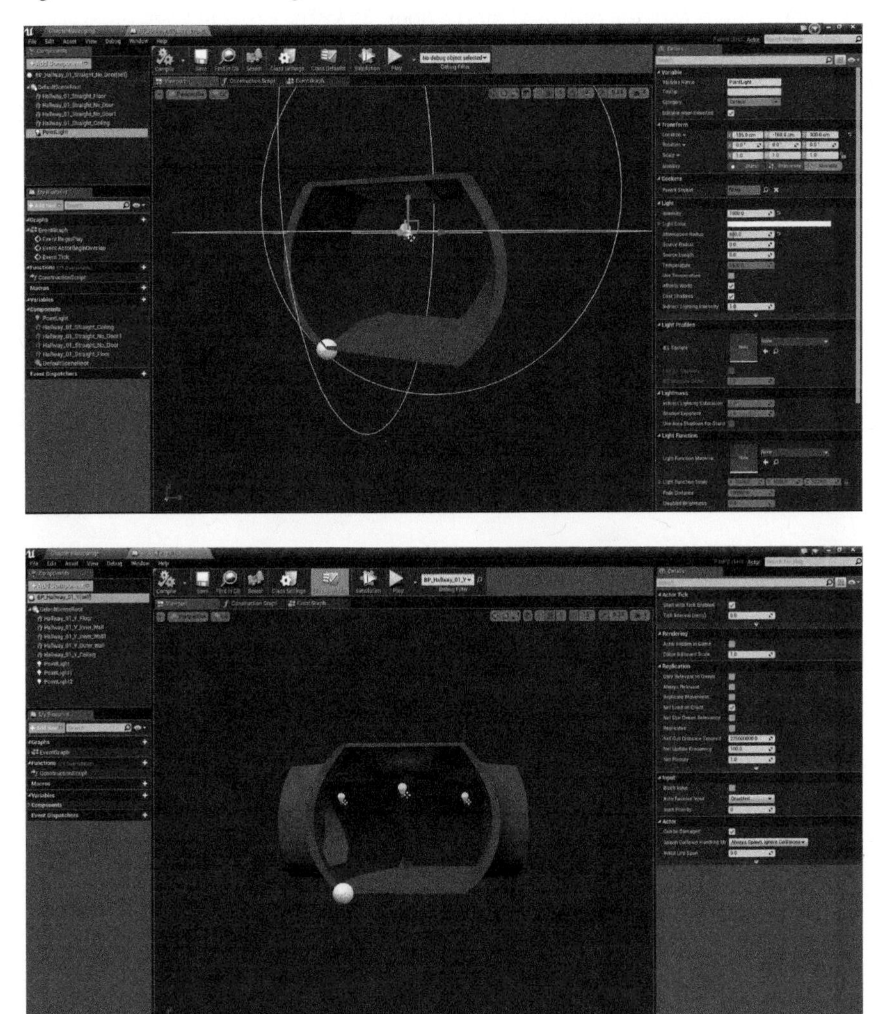

Chapter Challenge

So far in the chapter you have created a number of blueprints. However, there are more to be made. Using the importing steps discussed earlier, import the four parts to create a new blueprint based on the *Hallway_01_T sections*. After you have all the parts imported, create a new blueprint named *BP_Hallway_01_T* and then add those parts to the blueprint. Do not forget to add any point lights needed.

Adding Hallway Blueprints to the Level

Earlier we took a look at the swapping process. You can use those same steps to swap out different sections of the hallway. You will wait until you have all your hallway sections in place and have created doorways before converting your BSPs into blocking volumes. Start by adding the *BP_Hallway_01_Straight_No_Door*. You can place one section using the Perspective view, making sure to align it properly to the ground, then duplicate and move the sections to create the hallways. If you have been following along, the Z location of the hallway section should be around 15 to make it properly align with the BSP used for the floor. It may be easier to align the sections using the Top view. Use the following image to have a better idea where to place them.

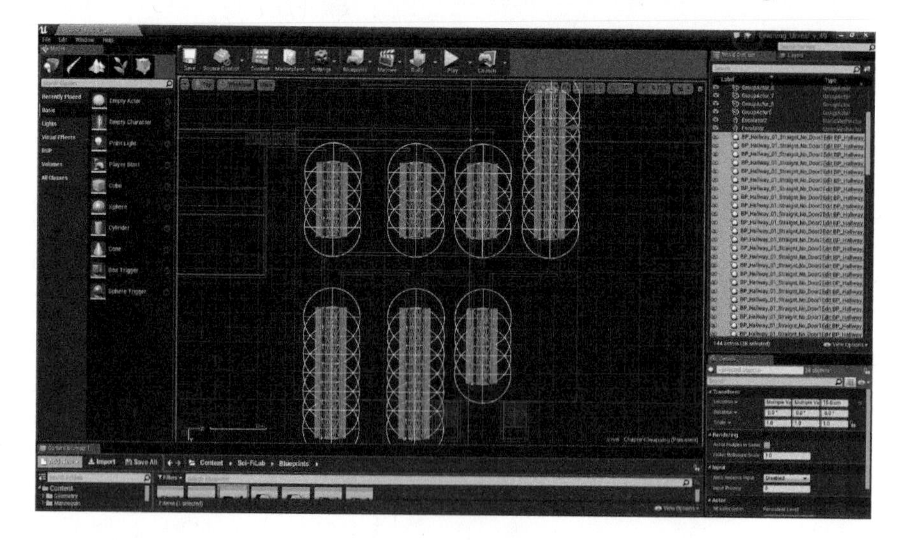

Note: When you are laying out your hallway sections, there will be small gaps between each section. This will be addressed shortly.

Now that you have the majority of the straight sections in place, you can begin to add some of the 90 degree hallway sections. Use the image below as a guide.

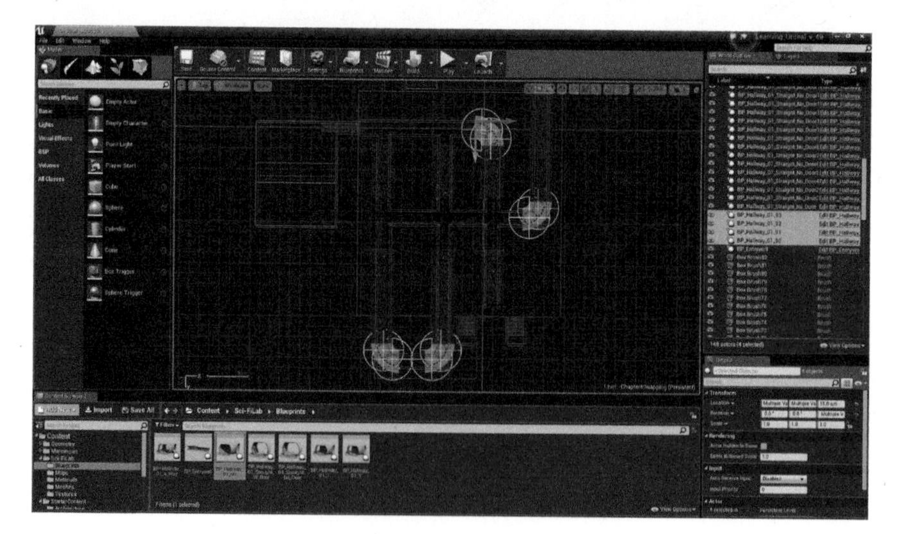

Next, add the four-way sections.

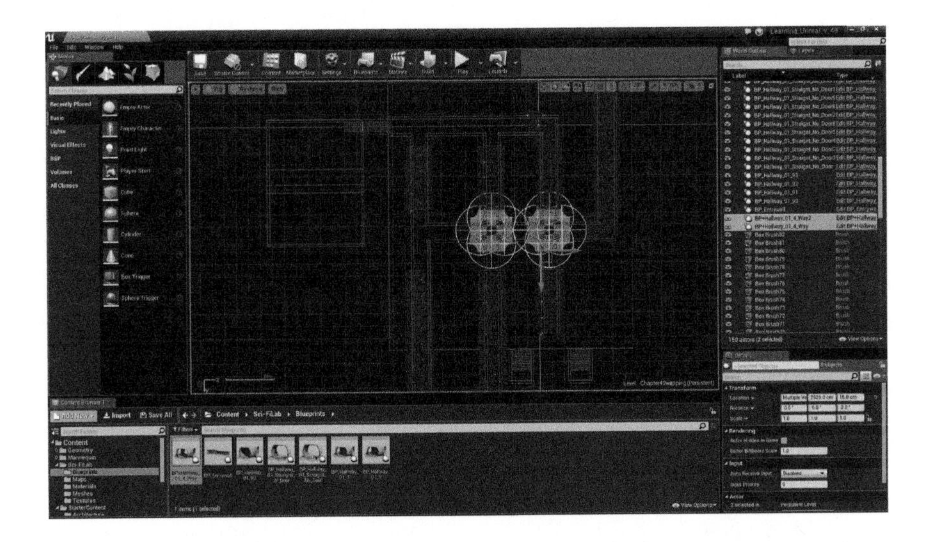

You have just a few sections left to address. You can add the Y sections now as shown in the following figure.

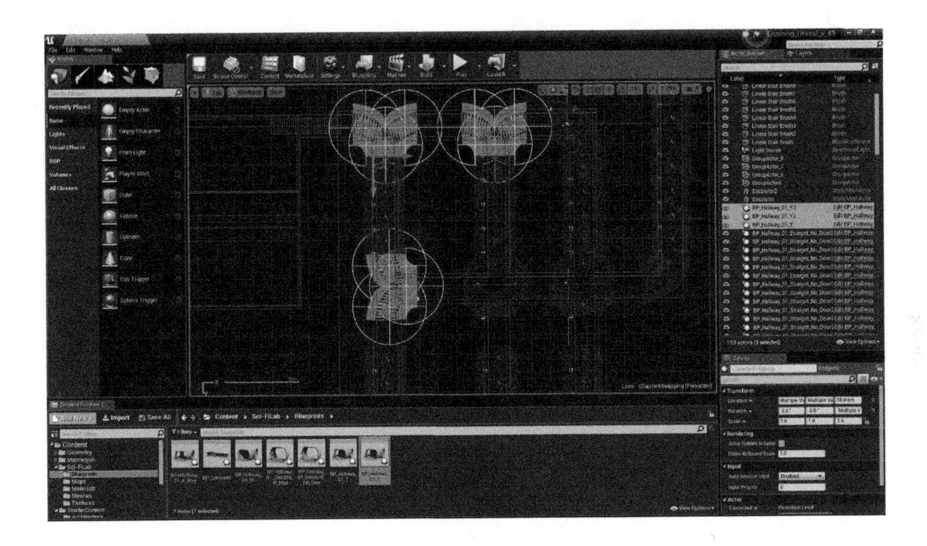

You should notice that there are still a few areas without a hallway section. You will correct this issue shortly. Before you continue, take time to play-test your level to see how it is changing. Once done, save your work. Now you can refer back to your initial sketch.

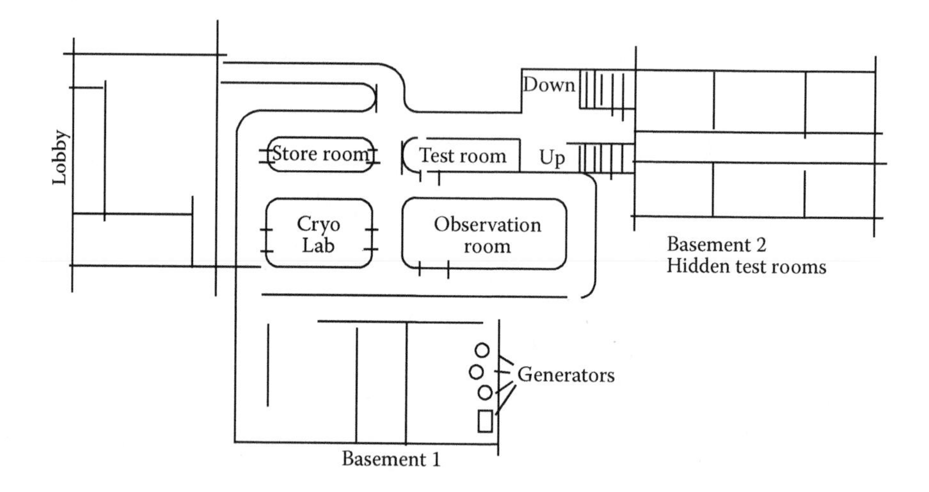

Using the sketch above, you can see where to place the doors. The doors go where there are double lines intersecting the hallways. Add *BP_Hallway_01_Straight_W_Door* to your level. Take special note of which side the doorway is on.

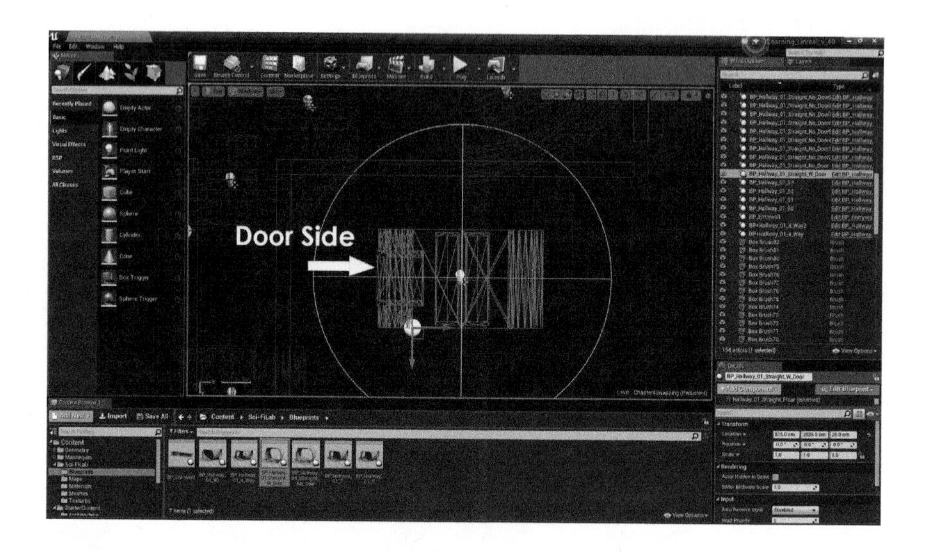

Place the door sections as shown in the next figure.

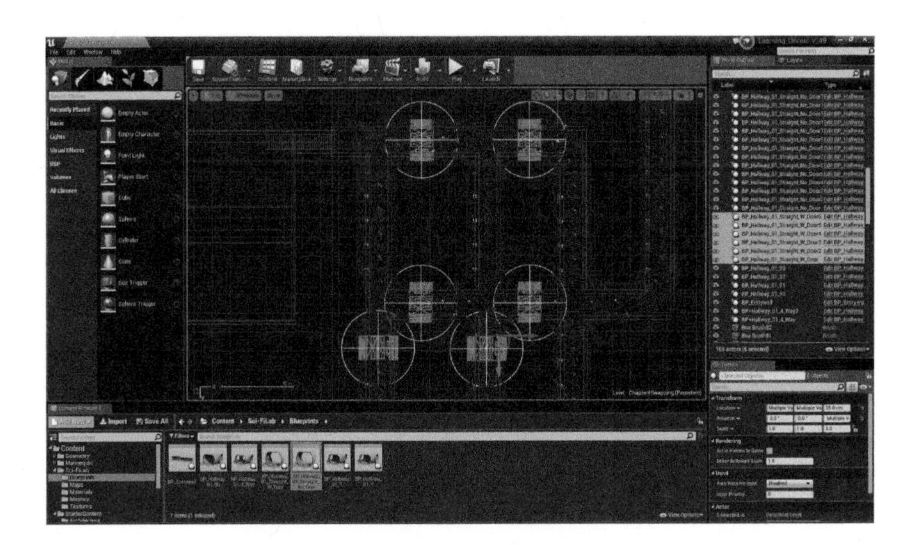

To finish adding the hallway sections, you need to add a few more straight sections without doors at the locations shown in the following figure.

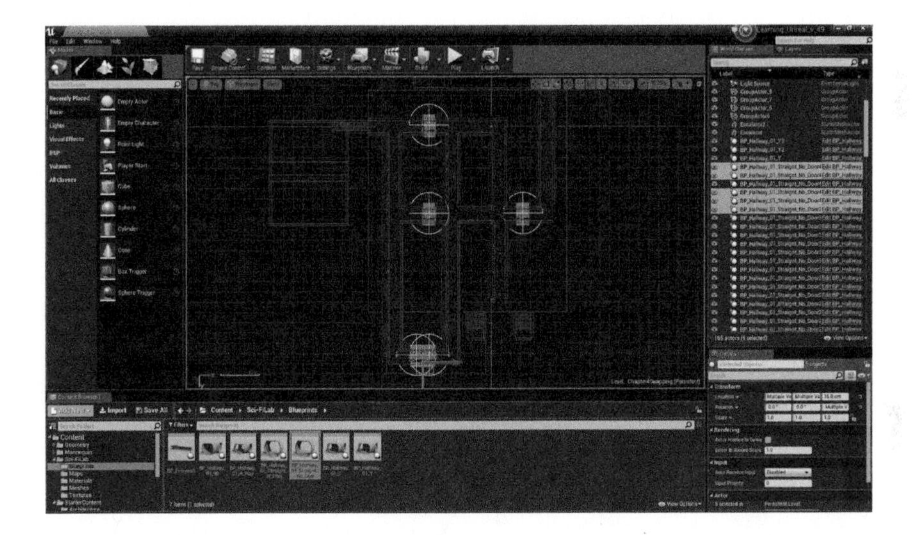

The finished hallways should resemble the next image. Take time to adjust as needed.

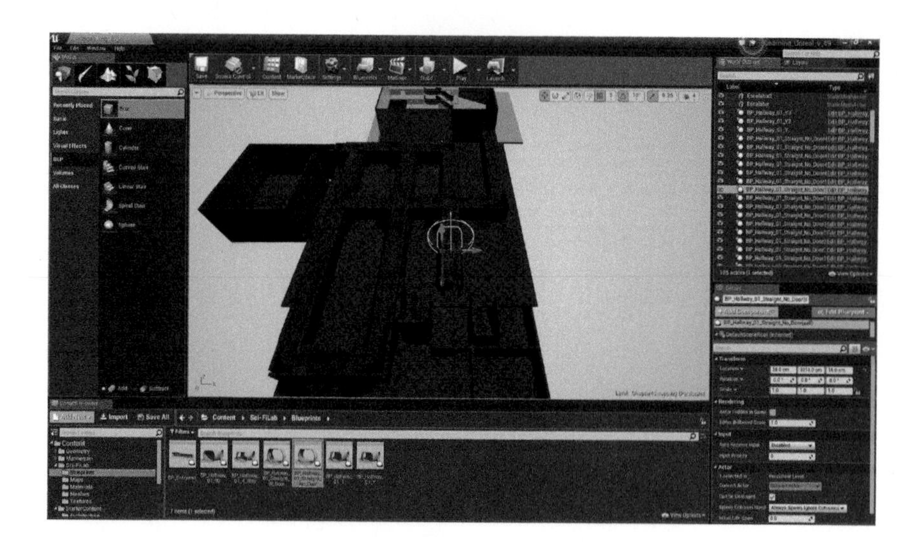

Using Layers to Group Objects

Since you have some doorways to create before you can change the BSPs to blocking volumes, you need an easy way to hide sections of the level. In an earlier chapter you looked at grouping objects together. While this is an easy way to manage a few objects at a time, you need a more encompassing solution now. There is a new tab you will look at now, named Layers, which can be found under the Windows menu→Layers.

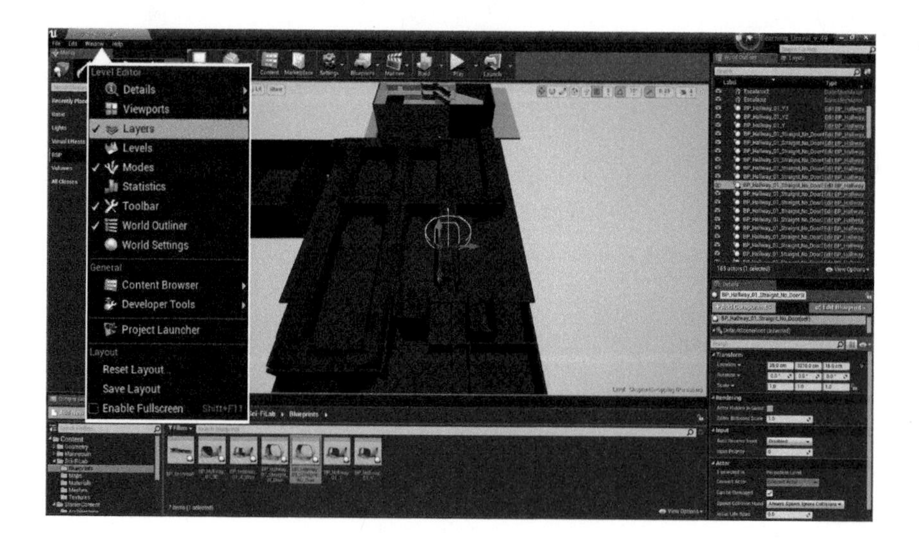

The Layers tab will open sharing space with World Outliner. You can switch now by clicking the Layers tab.

You can add objects to new layers or existing layers by selecting them in either the Viewport or the World Outliner. You are going to be putting all the hallway sections into a layer. Start by selecting at least one of the hallway sections now. Right-click in the Layers tab and choose Add Selected Actors to New Layer. Name the new layer Hallway01. Once you have the layer created, you can finish adding all the Hallway 01 sections to it by selecting them in either the Viewport or the World Outliner and then right-clicking on the layer and choosing Add Selected Actors to Selected Layers.

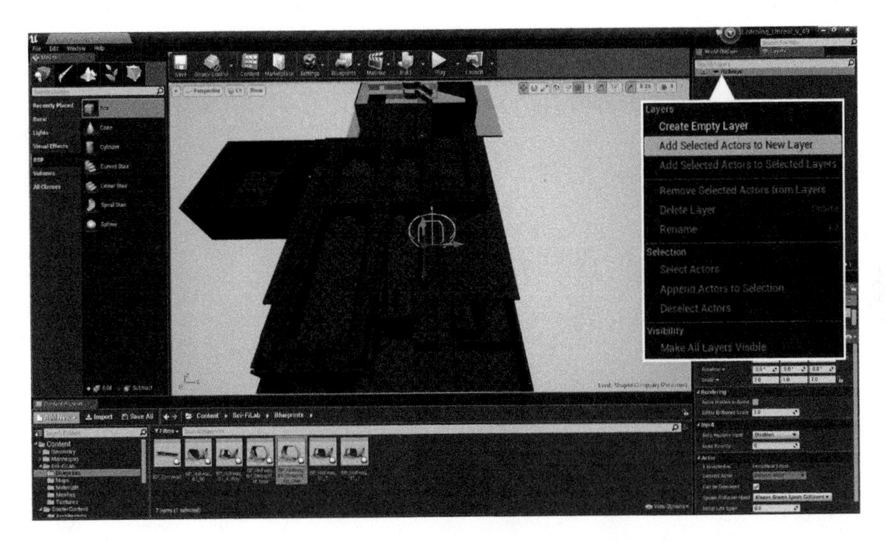

Now that you have added all the hallway sections to the layer, you can hide them all at once by clicking the eye beside the Layers name. This is a good time to note that objects hidden in either the World Outliner or Layers tab will reappear when playing the game.

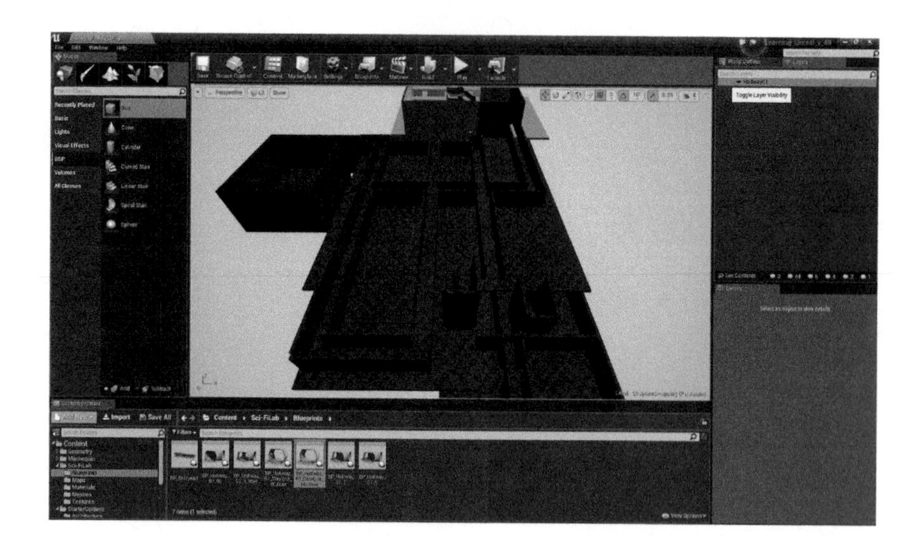

Before you can make the doorways for your hallway doors, you need to look at one issue that will arise. When you convert a BSP to a blocking volume, the additive and subtractive relationship no longer applies. This means that you cannot use the subtractive BSP to create a doorway in a wall that you will convert to a blocking volume. If you remember, in a previous chapter you worked with the Geometry Editing mode. You can use the same techniques here to change the shape of a BSP so that you do not need to use a Subtractive box. You will start on a small wall to get a better idea of what you will be doing. Find the wall highlighted in the following figure.

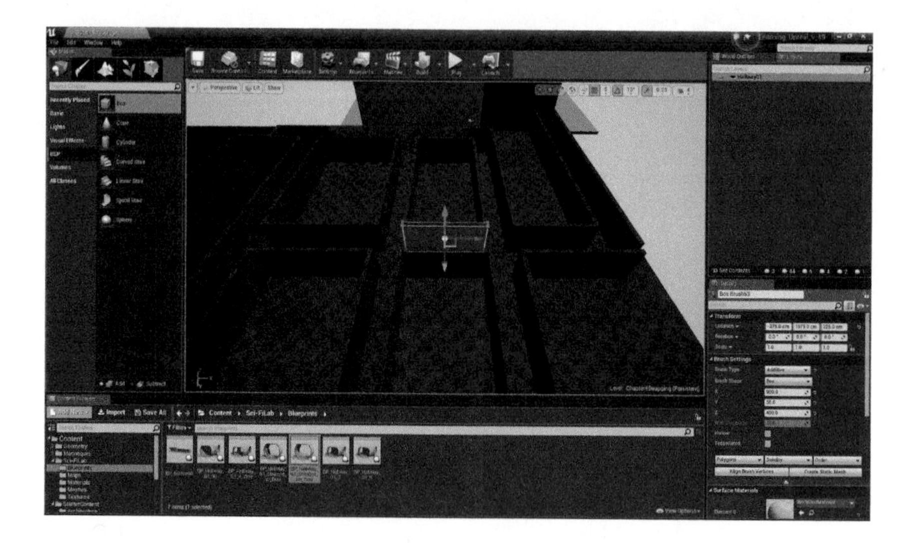

If you have turned visibility off for your Hallway01 layer, turn it back on now.

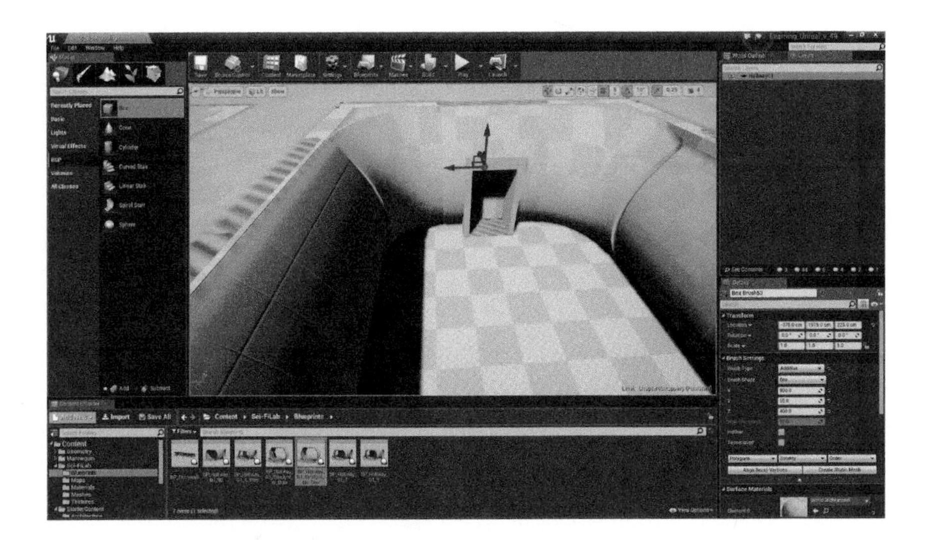

You should be able to see the wall running through the doorway here. To start, switch to Geometry Editing mode. Select the face on the right side (from inside the hallway) of the BSP and move it to the left so that it stops just before the doorframe.

Next, you need to lower the top side to just above the door height.

Note: If you are having difficulty selecting the faces, try turning the visibility for the hallway01 layer off, selecting the face, and then turning the visibility back on.

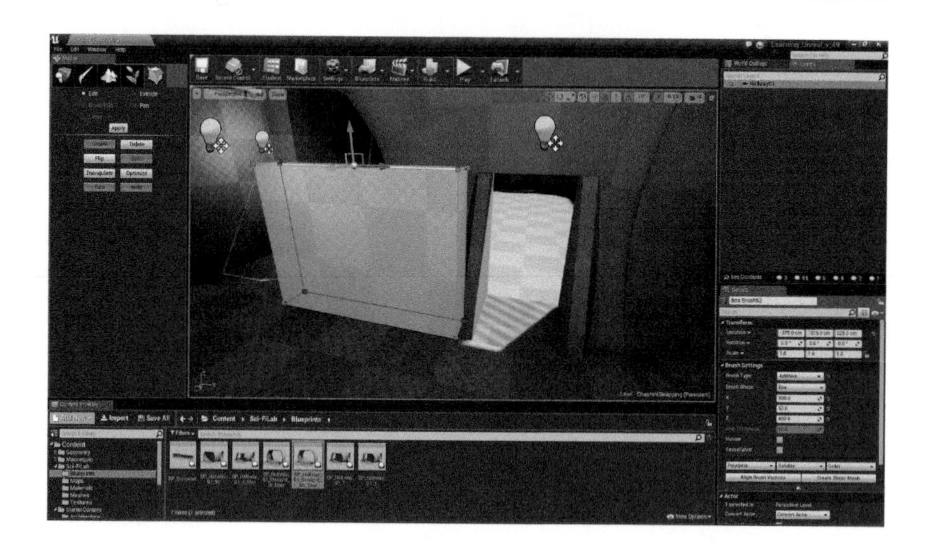

With the top face still selected extrude upward. This will create another section to the block that you can adjust separately. After you are done with the extrusion, remember to switch back to edit mode before making any other adjustments.

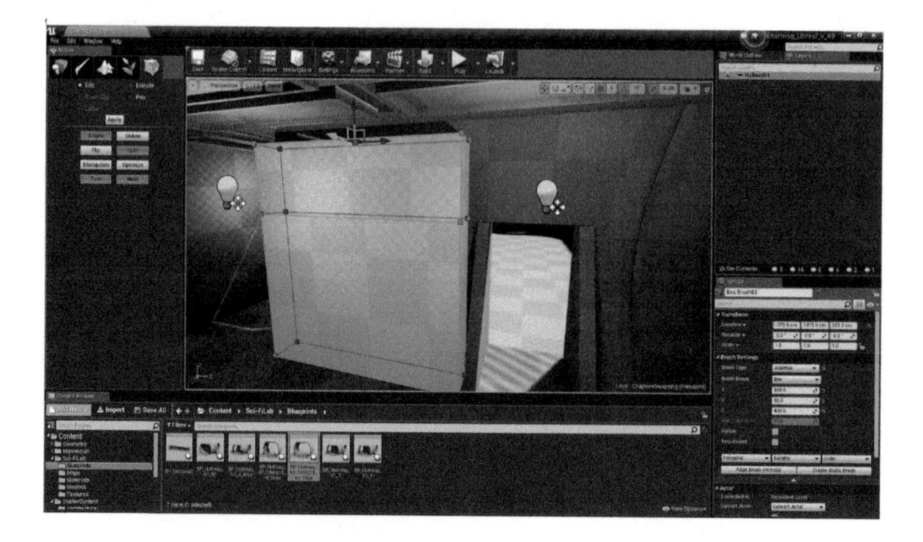

Next, select both faces on the door side by selecting one, then Ctrl + clicking the second.

Extrude these faces to the inside of the doorway.

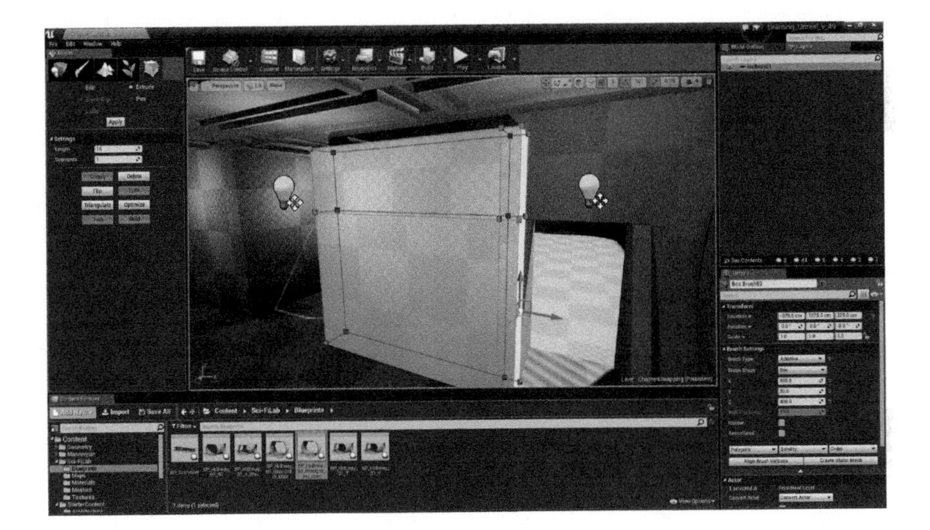

Select only the top section and extrude across the width of the doorway.

Extrude again to the outer edge of the doorframe and then extrude the bottom face downward to the ground.

Select both the top and bottom faces and extrude to the front wall.

The final step here is to extrude the back side of the narrow sections to cover the inside of the doorframe.

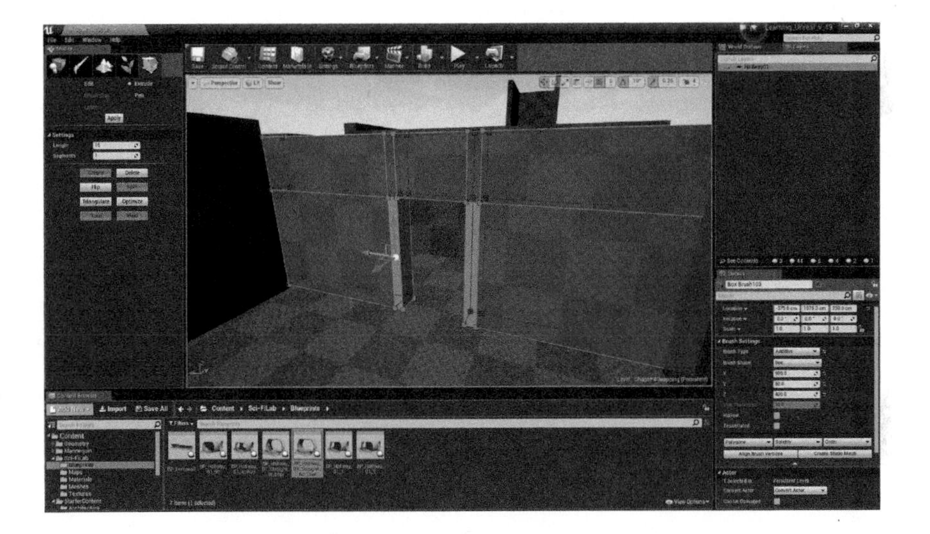

Now you just have to repeat the process for the rest of the doorways. Just kidding! Now that you have one built, you can use it in any other section where you have doorways. Switch back to Place mode and then you can copy the wall and move it wherever you need another doorway. When moving the wall into place, be sure that you use Geometry Editing mode to adjust the different sections of the wall if you find that they are not in the right position. The simplest method is to align the doorway of the BSP with the doorway of the Hallway 01 section and then use Geometry Editing mode to move the ends of the wall into place.

You should now have these modified walls in place where every door is as seen in the figure below.

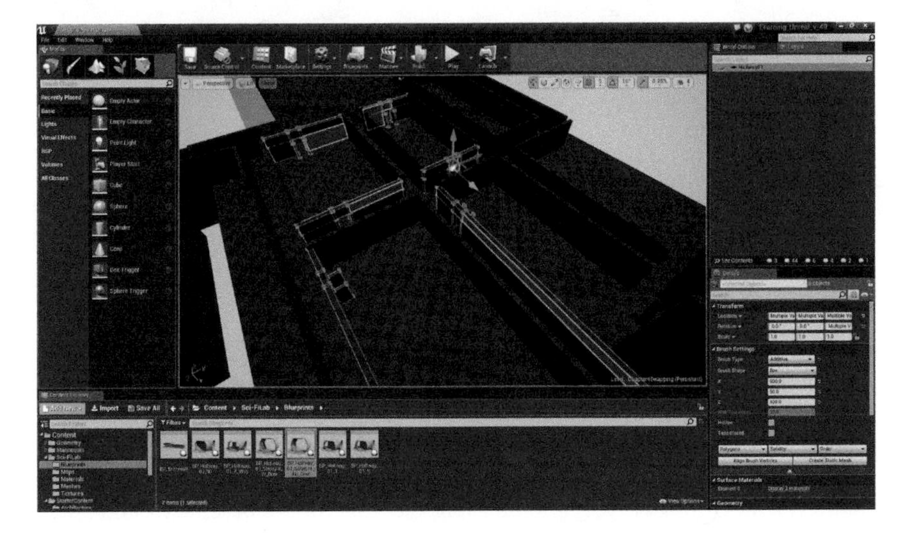

Chapter Challenge

We have looked at one way to get around the doorframe issue. Can you think of another way to solve the issue? Try building a new section of wall that has an opening for the doorway without using the steps outlined earlier.

Note: While there are a number of solutions, another relatively simple solution would be to use three boxes. With this method, you would need to put one on either side of the door and one above the door.

Error Checking through Play-Testing

Finally! You get to actually play your level once again. Run through each section of the level to be sure there are no issues. For this play-test I would like to draw your attention to another helpful tool. When you click Play, you spawn at the Player Start. Alternately, you can place the mouse over a section where you would like to start, right-click, and choose Play From Here. As it implies, the Play From Here option allows you to start at the location you selected in the viewport rather than the spawn point for the level. If you find that when you spawn you automatically fall through the floor, try moving the camera upward slightly and make sure you are selecting an actual floor section.

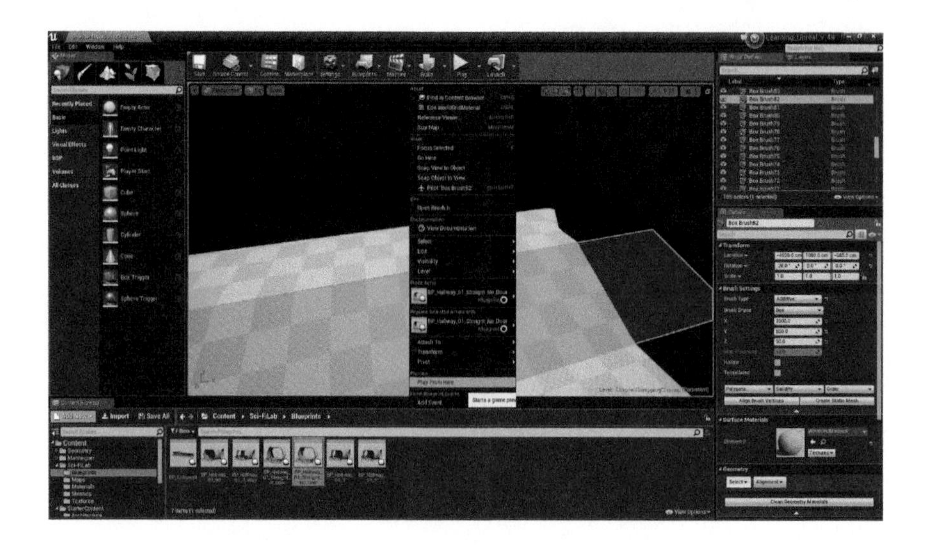

You are finally at a spot where you can start to convert some of these BSPs. Before you proceed any farther, I suggest saving your level under a new name so that you have a backup if any major errors or issues arise.

You are only going to convert the walls and floors that directly relate to your hallways. Since you are going to be using the walls in the basements and entryway you do *not* want to hide those. You can start by working from the beginning of the hallway section (near the entryway) and gradually working toward the basements. Remember that you may have to use the Build button before the converted blocking volumes become invisible. However, as you convert them, you should notice that the outline changes from orange to purple/pink. The pink outline will confirm that you have successfully converted the BSP. Take your time. You cannot undo edits after the level has been rebuilt, so if you were to make a mistake and build the level at the wrong time, you will not be able to use the undo command to correct it. If you are unsure of how a particular section is functioning, play-test.

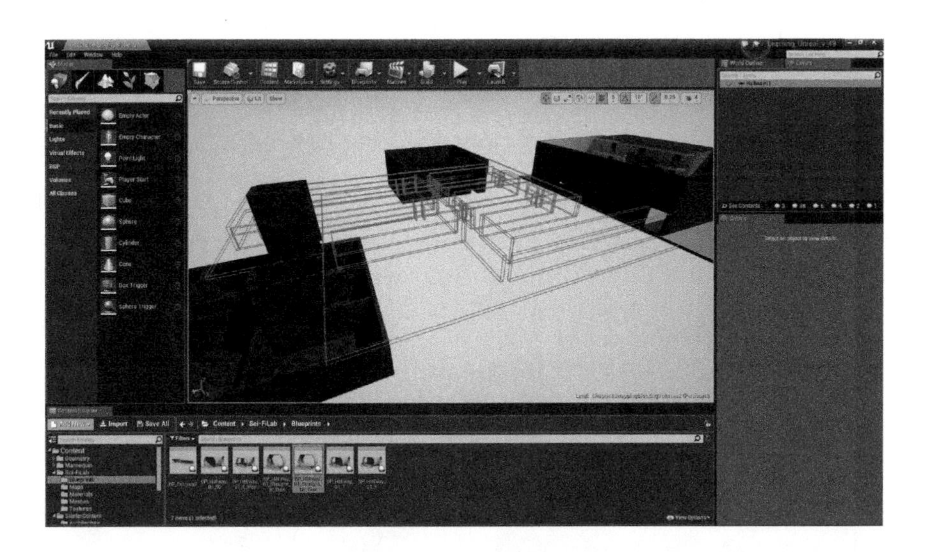

The purple/pink lines represent the blocking volumes. Play-test one more time after you have completed the conversion and look for any irregularities.

You may notice that in some areas there are slight gaps similar to the ones seen in the figure below. Take note of their location as you run through the level. This is actually by design to express a particular point about the power of blueprints. You will be correcting the issue shortly.

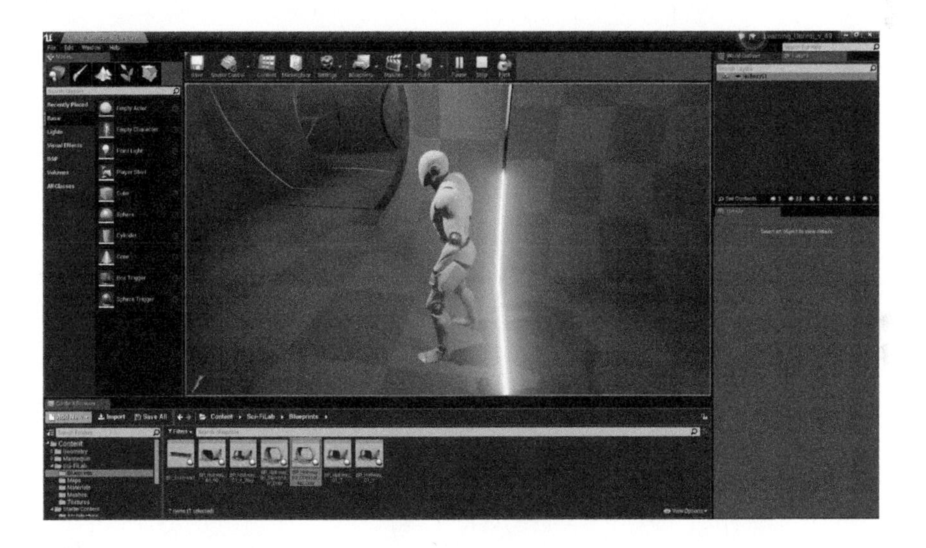

Modifying Your Blueprints and Adding Doorframes

By now you should be starting to realize how powerful blueprints can be. You have already used them to combine multiple meshes together to use as a unit. Now you will see how simple it can be to correct issues by modifying your blueprints. Before you can start on the corrections, you need to import a new mesh. In the Meshes folder, right-click and choose Import. Find the *Hallway_01_Door_Frame* object in the support files. The import options should be the same as before, so once you have it selected, click on Import.

You could take the time to go through the whole level, adding doorframe after doorframe until you have covered every gap. You can imagine, though, how long and boring a job that would be. Instead, you can drastically reduce the number of corrections needed by modifying your *BP_Hallway_01_Straight_No_Door* blueprint. Open that blueprint now. You should notice that your blueprint viewport has change dramatically. Instead of opening directly into the regular viewport, it opened into a graph. You will get to know graphs soon enough, but for now you can change back to the normal viewport by clicking the Viewport tab.

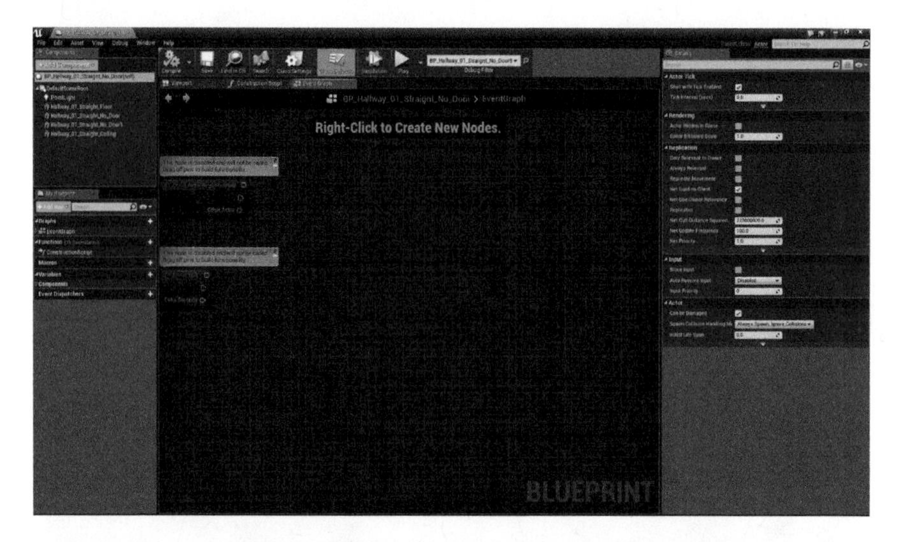

Find the doorframe you just imported and add it to the blueprint.

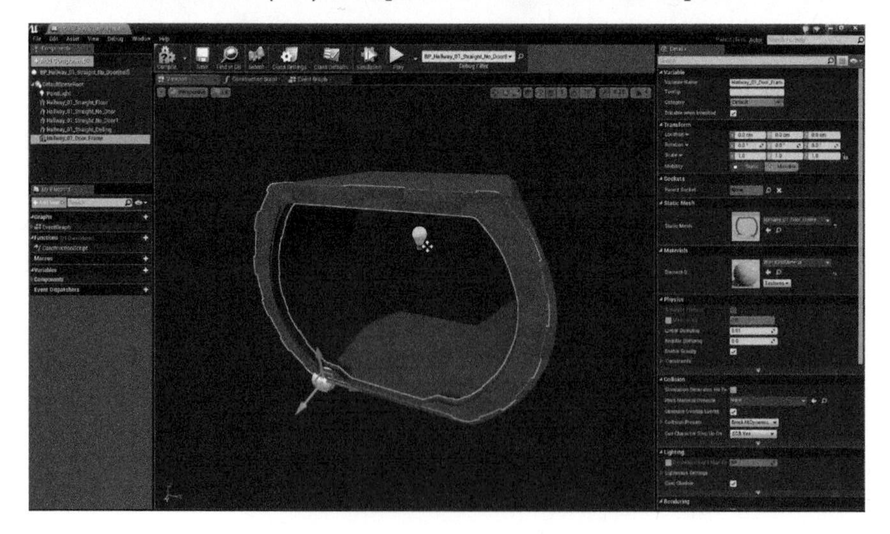

Move the doorframe to the following location:

- X—15
- Y—20
- Z—2

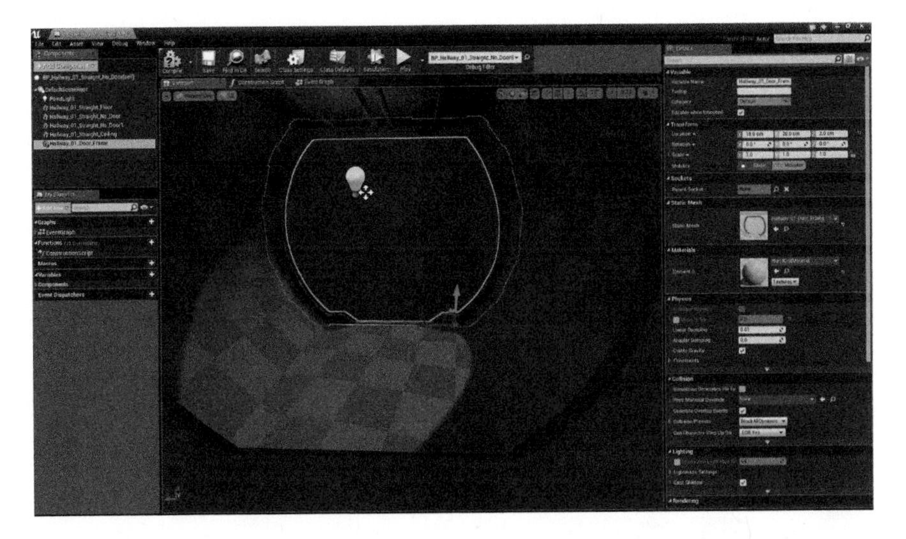

Compile and save the blueprint and then close the Blueprint Editor. Now play your level and look at how it has changed.

You should see a pretty drastic change to your hallways. Not only did you correct many of the gap issues you were seeing earlier, but you added a little more detail to the hallway as well. There are still a few more gaps that need to be covered. To fix these, you can add the *Hallway_01_Door_Frame* and move around as needed to cover them up.

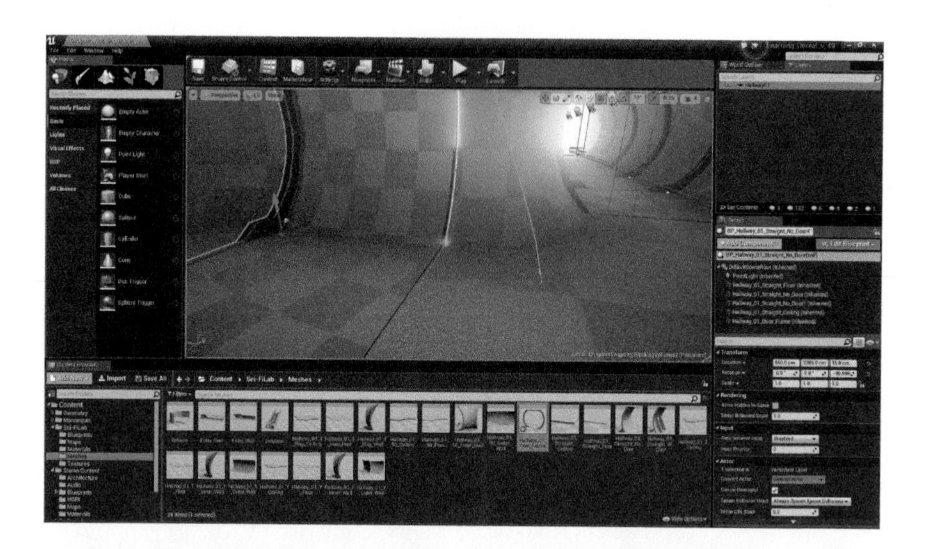

Once you have added all the doorframes, you can play-test again to look for any more trouble areas.

Correcting Collisions

If you ran across a Y section of the hallway on your last play-test, you may have noticed that you can walk through the wall.

This is happening because the blocking you made earlier does not extend inward far enough to cover this area. You could add more blocking here, or you could take a look at another editor available to you.

Find *Hallway_01_Y_Outerwall* in the Meshes folder and open it by double-clicking on it. This opens the **Static Mesh Editor**.

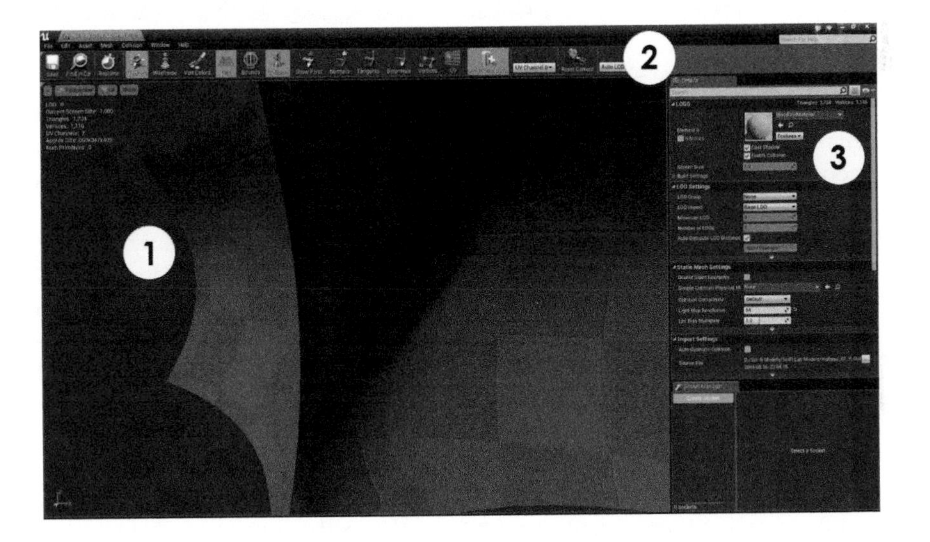

Looking at the Static Mesh Editor, there are a few sections you need to review:

1. Viewport is similar to the viewport in the Blueprint Editor or Level Editor.
2. Toolbar contains many of the same buttons as other editors and new tools also.
3. Details contains all editable properties of the currently open mesh.

All these sections function as they do in the other editors we have reviewed. There are a few additions to the viewport here that you will look at as you correct the issue with the collisions. To begin fixing the collision issue, you first need to make sure that collisions are visible. On the toolbar, make sure the Collision button is highlighted orange. With Collision on, you will be able to see the changes take place.

First you can take a look at some common collision types. In the title bar, click Collision to expand the menu options.

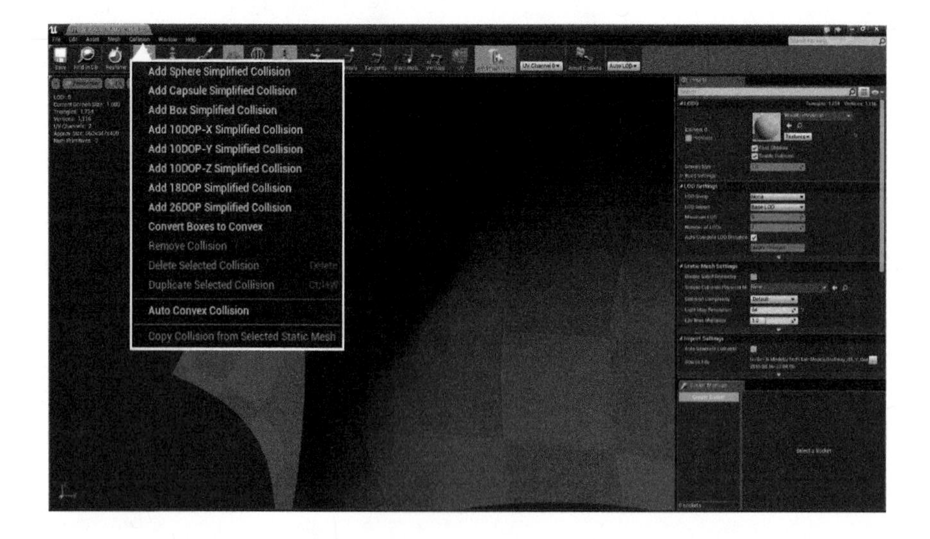

As you can see on the list, there are a number of different choices. All of the Add options will add Collision based on their specific properties. The first three are relatively simple to understand. They create a bounds base on the shape you choose. For example, if you choose Sphere Simplified Collision, it will build a sphere around your object.

The next section (10DOP through 26DOP) works a little differently than the simple shape types. All of the DOP collision types are called **discrete oriented polytope** collisions. Let us go over how these are created. The overall goal is to encase the object completely by using the sides provided. For example, **10DOP-(X, Y, Z) Simplified Collision** will build its collision model around the object using 10 faces based on the direction specified.

The next option you want to look at is **Remove Collision**. This option will delete all collisions associated with the object. So if you accidently add a collision volume you do not want, you can use Remove Collision to get rid of it. When you use Remove Collision, it will remove *all* of the collision volumes that are currently associated with the mesh.

The final option here is **Auto Convex Collision**. If you cannot create a suitable collision through any of the other options, you can try the Auto Convex Collision.

Let us begin by looking at some of the collision models in action. First, look at Add 10DOP-X.

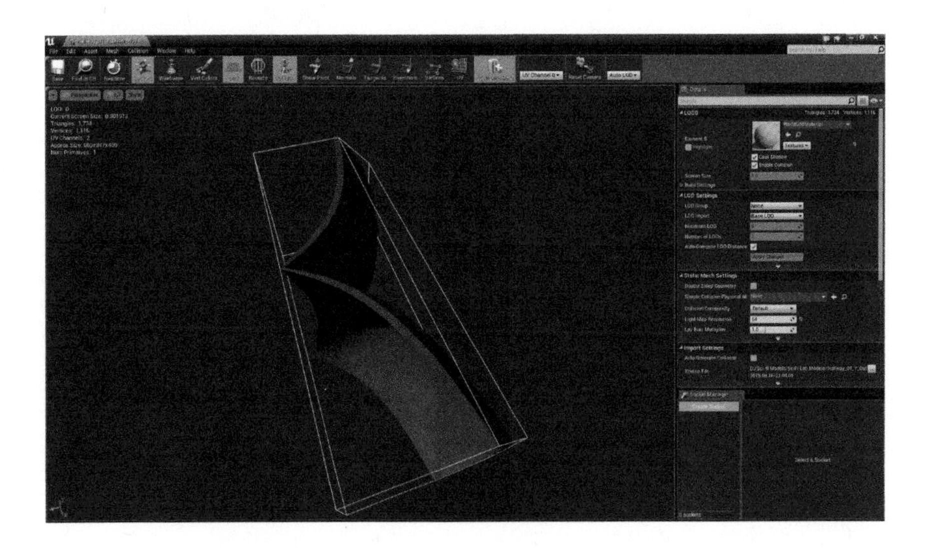

As you can see, there is not much complexity to this collision and it encompasses a lot of area you do not want included.

The next one you will look at is the 10DOP-Y option.

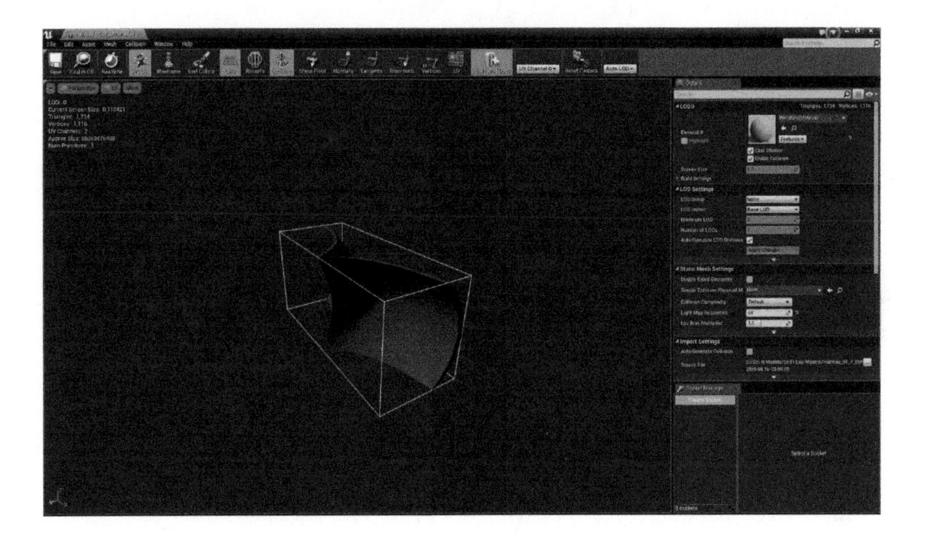

Next, try the 10DOP-Z.

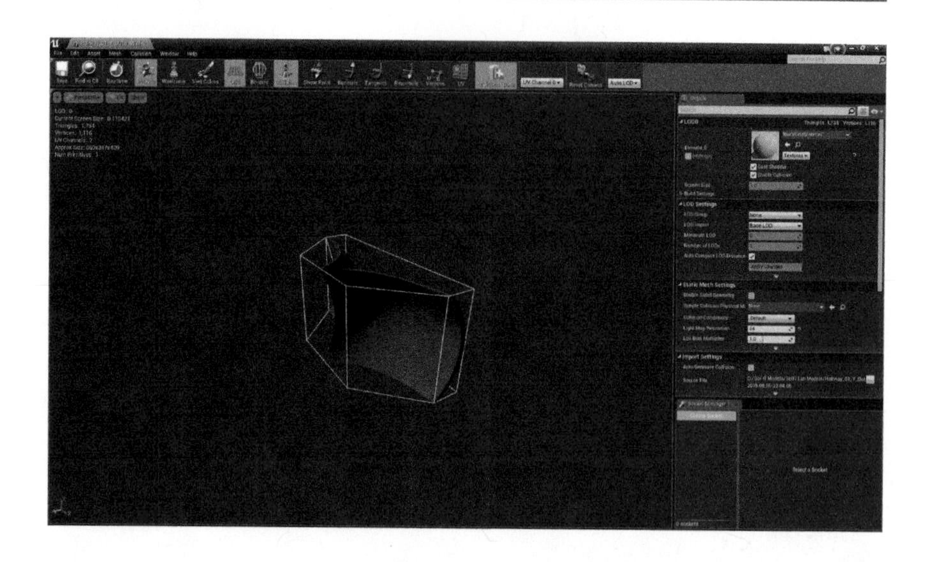

Note: Remember that if you are adding a new type, you should delete the collision first.

Almost done now, you will look at the last of the locked types with the 26DOP.

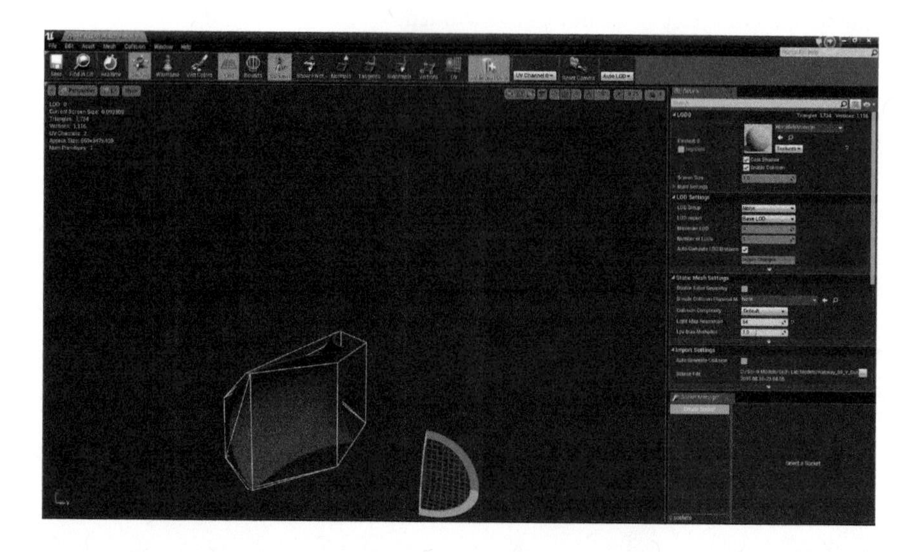

Now you get to work with the really interesting one: Auto Convex Collision. Unlike the others here, Auto Convex does not have a locked-in set of sides that has to be made. Auto Convex Collision generates a wholly different type of beast. Let us look at how it does this. When you first select Auto Convex Collision from the Collision menu, nothing happens in the viewport. Instead, a new tab, named Convex Decomposition, shows up in the bottom right corner below the Details tab. This tab has only two options: **Accuracy** and **Max Hull Verts**. Accuracy as it is used here determines the fewest number of hulls that can be used to best suit the needs of the mesh. The lower the accuracy is, the closer to the mesh it will attempt to be. Max Hull Verts is the maximum number of verts that can be used to create the collision. With the default settings still default, you can click on Apply.

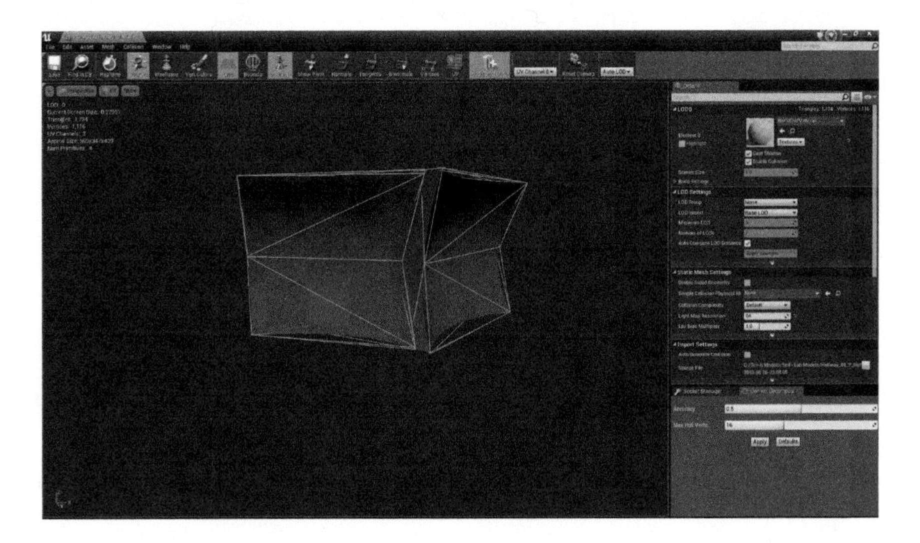

As you can see in the figure above, that was a pretty substantial change from the previous version. Save the mesh now and play-test again to check for any other issues. If you are happy with the results, you can close the Static Mesh Editor and move on. If for some reason your results were different, you can remove the collision and try building again.

Another glaring issue arises when getting close to certain corners. You may notice that because of the blocking volumes shapes, some corners extend well inside the hallway.

You can use the Geometry Editing mode to correct these issues by moving the faces on the ends of the blocking volumes back some and then extruding and moving the new face diagonally across the corner.

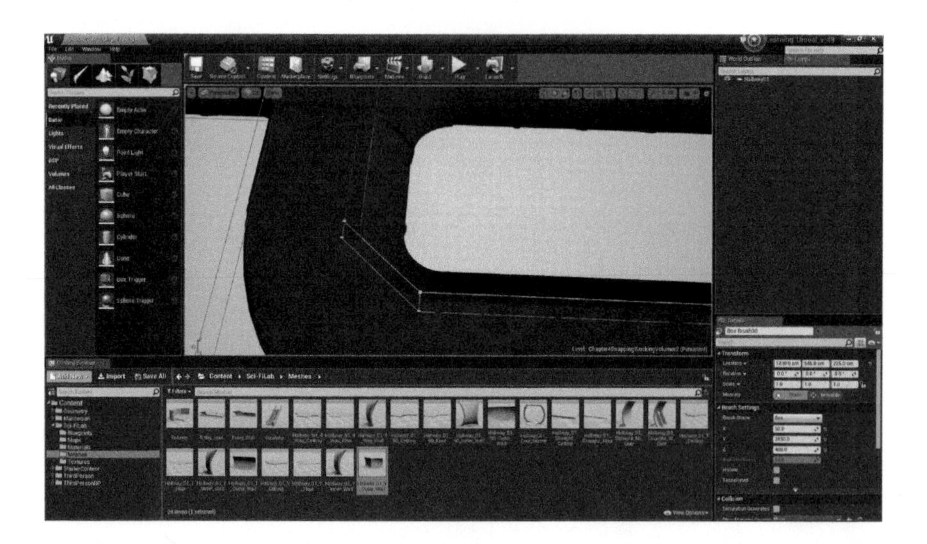

After completing the extrude on the trouble corners, you should end up with something similar to the following figure.

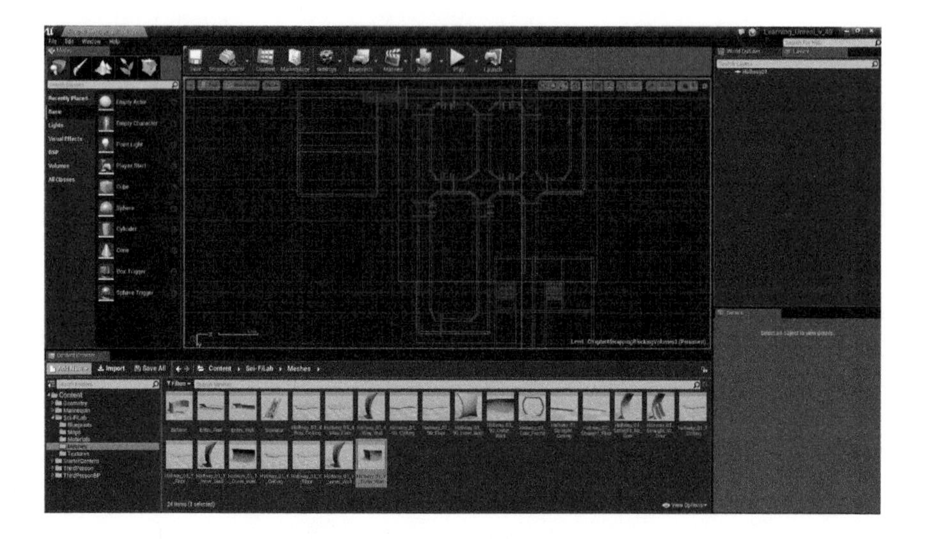

Before you move on to the next section, you need to add a collision to one more static mesh. Open the *Hallway_01_90_Outer_Wall* and add an Auto Convex Collision with the following settings:

- Accuracy—0.5
- Max hull verts—16

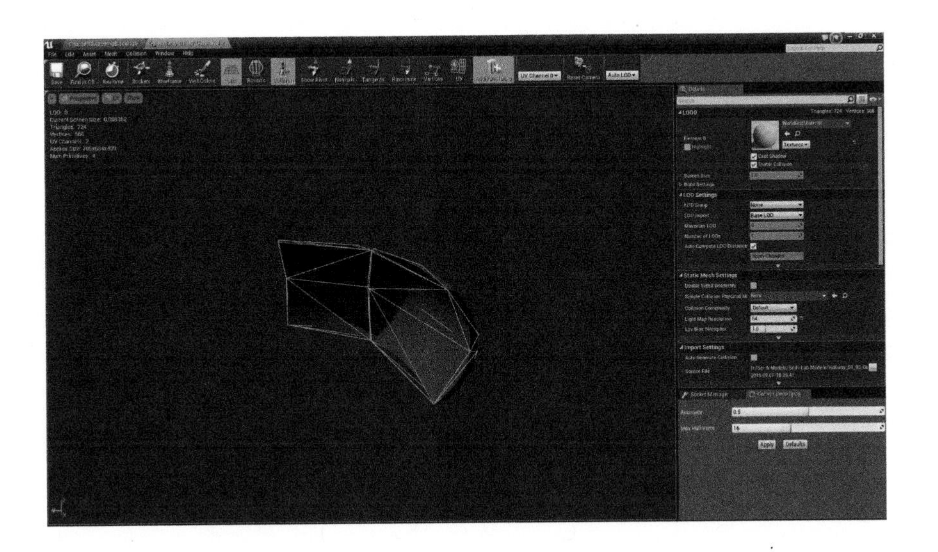

Play-test your level once again and look for any more standout issues. Once you are satisfied with your level, save your work and prepare for some materials fun!

Chapter Review

This chapter took a much more in-depth look at blueprints. You used geometry editing tools to create doorways in your blocking volumes. You also used geometry editing to clean up the corner sections of your hallways and looked for issues through play-testing. You also took a closer look at static meshes by modifying collisions with the Static Mesh Editor.

6

Materials

Introduction

In Chapter 4 we took a quick look at the Material Editor in Unreal Engine 4. In this chapter we will take a much more in-depth look at how to use textures to add detail to your materials. **Textures** are simply two-dimensional images that you can use to change the appearance of a material. We will also explore the multitude of different options available in the Material Editor that will help add detail and create glows and glass, among other things.

Textures versus Materials

There are a few main types of textures that you will be using. The three primary texture types are

- Diffuse—the color texture of a material
- Mask—a texture that is used to block sections within a material
- Normal—a texture used to create high-quality detail

Unreal can use a number of different file types for textures, including:

- .bmp
- .float
- .pcx
- .png
- .psd

- .tga
- .jpg
- .exr
- .dds
- .hdr

When importing textures, you must make sure that the file being imported has dimensions that are powers of 2. This means the texture should be 512 × 512, 1024 × 1024, 2048 × 2048—pixels, and so on. When creating your textures, if you have multiple textures for the same object, it is a good idea to keep them all the same size. While Unreal will have no problem applying textures of different sizes to an object, if you were to adjust the tiling, for example, it may not line up correctly.

Now that you have a little better understanding of what textures are, we can begin to discuss the overall difference between a texture and a material. While textures contain a lot of the detail information, they cannot be applied to an object in Unreal Engine 4. This is where materials come in. A material can have multiple textures or none at all. This helps to make material creation very flexible. You also have the ability to mix different components together as you see fit. For example, you can use a normal map in a material without using a diffuse or mask texture. You will be creating a number of base materials that you will then be able to use throughout your level.

Material Types

In the Content Browser, open or create a Materials folder in your project. In the Materials folder create a new material and name it *M_Hallway_Base*. Double-click your new material to open it in the Material Editor.

Before you start building your new materials, let us explore some of the available options materials have. Looking at the Details tab, you will investigate a few key properties specific to your material. Starting at the top, these options are

- **Phys Material** can be used to create different types of physics reactions applied to the material; some common uses are special sounds and friction types.

- **Material Domain** determines the usage of the material.
- **Blend Mode** controls how the material will be blended with the background.
- **Decal Blend Mode**—If the material domain is a decal, this will control the blending.
- **Shading Model** controls how the material inputs are combined to create the final color of the material.
- **Two Sided** controls the back face culling of the material (when checking if the material will be visible from both sides).
- **Use Material Attributes**—When checked, the material will use the Material Attributes pin rather than the regular pins.

While this is not the complete list of properties available, it is the core of what you will be working with. You should be able to accomplish virtually everything you will need throughout this book using only these properties.

Input Types

For this material, you will use a domain of Surface, blend mode of Opaque, and shading model of Default Lit. This is one of the most common setups and is the default setting for a new material. In the graph portion of the material you should see the Material Attributes node. There are also a number of different properties here that you will look at, but for now you need to focus on three of them. This first material will be very similar to your first material since you want the entry and hallway sections to flow together. Create a Vector node by holding the "3" key and clicking in the graph. Create two Constant nodes by holding the "1" key and clicking in the graph two times. Connect the Vector node to the Base Color input; connect one of the Constant nodes to the Metallic input and the other to the Roughness input. See the figure below.

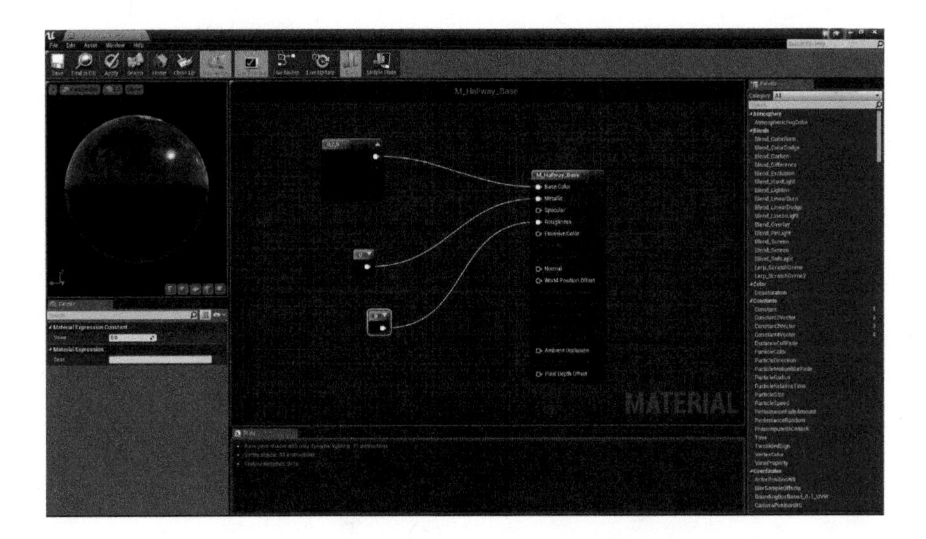

You now can adjust your color by changing the vector to an off-white/light blue color. Click on the Vector node; then, in the Details tab, click on the Constant color block to open the color picker.

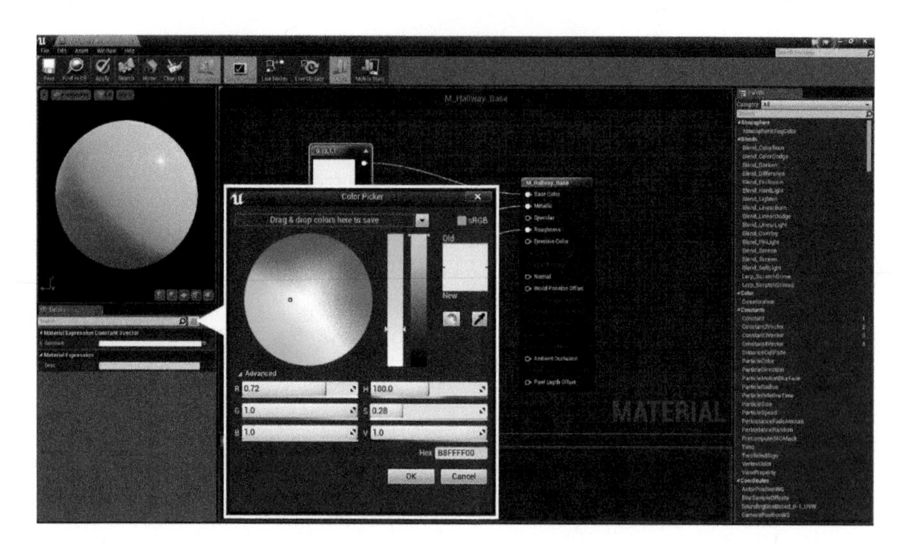

That is everything you need for this material, so you can save and close the Material Editor now. While you did not make any adjustments to the Roughness or Metallic values, they are still affecting the material.

Adding Textures

Before you can add textures to your material, you need to import them. Create a new folder and name it Textures. In the Textures folder, import *Tile_M* and *Tile_N* from the Chapter 6 Assets folder. Looking at the names, you should notice a single letter at the end of the name. These letters indicate the type of texture. As discussed earlier, "M" refers to a mask, which is used to limit color information to certain sections. The "N" marker stands for normal and is used to add detail to the object.

Now you can start on the new material that you will be adding your normal texture to. Since you want a material similar in color to the previous material, you can right-click on *M_Hallway_Base* and choose Duplicate from the pop-up window. Name the new material *M_Tile_Base*. Open your new material in the Material Editor.

With the *Tile_N* texture selected in the content browser, hold the "T" key and click in the Material Editor graph to add the texture.

Drag off the top pin from the texture and connect it to the Normal input of the material. You should notice in the Material Editor viewport that your material now has lines or grooves running through it. The normal map you added contains the detail information that gives you these grooves. See the figure below for an example.

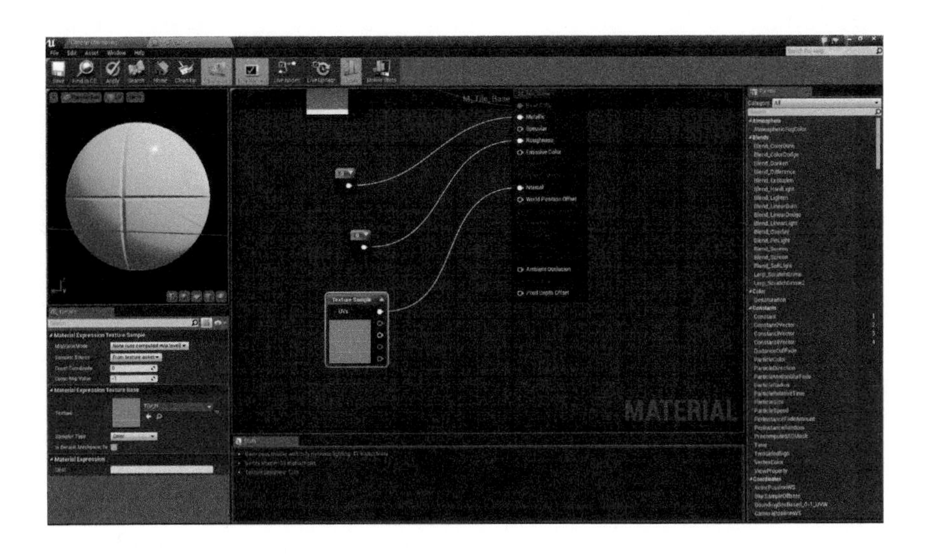

Save the material. Switch back to your viewport and find the entryway of the level. You can add the new material to the floor temporarily to see the difference the Normal makes. The figure below shows the floor with the original material, while the next figure shows the new material. As you can see from the figures, a simple texture can give your level more detail and help to break up larger areas.

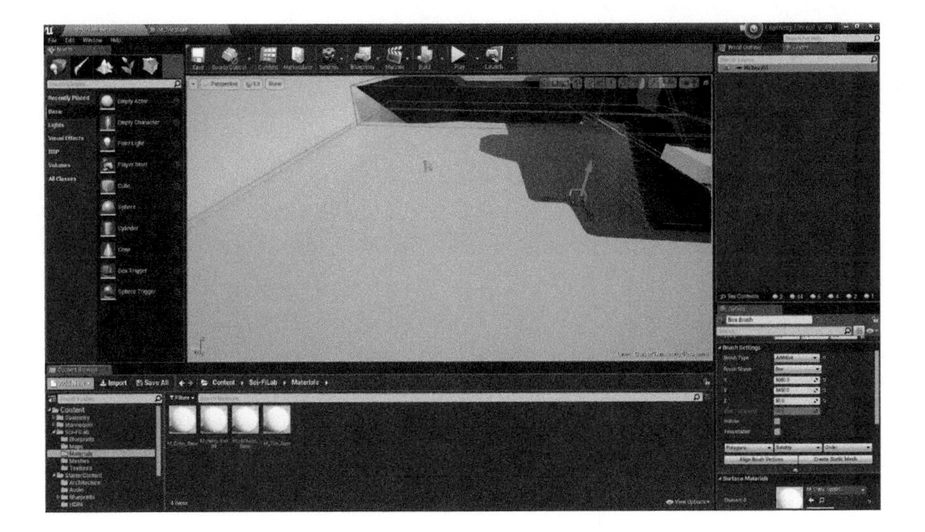

Back in the Material Editor you can make a couple more changes to the material to add even more diversity. Start by adding the *Tile_M* texture to the material. Looking at the *Tile_M* texture, you can see that there are two different colors (black and white). You can use this texture to mask out sections, allowing you to use multiple colors.

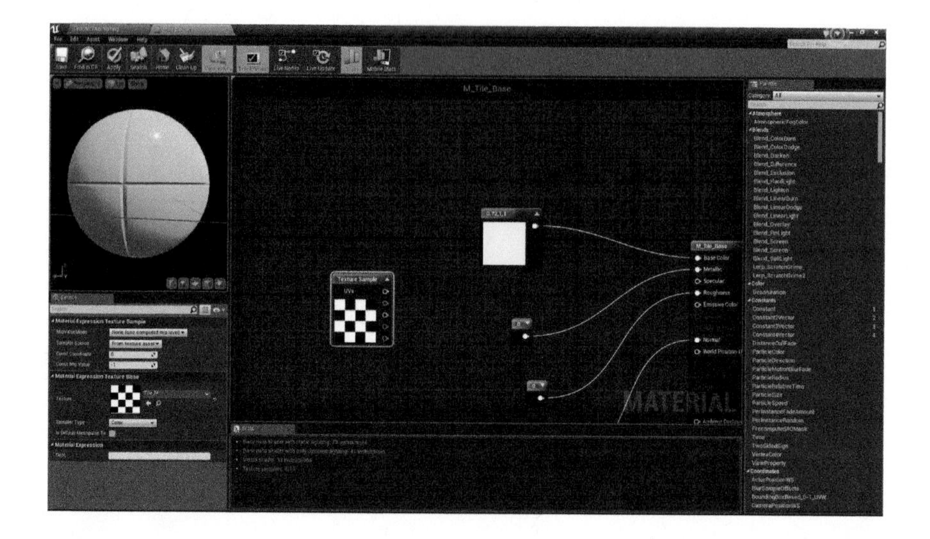

Before you can continue, you need to add another Vector node so that you can use two different colors in the material. Hold the "3" key and click in the graph. Set the color of the new node to a light gray color.

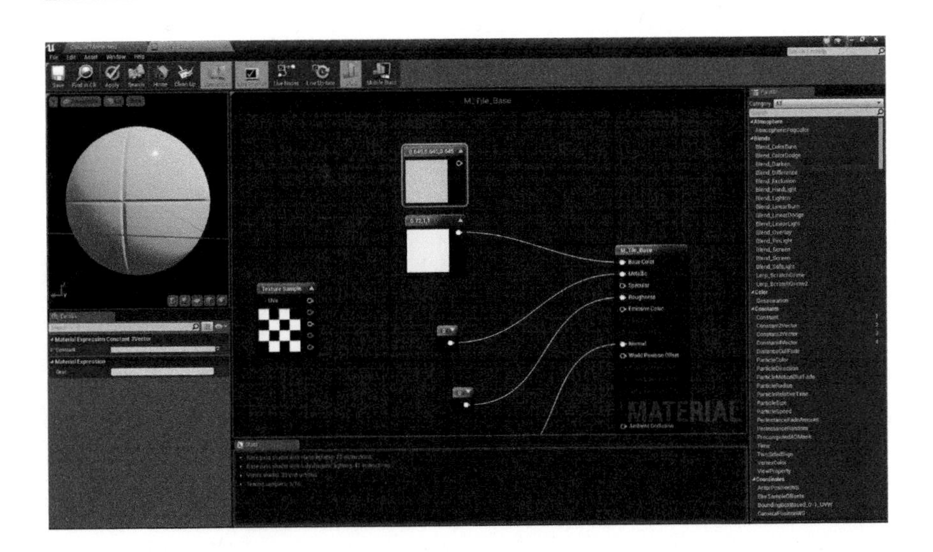

You need one final node before you can start connecting everything together. Right-click in the graph and type "lerp." Find the Linear Interpolate node and add it to the graph by clicking on it.

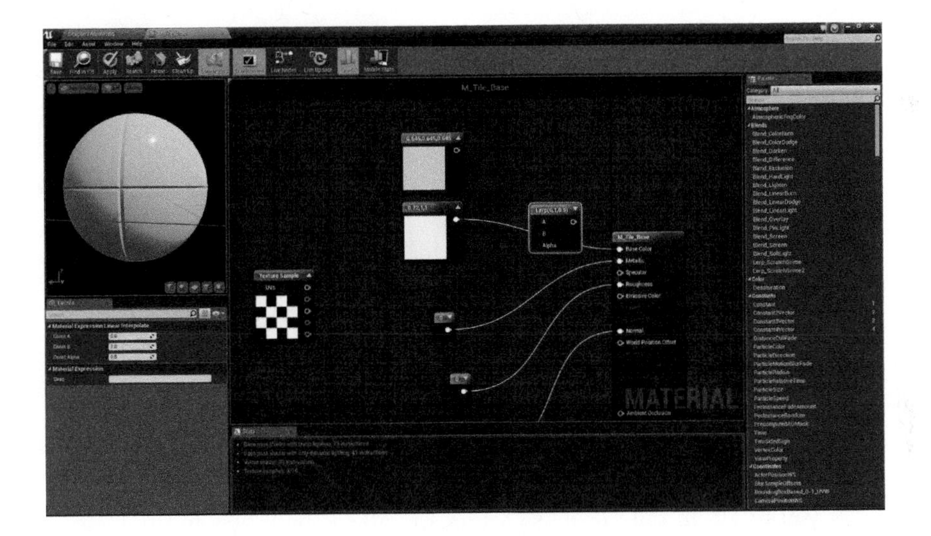

Linear Interpolate nodes allow you to switch between two colors using an alpha or mask. Connect one of the colors to the A input and the other color to the B input. Connect the output of the *Tile_M* node to the alpha input on the Lerp node. Finally, connect the output of the lerp to the base color of the material.

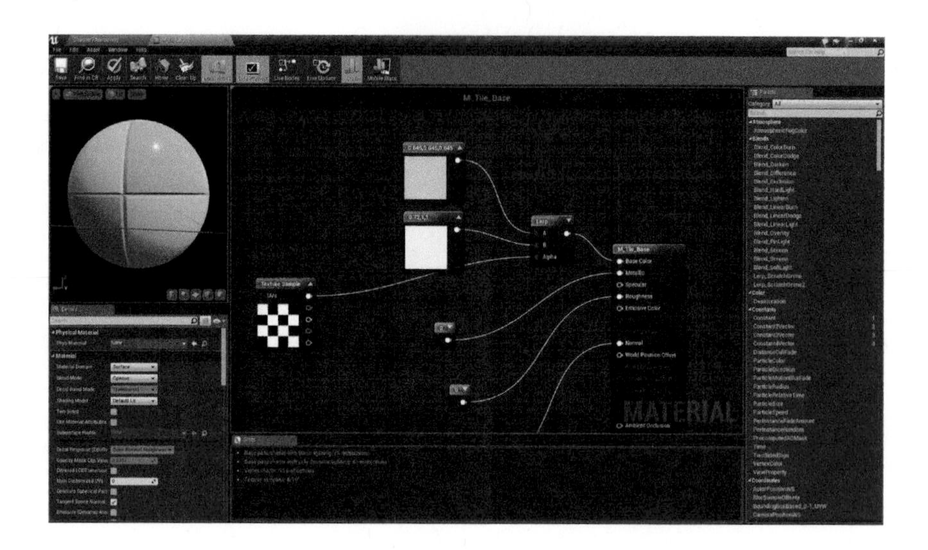

Now you should have a floor similar to the image below.

If you recall, in the previous chapter we talked about how to use material instances to add more adjustment without changing the material. To add these adjustments, you need to make some modifications to your material. Back in the Material Editor window you need to convert some of the nodes into parameters. Select the two Vector nodes and convert them to a parameter by right-clicking on them and choosing the first option (Convert to Parameter). Select the first of the Color nodes. In the Details tab, change the Parameter Name to Color 1. Repeat the process, renaming the second color Color 2. By converting the colors to parameters, you can now adjust the color of any instances *without* changing the material itself. This means that you can have multiple versions of a material while only having to build the material once during runtime.

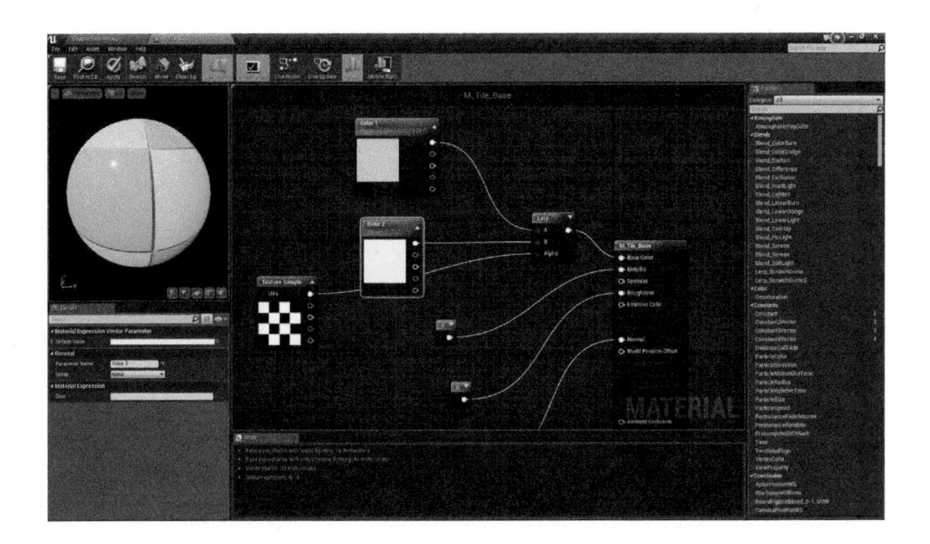

Modifying Channels

You can save and close the Material Editor now. In the content browser, right-click on the material and choose Create Material Instance. Name the new instance *M_Tile_Inst*. Add the new material instance to the floor. Open the Material Instance Editor by double-clicking on the instance.

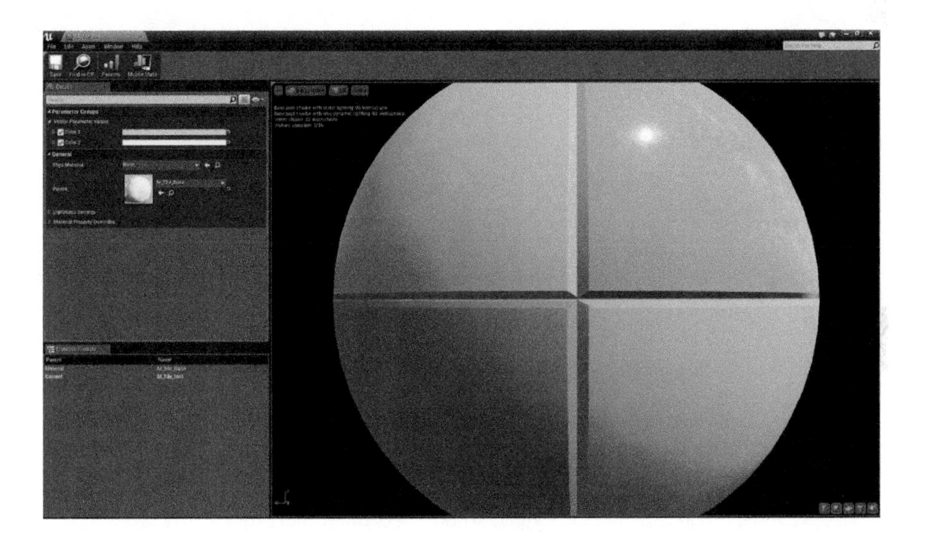

In the Details panel, there is a section containing the names of the properties that you added in the base material earlier. You can check the boxes beside the two color inputs and then change the colors to see how the instance can be modified without affecting the base material. One thing you should notice right off the bat is that, with the color picker open, you can adjust the color and it will update instantly without your having to click OK.

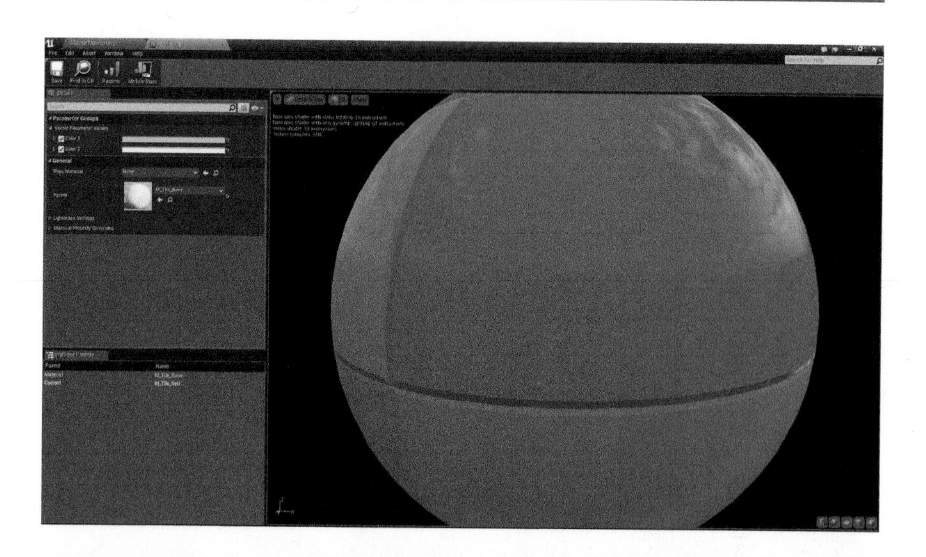

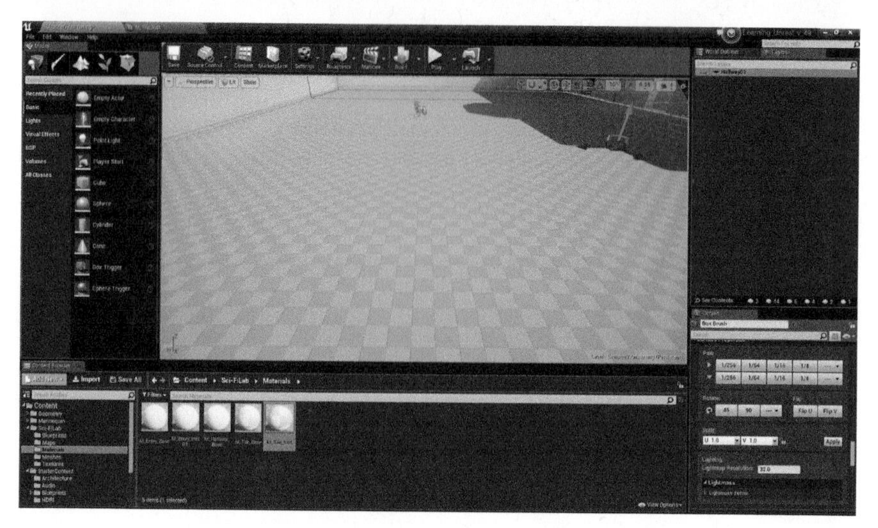

Chapter Challenge

Now that you have a good starting point and a basic understanding of how materials and material instances work, try creating a few more. It is not uncommon to see blocking levels that have different materials on the walls, ceilings, and floors. Using the material you just created, make two more instances that are easy to distinguish from one another by changing the colors. Apply them to some of the walls and ceilings in your level to get a better feel for how changing the color can help to break up the different areas.

To finish out this chapter, you will need a few more base materials for your hallway section: a glass material, a metal material, and a glowing material for the light fixtures. You can start by creating a new material named *M_Glass_Base*. Open your new material in the Material Editor. Add a Vector node and a Constant node. Connect the Vector node to the Base Color and the Constant node to Opacity. You may notice that Opacity is grayed out and, when you connect the constant, it also grays out the connecting line. Because your material's Blend mode is set to Opaque, you cannot modify the opacity. With the material selected in the graph, change its Blend mode to Translucent.

Now you can adjust the opacity of your material. Set your opacity to 0.5 and choose a bluish color.

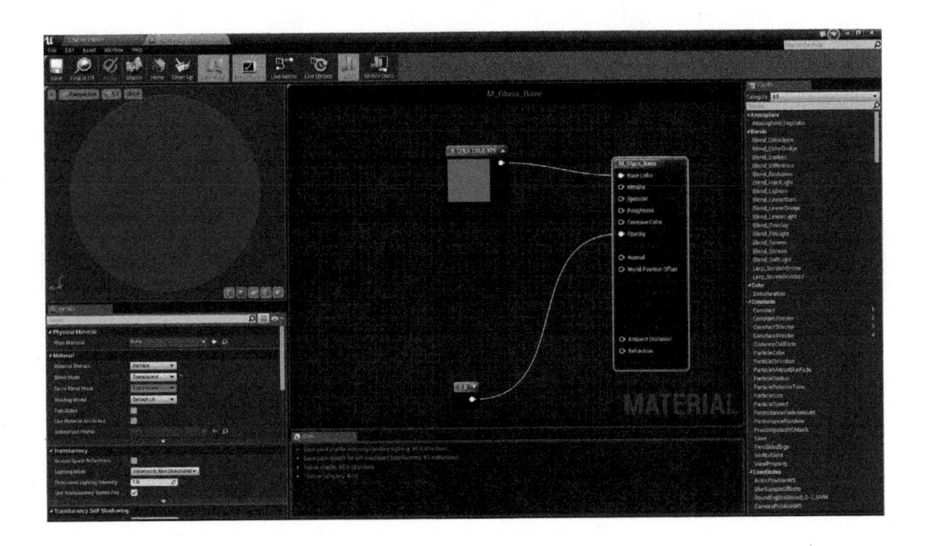

The next material you will work on is the light material. Create a new material and name it *M_Light_Base*. Open the material in the Material Editor and build a graph similar to the next image. You will need a Vector node, Constant node, and Multiply node. Notice that the Color and Constant nodes have been converted to parameters.

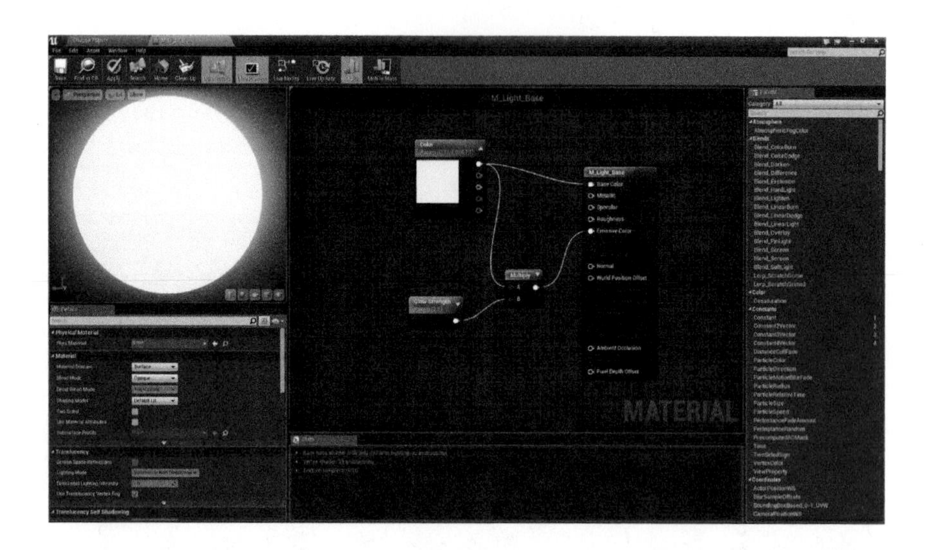

The last material you need for your hallway is a basic metal. Create a new material and name it *M_Metal_Base*. Open the new material in the Material Editor. Add a Vector node and two Constants. Connect these nodes as you have before. Set the color to a grayish color. Change the constant connected to Metallic to 0.8 and the constant connected to Roughness to 0.25. Convert all three nodes to parameters. Rename the Vector node to Color and name the constants Metallic and Roughness accordingly. Use the following figure as a reference.

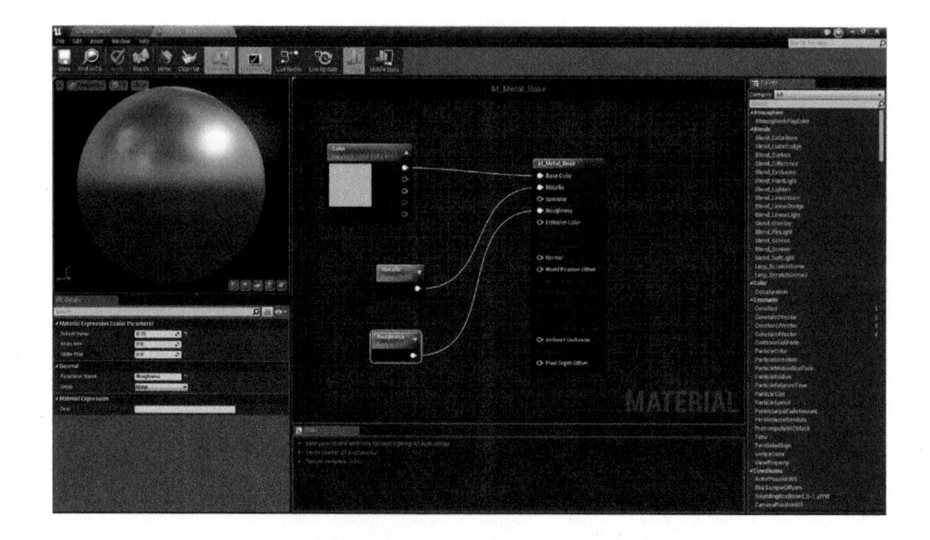

That completes the materials needed for the hallways. You do have one final material left to create to complete this chapter. Before you create the last material, we can take a look at how to apply the materials to some of your hallways. Start by creating an instance of the three materials you just made. Make sure that when you rename them, you use a name that tells its location and type. For example, to make an instance of the metal, I will name it *M_Hallway_01_Metal_Inst01*. This helps to separate any other instances in a way that lets you know quickly where the material belongs.

In your Meshes folder, find the mesh named *Hallway_01_4_Way_Ceiling* and open it in the Static Mesh Editor by double-clicking it. Move the camera around so that you can see the bottom side of the mesh.

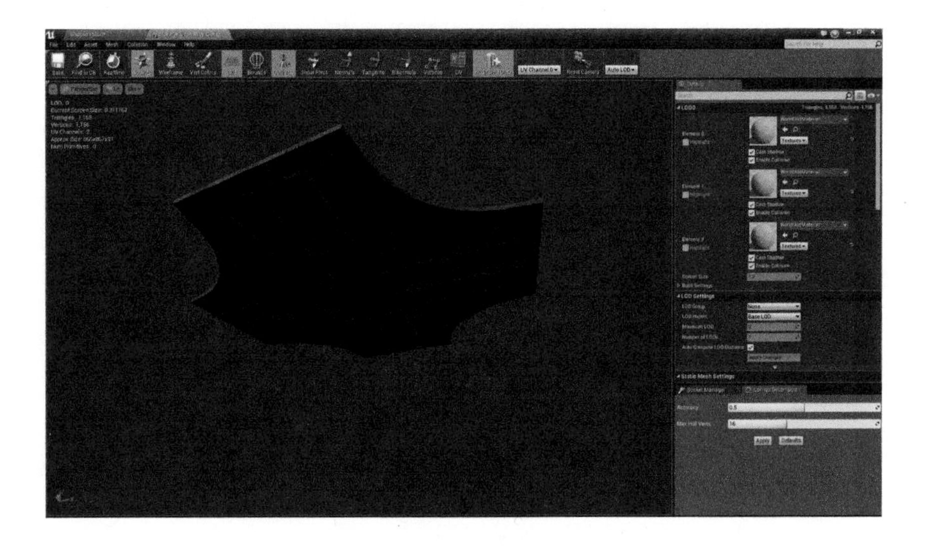

In the Details tab, you should notice that the first section has an area for three different materials. You can use the Highlight checkbox to determine where a particular material corresponds on the mesh. Using the Highlight boxes, apply a metal instance material to the framing around the lights, a light material instance on the lights, and a hallway base instance on the ceiling.

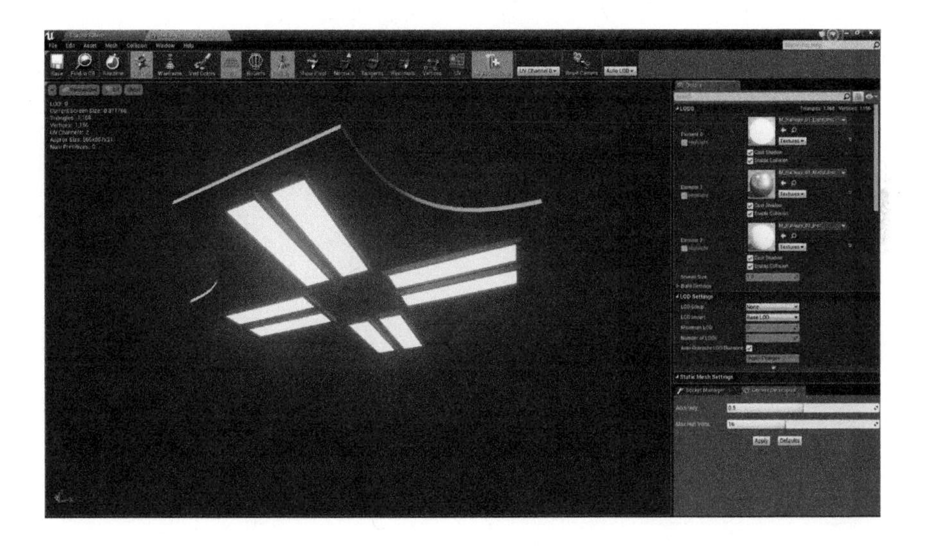

Using this same method, you can apply materials to all the different meshes you have imported so far. Remember that you can change aspects of any of the instances to make them appear differently. This will be useful for the Escalator and Entry_Wall. When you have finished applying your materials, take the time to save your work.

Go back to your Textures folder and import Concrete_D and Concrete_N from the Chapter 6 folder. You have a new texture type here using the "D" moniker. The "D" stands for diffuse and, as discussed earlier, is used as a color input.

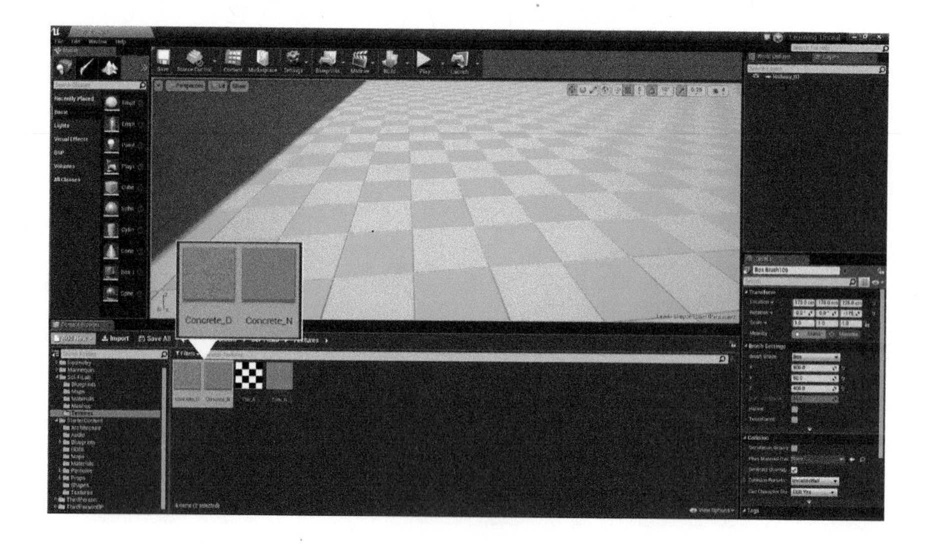

In your Materials folder, create a new material named *M_Concrete_Base*. Open the new concrete material in the Material Editor. Add your concrete textures to the material. Connect the *Concrete_D* texture to the Base Color input and the *Concrete_N* texture to the Normal input. Add a constant for Metallic and one for Roughness. You can set the constant connected to Roughness to 1. You should have a material similar to the image below.

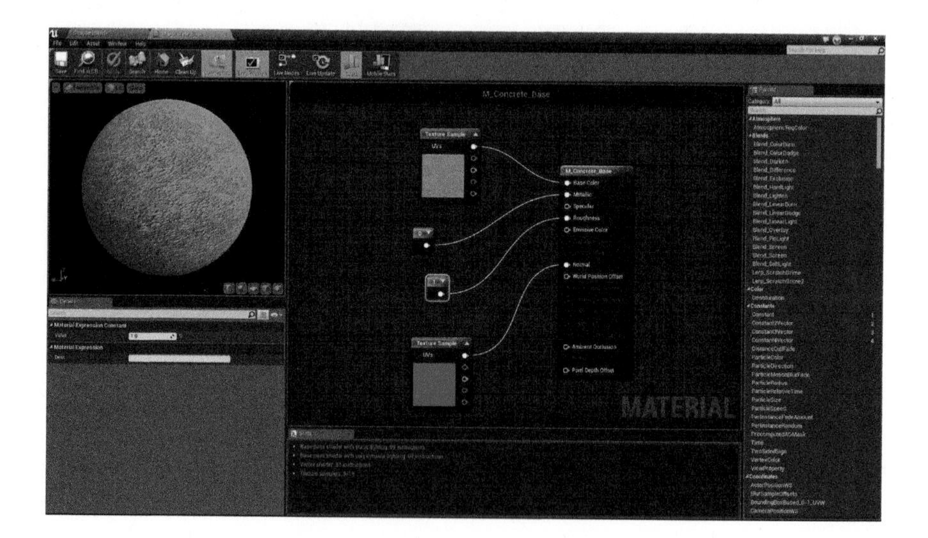

To add a little color to your concrete, you can add a Vector node and Multiply node to your graph. Connect the output of the Vector node to the "A" input on the Multiply node. Connect the color texture to the "B" input on the Multiply node. Finally, connect the output of the Multiply node to the base color of the material. Convert the Vector node to a parameter named Color.

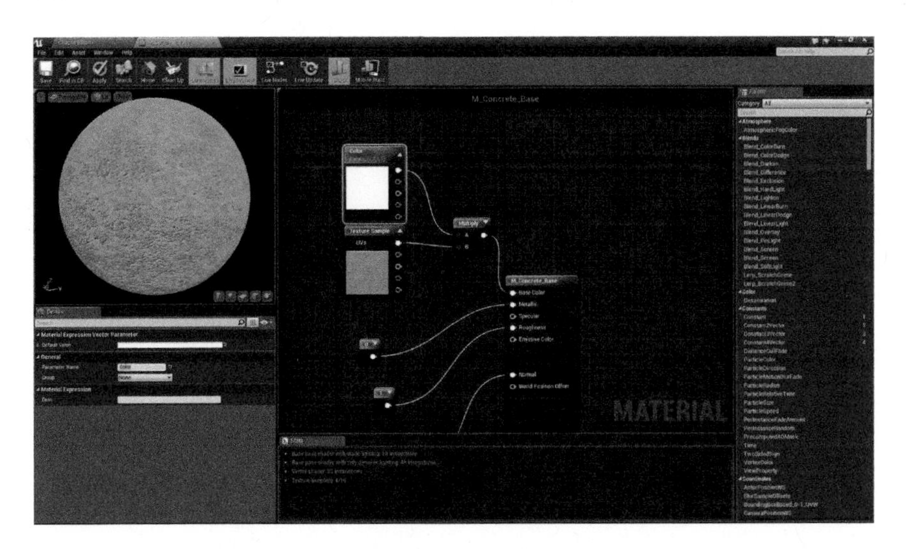

You can use this concrete material on both of your basements. Remember that you want to apply material instances to the BSPs rather than the base material. When creating the instances, you can use the Color input to change the tint of the material. Apply some instances to the basements now.

Chapter Review

In this chapter we took a closer look at the Material Editor. You learned how to add textures to a material. You looked at how you can use an alpha or mask to switch between two colors and used the Material Instance Editor to modify an instance of a material. You applied materials to some of your meshes. You also began applying more materials to your level. By this point, you should have a level that has a number of different hallways, a lobby area, and two basements. For the next few chapters you will be working to add some more detail and begin to modify the lighting to adjust the overall feel of the level. Remember that as you progress through the different chapters, you should save your level under a new name so that, if any issues occur, you can go back to a previous save.

7

Lighting Concepts

Introduction

Lighting can be a large undertaking on some levels. Because you added lights to your blueprints earlier, you already have a pretty good jump on the task at hand. You will need to add some lighting to the basements and will be adding a new type of volume as well. If you have been following along in the book, you should have a level that is ready for some detail. You can continue using your level or you can open Chapter7Start in the Maps folder.

Common Lighting Techniques

The lighting process often takes a number of iterations to complete. There are a number of aspects that need to be considered when setting up the lighting. For starters, you need to take into account the light sources. This means that if you have a light shining on a wall, but there is no light source, the player will notice that something is wrong. Likewise, if you have made a mesh that appears to shine light but there is not any light, it will also be distracting. Make sure you have a good idea of how and where you want your lights and then work from there. Oftentimes I will go through and add the light sources in about the location I want them to be prior to adding the actual lights. This can help give you a clearer picture of what you need. It is not uncommon, however, to have to add more sources as the level creation process continues, so do not feel like you have to have everything perfect right away.

Another area of lighting that needs to be addressed is the ambient light of a level. Ambient light is the residual light that fills a given area. An example of ambient lighting could be a room that has windows with curtains. During the day the sun can light the room without actually shining directly into the windows. When you finish placing the windows in the lobby, there will be a lot of ambient light shining in. In the basements, however, there will be no ambient lighting from your main directional light.

The type of light being used is very important. Using a directional light for a lamp, for example, is not going to work at all. You could, however, use a point light or spotlight depending on the situation. Understanding how each light will be displayed is a key part of the selection process. You need to look at each type of light closely to understand how and when you should use it. There are four commonly used lights. You can find them located under Lights in the Modes tab and they are as follows:

- **Directional light**—A directional light affects the entire level equally and travels in one direction. The sun is a good example of a directional light.
- **Point light**—A point light radiates light in all directions. A common light bulb is an example of a point light.
- **Spot light**—A spot light emits light from a set point in one general direction. A car's headlight would be a good example of a spot light.
- **Sky light**—A sky light takes into account the entire level and uses it to create simple reflections and lighting.

The final piece to the puzzle is the intensity of the light. Having high-intensity values for light sources that are small will detract for the look of the level. This works both ways, so be mindful not to decrease the intensity too much either.

Lightmass Importance Volumes

The lightmass importance volume is used to help define which areas of a level need more lighting detail. Typically, you can use one volume to surround the level. When placing the lightmass importance volume, you want to keep it as small as possible while still surrounding the entire area you want to be affected. Areas outside the volume will only be affected by one bounce of lighting, which can help to drastically reduce the build time. If you have parts of the level that extend beyond the playable area, you typically do not need to include them inside the volume.

Before you add the volume, you will need to build your lighting. Click on the Build button on the toolbar to build your level now. When you have finished building your level, save under a new name. Now you can add your volume. In the Modes tab, select Volumes and then drag a lightmass importance volume into your level. Scale your volume so that it surrounds your level. Try to keep it as small as possible while containing everything. Use the top and side views as needed.

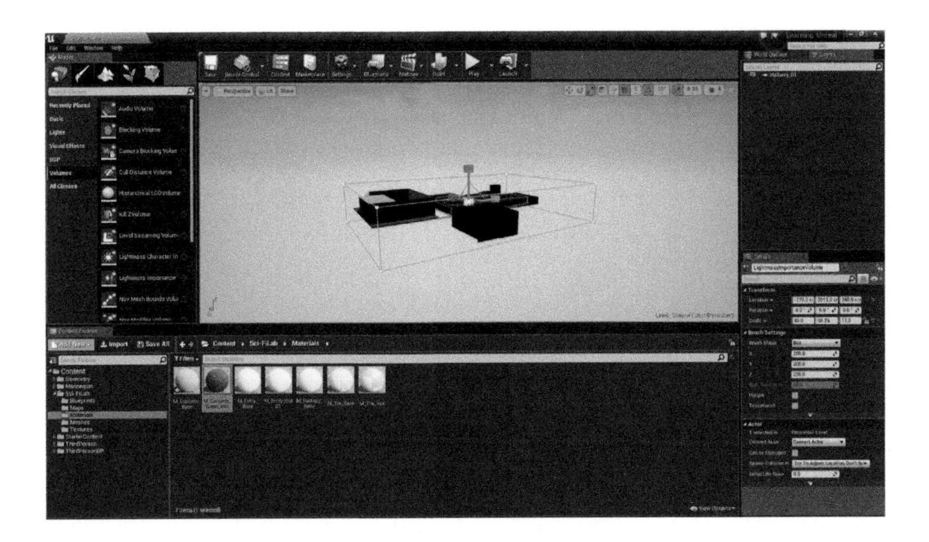

Reflection Nodes

Reflection nodes are another great addition to Unreal Engine 4. You can place Reflection nodes around your level to specify how you want that area to be affected by its surroundings. When deciding where to add Reflection Capture nodes, be sure that there is enough contrast between light and shadow. There are two types of reflection shapes. The first and most commonly used is the Sphere Reflection Capture node. The sphere shape is typically the preferred method because it has no corners; this helps to keep the reflections more uniform. The Box Reflection Capture node, on the other hand, is used far less because its shape is really only suited for rectangular rooms. While it is up to you to determine which one is better for your current environment, you will be focusing on the sphere rather than the box.

Before you start placing your reflection nodes, you do need to look at how they will work. The first rule for these nodes is that they work on a hierarchal type of structure. This means that smaller, more localized spheres will override larger ones. You can add a few large nodes to get a general reflection environment and then place smaller nodes in the areas that you want to have more focused reflections.

You can start by adding three main nodes: one to cover the lobby and one in each basement. You will be adding nodes in the hallways on a much more local scale later in the chapter.

In the Modes tab change to Visual Effects. Drag in a Sphere Reflection Capture node and place it in the middle of the lobby. In the Details tab, under Reflection Capture, set the following:

- Influence radius—2200
- Brightness—1.5

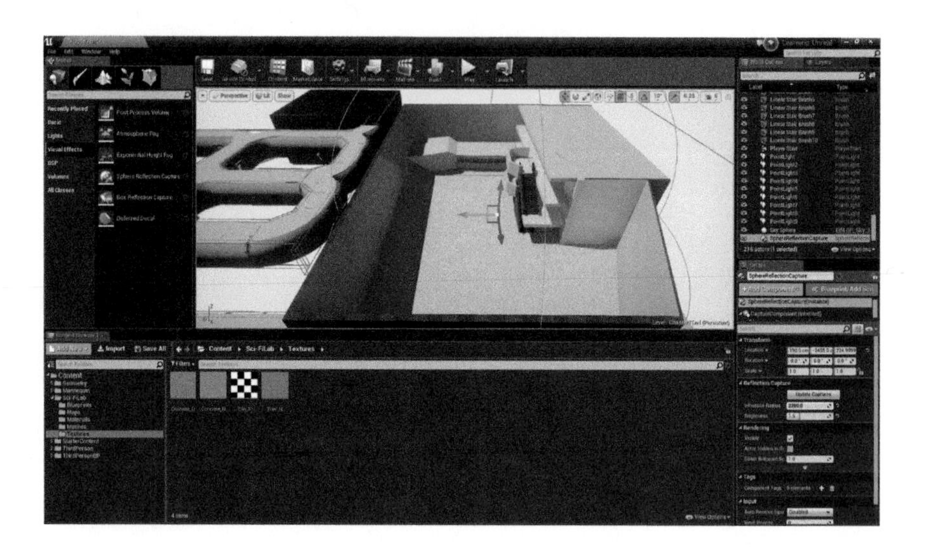

Move the node so that its radius encompasses the lobby. Once you have the Lobby node in place, add two more nodes—one for each basement—and set them as you see fit.

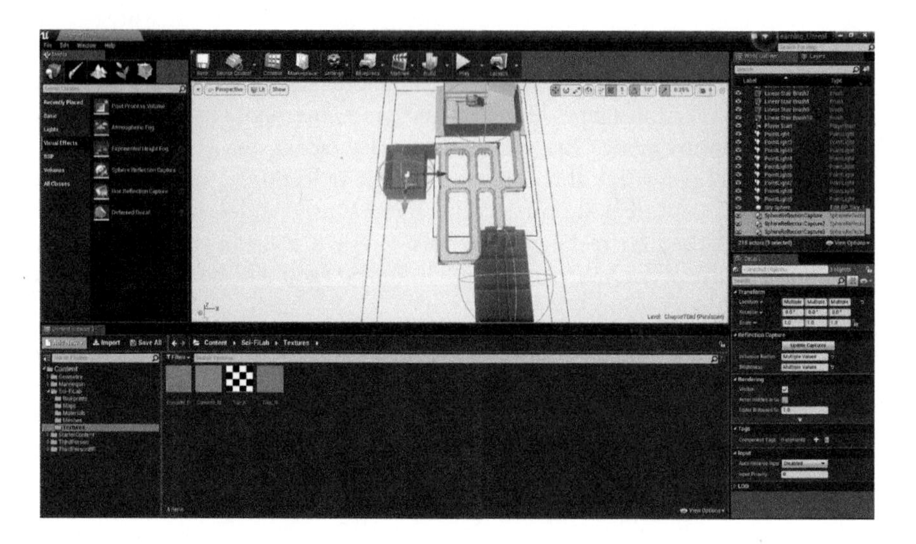

Now you can begin to work on the hallways. Move into one of the four-way intersections. Before you add reflection, you can take a moment to build the level. Click the Build button on the toolbar. When the build is completed, save your level.

Drag in a new Reflection node and place it in the middle of the intersection. Set the following:

- Influence radius—800
- Brightness—1.5

Once you have placed your reflection nodes, click on the Update Captures button in the Details tab. You should notice a moderate difference in the reflections on the floors, walls, and ceilings. Use the first image below as a guide *before* and the second one as a guide *after*.

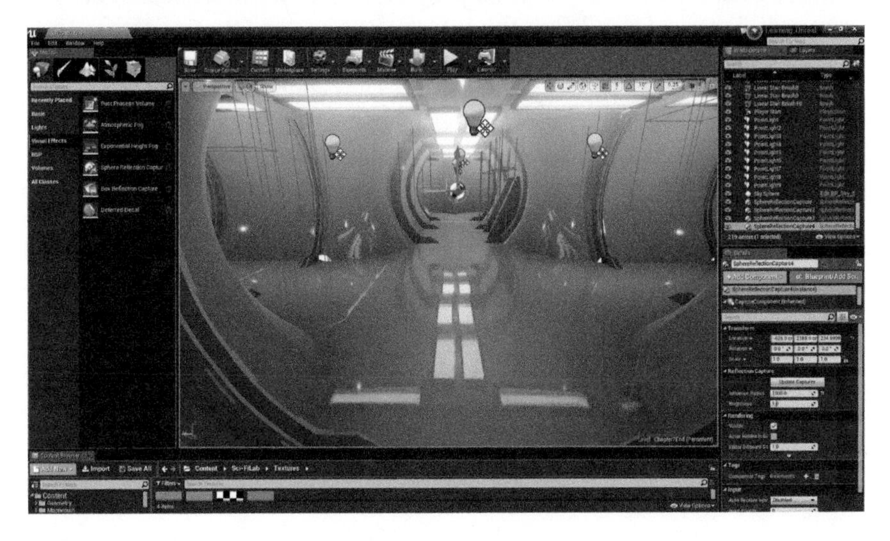

You can add a few more reflections nodes throughout the hallways now. There is no need to overdo it here, so adding a node to each intersection should serve as a good base. Take the time to adjust them as you see fit. While adding the nodes, if you notice that your level is progressively slowing down, you can stop adding the reflections, or you can use the Settings button on the toolbar to adjust the overall quality.

To adjust the quality, click on the Settings button and scroll down the Engine Scalability Settings options; lowering the quality here will reduce lag while editing. You should see a very noticeable difference in the overall appearance of your level. Do not worry, though; this is just a temporary adjustment that can be changed at any time. Lowering the settings can often help to make the level more responsive while editing. Remember that you need to change it back before playing if you want to have the full effect of your work appear.

Toggleable Lighting

So far you have worked only with static lighting—lighting that does not move or change during game play. While this is the most common form of lighting, there are some alternates you can use.

Toggleable lighting is similar to lighting that is connected to a light switch—a light that can be turned on or off during game play, either through a chain of events or by player interaction. Toggleable lighting could be useful in sub-basement 1. Since it is a basement, maybe you want the lighting to reflect a dark, foreboding region of the level. You can set up some lighting that the user has to trigger in order to turn it on. You can trigger it in a number of different ways. You could give the user an actual switch or set up a trigger volume that is activated when the player walks through it.

First, you need a trigger to turn on the lights in the basement. In the Modes tab, select Volumes. Scroll to the bottom to find Trigger Volume. Drag in a trigger volume and position it at the bottom of the stairs.

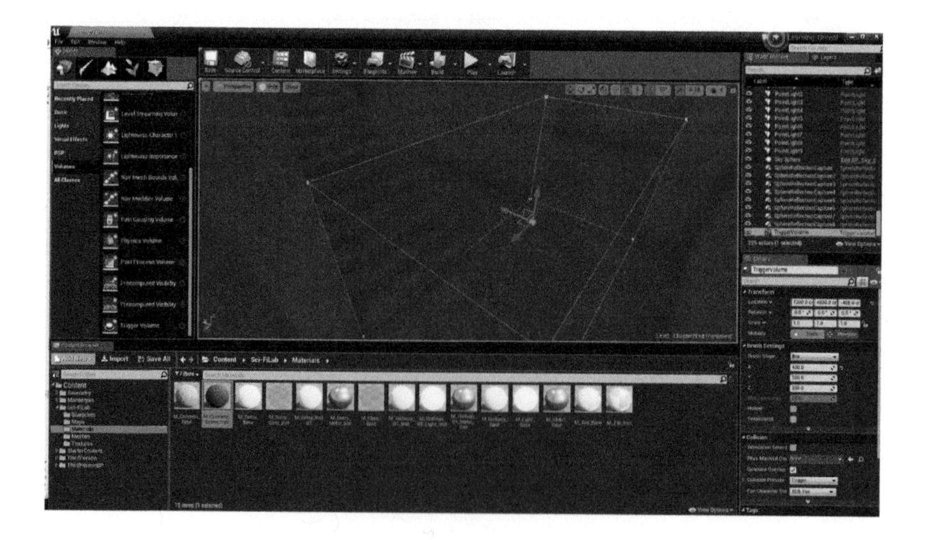

Make sure that it is large enough that the player cannot bypass it. Set the trigger volumes shape to the following to get plenty of coverage:

- X—400
- Y—200
- Z—200

You can duplicate the volume by holding the Alt key and left-clicking the mouse, dragging it upward. Position the second box at the top of the stairs. You will use this second box to turn the lighting back off as the player exits the basement. Since the area at the top of the stairs is smaller, you can adjust the X value of the shape to 200.

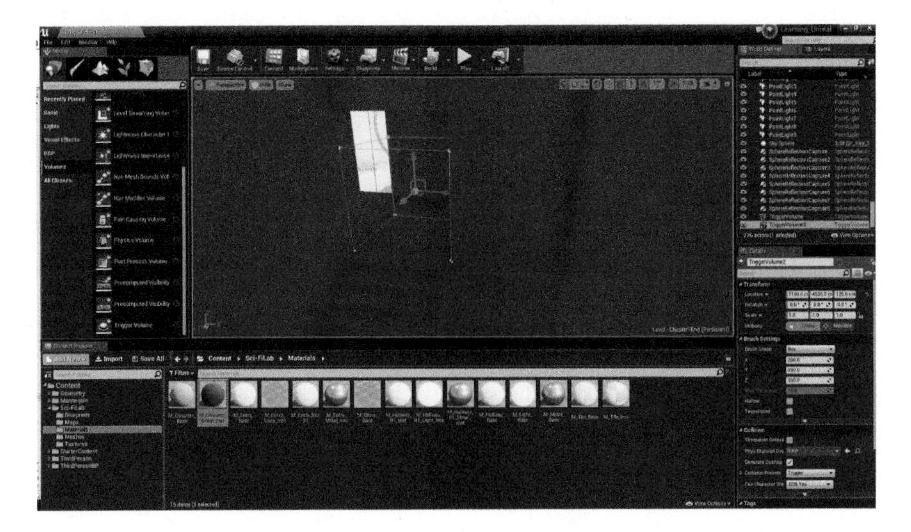

Now that you have your triggers in place, you need to create some lights. Add five point lights down the length of the center hallway for the basement as seen in the figure below.

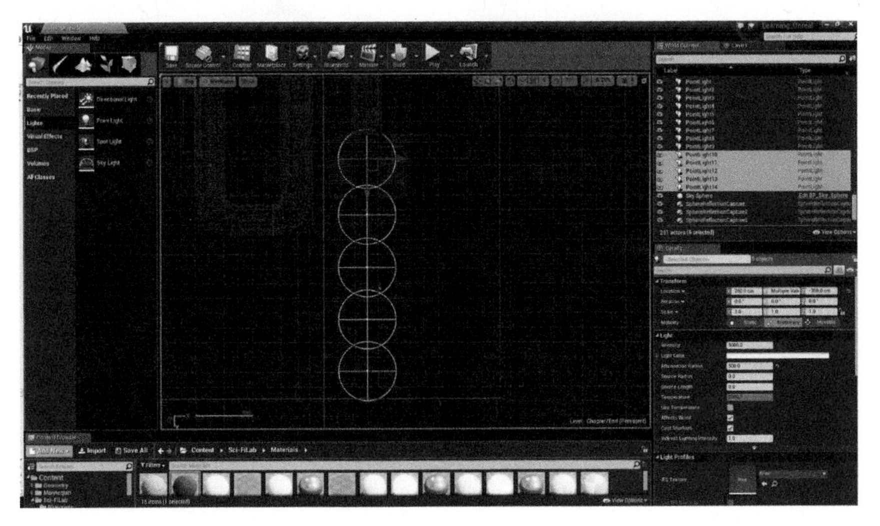

In order to be able to modify the visibility of these lights, you need to connect your triggers to each light. You can do this through the **Level Blueprint**, which acts as a global blueprint. Each level in a project has its own level blueprint. The level blueprint can also access nearly everything in the level. On the toolbar, click on the Blueprints button and then scroll down to find Open Level Blueprint.

In the level, select the lights that you just added. With the lights still selected, right-click in the Level Blueprint and choose Create References to five selected actors to add the lights to the blueprint. In the Level Blueprint, creating a reference to an actor allows the blueprint to access and modify any values you would find in the Details tab. You can create references to virtually any actor that has adjustable attributes, including other blueprints.

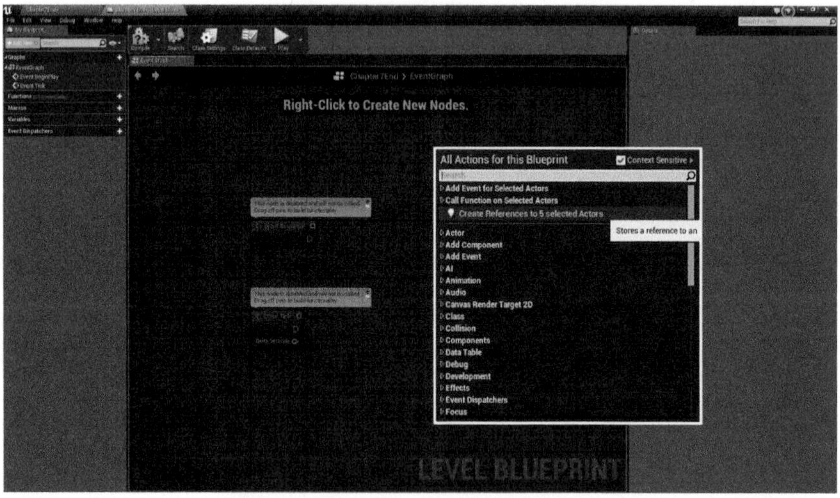

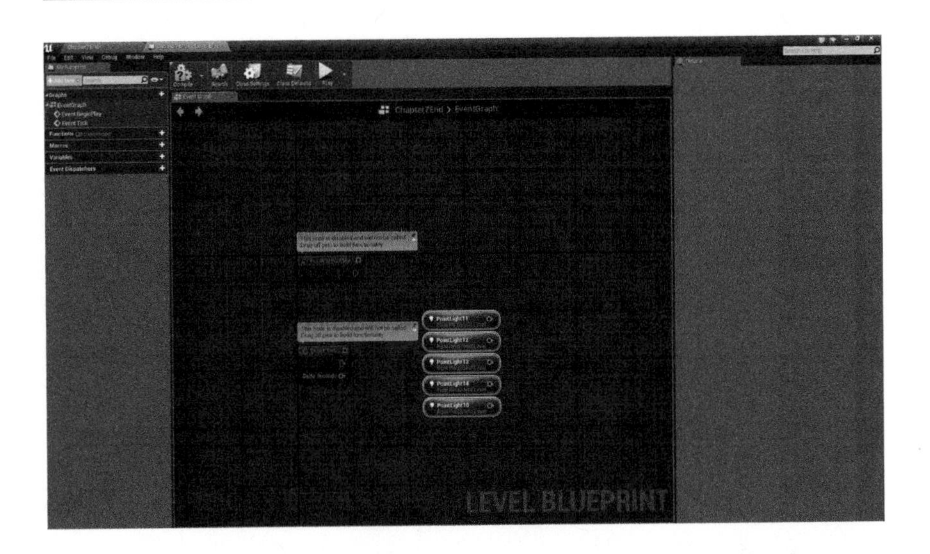

Switch back to the level and select both trigger volumes (see the figure below).

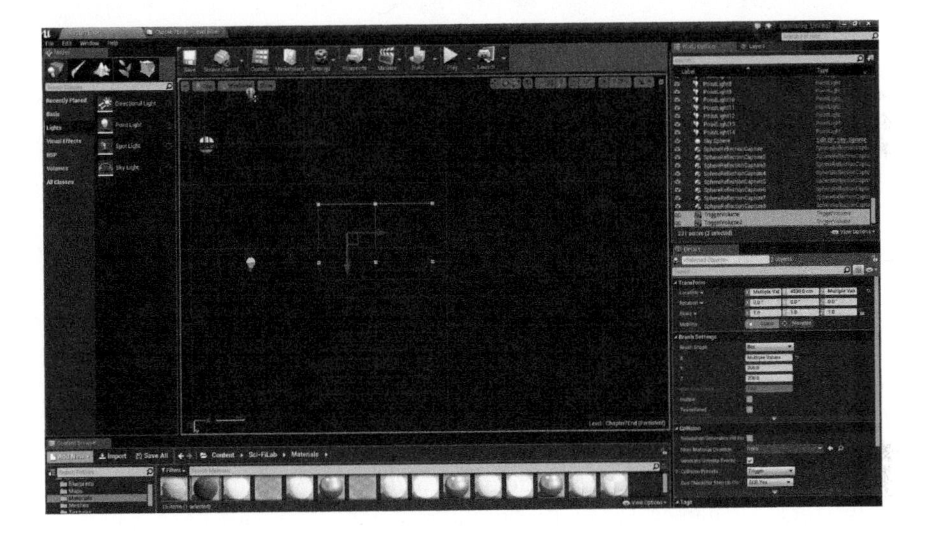

Return to the blueprint and right-click to bring up the Context menu. Type "begin over" to narrow the search result. Find the **Add On Actor Begin Overlap** node under the Collision section to add the overlap events to the blueprint. These nodes work basically as their title would imply. When the player overlaps or enters the box, it will trigger the chain of events you connect to it.

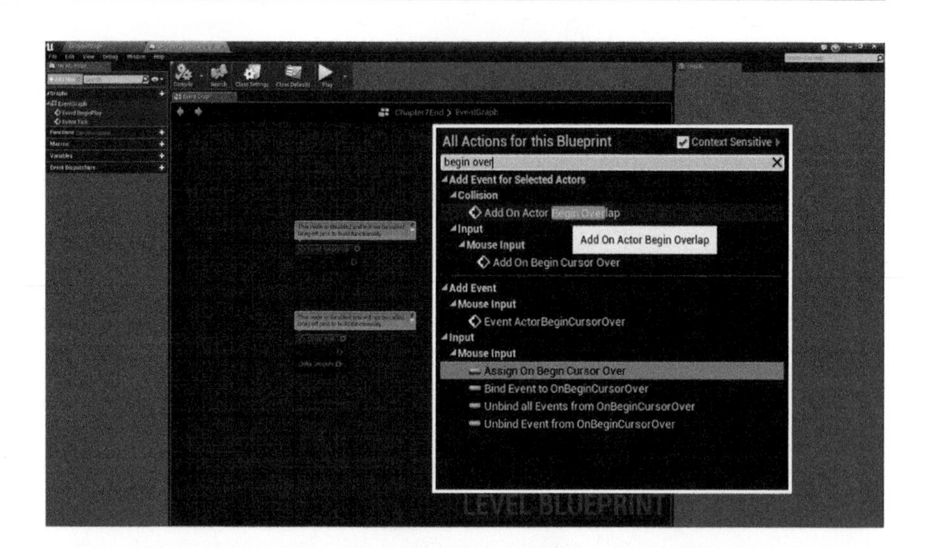

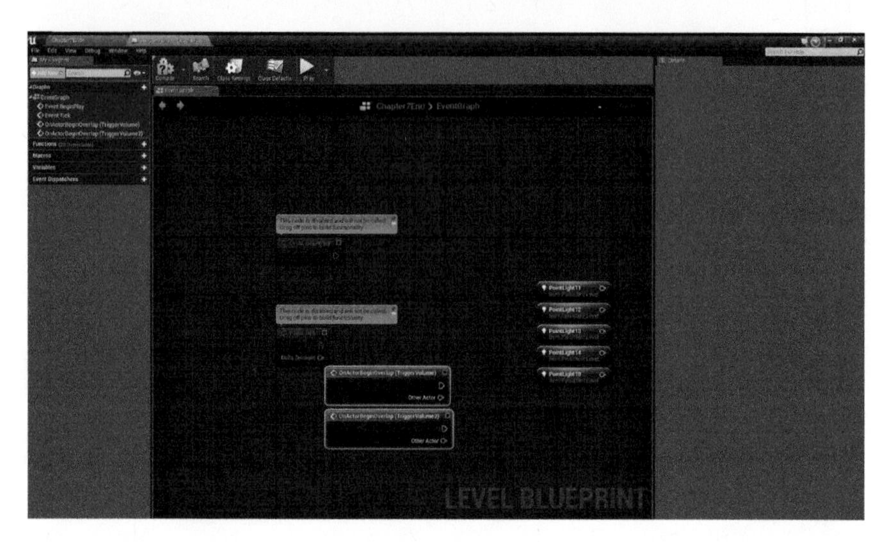

From the out-pin on one of the *point lights*, drag off and search for toggle. Find the node named Toggle Visibility (PointLightComponent) and select it to add to the graph. You should notice that there are two options; the first is Toggle Visibility (LightComponent), which is the one you will use. When you select it, you should notice that it will add two nodes to the graph. The first of these nodes is used to specify the exact property you are modifying, while the second is the modifier. Use the next two images as a guide.

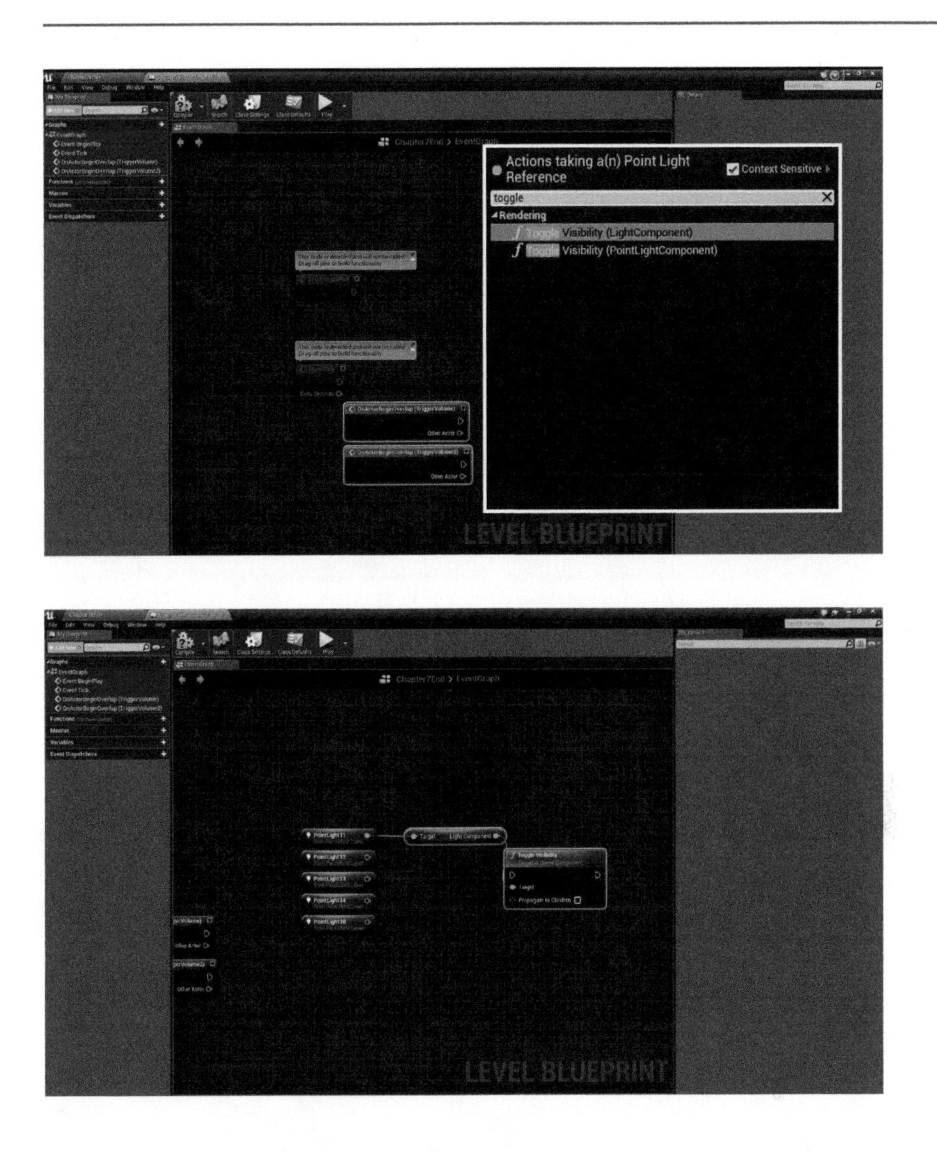

Since you want to affect all the lights at the same time, you can now connect each light's out-pin to the target input of the Toggle Visibility node. When the connection is made, it will automatically add the property node.

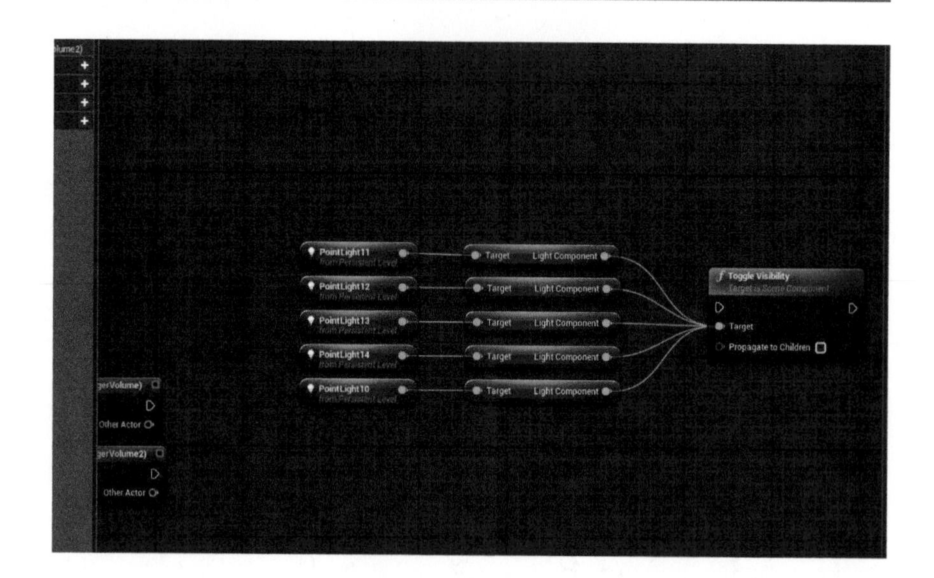

Now that you have all the lights connected, you can connect the first trigger to your toggle node. Make sure that you are connecting the Trigger Volume node from the bottom of the stairs. You can double check this by looking at the name of the volume in the World Outliner.

You now have a way to turn the lights on, but you do not have a way to turn them off. This duty will lie in the hands of the TriggerVolume2 volume at the top of the stairs.

Because your second trigger should activate only if the lights are already on, you need to check the visibility before connecting to the toggle. Since all your lights are set up to turn on or off together, you only need to check the visibility of one. Drag off of the out-pin of one of the lights and search for *Is Visible*. The Is Visible node returns a **Boolean** value, which is simply a variable that contains either true or false.

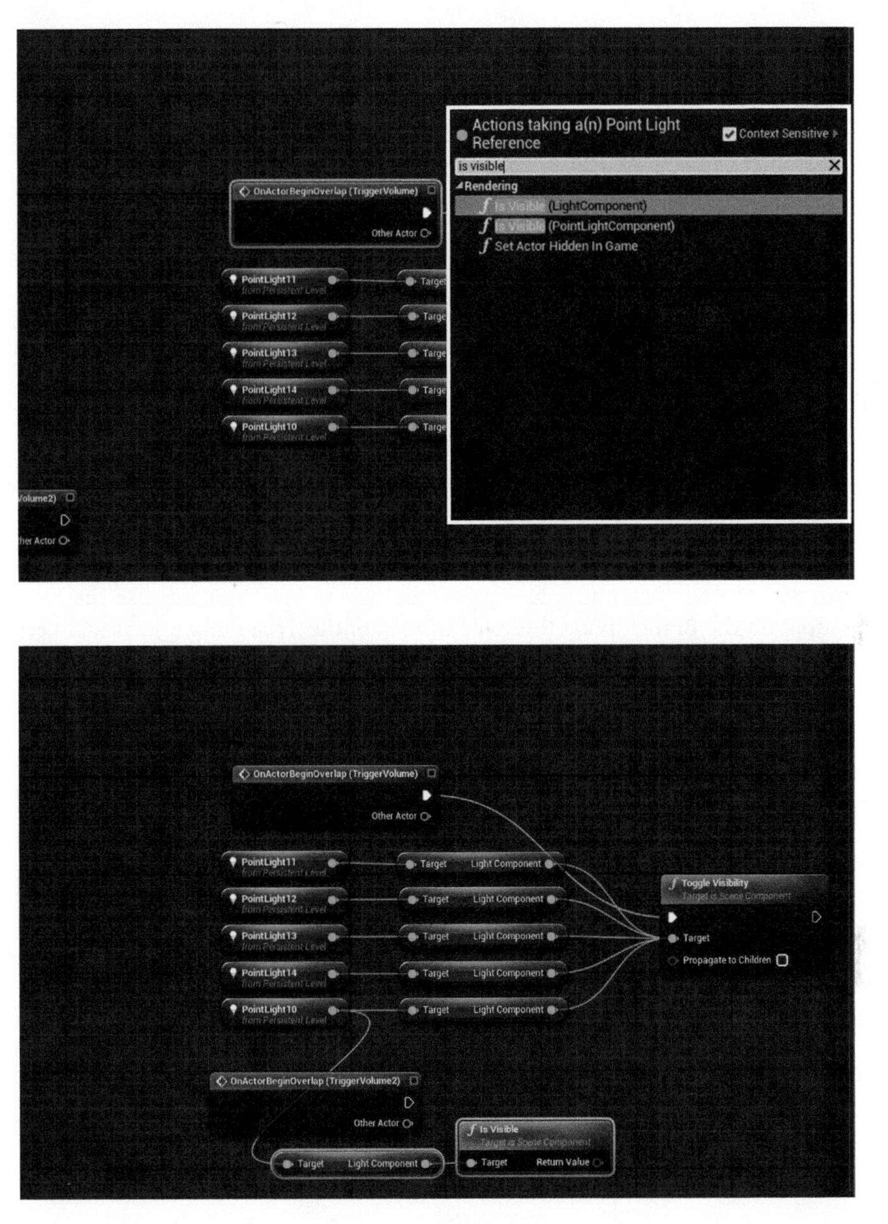

The last piece of the puzzle is a Branch node, which reads a Boolean variable and outputs the result as an execute pin. From the Return Value of the Is Visible node, add a Branch node. Connect the second trigger to the exec input of the Branch node and the True output of the Branch node to the Toggle Visibility node.

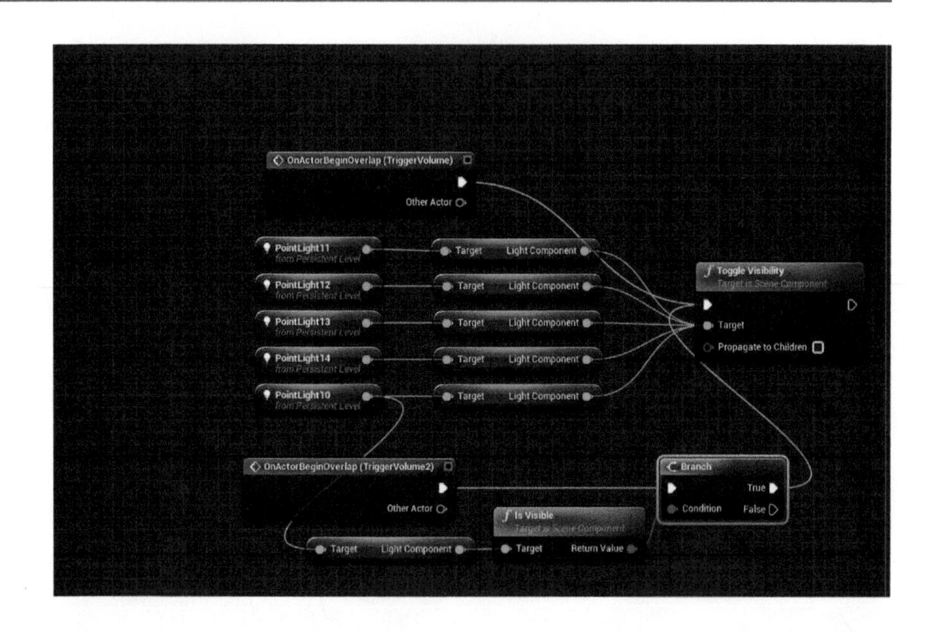

If you were to play-test now, the lighting should turn on as expected. However, you may also notice that as you run in and out of the first trigger, it will constantly toggle the lighting on and off. Since you do not want that to happen, you can add another Branch node setup to the first trigger. You will use the False output on the Branch node this time instead of the True output. This will keep the triggers working correctly with the bottom trigger activating the lights and the top trigger deactivating the lights.

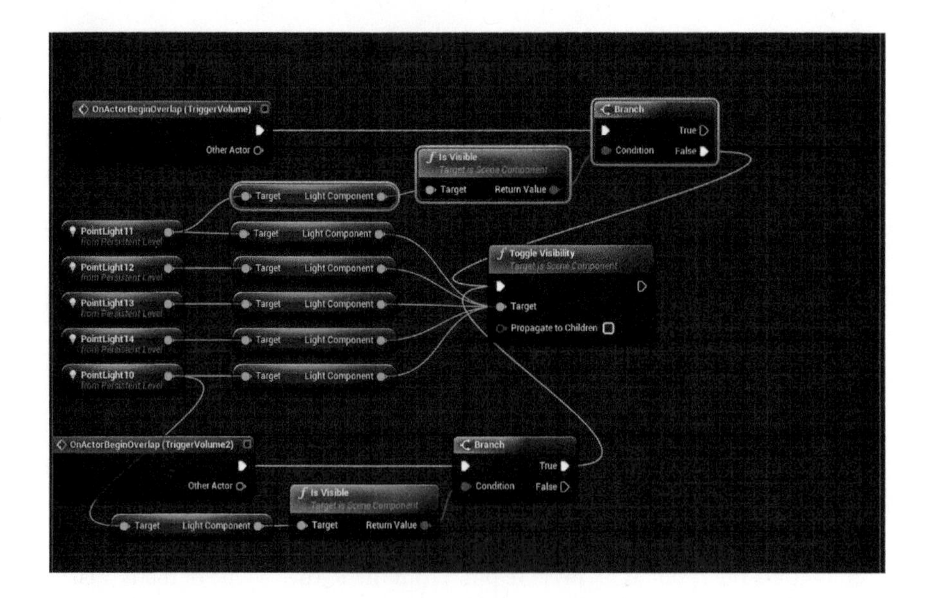

Compile the blueprint. Close the blueprint and play-test your level. Your basement lights should all turn on when the trigger at the bottom of the stairs is hit, and they should turn off again when the trigger at the top of the stairs is hit.

Chapter Challenge

Using what you have learned in this chapter, create the lighting for the second sub-basement. Try using a single trigger at the top of the stairs to turn the lights on and off. Instead of using point lights, try using spot lights *and* point lights. Taking what you learned in the earlier chapters, create and modify a few new material instances and apply them to the second sub-basement.

Chapter Review

In this chapter we took a closer look at how to modify lighting within a level. You added a new type of volume, called a lightmass importance volume, to help localize the area affected by the different lights in the level. You added a few Reflection Capture nodes as well. Finally, you added some lighting that is turned on and off by walking through a trigger placed in the level. You learned about a new type of blueprint called the Level Blueprint. Using this blueprint, you learned how to add and modify actors in the level.

8

Blueprint Animation

Introduction

In this chapter, we will spend a lot of time looking at some commonly used animation techniques. We will be focusing on a more localized version in blueprints. We will also take a quick look at the Matinee Editor. There is a lot of information to cover here, so let us get started!

Creating Automatic Doors

Blueprints are great for grouping objects together to use over and over again, but the real power lies in the ability to add events to them. While playing a game, have you ever walked up to a door only to have it open automatically? That is an example of a scripted event. While relatively small in the scope of a full game, a broken script can ruin the experience.

Before you can start on your doors, you need to add some new meshes to your project. In the Meshes folder, import:

- Hallway_01_Left_Door
- Hallway_01_Right_Door

These doors are going to be an important part of the intersections in the hallways of your level. You will learn how to add triggers and events that will open and close the doors for you as the player approaches, similarly to the toggleable lights created in the last chapter. Unlike those lights, however, you will not be using the level blueprint. Instead, you will be adding your triggers and events directly to the actor blueprint, which will allow you to place multiple copies of the blueprint into the level while still allowing them to work independently of each other.

Before you begin creating your animated blueprint, let us take a minute to add the materials to the doors as needed. Open *Hallway_01_Left_Door* in the Static Mesh Editor. Apply material instances to the door so that it is similar to the image below.

Looking at the image, you should notice that there is a new material being used. A dark, rough material was created to simulate a rubber type of texture. Using the same methods as before, create a new material that has a dark gray color with high-value roughness and low-value metallic. Remember that you want to apply material instances to your object, so create instances as needed. You can continue to use the same instances used on the hallway if you so desire. You should also notice a green glowing material on the center of the door. This is just an instance of your light material made earlier with the color changed to green. Once you have completed the left door, move on to the right door and repeat the process.

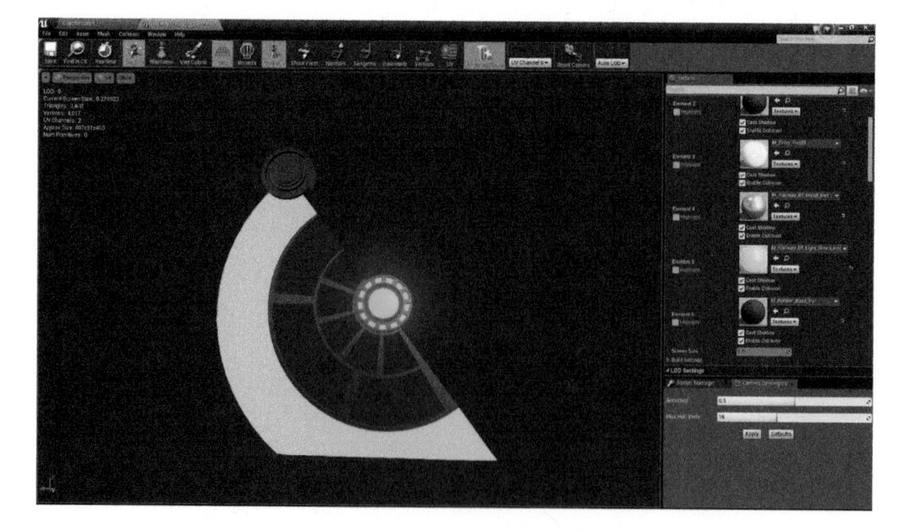

Create a new blueprint in the Blueprints folder and name it *BP_Hallway_01_Doors*. Open the new blueprint in the Blueprint Editor. You need to add a new type of object to this blueprint before you can add the doors. In the Components tab, click on the Add Component dropdown menu and find Box Collision. **Box collisions** can be used similarly to the trigger volumes you created earlier.

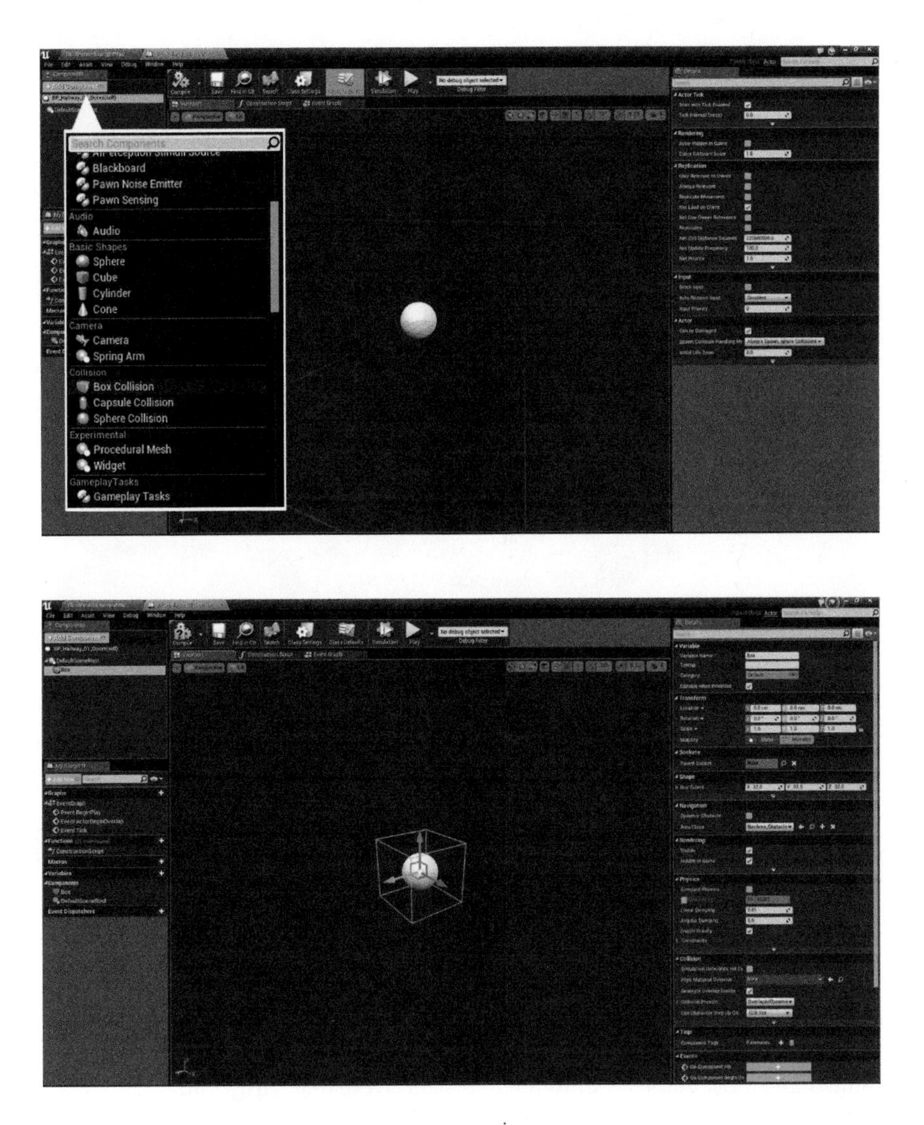

Since doors typically open from both sides, you will need two box collisions. In the dropdown menu add a second box collision. Move the second box along the Y axis to about (–300).

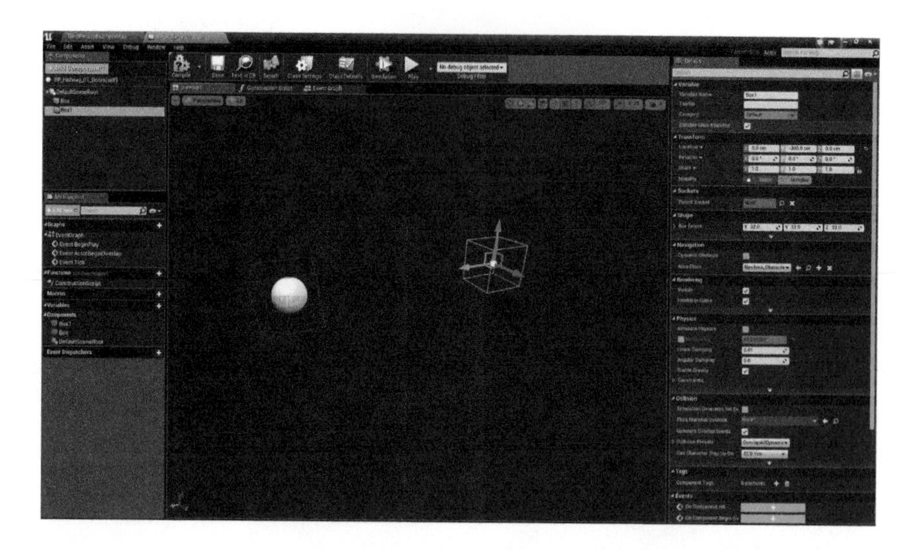

Now that you have both of your boxes in place, you can add the doors to the blueprint. In the Components tab, use the Add Component dropdown to add a static mesh.

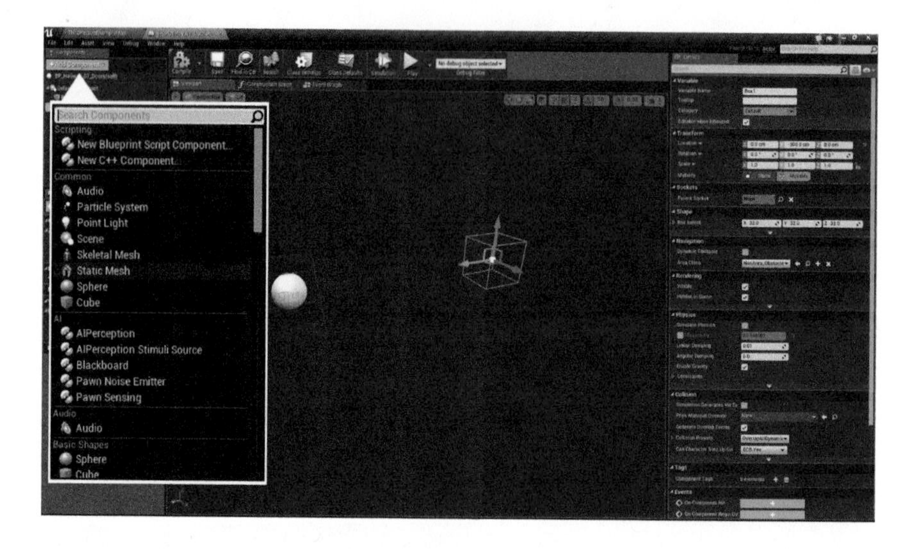

Since you did not have a static mesh selected in the content browser, you only added an empty static mesh to the blueprint. In the Details tab find the section labeled Static Mesh.

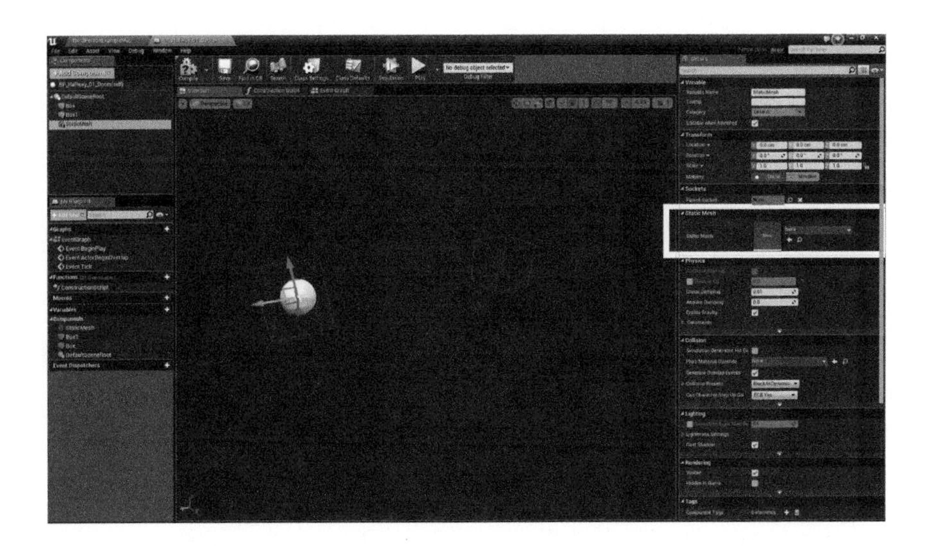

You can change the static mesh being used by dragging one into the static mesh box from the content browser. Find *Hallway_01_Left_Door* in the content browser and drag it into the Details panel under Static Mesh. While this method does work perfectly fine, you have to complete one last step before you can continue. In the Components tab, rename StaticMesh to *Hallway_01_Left_Door*. Set the location of the left door as follows:

- X—(-150)
- Y—(-90)

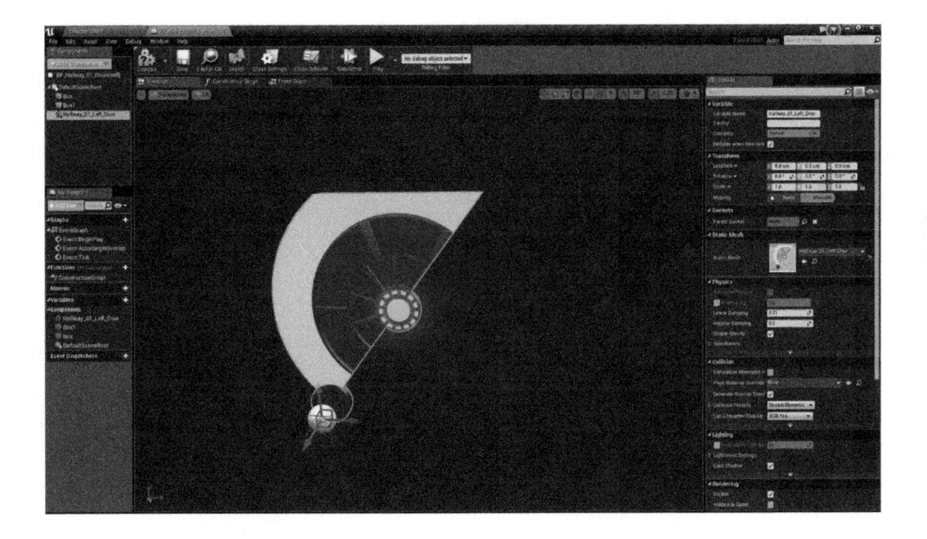

Back in the content browser, find the *Hallway_01_Right_Door* and select it. In the blueprint under Components, choose Add Component and then add the static mesh (Hallway_01_Right_Door).

Notice how the doors are offset from each other. This is due to the location of the **pivot point**, where the gizmo handles will appear; it is the location from which the object will move, rotate, and scale. You need to adjust the location of the right door to line up with the left. Move the right door to the following:

- X—150
- Y—(-100)
- Z—420

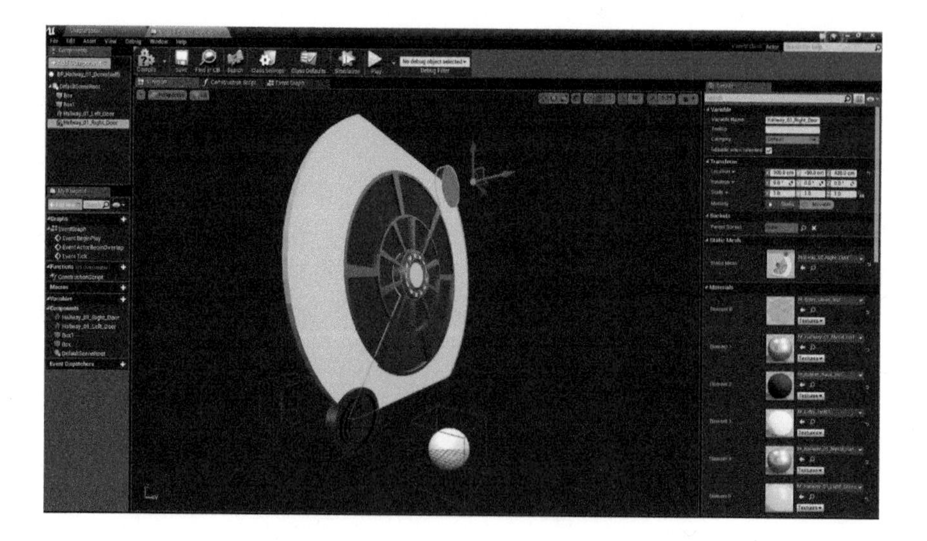

Save all of your work before continuing.

Now you are going to begin working with graphs in your blueprint. You will be using the **event graph** to add movement to your doors when the player approaches.

To start, you need to add an event for your trigger boxes. Click on Box in the Components tab. In the Details tab, scroll down until you find the Events section, which contains any events that you can add to the selected object. For your purposes, you will select *On Component Begin Overlap*. By clicking the green box with the +, you will add a new event to the event graph.

Once you click on the button, your viewport will change to the event graph tab.

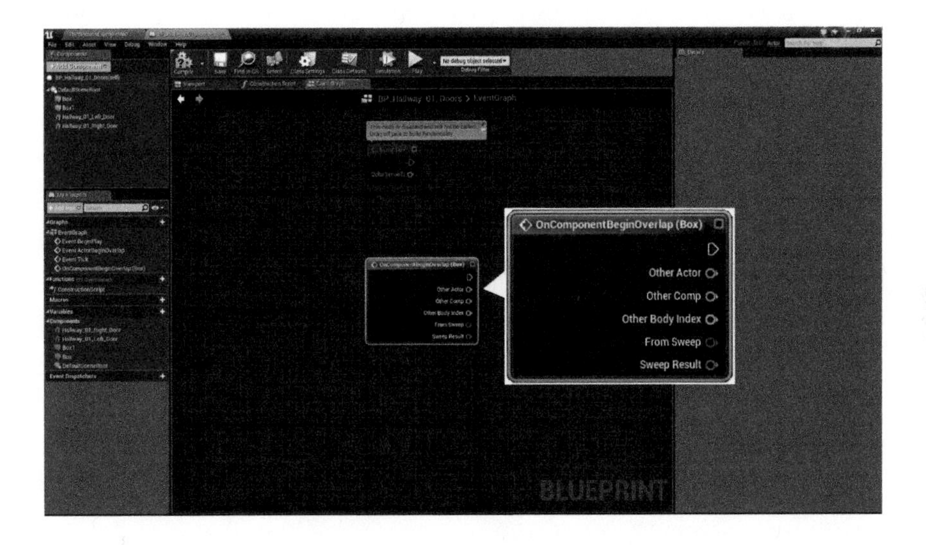

Before you start working in the event graph, you can do some planning to help organize your thoughts. The first thing you need to establish is what you want to happen when the player enters your trigger box. Your initial reaction may be, "I want the doors to open." While that is not wrong, what would then happen if the doors were already open? Depending on how you set up the rest of the graph, the doors could open even farther, or they could slam shut and then open again. Neither of these responses is going to help you at all, so the first thing you need to do is to check to see if the doors are open. This is a good time to use a Boolean variable. As discussed earlier, Booleans can represent two states: true or false. By using a Boolean here, you can set it up to check if the doors are open and, if that is true, stop the doors from trying to open again. To add a variable, you need to click the + icon on the right-hand side of the **Variables** section in the My Blueprint tab.

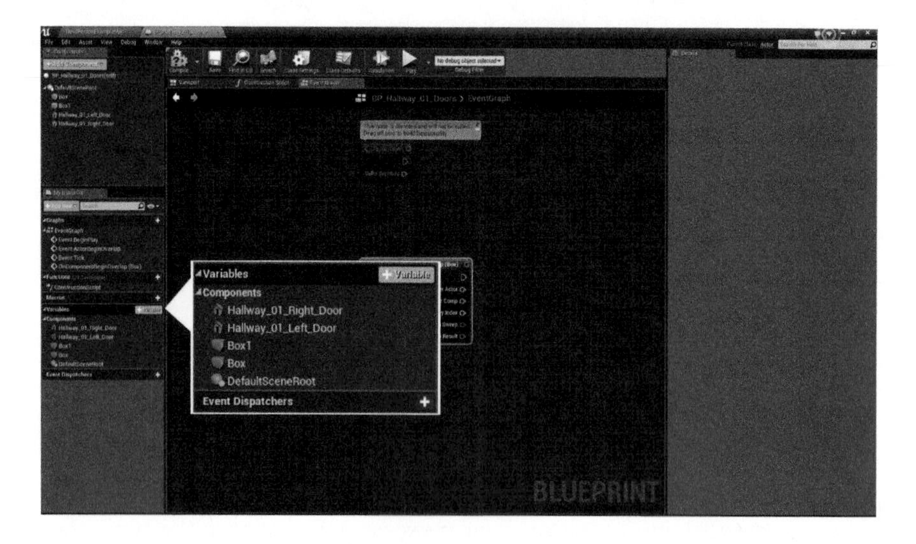

When you click on the new variable button, it will add the variable to the list in the figure below. Name the new variable *b_IsOpen*. In the Details panel, make sure that the Variable Type is set to Boolean.

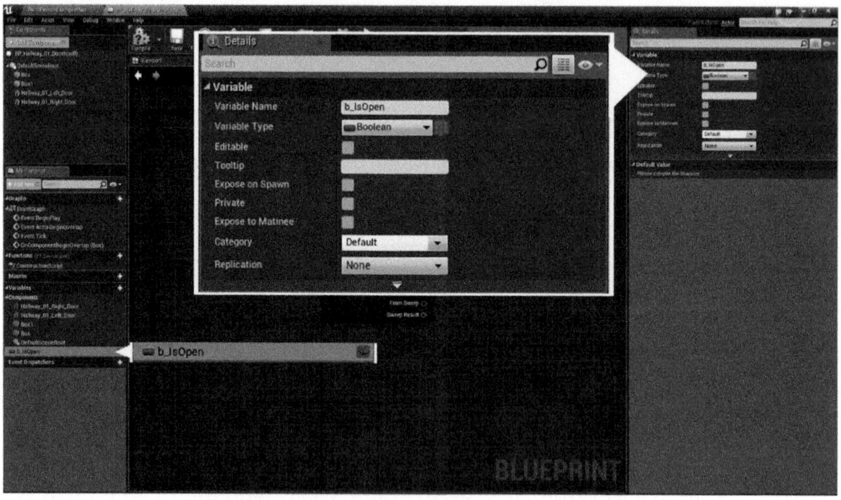

There are a number of different methods to add a variable to the graph. You can drag the variable into the graph, where you will be prompted with an option box. The options are **Get** and **Set**.

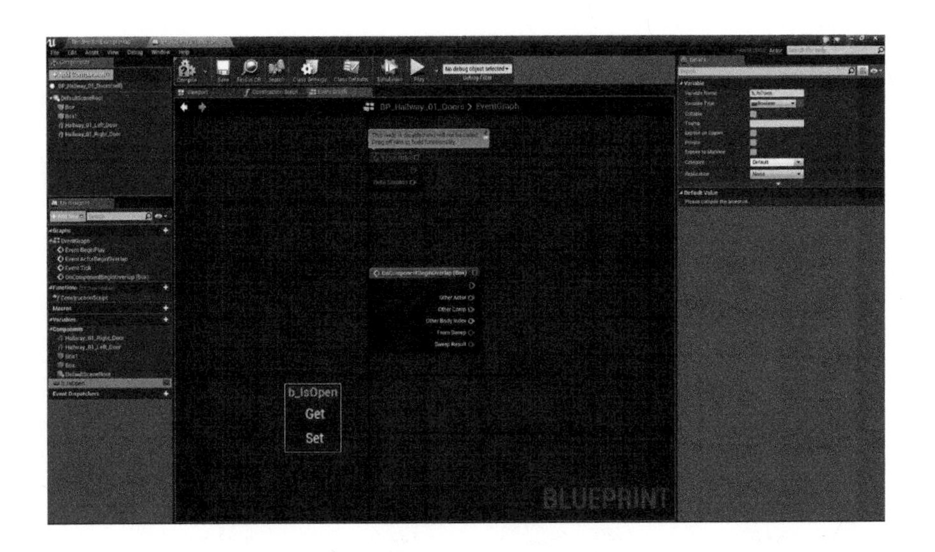

These options work just as they appear. The Get option will *get* the value of the variable, while the Set option will *set* the value of the variable. You want to know if the doors are open, so, to begin, you need to get the value. Click on Get to add a Get node now. Looking at the newly created node, there are two main parts. The first is its color and the second is the Out pin on the right side of the name. The color of the node is a good indicator as to what type of node it is. Each variable type has its own specific color, and I recommend that you take some time later to look at the different types of variables available.

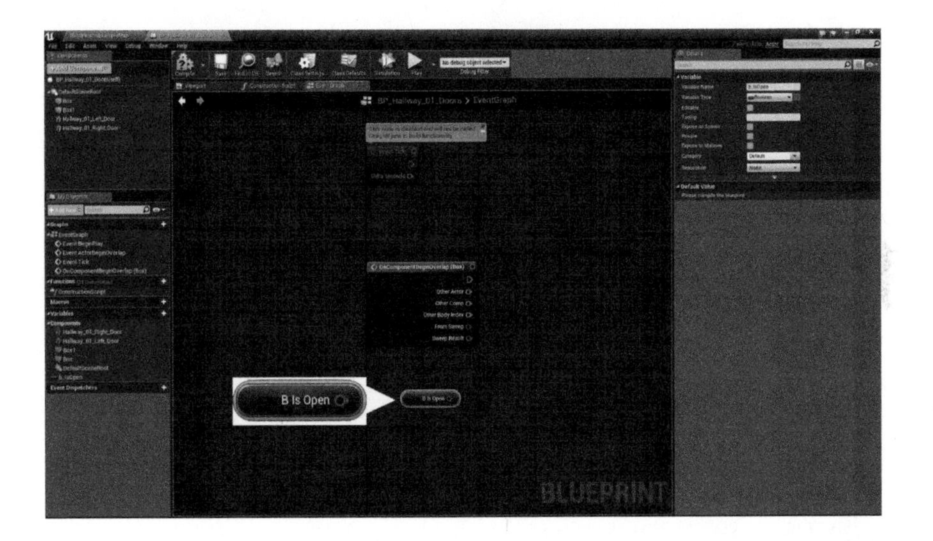

Now is a good opportunity to take a closer look at the context menu available in Blueprints. The context menu changes its options depending on how and when you access it. For example, if you were to right-click in the graph right now, you would get something similar to what is shown in the next figure.

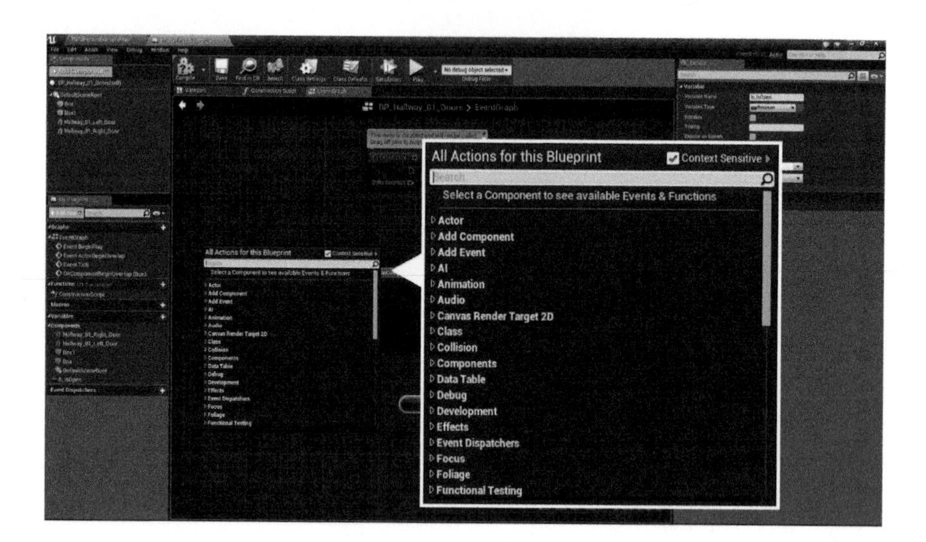

However, if you were to drag off the out pin on the Boolean, you would get a menu similar to that seen in the image below.

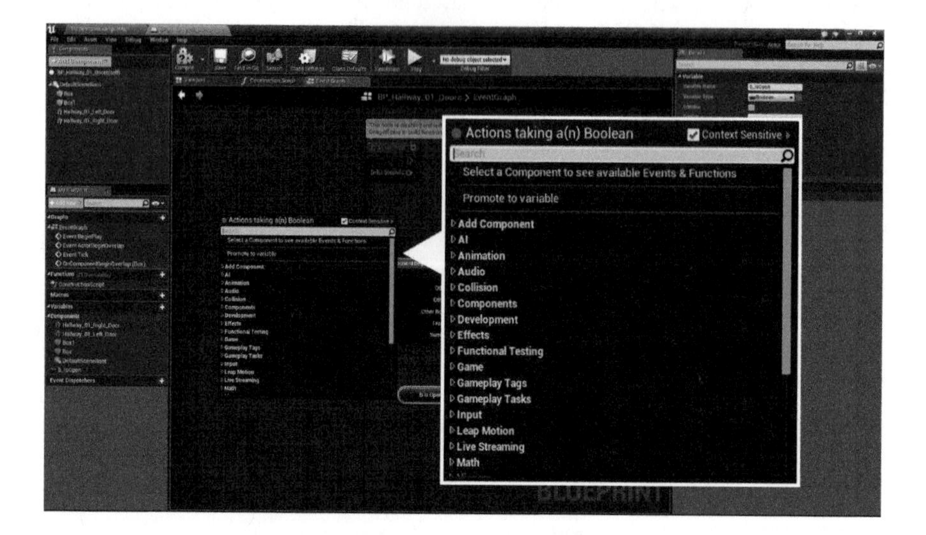

The menus do look similar; however, when dragging off the out pin, the options are slimmed down a bit. This is because Unreal will not allow you to connect two nodes together if they are incompatible. You can use this to your advantage as you progress.

Using the context menu (while dragging off the out-pin), type in "branch." You do not need to click in the search box; you can simply just start typing.

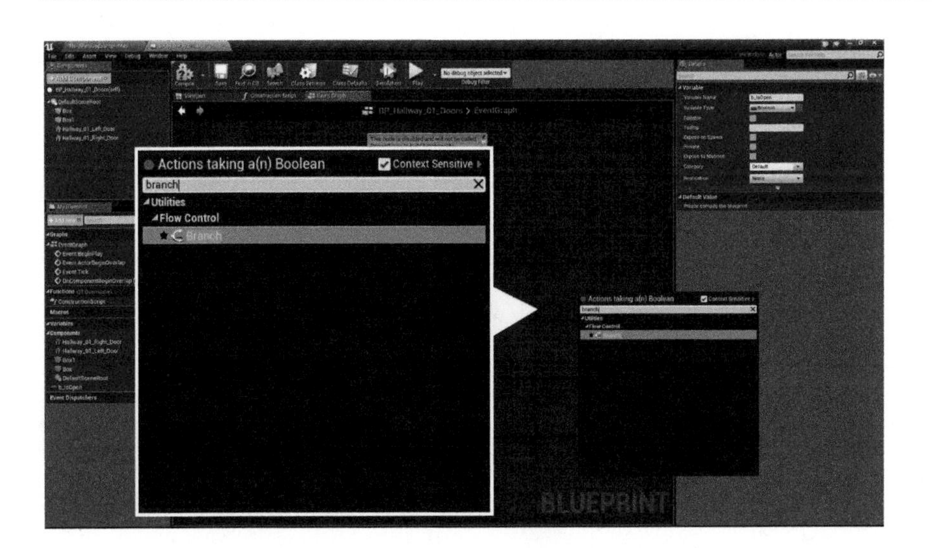

Once you have found the Branch node in the menu, you can click on it to add it to the graph.

Notice that the Boolean node has a line connecting it to the Branch node. Also note that the Condition pin on the Branch node is the same color as the Boolean variable node. Looking at the Branch node, you can see that it has the same output values that a Boolean has. This means that, as you run through the Branch node, it will read the Boolean value and then trigger the corresponding out-pin.

You need to connect the OnComponentBeginOverlap (Box) node (trigger node) to the Branch node. The arrow at the top right of the trigger node is an exec pin and should be connected to the in-exec pin of the Branch node.

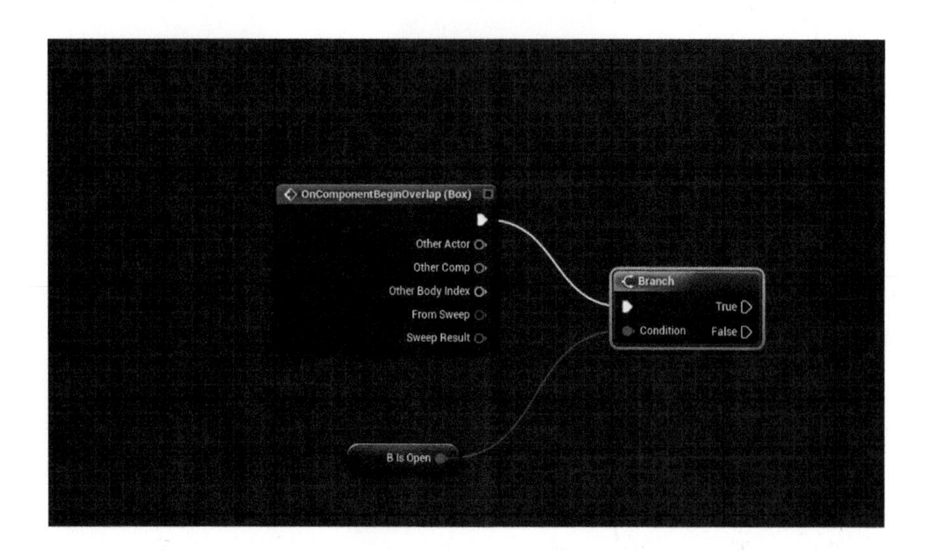

Before continuing, we should take a minute to talk about the execution path of the graph. Using the above figure, you can see the white line running from the trigger to the Branch node. This is the line of execution. Execution lines will always be white and will always run between two arrow shaped pins.

Because you want to continue only if the door is closed, you need to work only with the false out-pin on the Branch node. The first thing you want to do after the Branch node is to set your Boolean to true. (This will stop the graph from repeatedly running when you do not want it to.) From the Variables section, bring in a Set node for the B_IsOpen node by dragging it into the graph while holding the Alt key. Once you have added the Set node, you can connect the False out-pin from the Branch node to the in-exec pin on the Set node. Also check the box beside B_IsOpen to set the value to true.

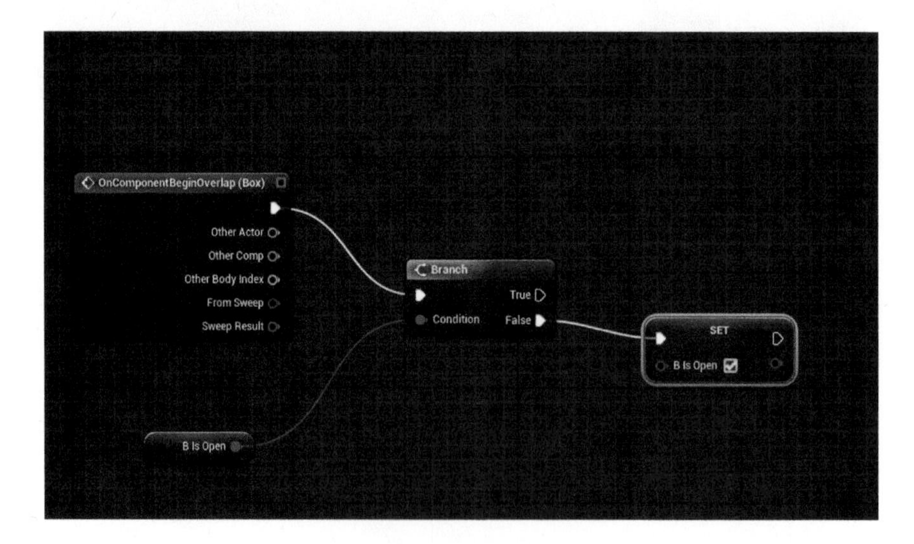

Now is a good time to review what you have done so far. You have a trigger box that will activate when the player has entered it. From there it will check to see if the doors are already open. If the doors are closed, then you will start the path that will open them by setting the state of your Boolean to true.

In an open area of the graph, right-click and then scroll all the way to the bottom of the context menu to find **Add Timeline**.

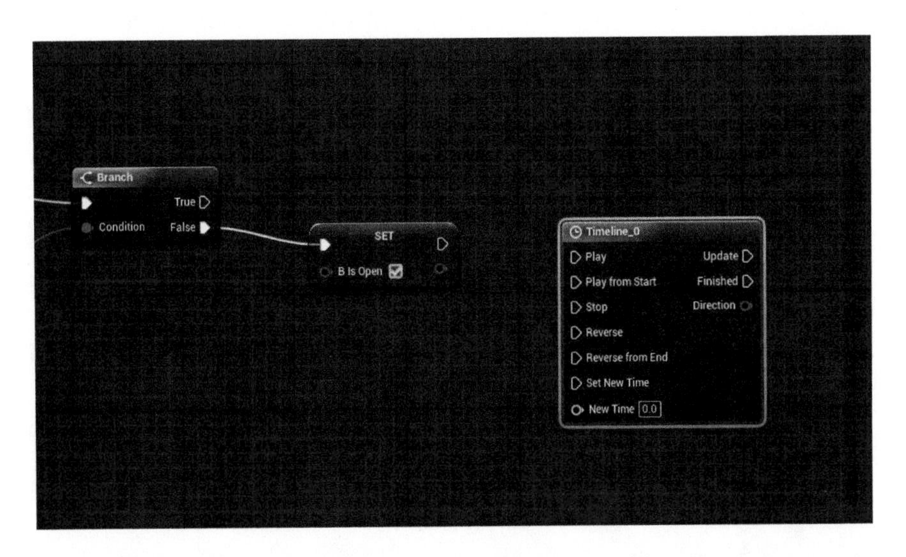

Clicking on Add Timeline will add a new node to the graph. **Timeline** nodes are used for many different things in Unreal. Before you go any farther, open the timeline by double-clicking it.

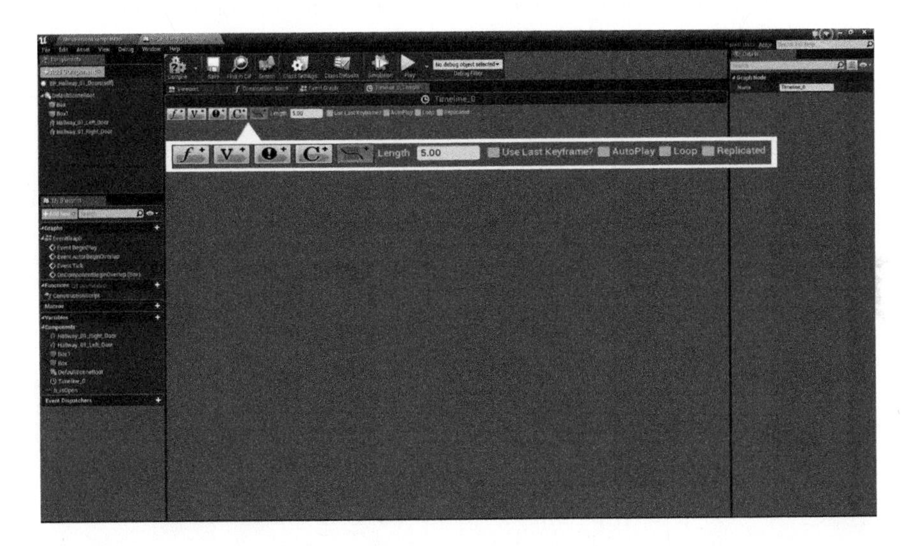

A new tab and toolbar appear when you open the timeline. From left to right, the buttons are as follows:

- Add Float Track
- Add Vector Track
- Add Event Track

- Add Color Track
- Add Selected Curve Asset

While each track has a different purpose, you only need to work with a float track for your doors. A **float** is just basically a number that can include a decimal. Click on the *Add Float Track* button now to add a new float track to the timeline.

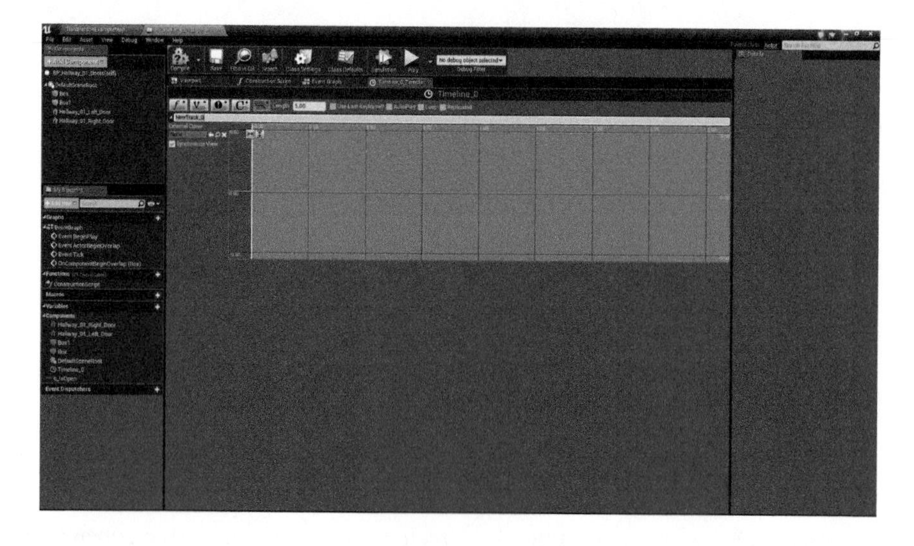

Right now, your track cannot do anything. You need to add some keys first. Holding the Shift key on the keyboard, click inside the new track to add a key.

Once you have added the key, you should notice that two new options have appeared. You now have the ability to set the *Time* and *Value* of the currently selected key. Because you want to start your animation as soon as it is triggered, set the time to 0. The value is what will output while the timeline is running. You will be using the track as a percentage value; you want it to start at 0 and run to 1. For this key, you want to set a value of 0.

Now you can add your second key. Again, hold the Shift key and click anywhere inside the timeline. Set the time and value to 1. This indicates that the timeline will run for 1 second, and its value will end at 1.

Note: If you are having a hard time seeing the keys after you type in your values, you can use the two sets of double arrows beside Time to recenter the timeline.

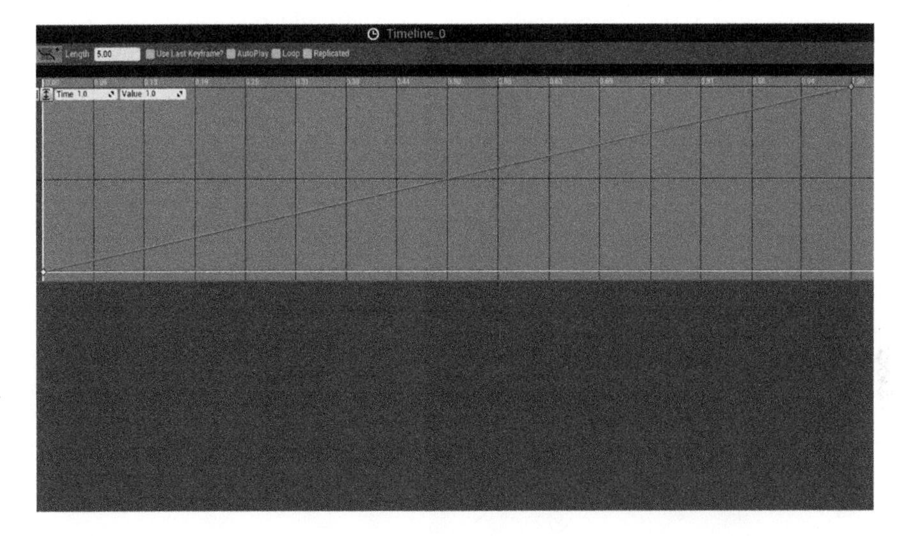

You are almost ready to start using your timeline. Before you switch back to the event graph, you need to set one last thing on the timeline. At the top of the timeline, check the box beside Use Last Keyframe? This tells the timeline to stop once it has reached the final key. Without checking this box, the timeline will run for the duration of the graph (currently 2 seconds). Once you have checked the box, switch back to the event graph by clicking its tab.

You can now connect the Set Boolean node to the Timeline node. You may notice that there are two play options. Play will run from the last used time; for example, if you previously ran the timeline for 0.5 seconds, activating Play again would start from 0.5. Play from Start, on the other hand, will *always* start the timeline from the beginning. You do not want to run only a portion of the timeline when you activate it, so connect to the Play from the Start in-pin.

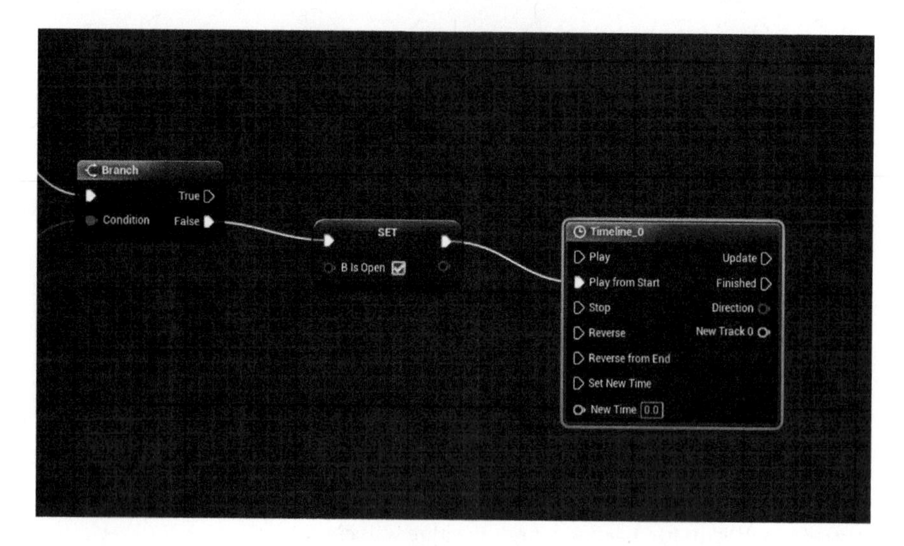

What is next? Thinking of what you are trying to do, the next step would be to move the doors, right? To begin this part, you will need to add the doors to the graph. From the Variables section, hold the Ctrl key and drag in *Hallway_01_Right_Door* and *Hallway_01_Left_Door.* This will add two new nodes to the graph that will give you access to all the attributes available for modification relating to the doors.

You will be changing the rotation of the doors. To start, you need to know how you will be rotating the doors. You can switch back to the Viewport tab and try different rotations until you find the correct rotation.

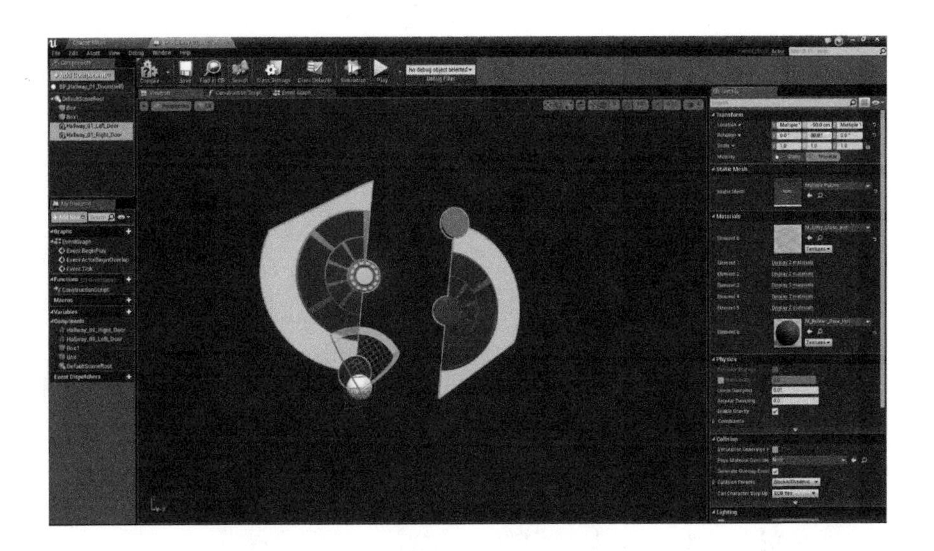

You can rotate both doors along the Y axis to 30 degrees to get a nice opening. Once you are done rotating the doors, reset their rotation to 0 on all axes. You can build one chain to set the rotation of the right door, and then copy it to set the rotation of the left door. Starting with the right door node, you need to add a *Set Relative Rotation* node.

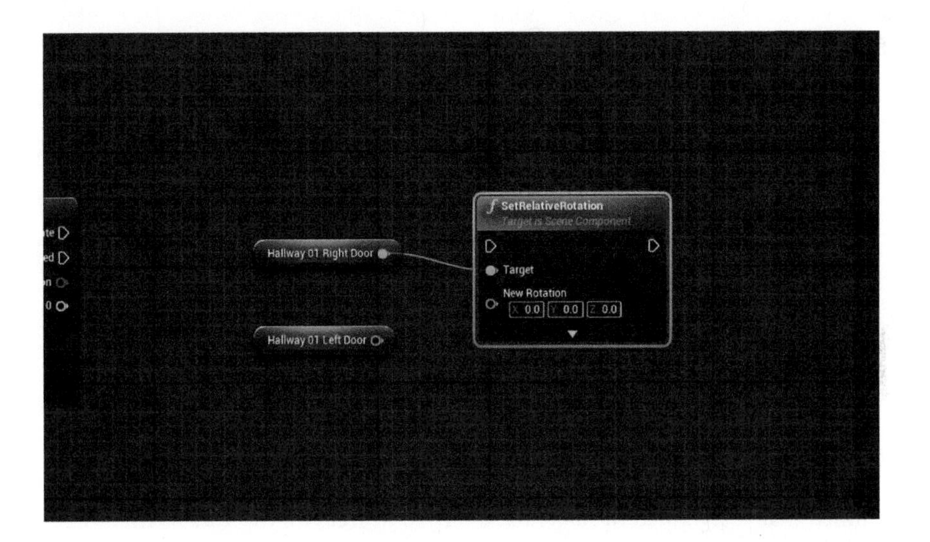

Next you need to add a Lerp (Rotator) node. In a blueprint, "linear interpolate" is a fancy way for saying "from one to another." Right-click in the graph, type "lerp," and then look for the correct node before clicking on it to add it to the graph. Remember that you are adjusting the rotation of an object, so be sure to select the Lerp (Rotator) node.

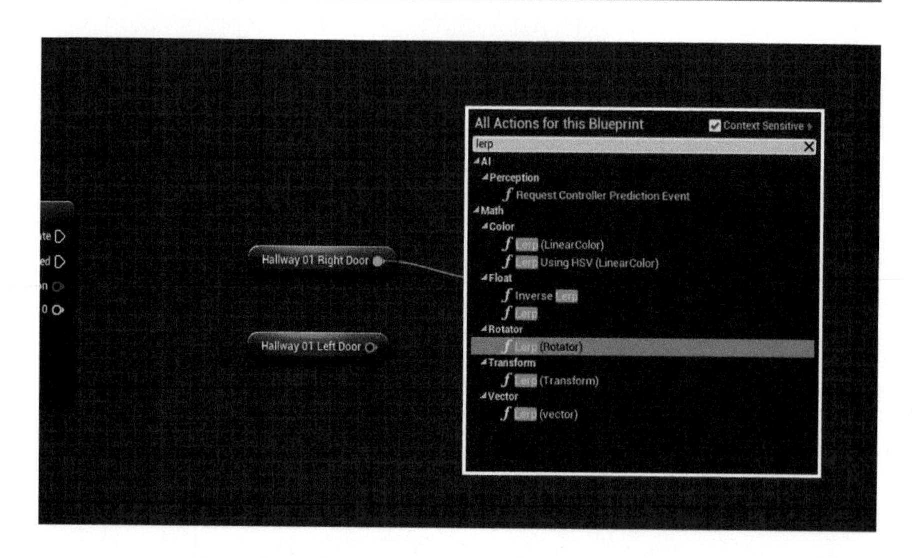

Looking at the Lerp node, you should notice that its return value is of the same type as your Set Relative Rotations New Rotation type. Connect these two pins together.

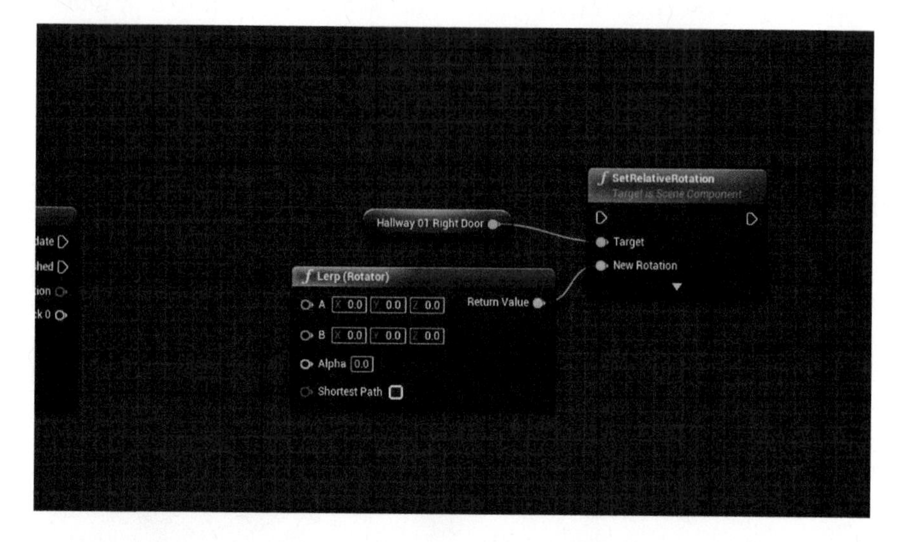

Again looking at the Lerp node, you should also notice that it has two inputs for rotation (A and B) as well as a float (alpha) that you can use. Earlier we determined that you wanted to rotate the doors 30 degrees on the Y axis. This will be your B value, so you can change the Y axis of B to 30. A is your starting point, which is 0 on all axes. Your timeline will be your alpha, so you can also connect those together as seen in the next figure.

The final step in controlling the right side door is to connect the Update out-pin from the timeline to the in-exec pin on the Set Relative Rotation node.

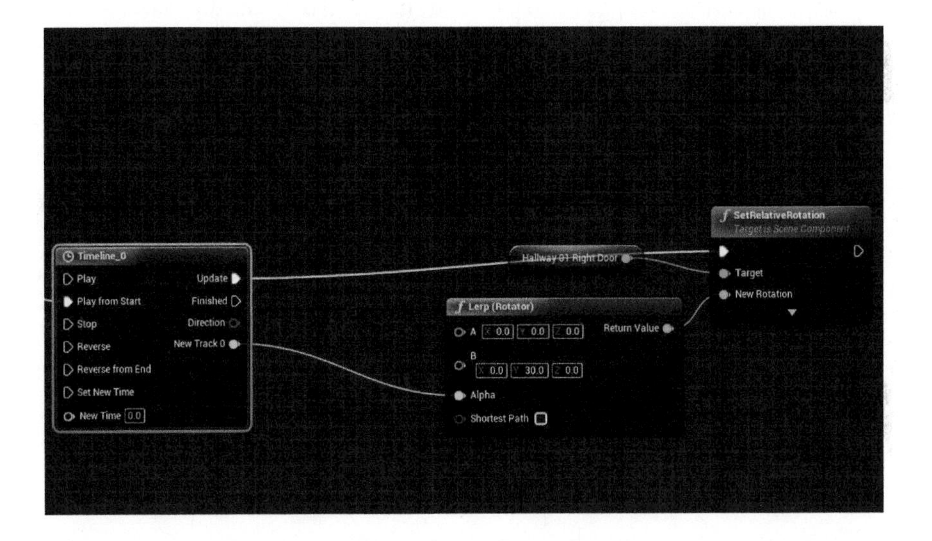

To copy the setup to your left door, you can select the Lerp and Set Relative Rotation nodes and then use Ctrl + C to copy and Ctrl + V to paste. Once you have pasted the new nodes, you can connect them as seen in the next figure.

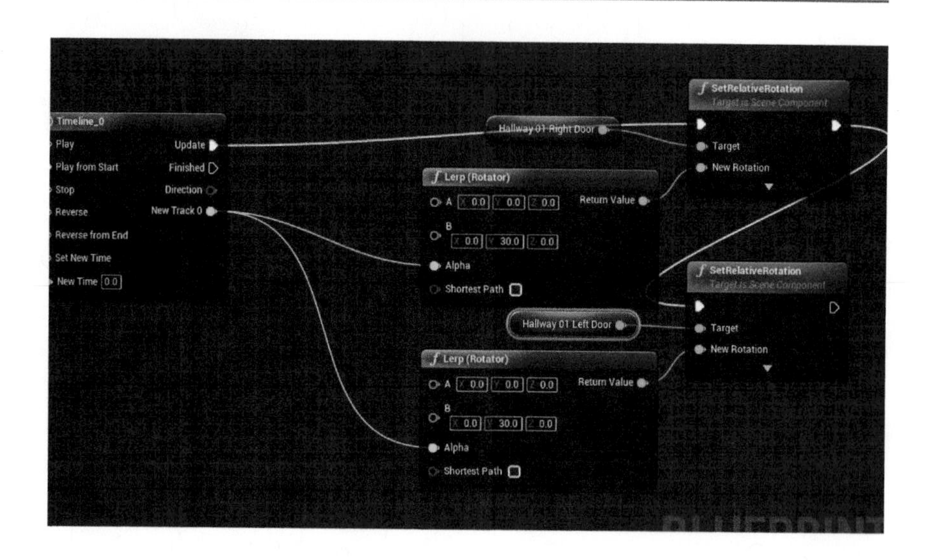

Note: An alternate method would be to connect both doors to the same Set Relative Rotation node. While this will work just fine, it would reduce the amount of control over the individual doors.

If you saved this blueprint and added to your level now, the doors would open from one side, but not the other. To correct this issue, you need to add an overlap event for Box1 also.

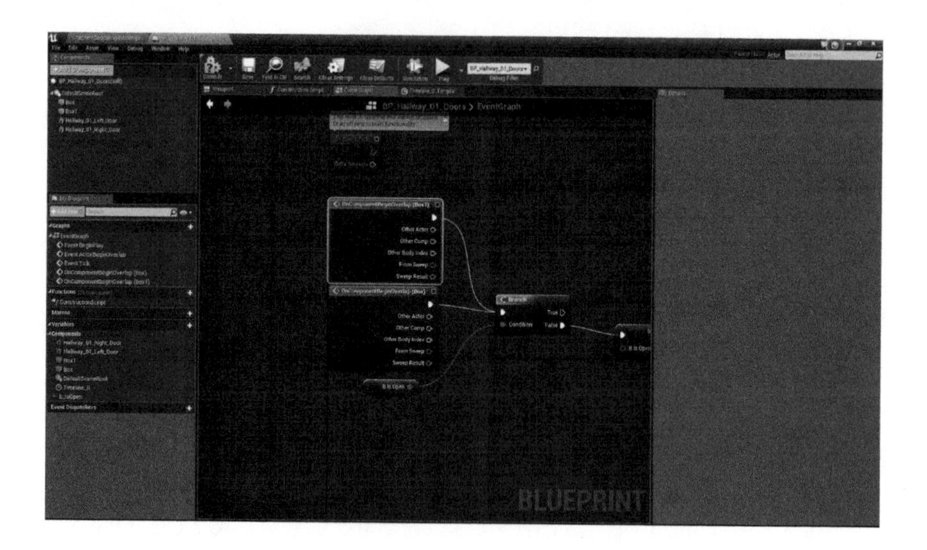

With both triggers added to the graph, you can now add the door to your level and test it out. Take a minute to try them out before continuing.

If you were only concerned about your doors being able to open once and then stay open, you could stop here. However, your goal is to have the doors close after a short time. Here, you can use a **Delay** node, which works just as it sounds. You can specify a time for the delay and then, once the clock has run out, it will continue.

To be on the safe side, you can check again to make sure the doors are open before trying to close them. This will help to avoid triggering the close action if the doors are closed. You can copy the Branch and corresponding Boolean nodes and move them below the Lerp node as seen in the figure below.

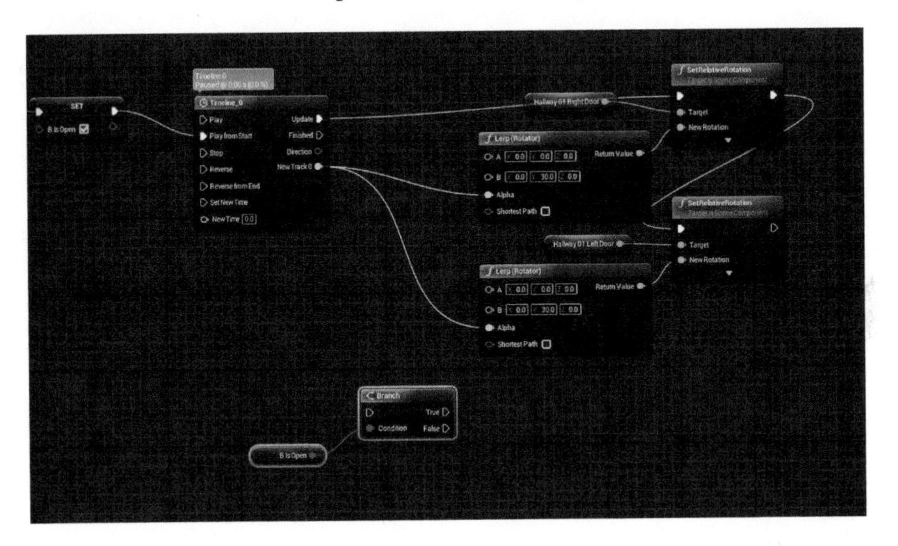

This time you are making sure the doors are open rather than closed. Instead of pulling from the False pin on your new Branch node, you will pull from the True pin and find Delay.

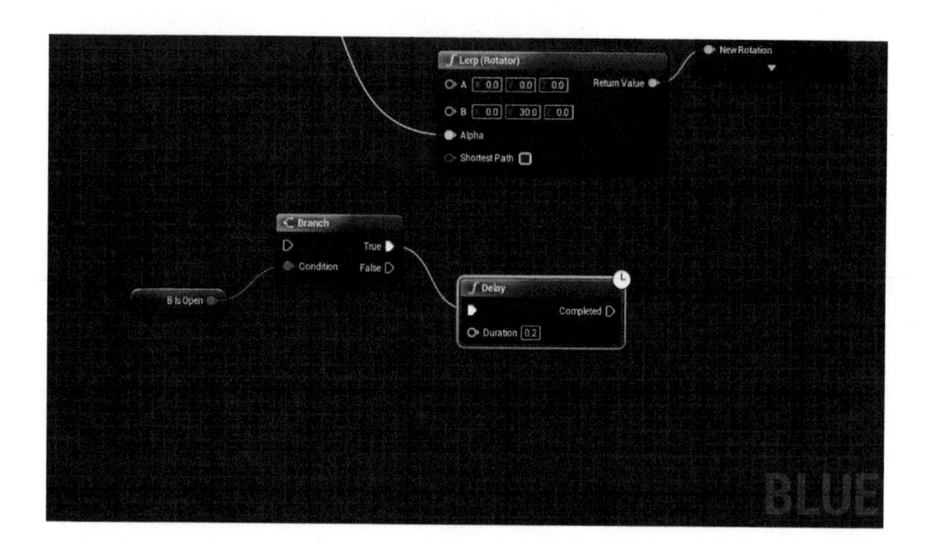

You know that your doors take 1 second to open. You would also like a little extra time to actually make it through the doors. You can set this delay's duration to 3 seconds. To continue the door closing operation, you will add another new node called a **Sequence** node, which has a series of out-exec pins that it will run in order. This allows you to run multiple operations from a single node while ensuring their order. Drag off the Delay's out-pin and find Sequence under Flow Control.

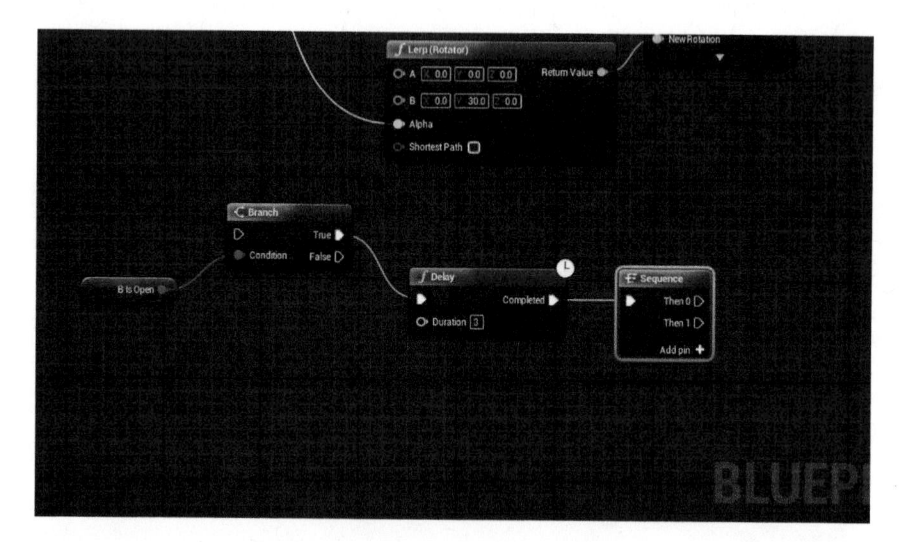

By default, the sequence node has two outputs. You will connect the Then 0 exec pin to the Reverse in-pin on your timeline. The reverse pin will play your timeline backward, allowing your doors to close in the same manner they opened. While the timeline should have already ended by the time you reach this point, by using Reverse rather than Reverse from End you can avoid any snapping effects from incorrect timing. Finally, you will add another delay to the graph to stop you from triggering the doors to open instantly after they have closed. From the sequence node, use the Then 1 pin to connect to a delay of 1 second. From the new delay, connect the Completed pin to a Set Boolean node as seen in the next figure.

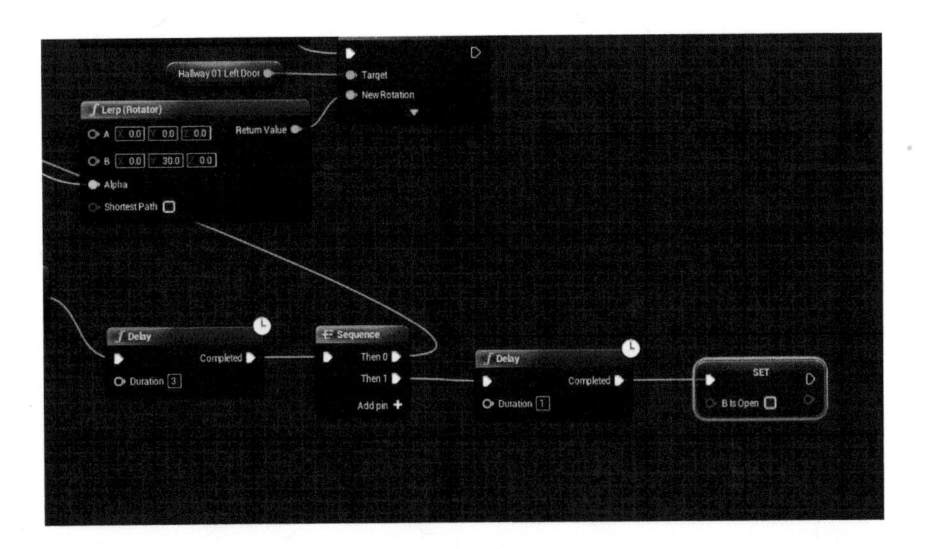

Before your doors will actually close, you need to connect the Finished out-exec from your timeline to the in-exec of your last Branch node. The completed graph should be similar to the image below.

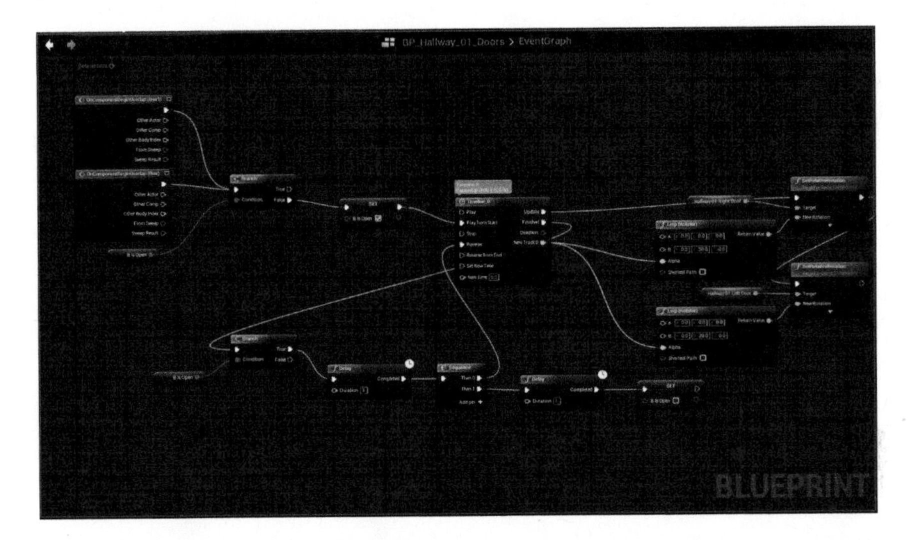

Compile and save your blueprint. If you have not added the door blueprint to your level, you can do so now. Test your doors to make sure they are working correctly. If you have any issues, refer back to the above image to make any adjustments. Before we close out the chapter, you can add your doors to a couple different locations. You can add a door to each hallway of the four-way sections.

One final thing we need to cover here are the restrictions of the event graph. While you have not had any issue adding the different nodes to this point, there is one significant difference between the event graph and all other graphs in a blueprint. If you were to switch to any other graph on a blueprint, you would *not* have access to the Timeline or Delay nodes. This is because *only* the event graph has the ability to modify timed events. If, for whatever reason, you become stuck without the ability to add timelines or delays, make sure that you are not in another graph.

You may notice during testing that you can walk through the doors. To correct the issue, you can open the doors in the Static Mesh Editor and apply an auto convex collision to each door.

Matinee

Unlike blueprint animations, you can use Matinee to create different types of animations—for example, cut scenes. Matinee has a number of different tools and options, but for the example in this book you will focus on the camera animation. Adding a new matinee to the level is as simple as clicking on the Matinee button on the toolbar and then selecting Add Matinee. Upon selecting Add Matinee, the Matinee Editor window should open.

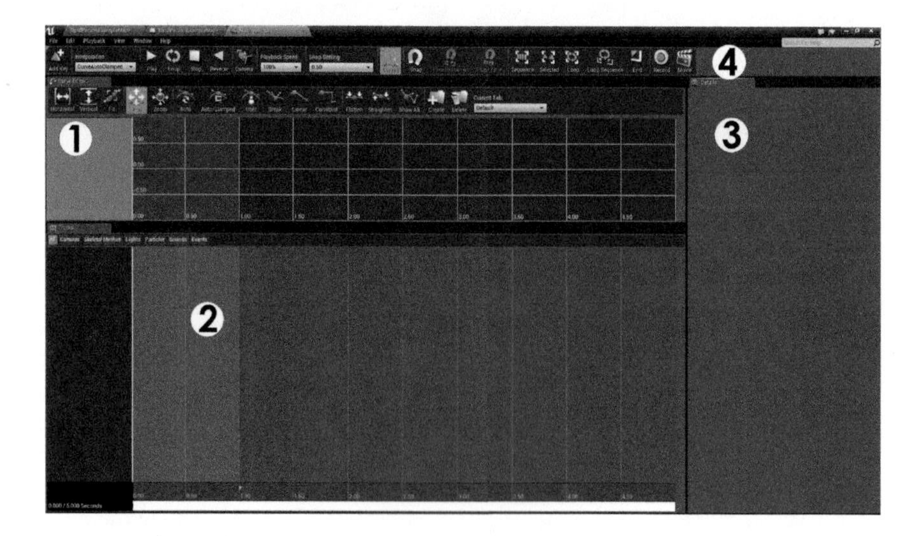

The sections in the Matinee Editor are as follows:

1. Curve Editor
2. Tracks
3. Details
4. Toolbar

While not unlike some of the other editors you have used so far, you do have a Curve Editor and the Tracks tab. We will be focusing on the Tracks tab for the remainder of this chapter. This tab is used to add all the needed matinee tracks to be used. The tracks are organized into groups.

The group you will be working with is the camera group. To add a group to the Tracks tab, right-click in the dark gray area on the far left. Select Add New Camera Group from the popup menu. Once you have selected the group, it will prompt you for a name. For this example, you will leave the name as the default; however, it is important to understand that you can use multiple groups of the same type. This means that you should take the time to use a naming convention to label each group as needed. Once you have finished naming your group, you should see three new elements in the Tracks tab. The first of these new elements is the camera group, the second is the movement track, and the third and final element is the FOVAngle group. You will be focusing on the movement track, but the methods used will work for other track types as well.

Before you start modifying the track, use the mouse wheel to scroll out so that you can see the whole track.

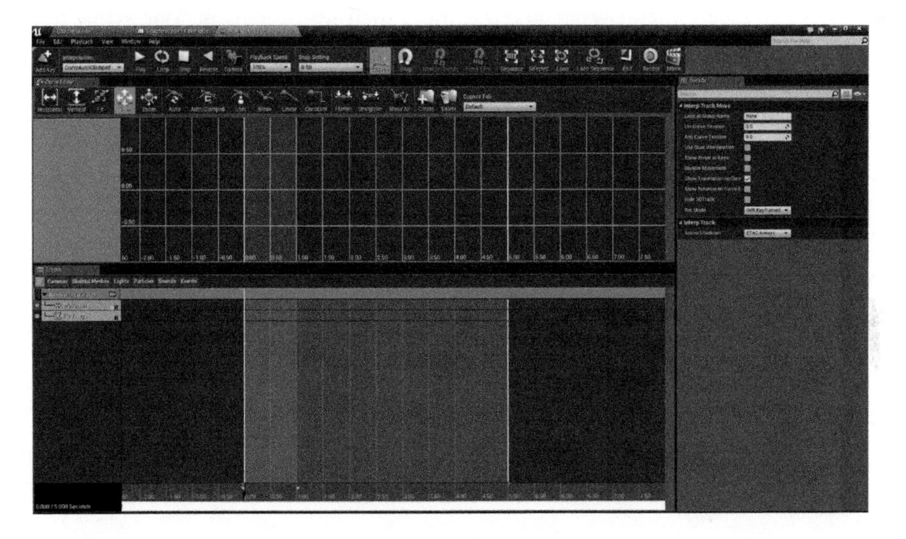

Looking at the Tracks tab, you should notice that there are two different colors for the tracks. The background color of light gray represents the full length of the currently set matinee, while the light green represents how long the track will be. In the above figure, the full length of the matinee is set to 5 seconds, while the track length is 1 second. To set the track length to the appropriate length, drag the green arrow at the bottom all the way to the right.

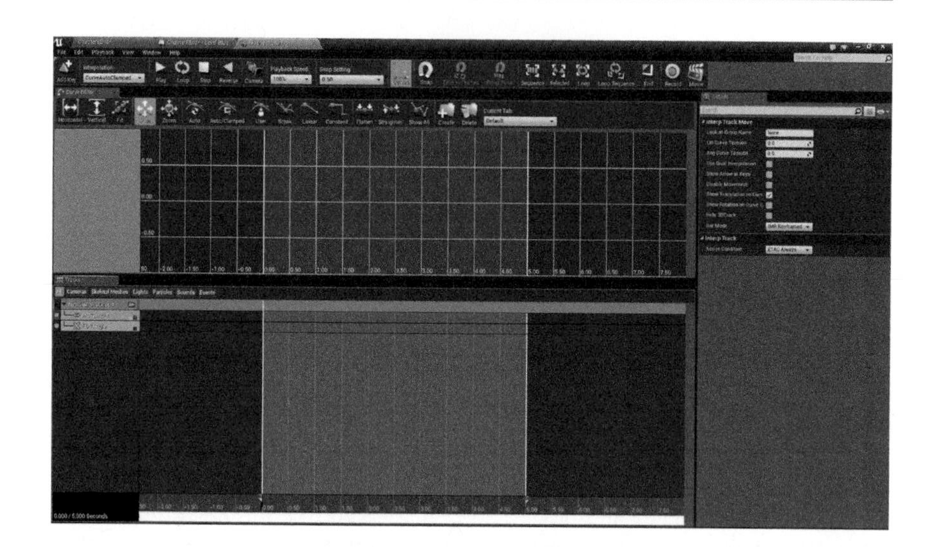

Now your track length matches the matinee length of 5 seconds.

Switch back to the Level Editor and move the camera back to see the newly added camera from the matinee. You can use the Level Editor and Matinee Editor to create a fly-through of the first section of the level. It takes a little time to get used to working with both, so take your time.

In the Matinee Editor, you should notice a solid black line below the tracks on the timeline. This line represents the current time. If there is a key (the red arrow in the Movement track) where the current timeline is, then any movement done to the camera will modify that key. If there is no key, the movement will not affect the timeline.

Without changing the current location of the timeline, move the camera to a good starting position. When you select the camera in the Level Editor, you should notice that a small window appears that shows you what the camera can see. You should use this to line up your camera's view. Since you are only working with 5 seconds currently, you do not have a lot of time to move through the level. For this part, instead of doing a level flythrough, you will simply look at the room you are in, moving the camera around.

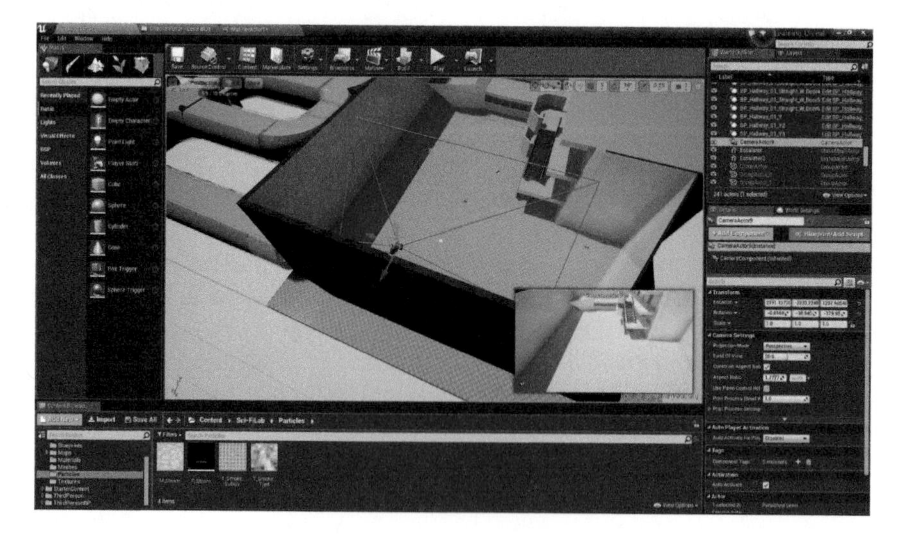

Before making any more adjustments to the camera (after you get a decent start position), make sure you change the timeline in the Matinee Editor. While you can add as many keys as you would like, you can get a smooth movement by only using the first key and creating the last key.

In the Matinee Editor, move the timeline all the way to the right.

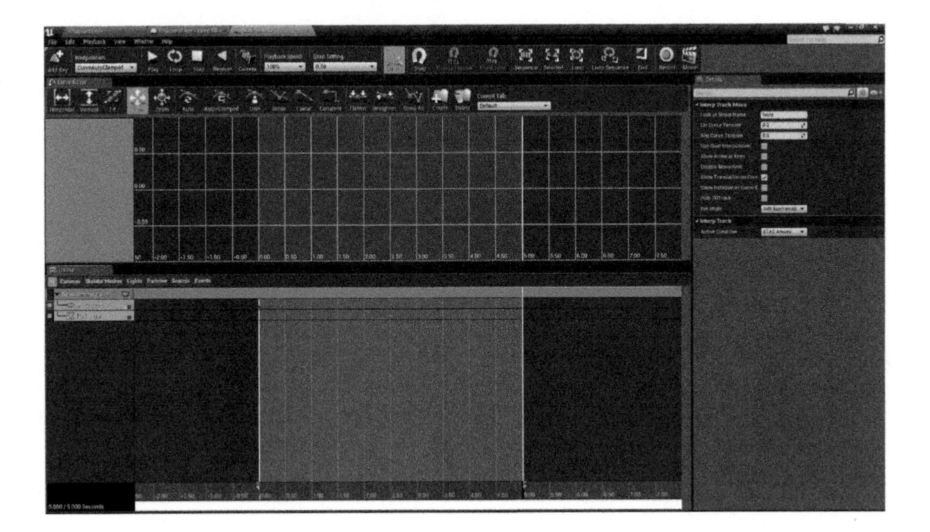

Switching back to the Level Editor, you can now move your camera to a new location.

Once you have your camera's new position set, switch back to the Matinee Editor. Make sure to click on the Movement tracks name to ensure it is selected. Do not move the timeline yet. Press Enter on the keyboard to add a new key. Once you have hit enter, you should notice that a new red arrow has appeared at the location of the timeline.

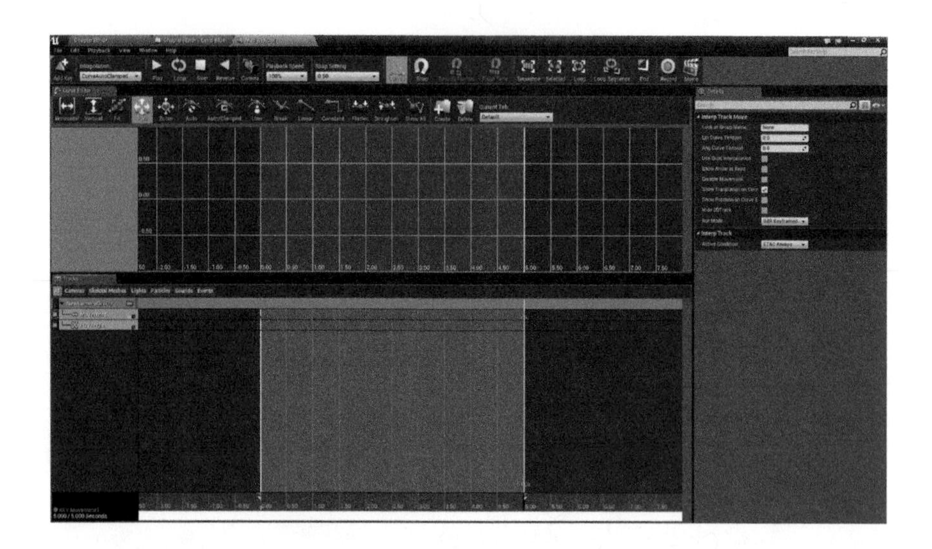

You should now be able to scrub through the timeline and watch your camera move from its starting location to its ending location.

You still have a big issue, though. If you were to play the game right now, it would simply go to the player and you would never see the matinee play. In order to view your matinee during runtime, you need to make some adjustments to the level blueprint.

On the main toolbar, select the Blueprints button to open the dropdown and choose Open Level Blueprint. You have already done some work in the level blueprint, so you will need to move to a new area so that you have a nice clean work area. Grab the Event Begin Play node and move it to an empty section of the graph.

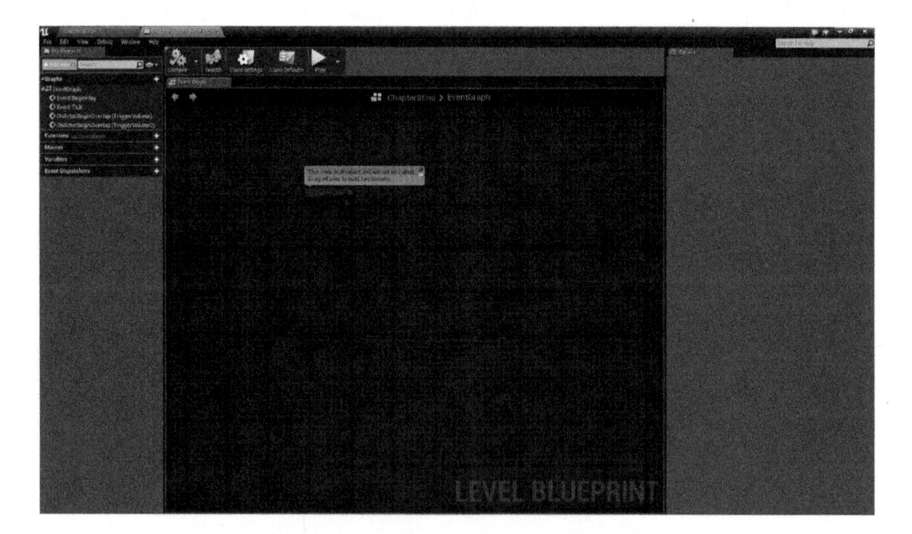

The first thing you will need to do is get your player controller and camera. In order to do that you need to add a node named Get Player Controller. Right-click in the graph, find the correct node, and add it to the graph. The Get Player Controller node can be used to get a number of different components related to the player. For your needs, you will be getting the default camera first.

From the Return Value of the Get Player Controller, drag off and find the Get View Target node to add it to the graph. Here you can use a new method of adding a variable. There are instances like the one you are currently in which it can be difficult to find the correct variable type. Instead of clicking on the Add Variable button and searching through all the different variables types, we can right-click on the Return Value of the Get View Target node and choose Promote to Variable. Rename the new variable to PlayerCamera. Connect the output of the Event Begin Play node to the exec input of the Set variable node.

Now that you have a reference to your camera, you can change it freely while still maintaining the ability to switch back at any time. In the Level Editor, select the camera added during the matinee creation. Switch back to the Level Blueprint. Right-click and select Create a Reference to CameraActor (this should be the third line down).

From the Return Value of the Get Player Controller node, drag off and find the Set View Target With Blend node and add it to the graph. Connect the exec-out of the Set node to the exec-in of the Set View node. Connect the output of the CameraActor node to the New View Target input of the Set View node.

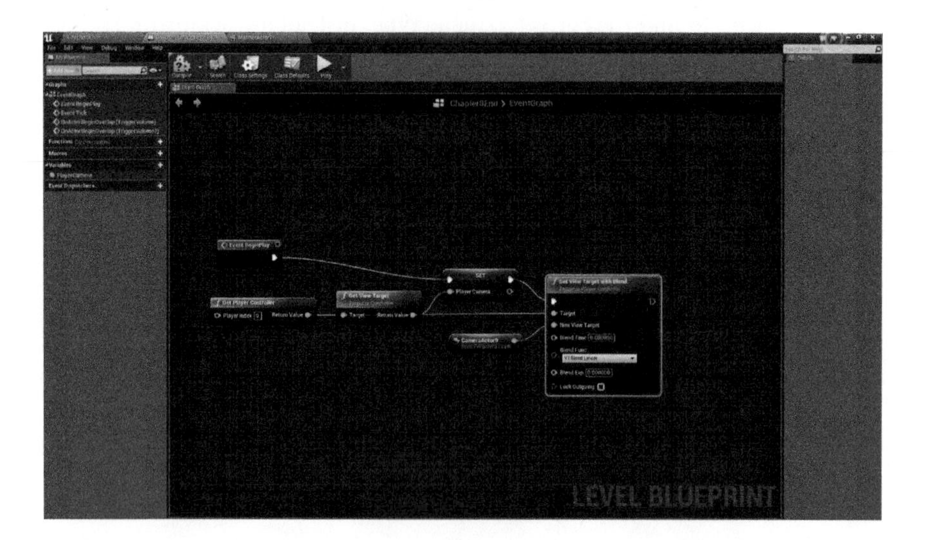

Next you need to add a reference to your matinee to the Level Blueprint. Select the matinee in the Level Editor by clicking on the matinee actor.

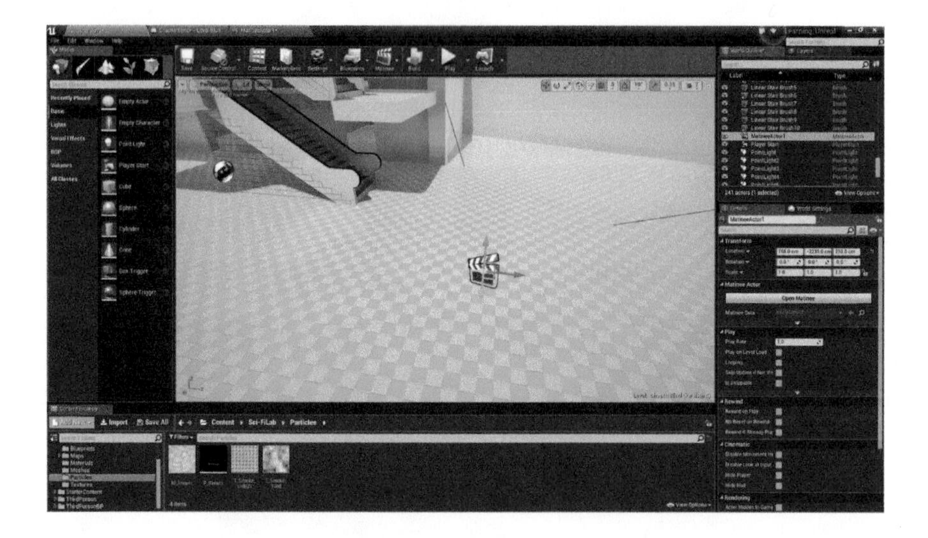

Return to the Level Blueprint and right-click in the graph. Expand the call function on the matinee actor section. Expand the cinematic section. Select the play function. Once you have added the Play node to the graph, you can connect the exec output of the Set View node to the exec-in of the Play node.

Play your level now to see how your matinee has affected your level. You should notice that the matinee plays without issue; however, you never return to the player camera. To correct the issue, you need to add a couple more nodes in the Level Blueprint.

From the output of the Play node, add a Delay node and set the duration to 5. Add another instance of the Set View Target with Blend node and the Get Player Controller node. Connect the output of the delay node to the exec input of the new Set View node. Connect the output of the Get Player Controller node to the target input of the Set View node. Finally, add a Get node for the PlayerCamera variable. Connect its output to the New View Target input of the Set View node.

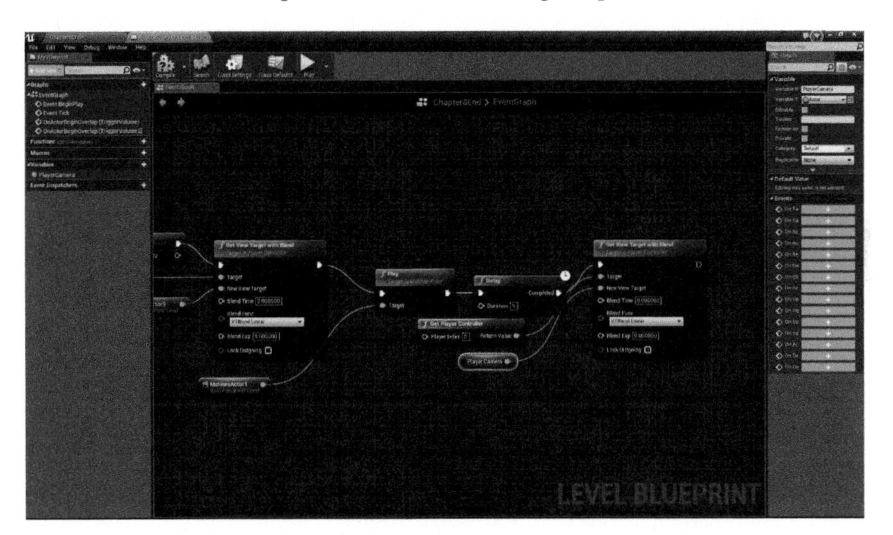

Play-test your level now and you should run through your matinee; then, when it has completed, switch to your player camera.

Chapter Challenge

Now that you have an idea of how to create a matinee cut scene, try creating a lengthier fly-through of your level. Remember that the Delay node you added to the Level Blueprint should match the length of the matinee. (If the matinee is 30 seconds, the delay should be 30 seconds.)

Chapter Review

In this chapter we took a much closer look at the event graph with a blueprint. You learned how to add triggers to a blueprint and how to add and manipulate timelines. You learned how to use a timeline to rotate an object. We also covered some of the more common restrictions found in the different graphs associated with blueprints. To close out the chapter, we took a brief look at the Matinee Editor. You created a short-cut scene that plays upon starting the level and then switches back to the players' camera when completed.

9

Populating Your Level

Introduction

From this point on, we will be looking at a few more advanced techniques. In this chapter, we will look at a couple more material concepts along with adding mode detail to a level.

While you have been building a pretty interesting level, it is still quite bare. In order to fill the empty space and beautify your level, you need to add some more objects. Before you can add them to the level, you must first import them.

Note: If you do not wish to go through the process of importing the objects and building their materials, you can instead open the Chapter_9_Mid Project and proceed to the Adding Actors portion of the chapter.

Importing the Rest of Your Objects

You can use the same method as you did in previous chapters. There are quite a few new objects, so you should import them in groups. While you can simply select them all and import them at once, splitting them up to around 10–15 at a time will reduce the chances of issues arising.

In the content browser open your Meshes folder. Right-click and select Import To. you will be importing the following meshes on your first pass:

- Angle_Beam
- Angle_Trim_90
- Angle_Trim_Long

- Angle_Trim_Short
- Book_Shelf_01
- Book_Shelf_02
- Ceiling_01
- Ceiling_Light
- Computer
- Cryo_Chamber
- Desk_Chair
- Desk_Lamp
- Detail_Panel_01
- Detail_Panel_02

Use the same settings as before; do not generate collisions, do not import materials, and do not import textures. Once you have all the options set correctly, you can choose Import All to add them to your project.

The next batch includes the following:

- Exhaust_Vent
- Ext_Window
- File_Cabinent_01
- Floating_Monitor
- Floor_Details_01
- Generator
- Generator_Square

The next import will contain:

- Hose_01
- Hose_02
- Hose_03
- Hose_04
- Hoses
- L_Desk
- Lab_Stairs
- Lab_Stairs_02
- Large_Computer
- Lock_Box
- Locker
- Locker_02
- Medbay_Bed
- Medbay_Monitor_Screen
- Medbay_Rays
- Medbay_Scanner
- Medbay_Station
- Medbay_Support_Beam
- Medbay_Table
- Medicine_Vial_Empty
- Medicine_Vial_Full
- Monitor_01

You may encounter a warning about a mesh being very small. This is because of the vials and can be ignored.

The next batch includes:

- Observation_Room_02
- Observation_Room_02_Brace
- Observation_Room_Ceiling
- Observation_Room_Curved_Wall
- Observation_Room_Floor
- Observation_Room_Straight_Wall
- Pipe_Elbow
- Pipe_Long
- Pipe_Short
- Pipe_Valve
- Pole_Generator
- Power_Core
- Rafter_90
- Rafter_Angle_Beam
- Rafter_Complete
- Rafter_Straight

The final selection contains:

- Railing_Curved
- Railing_Straight
- Rollup_Door
- Server_Rack_01
- Server_Rack_02
- Shelf_01
- Small_Console
- Small_Crate
- Small_Door
- Square_Vent_90
- Sub_Wall
- Sub_Wall_02
- Test_Floor
- Test_Floor_Long
- Test_Floor_Narrow
- Test_Room
- Test_Room_02
- Test_Room_Desk
- Test_Room_Window
- Trash_Can
- Turn_Lock
- TV
- Wall_Detail_02
- Wall_Detail_03
- Workbench

There are a lot of new meshes here and they are going to need some color. You can start by using the materials you have already created. The following meshes do not need new materials created:

- Book_Shelf_01
- Book_Shelf_02
- Ceiling_01
- Ceiling_Light
- Desk_Lamp
- Detail_Panel_01
- Detail_Panel_02
- Exhaust_Vent
- Ext_Window
- File_Cabinent_01
- Hose_01
- Hose_02
- Hose_03
- Hose_04
- Hoses
- Lab_Stairs
- Lab_Stairs_02
- Lock_Box
- Medbay_Support_Beam
- Observation_Room_02_Brace
- Observation_Room_Ceiling
- Observation_Room_Curved_Wall
- Observation_Room_Floor
- Observation_Room_Straight_Wall
- Rafter_90
- Rafter_Angle_Beam
- Rafter_Complete
- Rafter_Straight
- Railing_Curved
- Railing_Straight
- Rollup_Door
- Shelf_01
- Small_Door
- Square_Vent_90
- Sub_Wall
- Sub_Wall_02
- Test_Floor
- Test_Floor_Long
- Test_Floor_Narrow
- Test_Room
- Test_Room_02
- Test_Room_Desk
- Test_Room_Window
- Trash_Can

- Turn_Lock
- Wall_Detail_02
- Wall_Detail_03

Creating Time-Based Materials

One interesting effect that you create within a material is a time-based changing material. You may have run across an object in a game that has a pulsing glow. This is an example of a time-based material. While there are an innumerable number of uses for these materials, you will start by creating one for a small console. To begin, you need to create a basic material just as you have in the past. You will start by building a basic material and then look at the process of changing certain aspects to a time-based material. Before you can start, you need to import a few textures for your material. In the Textures folder, import the following three textures:

- Small_Console_BG
- Small_Console_Highlights
- Small_Console_M

Create a new material in your Materials folder. Name the material *M_Sm_Console_Screen*. Open the material in the Material Editor. The first step is to import the three textures that you uploaded into your material. Locate the textures in your Textures folder and drag them into the material graph.

You will need to add one more node before you can connect everything together. Right-click in the graph and type "lerp." Add the Linear Interpolate node to the graph. Once you have added the node, you can connect your textures to it. Connect the output of the *Small_Console_BG* node to the A input of the Lerp. Connect the *Small_Console_Highlights* to the B input on the Lerp. Finally, connect the output of the *Small_Console_M* to the alpha input of the Lerp. Now you can connect the output of the Lerp to the Base Color input of the material.

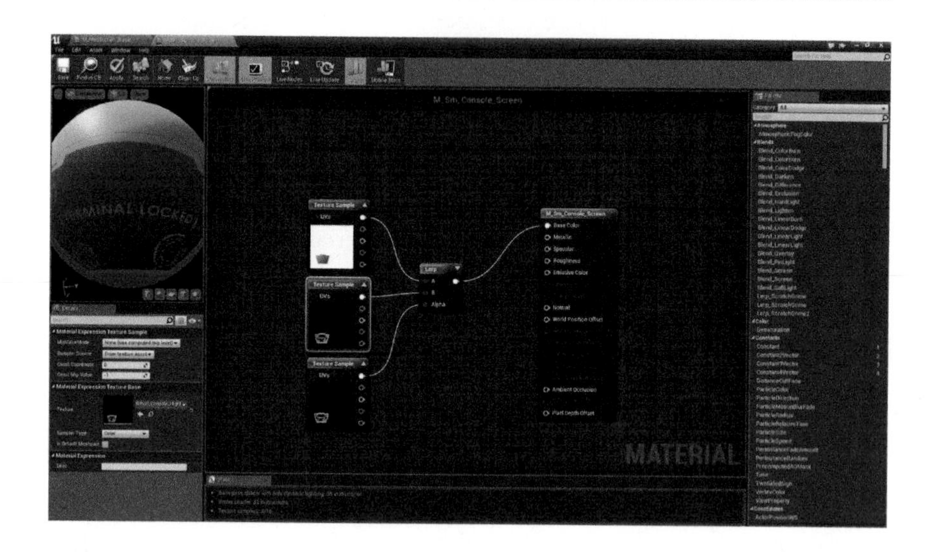

So far, the steps you have used are not unlike any other material you have created. From this point on, however, you will be working on the time-based portion of the material.

To start the process, you need to add two Vector nodes (hold "3" on the keyboard before clicking), a Constant node (hold "1" on the keyboard before clicking), and a Multiply node (hold "M" on the keyboard before clicking). You will connect one of the Vector nodes to the A input of the Multiply and the Constant node to the B input of the Multiply node.

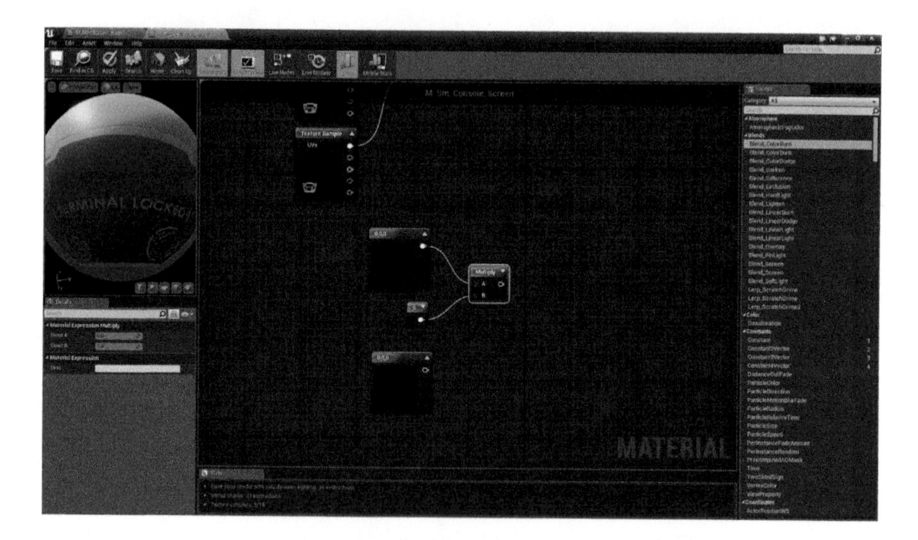

This will be your bright highlight color. You need to set the color to a light blue. I used the RGB (red, green, blue) value of 0, 1, 1 for this color. The second Vector node will be your dim highlight color. I used an RGB value of 0, 0.5, 0.5 for this color.

Now you can add the Time function. The Time node is used to add the passage of time to the material. Right-click in the graph and search for time. Once you have found the Time node, add it to the graph.

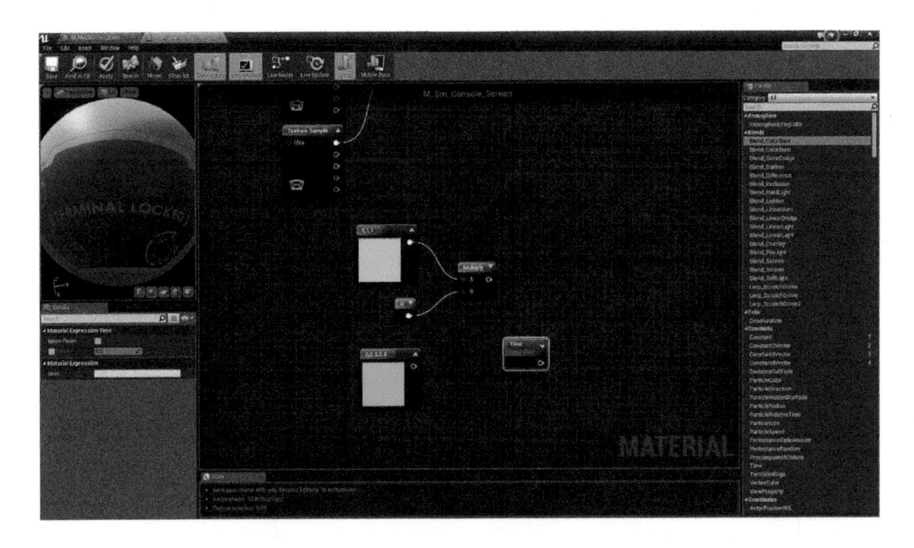

From the output of the Time node, drag off and find the **Sine** node, which converts the input into a continually oscillating waveform. You can use the Sine node to make the transition smooth as the glow increases and decreases. Add two more Lerp nodes now. You will also need another Multiply node.

The first connection you will make is from the dim color Vector node to the A input of the first Lerp node. Next, you can connect the output of the first Multiply node to the B input of the Lerp node. Connect the output from the Sine node to the alpha input of the Lerp node.

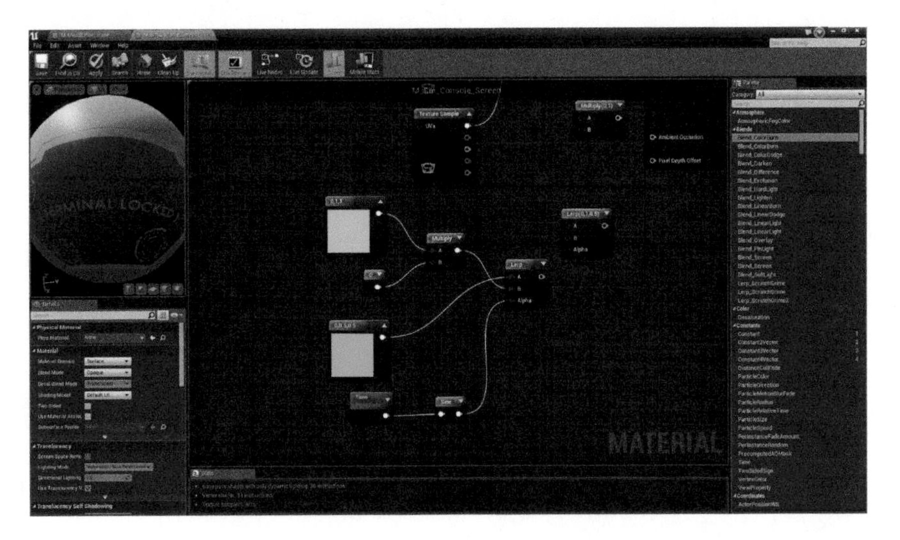

Now you can look at another use of the Lerp node. Lerp nodes do not need to have both inputs connected. You can use them to help mask off sections as well. Connect the Small_Console_M material to the alpha input of the second Lerp node. Connect the output of the first Lerp to the B input of the second Lerp node.

You are on the home stretch now. Connect the output of the second Lerp node to the B input of the newest Multiply node. Connect the output of the Lerp you used to create the base color to the A input of the Multiply node. Finally, connect the output of the Multiply node to the Emissive Color input node of the material.

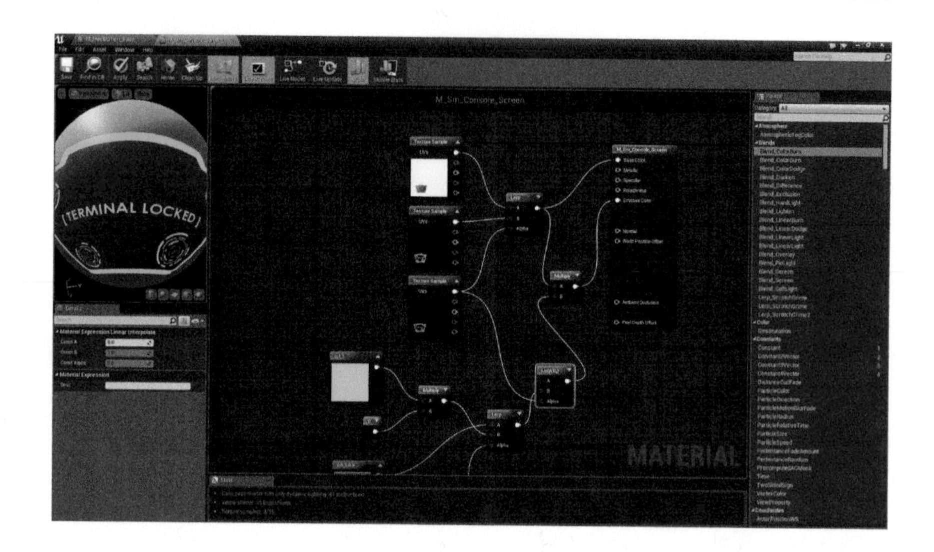

You should now have a pulsing material that makes the highlight sections glow. The pulse, however, is very fast. You can adjust the speed at which it pulses by modifying the Sine node's Period value. The higher the Period value is, the slower is the pulse. A value of 2.5 gives a nice steady speed. You can also use the Constant connected to the first Multiply node to increase the amount of glow during the bright section. A value of 5 should give you a nice bright glow.

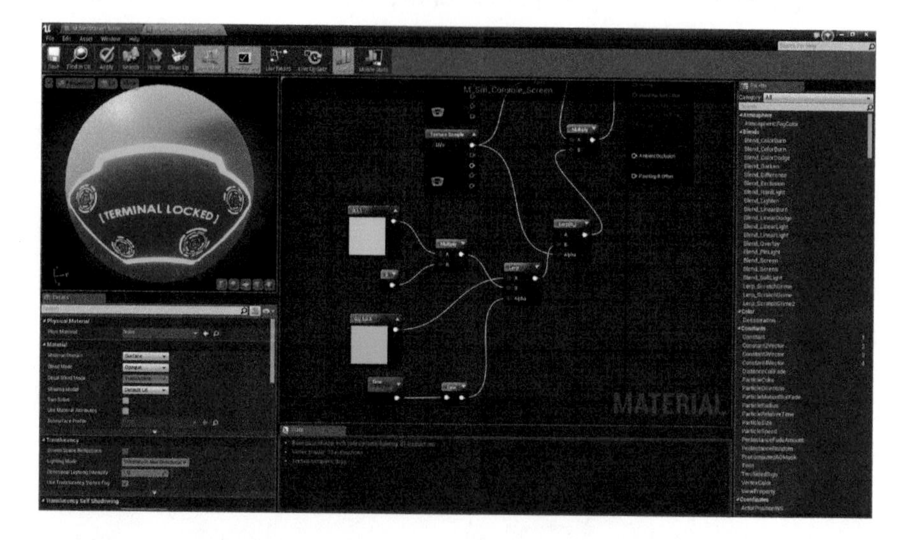

Creating Layered Materials

Layered materials in Unreal have a large variety of uses. You can use layered materials on landscapes; one material can contain mud, grass, and snow for example. You can use layered materials on characters, using the layers and masks to give sections of the character a different feel. We can also use layered materials to stack a paint type texture on top of a metal texture.

There are two ways to create layered materials. The first and simplest versions work very similarly to how we have been making materials up to this point. You use a mask texture to separate the two colors of the material. The second and more complex is to use Material Functions. Material Functions are a way to create complex materials that can be used by other materials in a very quick manner. While a Material Function can be used in layered materials, the creation of the function itself is very similar to the materials we have been working with.

Because you will be building a material that needs a shiny metallic surface in the background, you cannot build the material as you have in the past. The first thing you have to do is create a material function. Make sure that you are in the Materials folder. Right-click in the folder and find Materials & Textures→Material Function.

Name the new function *MF_Cryo_Base*. Opening the material function will open it in the Material Editor. When you open the new function, you should immediately notice that the graph is slightly different from a normal material.

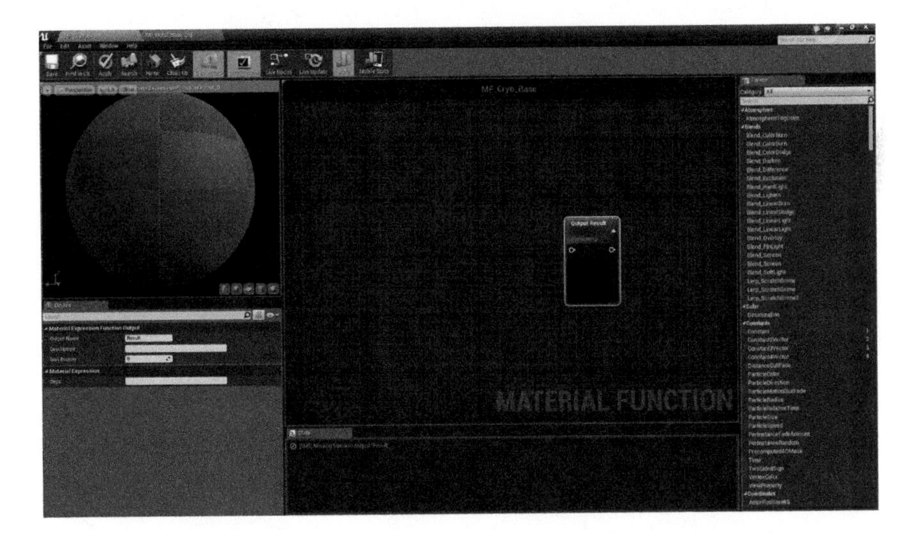

Looking at the graph, you should notice that there are no inputs for color, roughness, or metallic like you are used to. To create the material, you first need to add a **MakeMaterialAttributes** node. This node does have all the inputs required to make your material.

From this point, you can build your material as you have in the past. Add a Vector node and connect it to the Base Color input. Set the color to a light gray. Add two Constant nodes. Connect one to the Metallic input and the other to the Roughness input. Set the Constant for the Metallic to 1 and the Constant for Roughness to 0.25. Finally, connect the output of the MakeMaterialAttributes node to the input of the Output Result node.

You need to create two more material functions. The first should be named *MF_Cryo_Color* and the second named *MF_Cryo_Details*. To create these two functions, you need to import three textures:

- Cryo_Detail
- Cryo_Detail_M
- Cryo_Main2

The next material requires the use of the Cryo_Detail texture for the Base Color and the Cryo_Detail_M texture as the Opacity Mask. The MF_Cryo_Details material should be built as seen in the image below.

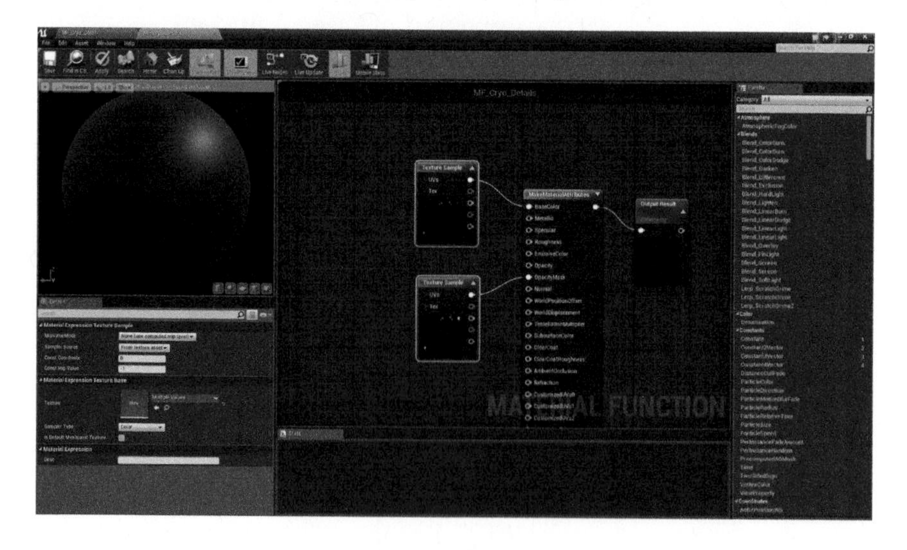

The *MF_Cryo_Color* material should be built similarly to that shown in the following image.

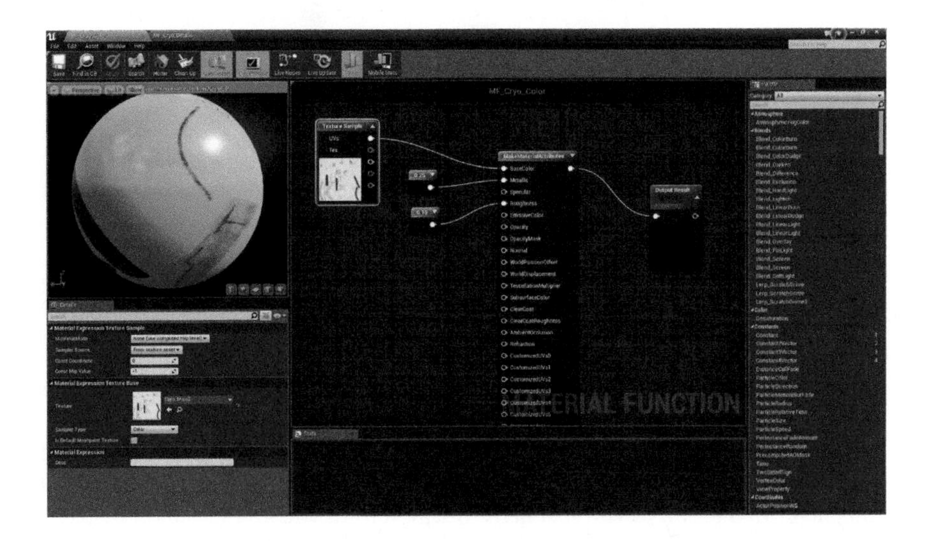

Now you can put them all together and create a material you can apply to an actor. Create a new basic material and name it *M_Cryo_Complete*. Open the material in the Material Editor. If you were to try to add the material functions to your material now, you would end up with errors. Before you move on, you need to check the Use Material Attributes option in the Details tab. This checkbox will make it possible to use your functions in the graph.

To add your functions, it is just a matter of dragging and dropping them into the graph. In the content browser find *MF_Cryo_Base* and *MF_Cryo_Color*. Drag them both into the graph of your material. To connect these functions to your material, you need a new type of node called a Material Layer Blend node. There are a lot to choose from, so you will need to scroll through and find *MatLayerBlend_Simple*. When you add the node to the graph, you will notice that it has three inputs. The node does require an alpha, so cover that first. In your Textures folder, import the *Cryo_Main_M* texture. Add the texture to the graph and then connect it to the alpha input of the Layer Blend node. You can also connect the *MF_Cryo_Base* node to the Base Material input and the *MF_Cryo_Color* node to the Top Material input. The last step here is to connect the output of the blend node to the input of the material. The final graph should be similar to the next image.

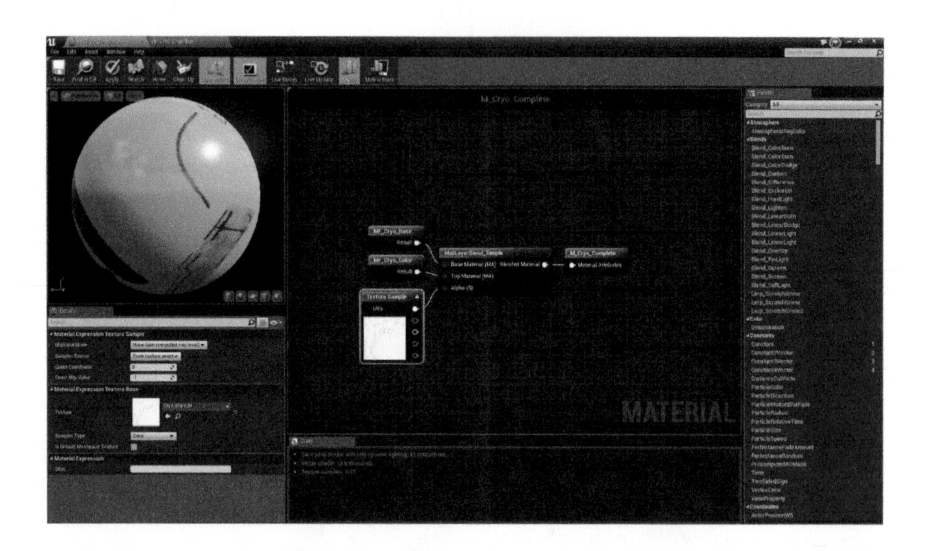

Now you can take a look at what you have accomplished. Find the mesh named Cryo_Chamber and open it in the Static Mesh Editor. There are a lot of material inputs for this mesh, so you will need to search until you find the main material input. Use the Highlight checkboxes to locate the material that highlights the same section as seen in the following figure.

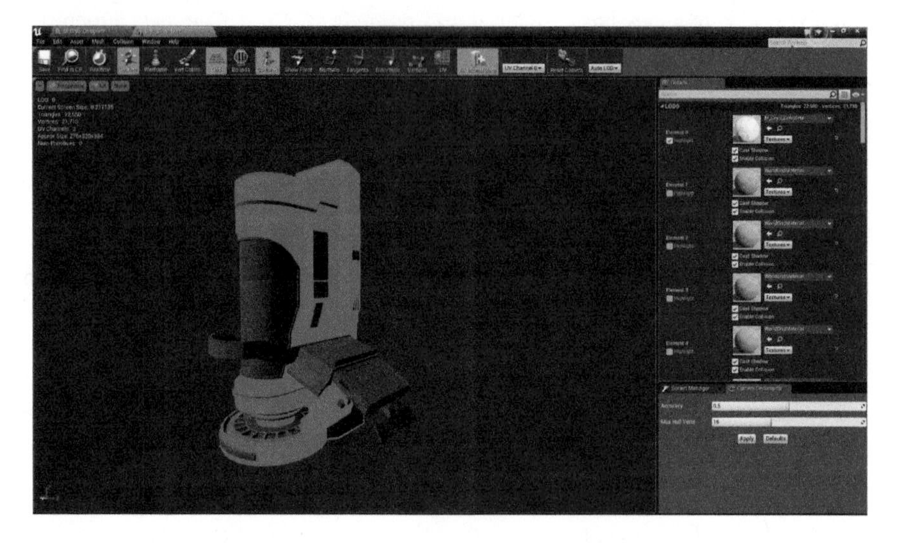

Once you have located the material input you can apply the M_Cryo_Complete material.

As you can see, the color has a lot of scratches where the metal below shines through. Without a layered material, you would not have been able to have the same overall effect. While you could have used a texture that had the metal color added into the actual paint, creating the material this way allows you to modify the color of the paint how you choose without changing the metal. Likewise, you could also modify the metal without changing the color.

To finish out the materials used on the Cryo Chamber you need one more material that contains your functions. Again, you could combine this with other materials, but you want to be able to have that extra level of control. To create the second material, in the Materials folder, add a new material named M_Cryo_Detail_Base. Open the material in the Material Editor. Again, before you start, make sure to check the Use Material Attributes option. Add the following functions to the graph:

- MF_Cryo_Base
- MF_Cryo_Color
- MF_Cryo_Details

You need one more mask texture. In your Textures folder, import the Cryo_Main2_M texture from the Chapter 9 Assets folder.

In order to connect all your different functions together, you need two MatLayerBlend_Simple nodes. You also need to add the Cryo_Main2_M and Cryo_Detail_M textures. Build the material as in the next figure.

This material should be applied to a few sections. As you cycle through the inputs, find the next five images to add the material.

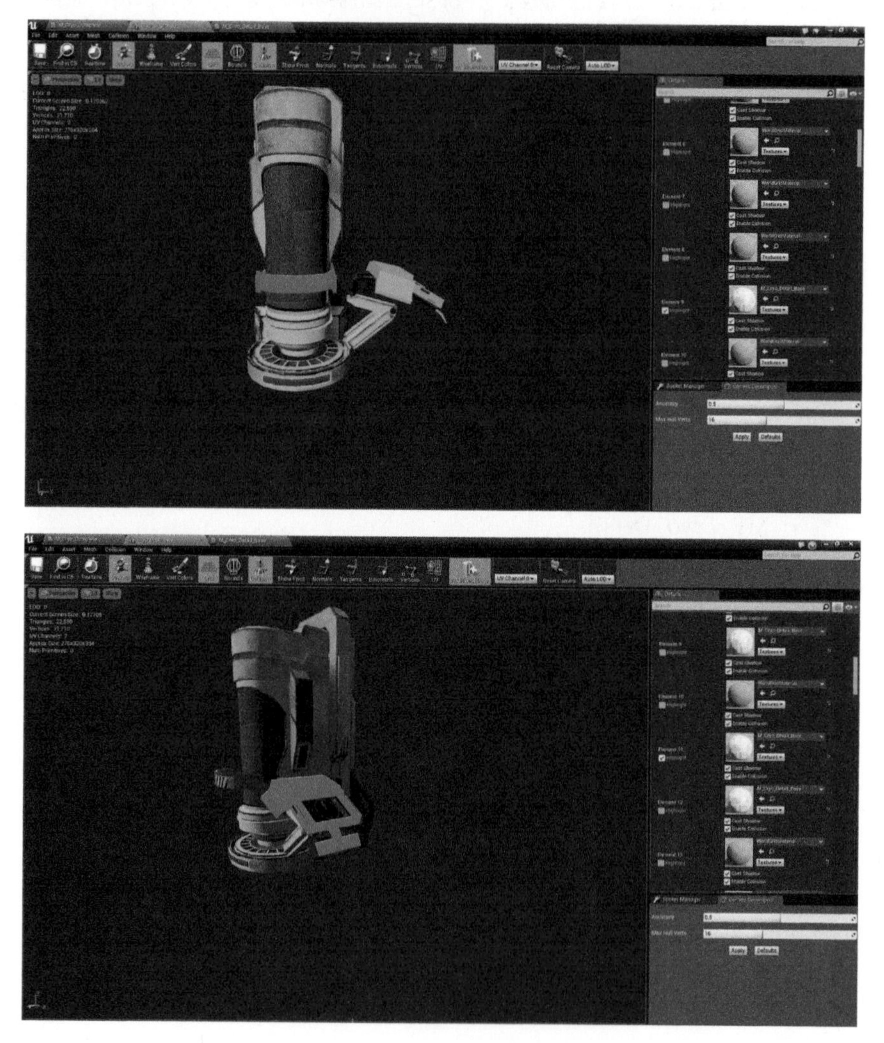

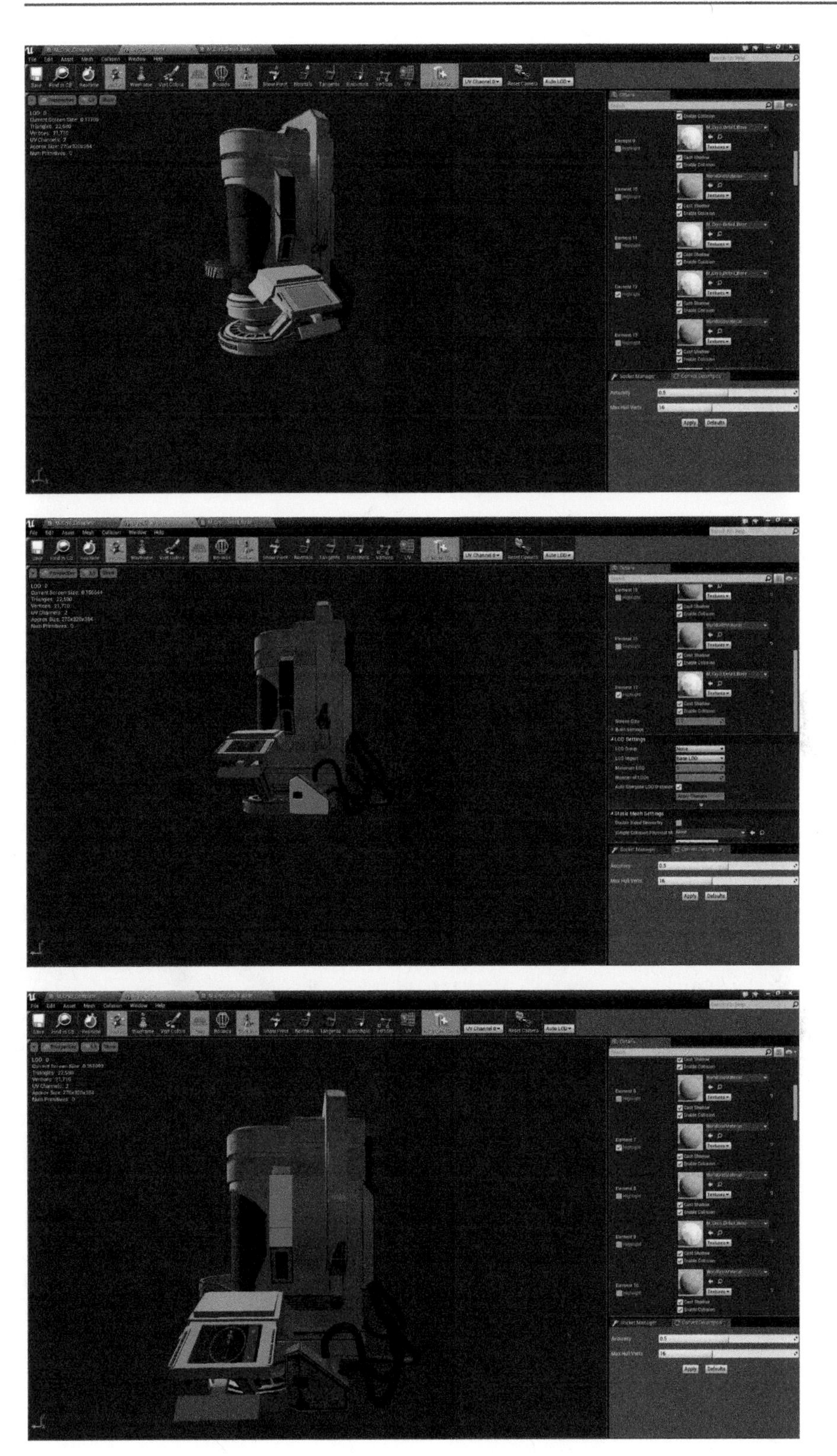

The rest of the materials on the Cryo Chamber can be built as you see fit. An example of the completed chamber is seen in the next figure.

You need to make materials for your square generator and small crate. You can import the following into your Textures folder:

- Generator_Square_D
- Generator_Square_M
- Small_Crate_Base
- Small_Crate_Details

Create a material for the generator named M_Generator_Base and build a graph similar to that in the image below.

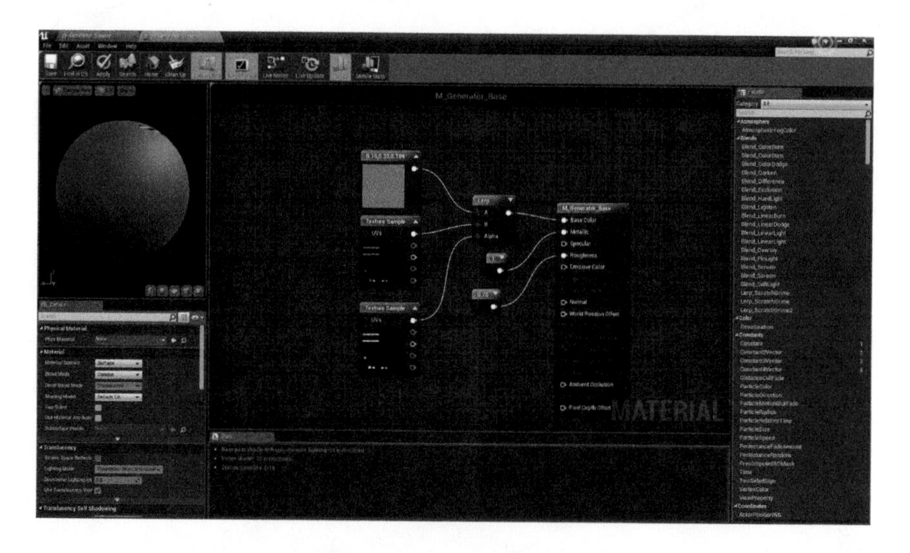

The second material is M_Sm_Crate and the graph should be similar to the one in the next image.

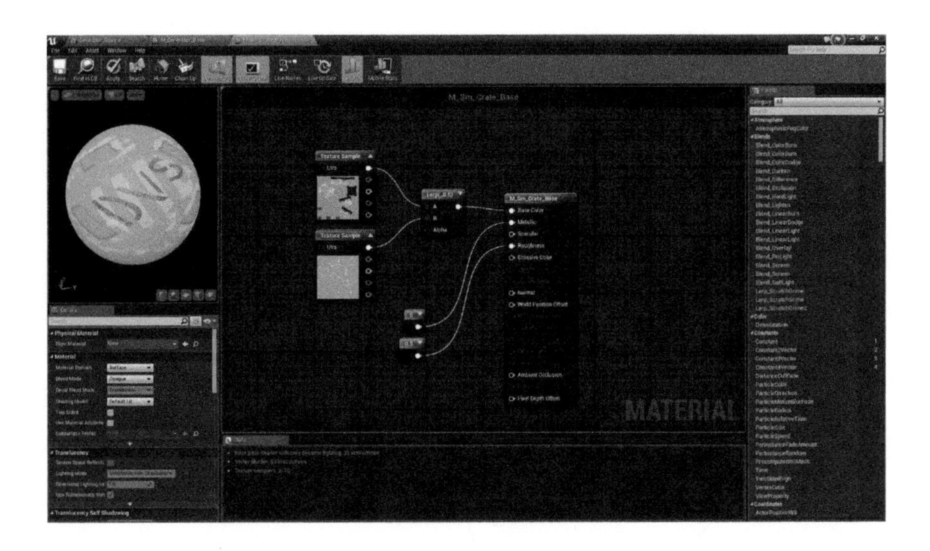

To build the rest of the materials you can import the following:

- Med_Station_BG
- Med_Station_Highlights
- Med_Station_M
- Pipe_Valve_D
- Pipe_Valve_M

Create a material for each and build the graphs as we have in the past.

Adding Actors

Once you have taken the time to build all the needed materials, it is time to start adding some actors to the level. When you are placing actors in the level, you should take into consideration a couple of things. First, if you are planning on grouping some actors together, you can consider putting them into a blueprint first. Second, do not forget to take into account the playable area of the level. If you just start throwing actors in the level, you are likely to disrupt the flow you have established.

If you refer back to the sketches, the first room in the hallway is the storeroom. You can start by adding some meshes there. Since you converted the floor to a blocking volume, you can walk around the storeroom, but you do not have a visible floor to stand on. You can take care of that with the Test_Floor_Long mesh. Place a few of them in the storeroom to cover the open space.

Looking at the above figure, you can tell that even with the floor in place, the walls are not going to line up. You should also notice that there is no ceiling. Address the walls first. There are plenty of meshes available to create whatever type of room you would like. Before you get too far, however, I would like to draw your attention to one thing. One key item of becoming a good level designer is learning how to use props in a manner that they may not have been originally designed for. For example, you could use the Test_Floor mesh as walls in this room. While placing your walls, you may need to scale or adjust them in certain ways to fill the space. There is nothing wrong with changing the scale or angle if it suits your needs. Unlike the BSPs we used earlier, we will not be converting the meshes, so any modifications will not affect the level in a negative way.

As you place your meshes, be sure not to encroach on other sections of the level (unless that is the effect you are looking for).

If you were to use the test floors as walls, you could place Test_Floor_Narrow on each side of your doors and use the regular Test_Floor as the walls running the length of the room. You should end up with a room similar to that in the following figure.

Because our blocking was only designed to cover the hallways we do need to add some collisions to our floor sections otherwise we would be able to walk through the walls. Open each test floor mesh in the Static Mesh Editor and choose Add Box Simplified Collision. This should give each floor section a small, simple collision volume.

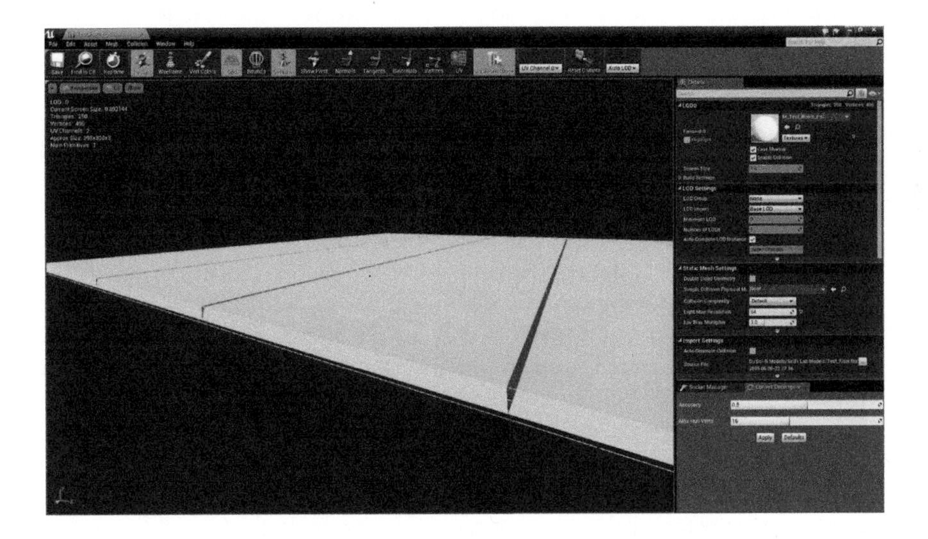

Now we should be able to travel the room without issue.

Chapter Challenge

Now that you have an idea of how to use different meshes to populate the area, try creating a ceiling for the storeroom using something other than the test floor meshes. Get creative. You have a lot to choose from, so take your time and fill in the space as you see fit. The following figure shows an example of the room completed.

Now that you have a room with some detail, you may notice that, for a storeroom, it is extremely clean. You can fix that with a few small tweaks to one of your materials.

If you look in the Starter Content folder, you should see a folder named Textures. Open that folder and look for two textures. The first is named *T_Metal_Rust_D* and the second is named *T_Smoke_Tiled_D*. Select both of them and drag them into your Textures folder. Once you drop them in the folder, you will get the option to Copy Here or Move Here. Use the Copy Here function in case you decide later to modify the textures.

Find M_Hallway_Base and duplicate it. Rename the new material to *M_Hallway_Dirty_Base* and then open it in the Material Editor. Add the two new textures to your material. You will also need a Lerp node, so add that to your graph as well. Connect the rust texture to the A input of the Lerp. Connect the original color to the B input of the Lerp and finally connect the smoke texture to the alpha of the Lerp. Now you can connect the output of the Lerp to the Base Color input of the material to create a slightly dirty version of the material. Save and close the Material Editor.

If you were to open the floors in the Static Mesh Editor and swap the material to this dirty one, it would affect all instances of the floor. If you were only planning to use dirty floors, this would be an acceptable option. However, you only want to apply the material to the instances of this room. In the Level Editor, select one of the floor sections. Take a look at the Details tab now. You should notice that there is a slot for the material. Remember to create an instance of the material and then drag that instance into the material slot in the Details tab. This will apply the dirty material to the floor without affecting any other instance.

Repeat the process of adding the material to the floor to any other meshes you wish to change.

To finish out this chapter you will build a blueprint for the Cryo Lab section of the level. In your Blueprints folder create a new blueprint name BP_Cryo_Lab. While building this blueprint, you can use the Level Editor to help get the floor, walls, and ceiling so that each will correctly line up with its section of the level.

Open the BP_Cryo_Lab blueprint in the Blueprint Editor and start by adding the floor. As mentioned before, there are many options, so choose the one you feel works the best. As you create this blueprint, I will only cover the basic concept of how to get the size down. There will be no exact measurements, so if you choose to use a different mesh than I do, take the time to adjust as needed.

I chose to use the straight hallway floor. After you have added the floor, compile and save the blueprint and then add it to the level where the Cryo Lab will go. You will need to adjust it to correct any placement issues. In the next figure, you can see that initially the floor was too high. To check your location, you can use the Play From Here option and test out your floor's location. As I stressed before, play-test, play-test, play-test.

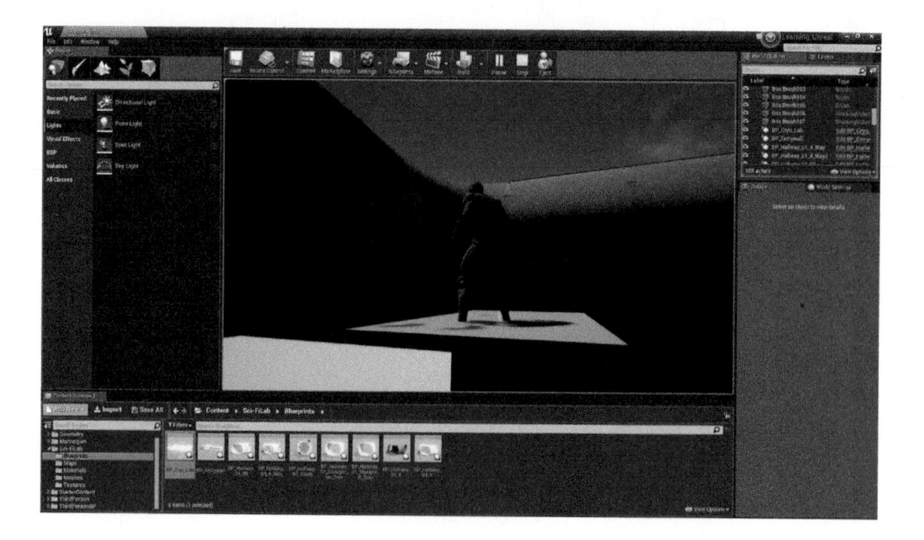

Once you have the first section in place, you can begin to add more. You should notice that as you add sections to the blueprint, they show up in the Level Editor. Because you have the blueprint already in the level, you can now modify the blueprint while watching the Level Editor to build the complete floor. Not only does this help to save time but you will also know that, in the end, you will not have to make any adjustments to the blueprint in the Level Editor. Continue to add sections to the floor until you are satisfied with the results.

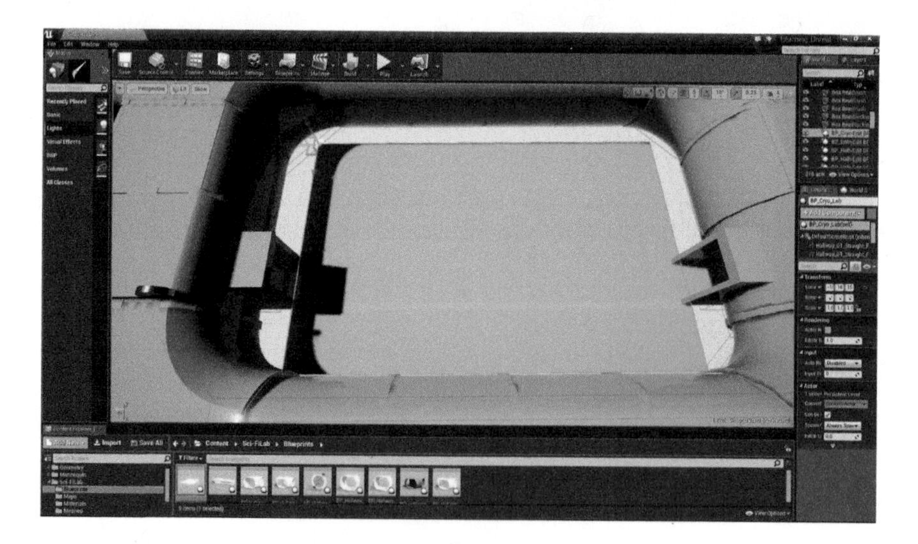

Repeating the process, add the walls now.

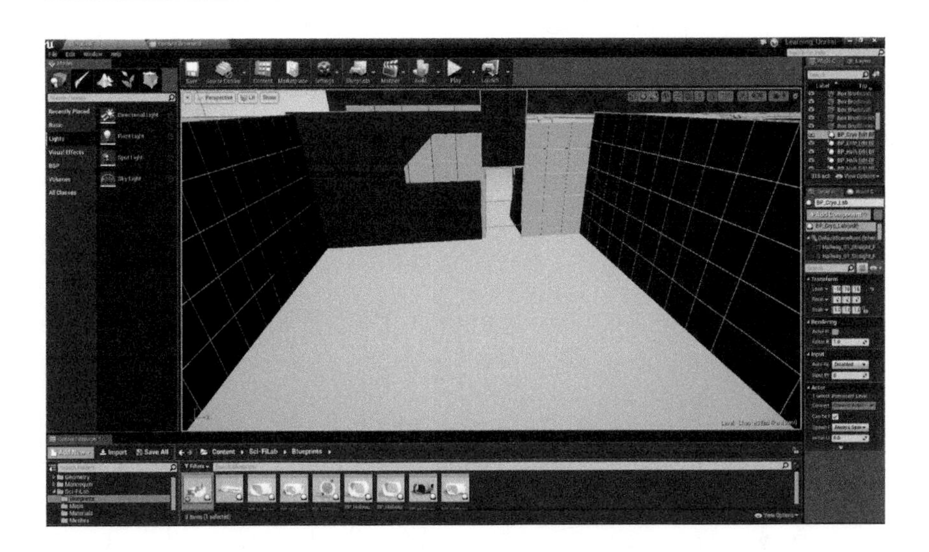

Once you have the base dimensions of the room, you can begin to fill it in. An example of a completed room can be seen in the image below.

Remember to play-test once you have the room completed. Check for any issues and correct them as needed. You should be able to fix any issues you come across in here without a problem. One thing that you should have noticed right away was that you could walk through the Cryo Chambers. You can correct this by using the Auto Convex Collision in the Static Mesh Editor.

By this point you should have a pretty good grasp on how to build some interesting rooms. To give you some examples, I have built a few of the other rooms. Use the images on the next page as guides.

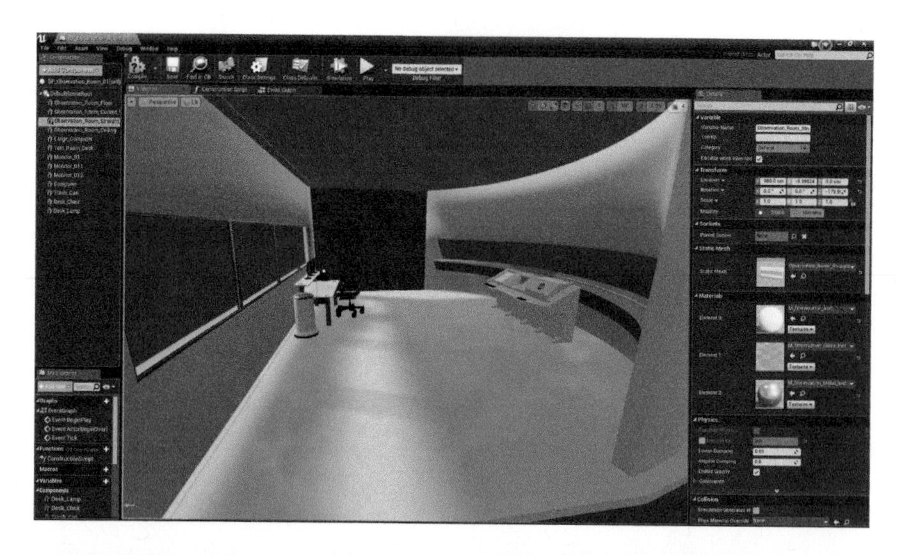

Adding Physics to an Actor

Up to this point, everything we have added to the level with the exception of the doors has been static. In other words, they cannot move. If you were to run into any of them, nothing would happen. You will begin to change some of the actors to include physics. Once you have added physics to an actor, you will be able to move it around the level, kick it, shoot it, or push it. When adding physics to an actor, there are a few things to consider. First and foremost is the weight of the object. You would not, for example, want to make a chair fly across the room by simply bumping into it. You also want to take into account the collisions. If you had a ball that had the simple box collision, it would not behave like a ball. How you build the collisions can greatly impact the overall result, so take your time.

To get your physics going, you will work with the Trash_Can mesh. Open it now in the Static Mesh Editor. The first thing you will test is the Add Box Simplified Collision as seen in the image below.

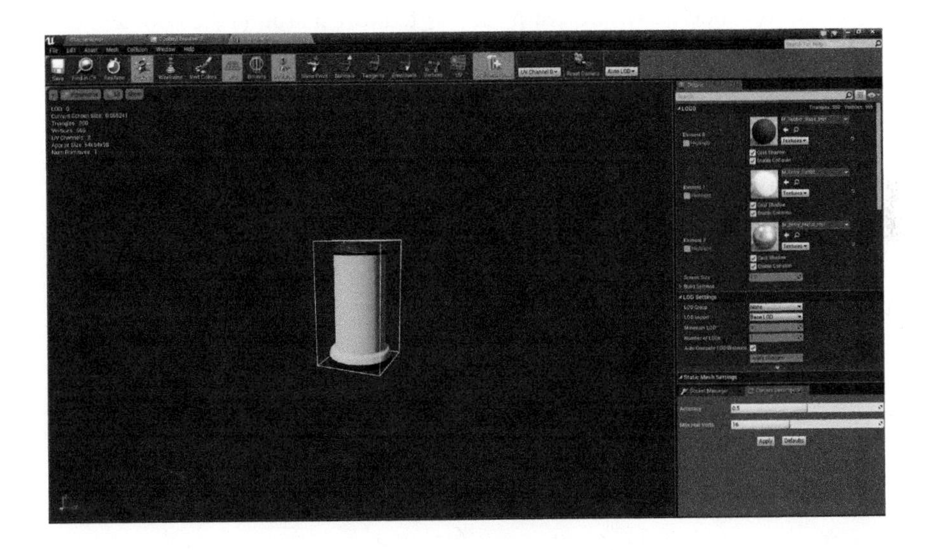

Save the mesh and switch back to the Level Editor. To give ample room and to be close to your starting point, you will be working in the lobby. Add the Trash_Can to the level by dragging it in from the content browser. With the mesh still selected, look at the Details tab. Two elements are necessary in order to make the mesh interactive. The first is the Mobility option. Mobility should be set to Moveable. The second option is Simulate Physics under the Physics section. (You may need to scroll down in the Details tab.) Make sure that Simulate Physics is checked. We will not worry about the options right now. We simply want to get the physics working. You should be able to play-test and kick the trash can around the lobby now.

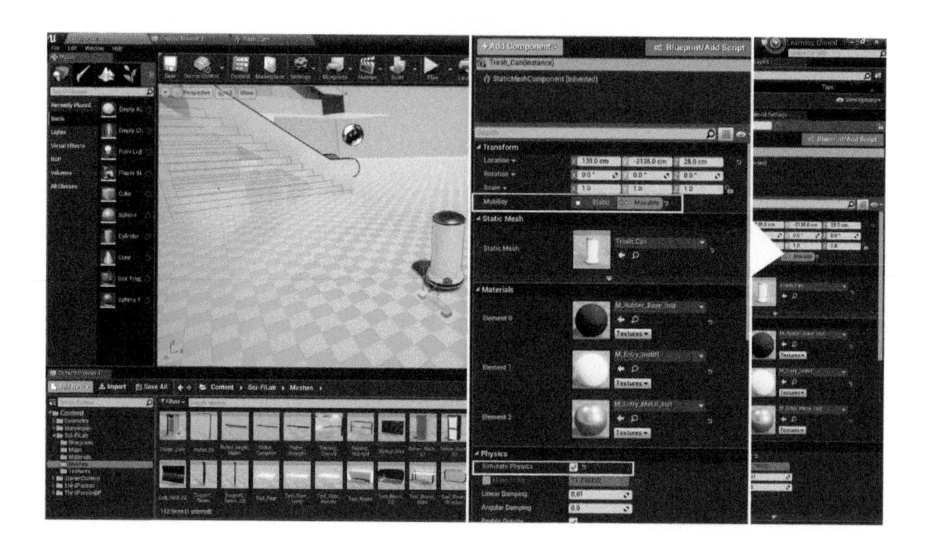

Once you knock down the trash can, try to move it around the floor and look at how it reacts. While it will move, it appears to be sliding instead of rolling.

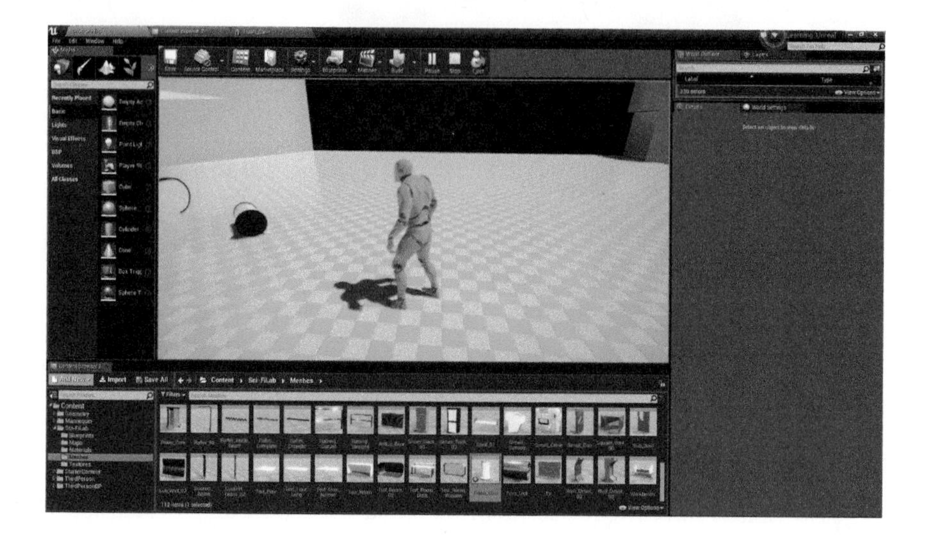

You are getting this effect because of the collision volume used. Switch back to the Static Mesh Editor. The first thing you need to do is remove the collision volume. Under the Collision menu select Remove Collision. Now that you are back to having no collisions, you can look at some more options. If you recall, in an earlier chapter we discussed what each type of collision does. Since your mesh is tall, you can use the Add 10DOP-Z Simplified Collision.

While this will probably work, the flat surfaces will cause it to stop rolling much faster than it probably should. Remove the collisions once again and try the Auto Convex Collision. Use the following setting:

- Accuracy—0.2
- Max Hull Verts—25

Now if you play the level and kick the trash can around, it should roll relatively well. You can test more settings in the Auto Convex Collision menu if you are unhappy with its movement. If you find that the can is flying around the level, you can adjust the mass in the Details tab. Under the Physics section activate the mass override by checking the Mass In Kg option box. Once you have activated the mass, you can adjust the weight by changing the value seen in the box beside it. Try a mass of around 80.0 to get a good starting point.

Chapter Challenge

Now that you have a good idea of how to add physics, take some time to add physics to the Desk_Chair, Small_Crate, Medbay_Table, and other objects you want to move around. Remember that you will need to modify their collisions to get a better reaction. Once you have them set up to your liking, try stacking some of them in the level to see how they react.

Chapter Review

In this chapter we took some time to import a few more meshes to help fill out our level. If you followed along with the whole chapter, you also learned how to make material functions and layered materials. After completing the materials, you filled a couple of the rooms with more detail. We looked at multiple options for adding detail. One of the options covered was creating large room blueprints using the Level Editor to help space the room out correctly. You also added the actors directly to the level without the use of blueprints. Finally, you took some time to add physics to an actor to make it more interactive during game time. By now, you should have a pretty well populated level. If you have been play-testing the whole time and checking the level thoroughly you should have most of the issues well in hand. You may have noticed one or two issues not directly covered (like the railings of the escalators). These issues have been left there in order to give you the opportunity to correct them on your own.

10

Particle Systems

Introduction

Particles in the Unreal Engine can take on a number of forms. A **particle system** is often used for things like fire, explosions, smoke, and sparks, to name a few. This is certainly not the limit of what a particle system can be used for, but should offer a good example of commonly used systems.

Overview of Cascade

To get started, you need to create a folder for your particle system. In the Content folder, find your created root folder and inside it add a new folder named Particles. Open the new Particles folder and create a new particle system by right-clicking and choosing Particle System from the popup menu. Name your new particle *P_Steam*. As you have done in the past, the first portion of the name denotes its type. Double-click the particle system to open **Cascade**, the particle system editor. With Cascade now open, you can take a look at the new editor window.

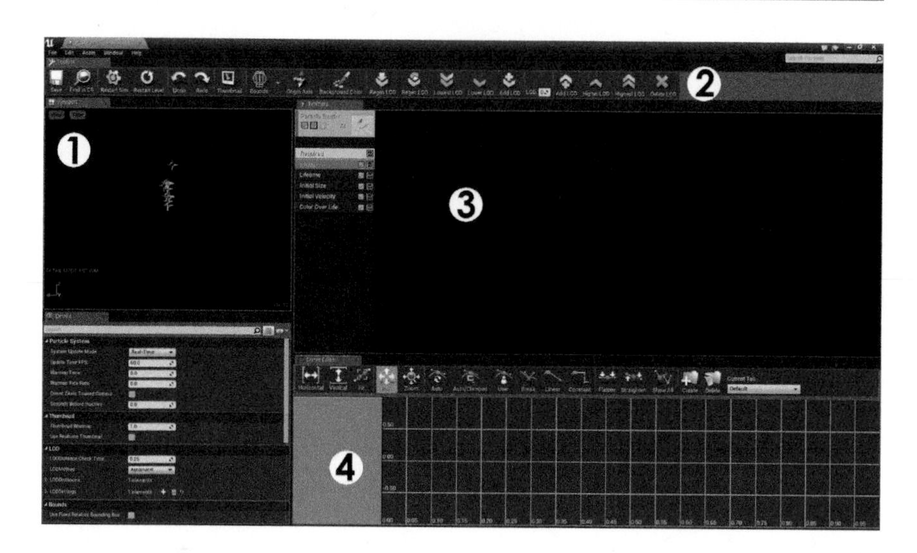

Looking at the above image, you can see each section identified as follows:

- 1—Viewport
- 2—Toolbar
- 3—Emitters
- 4—Curve editor

As the name would imply, you will be building a simple steam particle system that can be used throughout the level. Before you get too far into the different emitters, take a moment to look at your system in the level. You can do this by simply dragging the particle from the content browser to the level viewport. The default emitter does not take into account things like gravity. Take a moment to rotate the emitter and look at how it is affected. In the image below, I rotated the emitter so that the particles are emitted straight down.

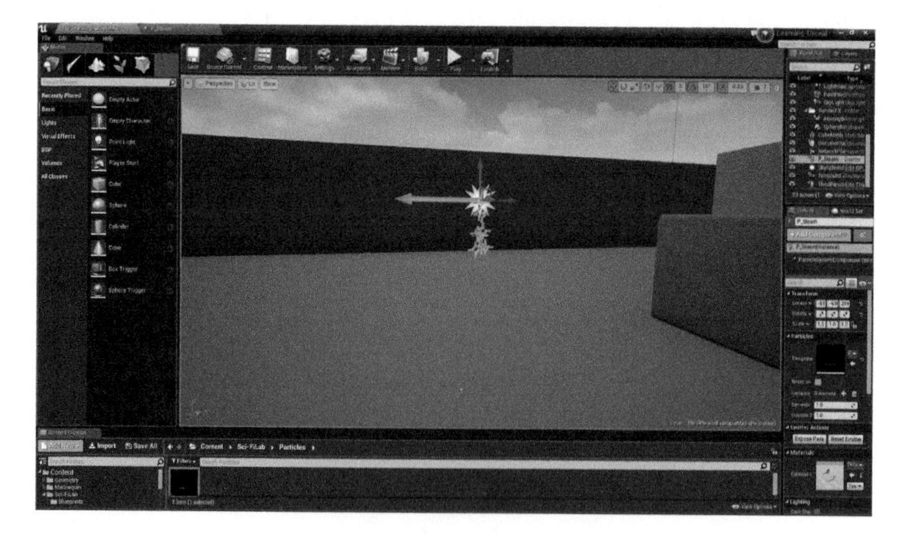

If you look back at the Cascade Editor, the particle system is moving straight up. Once you make a few adjustments to your system, it will not continue to behave so simply. Since you are making a steam particle, and steam rises, you do not want the particles to just fall straight down. While you could just rotate it so that the particles are emitted upward, this would still give you an undesirable effect later on.

To get started, you need to add a new texture and material to your project. Start by importing the *T_Smoke_Tiled* texture from the Chapter 10 Assets folder.

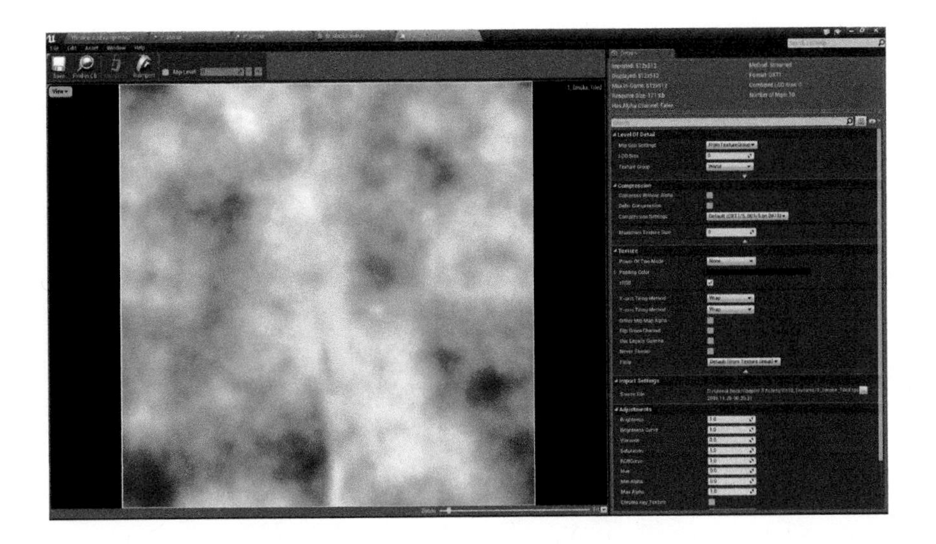

This is a special texture that is designed to be repeatable without leaving seams or breaks (tiled). You will also need to pull an asset from the started content. Browse to Starter Content, Textures, and find *T_Smoke_SubUV*. Drag the texture into your Particles folder and choose Copy Here.

Now you need to create a new material to use in your emitter. In your Particles folder create a new material and name it M_Steam. Open the material in the Material Editor. In previous chapters you used textures and texture coordinates to modify the look of the material. In this material you will also add a new function called **Particle Color**, which gives cascade access to the material to allow for color changes. Before you start adding your nodes to the material, you need to change the Blend mode to Translucent. Changing the Blend mode will unlock access to the Opacity input of the material. Once you have the Blend mode set, you can begin adding the necessary nodes. The first two nodes you need to add are the texture nodes. You can add the Texture node by holding the "T" key and clicking in the graph. Add two texture nodes now. The first of these nodes should have its texture set to your *T_Smoke_Tiled* texture, while the second should be set to the *T_Smoke_SubUV* texture. Once these are added, you can add the rest of the nodes as follows:

1. Texture Coordinate node—set both the UTiling and VTiling to 5.0 and connect the output to the UVs input of the tiled texture.
2. Add node—connect the primary output of both texture nodes to the A and B inputs.
3. Particle Color node

4. Multiply node—connect the output of the Add node to the A input and the primary output of the Particle Color node to the B input. Connect the output of the Multiply node to the base color of the material.
5. Multiply node—connect the alpha output of the Particle Color node to the A input and the alpha output of the SubUV texture node to the B input. Connect the output to the Opacity input of the material.

Your material should resemble the image below. Once you have added all the nodes and connected them correctly, you can save and close the Material Editor.

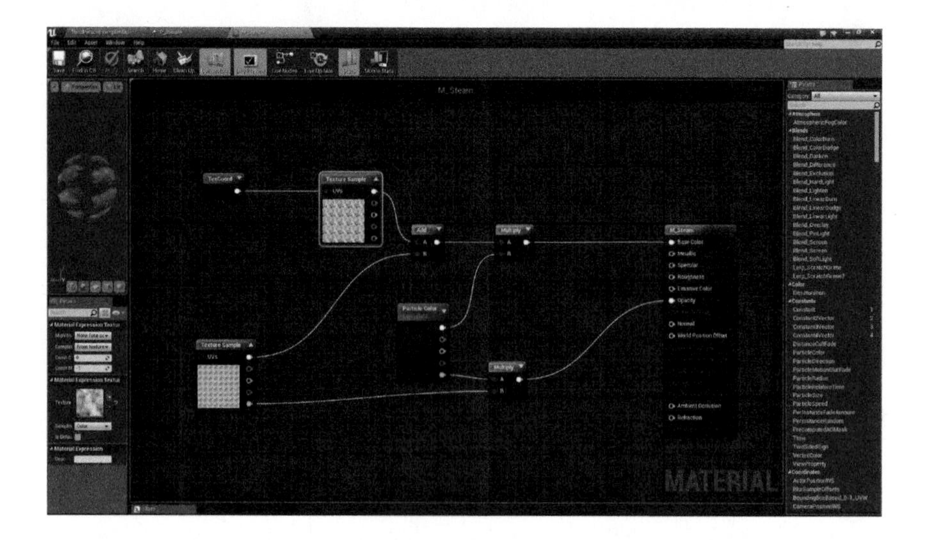

Emitters

Finally, you are ready to start working on your particle system. Switch to the Cascade Editor if you have not already. In Cascade, there is a window named Emitters. Emitters are used to add features to the particle system. By default, there is one emitter already present. This emitter currently is creating the series of crosshairs you see floating upward. You need to modify the emitter to suit your needs. In order to do that, you will have to change the modules within the emitter. Modules are similar to nodes in the other editors. They contain a number of properties that can be changed through the Details tab. By default, you should have the following modules available:

1. **Required** is the base settings for the emitter and cannot be removed.
2. **Spawn** contains properties like the spawn rate and rate scale and cannot be removed.
3. **Lifetime** controls how long the particle will live.
4. **Initial size** sets the start size of the particles.
5. **Initial velocity** sets the starting speed of the particles.
6. **Color over life** controls if/how a particle changes color as it travels.

With respect to lifetime, initial size, and initial velocity, each has both a minimum and a maximum value to allow for variance within the emitter. This will come in handy later, but you can imagine that steam that was always the same size, speed, and lifetime would not give the system an attractive look. You will be using these attributes shortly.

You will start with the Required module first. The first property you will change is the material the emitter will use. With Required selected, change the material property in the Details tab to the *M_Steam* material you created earlier. You will notice right away that the default settings here have a less than desirable effect on the emitter.

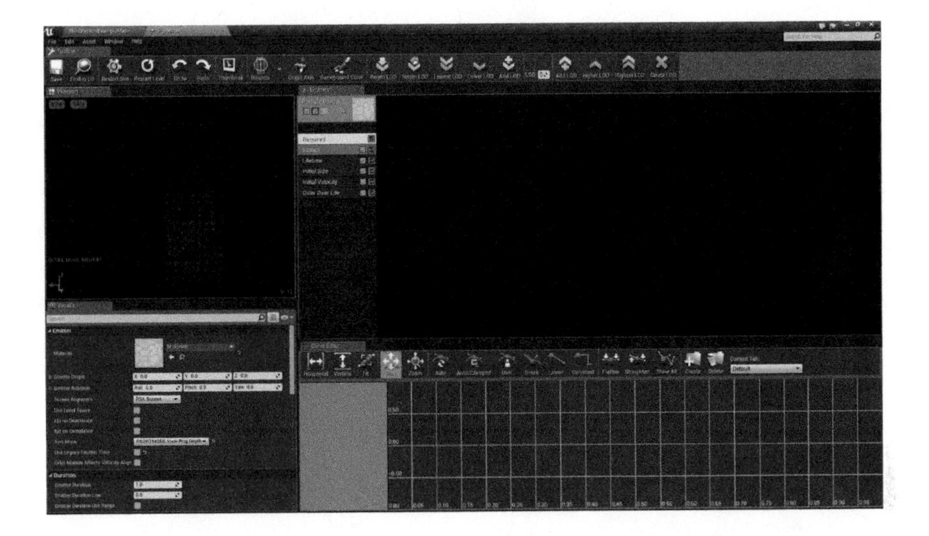

Have no fear, though; you will make some quick changes that will give you an entirely new look and feel to your steam. Set the Sort mode to PSORTMODE View Proj Depth. You still have a very odd looking particle. To remedy some of the bizarre effects you have going on, scroll down to the Sub UV section in the Details tab. Set the Interpolation method to Linear Blend. This should allow for a smooth transition between the different particles. Set the Sub Images Horizontal and Vertical to 8 to begin with. You can tweak this again later to improve the view.

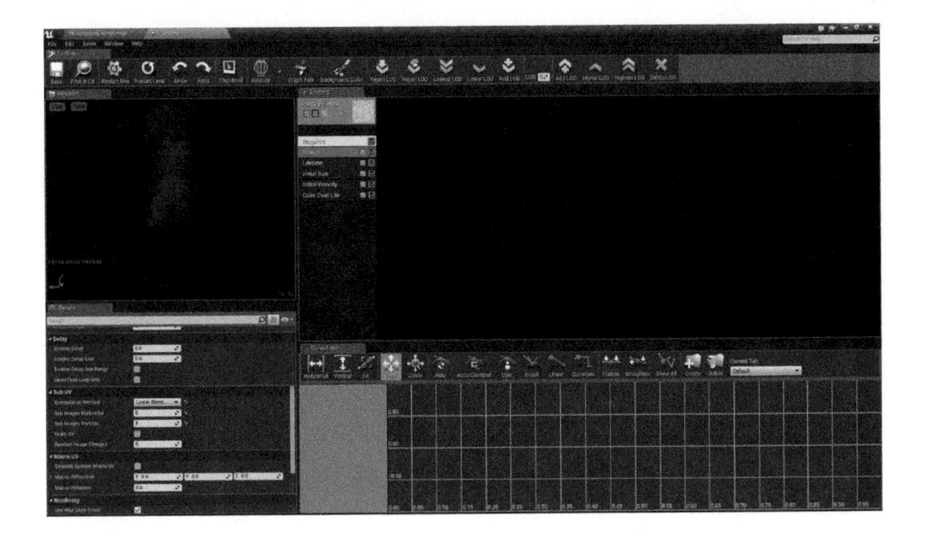

Switch to the Spawn module and expand Rate and then Distribution; set Constant to 10.

Next, switch to the Lifetime module and expand Lifetime and Distribution. Set the Min value to 2.0 and Max value to 5.0. This will create a variance in how long the particle will travel, giving it a more realistic feel.

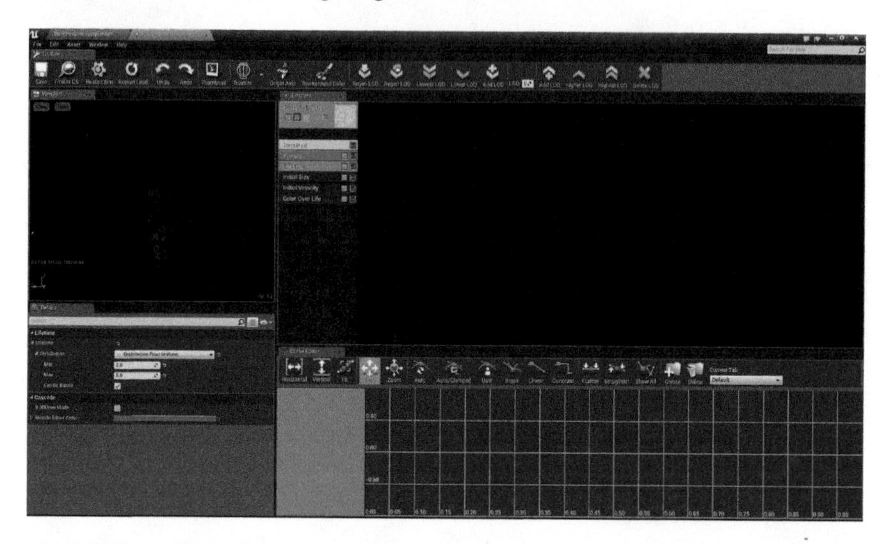

Now the real changes begin. Switch to the Initial Size module. Expand Start Size and Distribution. Set the Max values to

- X—200
- Y—100
- Z—0

Set the Mid values to

- X—100
- Y—50
- Z—0

Note: If there is too great a gap between the Min and Max sizes, there will be an evident popping effect.

The next module is the Initial Velocity. Expand Start Velocity and Distribution. Set the Max values to

- X—25
- Y—10
- Z—60

Set the Min values to

- X—10
- Y—0
- Z—30

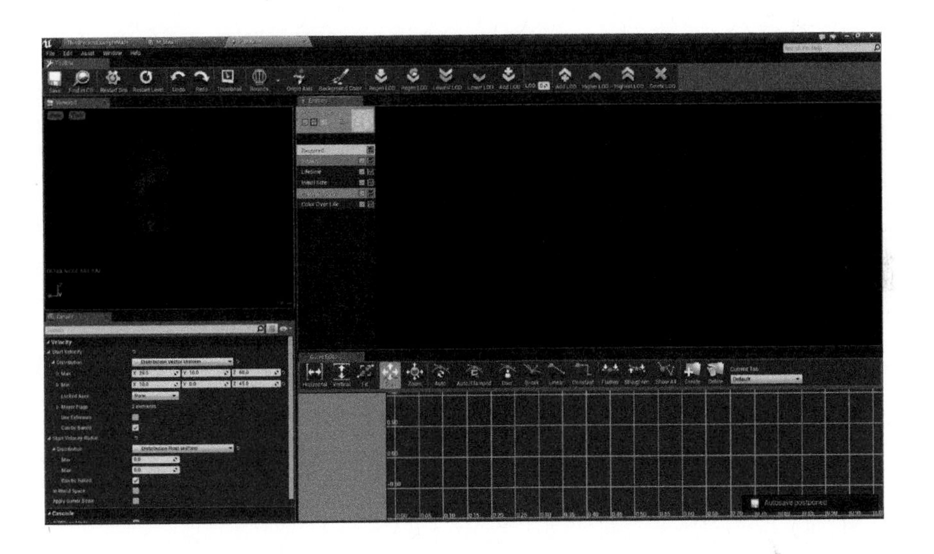

That is about as far as you can get with the default modules. The Color Over Life module was skipped for now, but will be addressed shortly. Before you do that, you need to add some more modules. In the emitter, right-click and find Size By Life (under the Size menu item). Click on it to add it to the emitter. Select the Size By Life module and set the following under the Life Multiplier, Distribution, Constant Curve, Points section.
For point 0:

- Out Val X—1.0, Y—0.0, Z—0.0
- Interp Mode—Curve Auto

For point 1:

- In Val—0.5
- Out Val X—1.0, Y—0.0, Z—0.0

You should have a particle system similar to that shown in the next image.

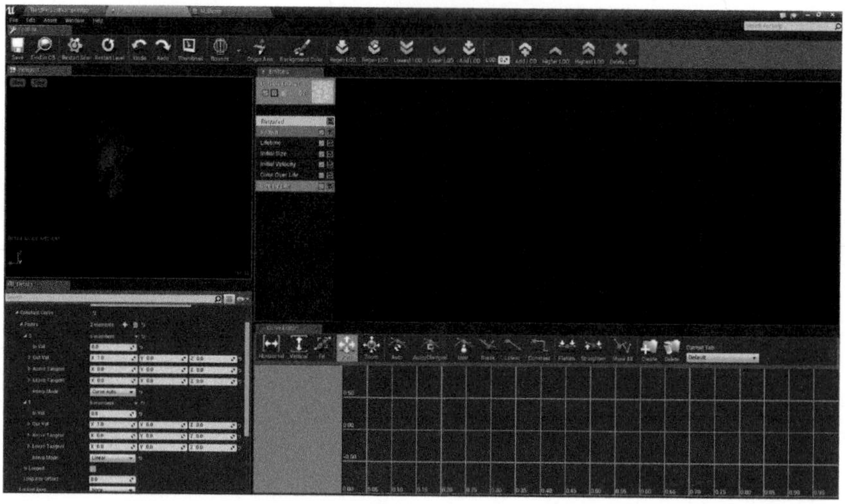

Now is a good time to take a look at the Color Over Life module. Select it now and expand Color Over Life and Distribution. Set the Distribution type to Distribution Vector Constant. Expand Constant and set the color to white.

Next, expand the Alpha Over Life, Distribution, Constant Curve, Points, 0 and 1. You need to set both these curve points one by one. Starting with point 0, set the following:

- In Val—0.1
- Out Val—0.8
- Arrive Tangent—0.0
- Leave Tangent—0.0
- Interp Mode—Curve Auto Clamped

Set point 1 to

- In Val—1.0
- Out Val—0.0
- Arrive Tangent—0.0
- Leave Tangent—0.0
- Interp Mode—Curve Auto Clamped

The last module you need to add here is the Acceleration module. Once you have added the module, select it. Set the following values:
Max:

- X—10
- Y—5
- Z—25

Min:

- X—5
- Y—2.5
- Z—15

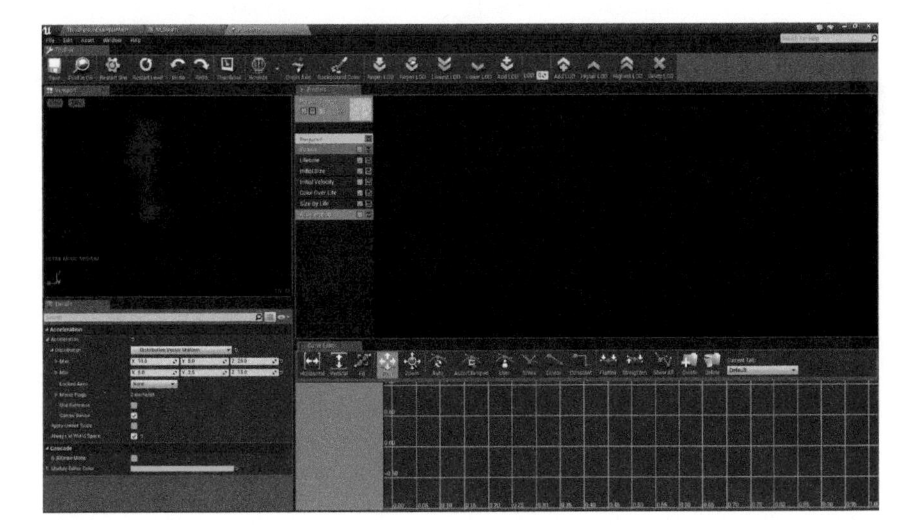

Curve Editor

Up to this point you have been relying on numerical inputs by typing in values. There is an entirely different way to add values using the Curve Editor. Before you can make any changes, you need to make the curves visible. You will be focusing on the Alpha Over Life section of the Color Over Life module. To view the curves, click on the curve icon of the Color Over Life module. Once you have clicked on it, you should see two curves appear in the Curve Editor. Because you have already set up a start and end value for the alpha section, you can easily add points by holding the Ctrl key and clicking on the curve itself. As you add points to the curve, it should be apparent how the particle system changes in the viewport.

The Curve Editor has two primary sets of values. Running vertically along the left side is the out value of the point, while the numbers across the bottom represent the in value of the point. Try adding a point in the middle of the curve. Move the point around to get an idea of how it will change the appearance of the particle. As you move the point close to an out value of 0, you should notice that the particles begin to disappear. You should also notice that there are two handles on each point. These are used to change the transition of the curve.

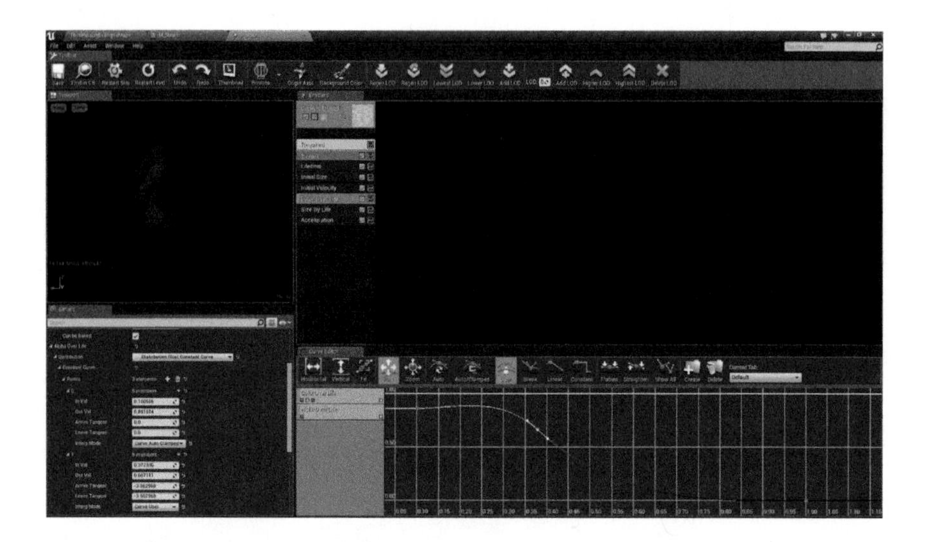

Make any adjustments you like and then save your particle. If you remember, when you started this chapter, you had a particle system that would only travel in the direction in which it was aimed. With addition and modification of different modules, you have made a particle that will always try to drift upward, just as steam does in real life. Add your particle system to your level and adjust it so that it shoots downward and watch how the smoke will slowly start to drift back upward. If you do not feel that it has enough upward movement, you can always go back and modify the Z attribute of the Acceleration module.

Chapter Review

In this chapter we took a look at the Cascade Editor. Using Cascade, you created a simple steam particle to use in your levels. You also took a moment to create a new material that the particle system uses. You looked at a number of different modules under the default emitter of your particle system and added new modules to adjust the overall look and feel of the particle system. Finally, you used the Curve Editor within Cascade to change the alpha appearance of the particle system.

11

Advanced Blueprint Techniques

Introduction

By now you should have a firm grasp of how blueprints work. You have built a number of different blueprints, including an animated blueprint in the form of automatic doors. In this chapter you will look at a few different types of advanced blueprints. You will make a new type of hallway section that will use a slider to determine its overall length. You will also make adjustments to your doors so that the glow color changes to red when the door is closed. Finally, you will build a blueprint that takes direct interaction from the user in the form of a keystroke. Let us get started.

Using Blueprints to Create Custom Length Hallways

While it may seem like a bit of a step backward, you will create a blueprint here that can adjust its length using a slider in the Details tab. You will build a number of different graphs that will allow you to add numerous sections with only the use of the slider. What difference does this make? If you remember, in the earlier chapters you added a number of straight hallway sections side by side. With the use of this new blueprint, you could place only one instance in each straight section of the hallway and then use the slider to increase the length filling in the overall space.

To begin, you need to create a new blueprint in the Blueprints folder. Name your new blueprint *BP_Hallway_01_R*. The R designation indicates that the blueprint is repeatable. Open the blueprint in the Blueprint Editor. Since you will be building the hallways through the graphs, you do not need to add anything to the viewport. In previous lessons you worked with the event graph. However, the event graph only activates at runtime, which means that it would not appear in the Level Editor. Instead, you will start by working in the construction script graph. You will be adding a number of different graphs in the form of functions as you progress, so take your time and be thorough.

Before you go any farther, we should discuss exactly what you want to do. Since you will be using a slider to control the length of the hallway, you will need a number to keep track of the number of sections. You can use an integer variable to store the number of sections. The next things you will need are some functions (represented by their own graph) for each part of the hallway section. This means that you need to build a function to add floors, another for walls, ceiling, etc.

You will start by adding the integer variable. In the My Blueprint tab, scroll down to the Variables section and click the + icon to add a new variable. By default, your new variable will be a Boolean. In the Details tab, change Variable Type to Integer now. While there is a default value for the variable, you will not have access to it until you compile the blueprint. Do so now.

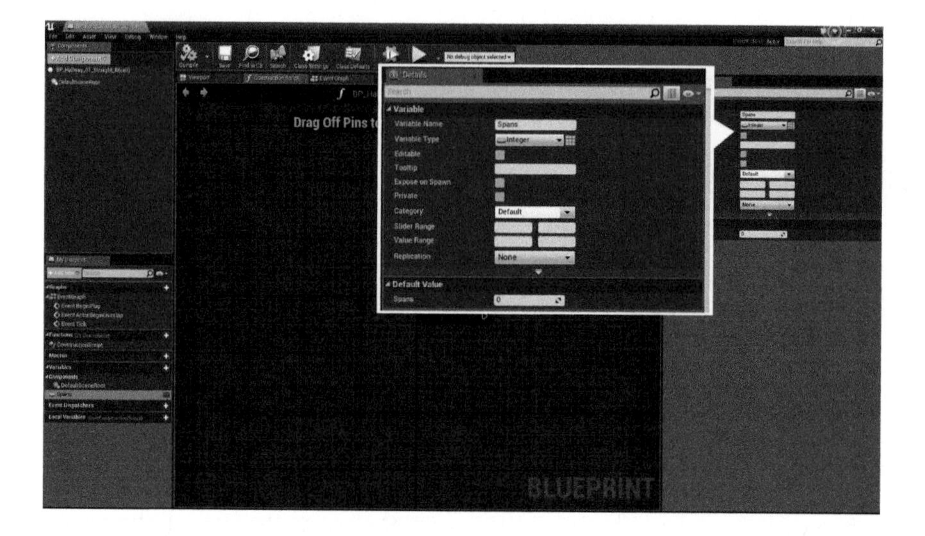

You can set the slider range in the Details tab to 1, 10. This means that you can have any number of sections from 1 to 10. An upper limit of 10 is used for performance reasons; however, you can change this later if you would like. Set the default value to 1.

In the graph you are going to add a new type of node called a For Loop. **For Loops** run in order from start to finish. Right-click in the graph and search for the for loop. Add the Loop node to the graph. You will also need to add a Get node for your Spans variable. Connect the Spans variable to the Last Index input of the For Loop node. Set the First Index input to 0. Connect the exec output of the *Construction Script* node to the in-exec on the *For Loop* node.

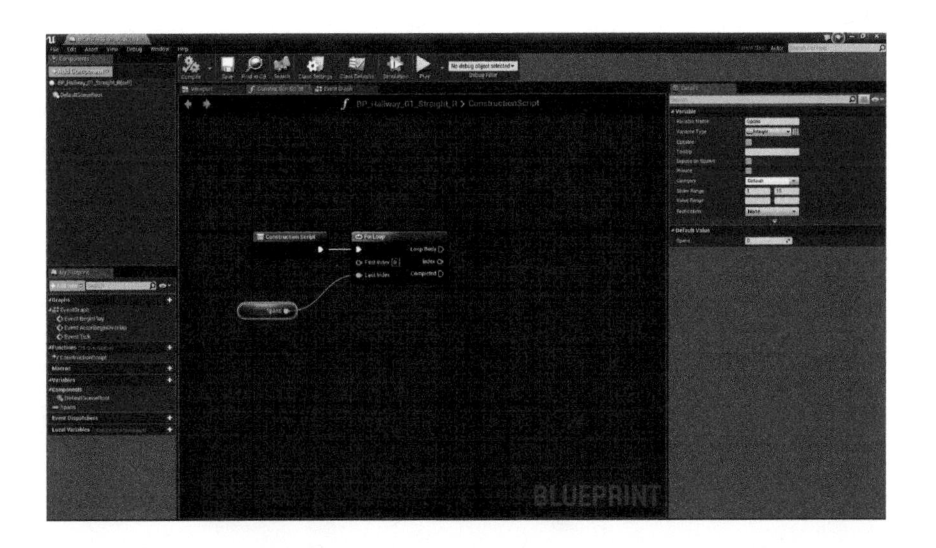

Because you have not created your functions yet, you cannot progress any further in the construction script. Let us create a couple functions now. In the My Blueprints tab find the Functions section and choose +Function. Name this new function *Add_Floor_Sections*. Once you press enter to save the name, your new graph will open over the construction script. As the name implies, you will be using this graph to add your floors. To do this, you need to add a node named **Add Static Mesh Component** to the graph. Once the node has been added to the graph, you will need to tell it what mesh to use. In the Details tab, find the Static Mesh section and set it to *Hallway_01_Straight_Floor.*

Connect the exec output of the *Add Floor Sections* node to the exec input on the *Add Static Mesh Component* node. Now you have a way to create the floor. However, if you were to switch back to the viewport, you would not see a floor yet because you have not connected the *Add Floor Sections* function to your construction script. Switch to the construction script and drag in the *Add Floor Sections* function. Connect the exec output on the For Loop to the exec input on the Add Floor Sections node. Once you have made the connection, Compile the blueprint and then switch to the viewport. You should now have a floor section.

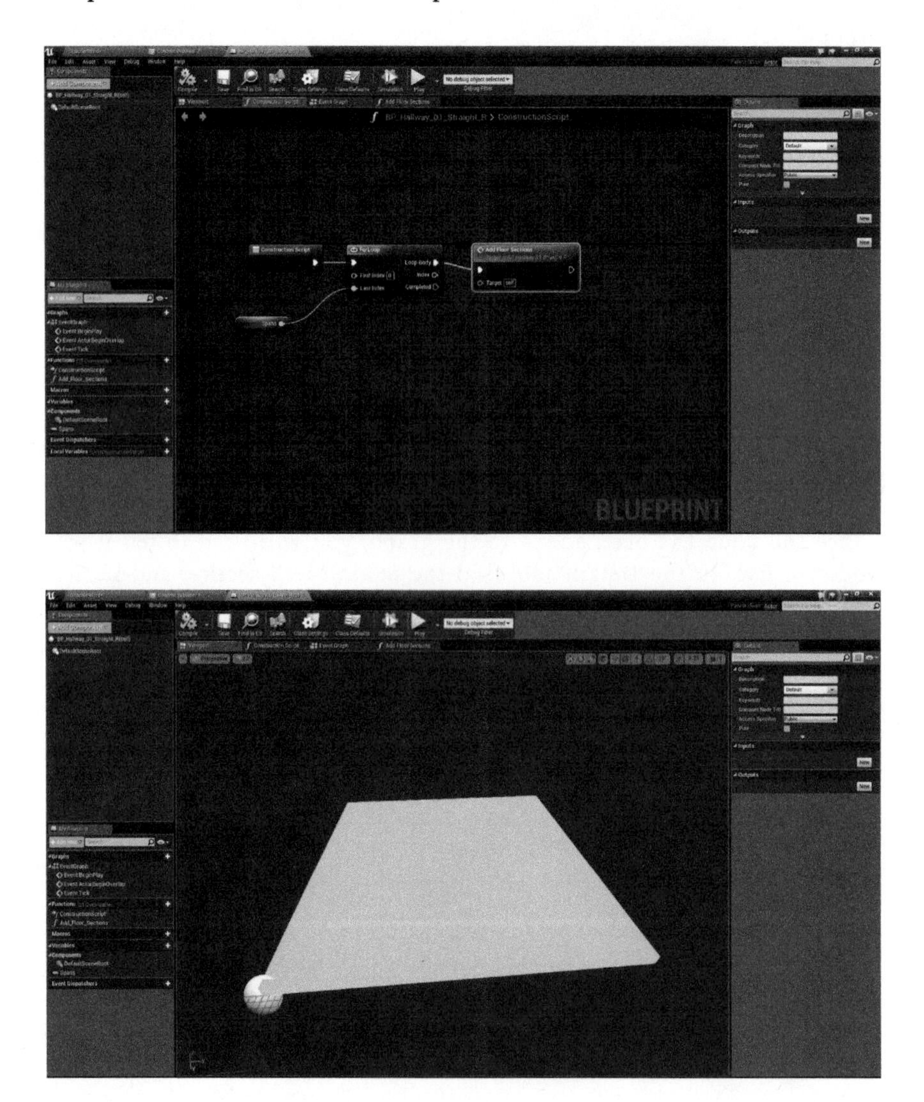

The next function you will work on is the *Add Wall Sections* function. Since you will always be adding both a left and a right wall to each section, they can both go into one function. Add a new function and name it *Add_Wall_Sections*.

In the new graph, add two *Add Static Mesh Component* nodes. Set both of these nodes' static mesh properties to *Hallway_01_Straight_No_Door.* Connect the exec output from the Add Wall Sections node to the exec input of the first *Add Static Mesh Component* node. Connect the exec output from the first *Add Static Mesh Component* node to the exec input of the second.

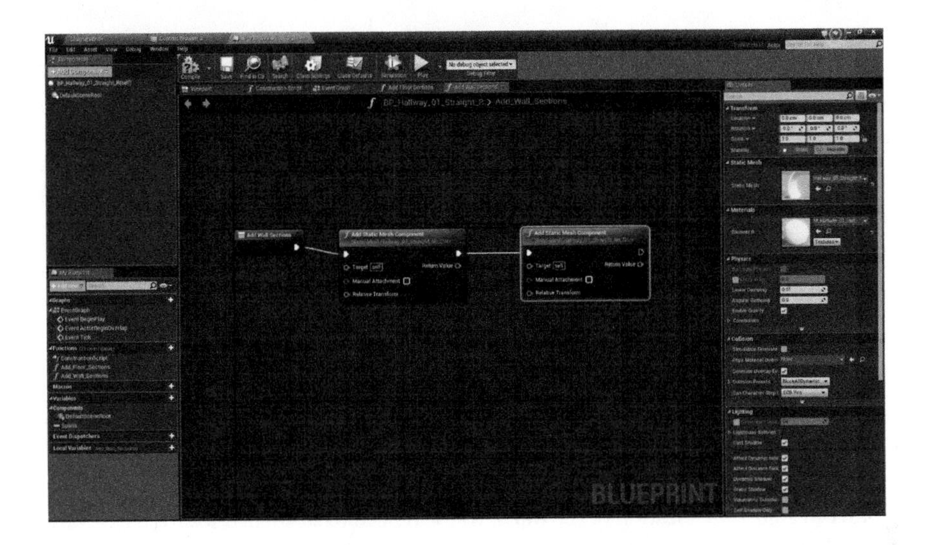

Switch back to the construction script, add the *Add Wall Sections* node to the graph, and connect it to the exec output from the *Add Floor Sections* node.

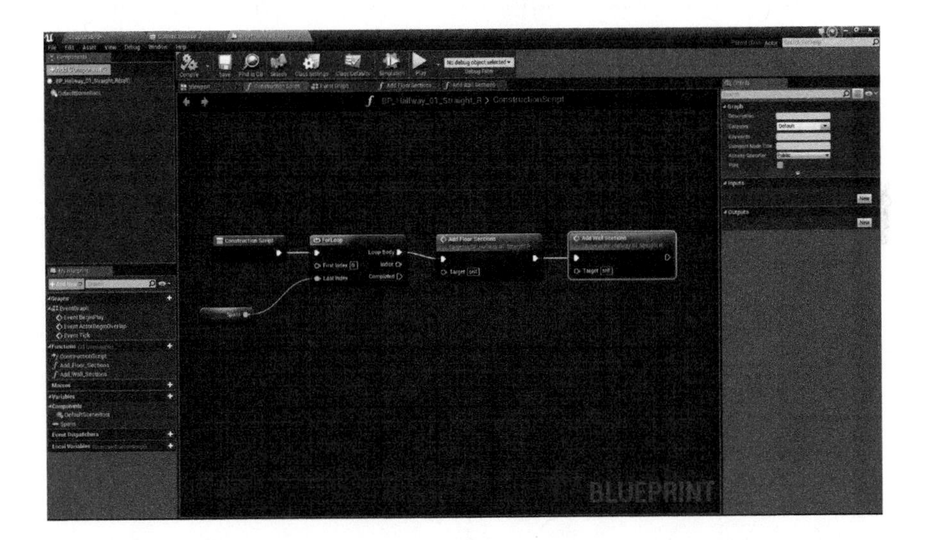

If you look in the viewport, you can already see that there is an issue.

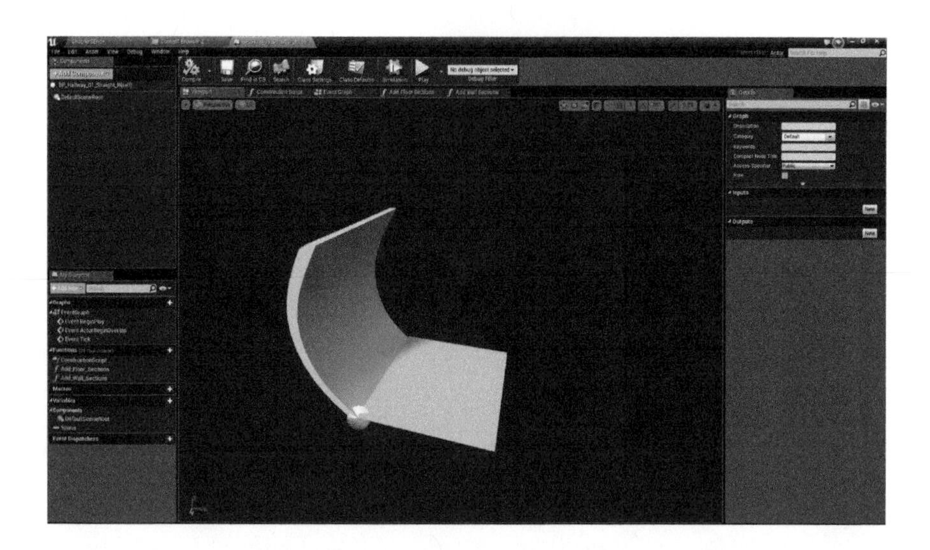

You added two walls to the graph; however, only one is showing up. Actually, they are in fact both there. They are in the exact same location. You should also notice that, if you try to move one in the viewport, you cannot select it because it is being built through the graphs.

To correct the wall issue you must first return to the *Add Wall Sections* graph. In order to adjust the location of the walls, you will need to store their location in a variable. You need to use a new variable here called a **Vector**. Similarly to using the Vector nodes you used in the Material Editor, a vector stores three numbers. For purposes here, it will be the X, Y, and Z locations of the walls. In the My Blueprint tab under the Variables section, create a new variable. Rename the variable *Left_Wall_Offset*. With the new variable selected, change the Variable Type in the Details tab to Vector.

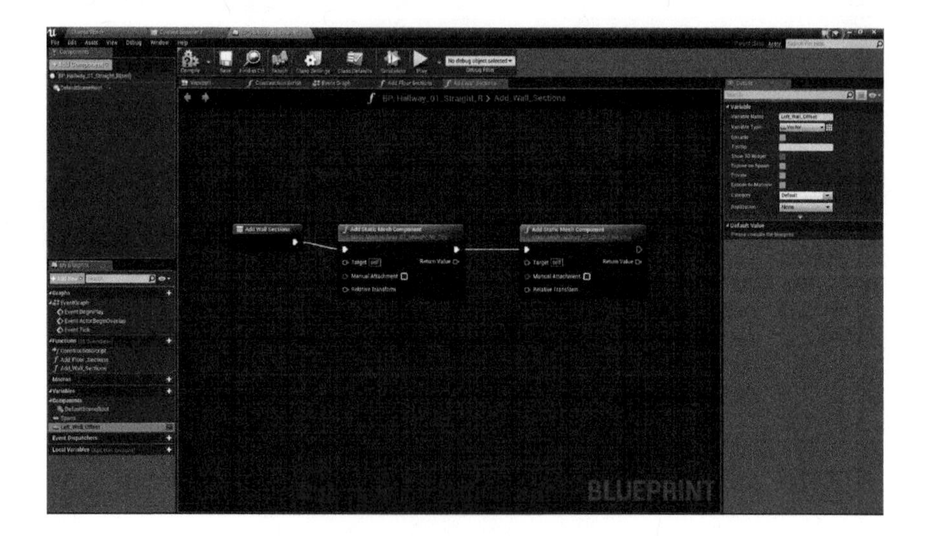

Since you have a wall for both the left and right, you need to add another Vector variable named *Right_Wall_Offset*. Add both of the Vector variables as Get nodes to the graph.

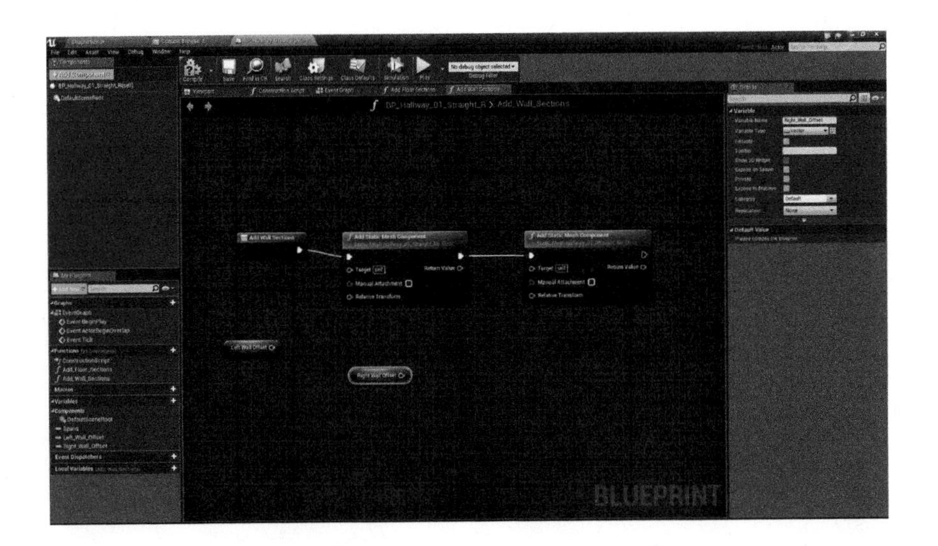

Taking a closer look at the graph will reveal that you cannot connect your Vector nodes to your *Add Static Mesh Component* nodes. You need to add a middleman of sorts. From the *Left Wall Offset* output, search for and add the *Make Transform* node. Connect the output of the *Make Transform* node to the Relative Transform input on the first *Add Static Mesh Component* node.

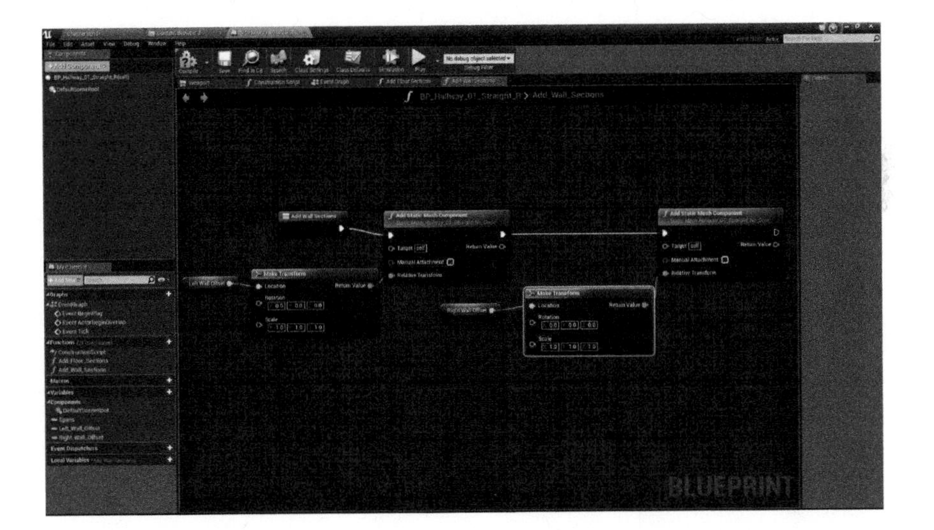

If you were to compile the blueprint now and check the viewport, you would notice that nothing has changed because you have not set the starting location for either of the Vector nodes. To set the *Left Wall Offset*, select it in the Variables section of the My Blueprint tab. In the Details tab set the following:

- X—10

Moving to the *Right Wall Offset*, set the following:

- X—310
- Y—(-320)

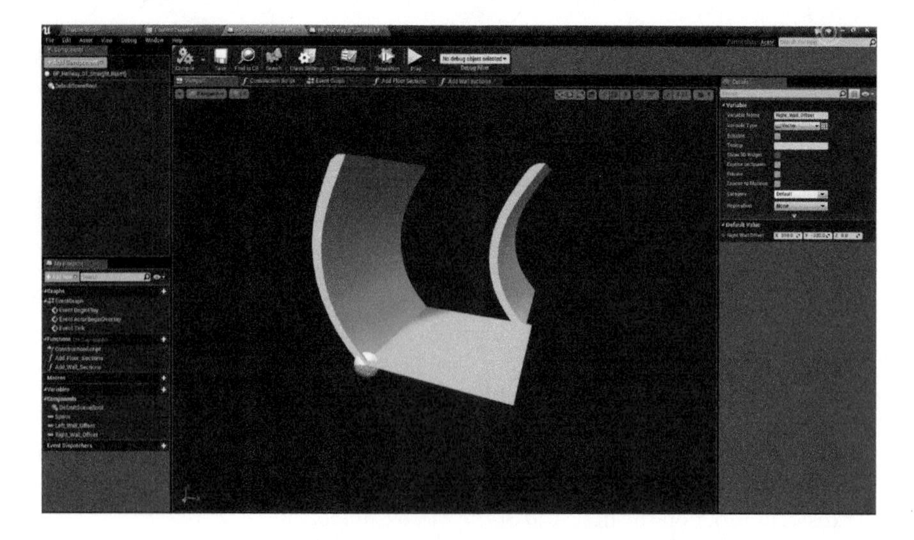

You are getting closer; unfortunately, you do not have a rotation attribute with your Vector node. Instead, you can use the *Make Transform* node in the graph to adjust the rotation of your right side wall. Make sure that you have selected the *Make Transform* node that is connected to the *Right Wall Offset* node. Set the Rotation Z value to 180. Compile the blueprint and then switch back to the viewport to see your handiwork.

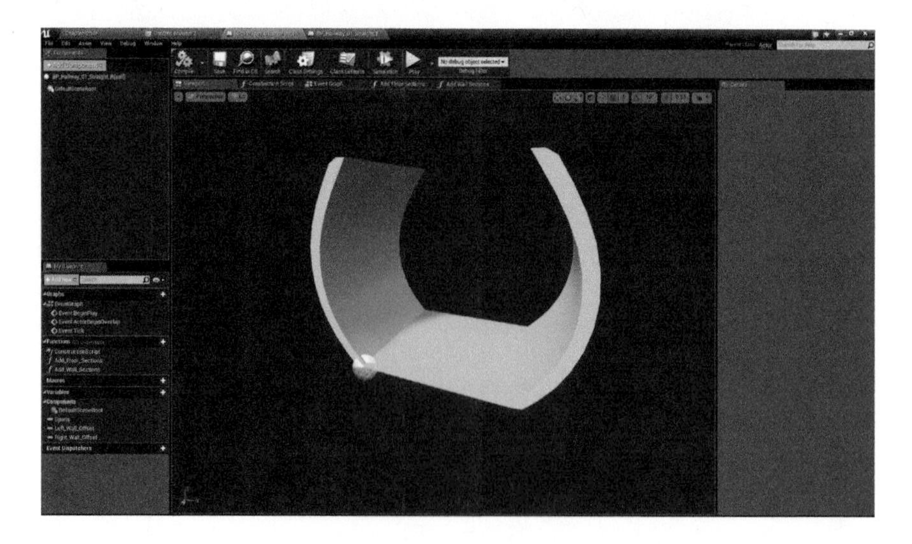

Now you are really getting somewhere! The next step is to add a new function for your ceilings. In the Functions section add a new function named *Add_Ceiling_Sections*. Set up the graph the same as before. Make sure that the mesh you are using in the Add Static Mesh Component node is the *Hallway_01_Straight_Ceiling*.

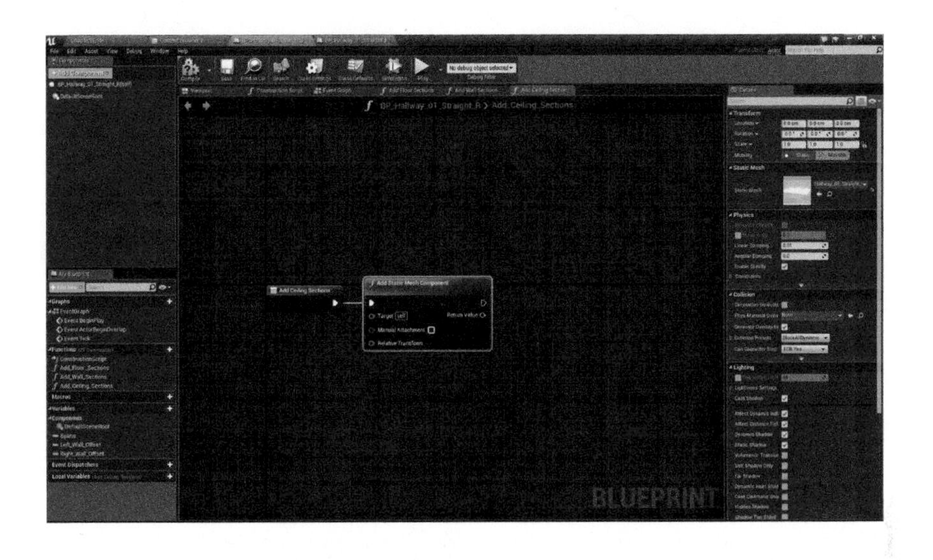

In the construction script, add the *Add_Ceiling_Sections* function to the graph at the end of the chain.

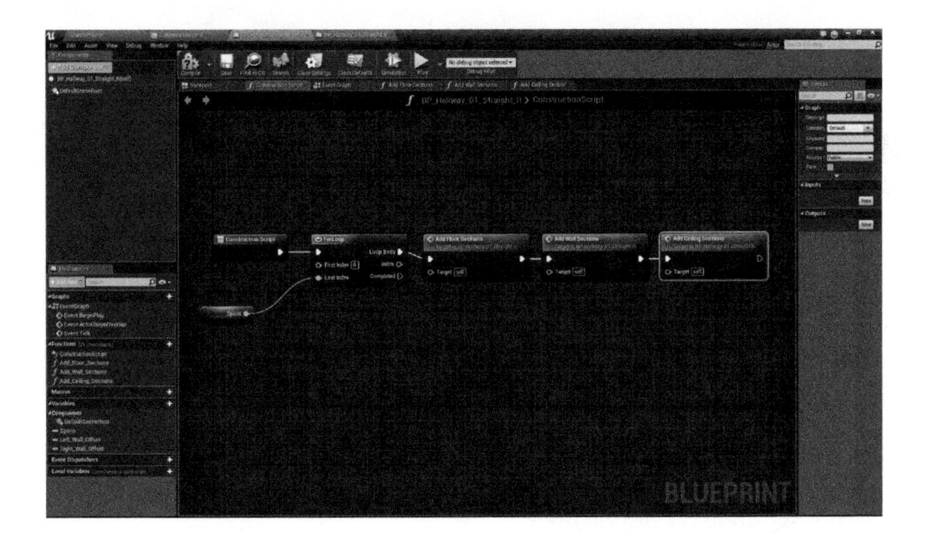

Compile the blueprint and then switch to the viewport. If you do not see your ceiling at first, try rotating the camera so that you can see the bottom of the hallway section.

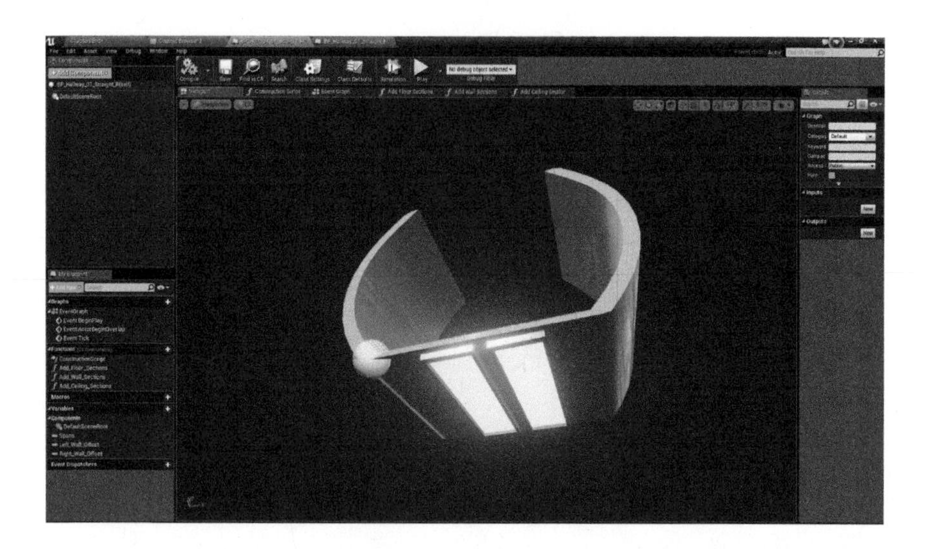

You will have to add an offset variable for the ceiling just like you did for the walls. Create a new vector variable and name it *Ceiling_Offset*. Set its default value to Z—400 (remember that you will have to compile the blueprint before you will have access to the default value). Add a Get node for the *Ceiling_Offset* vector node to your *Add Ceiling Sections* graph. From the output of the Get node, add a *Make Transform* node. Connect the return value of the Make Transform node to the Relative Transform input on the *Add Static Mesh Component* node.

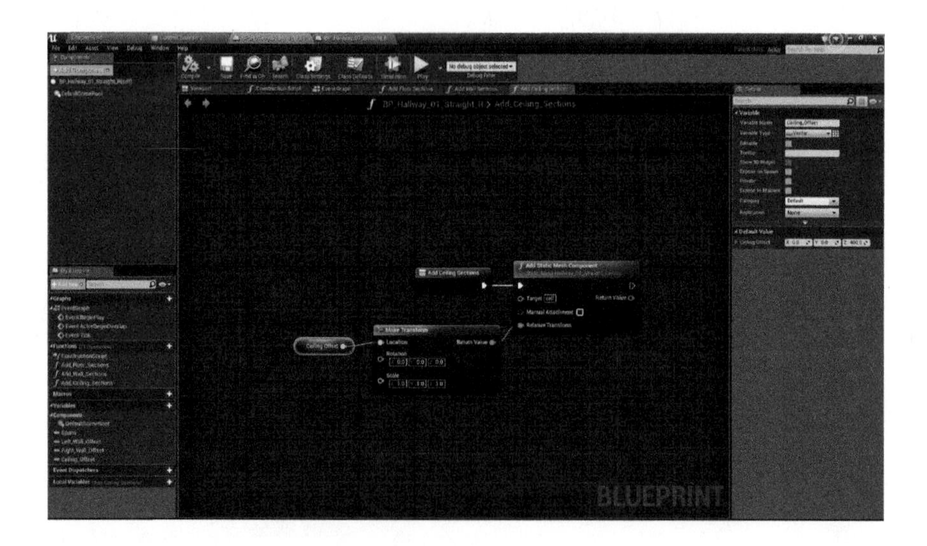

Now, if you switch back to the viewport, you should have something similar to what is shown in the next figure.

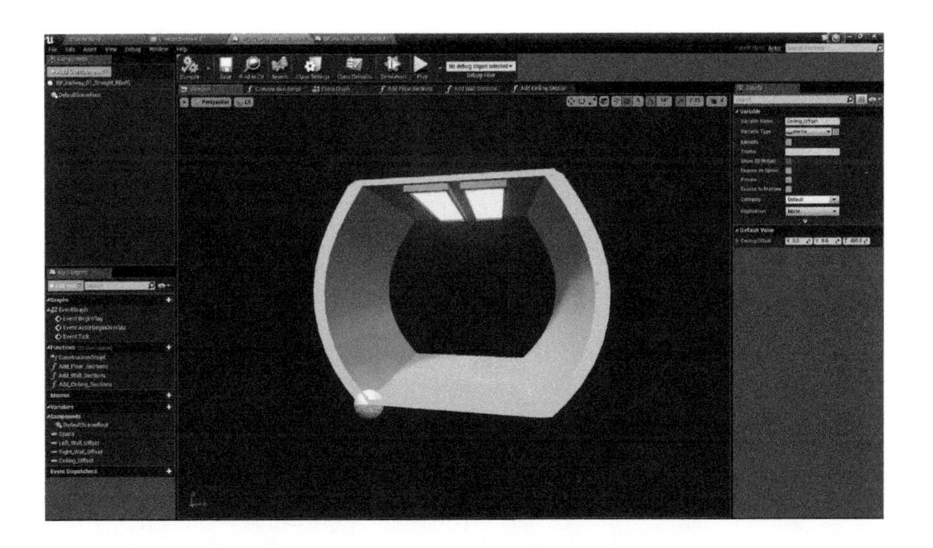

It is starting to look a lot like your original straight hallway blueprint now. You do have a couple more things to add; the doorframe mesh will be added next. Add a new function named *Add_Doorframe_Sections*. In the new function, add the *Add Static Mesh Component* node. Be sure to set the mesh to *Hallway_01_Door_Frame*.

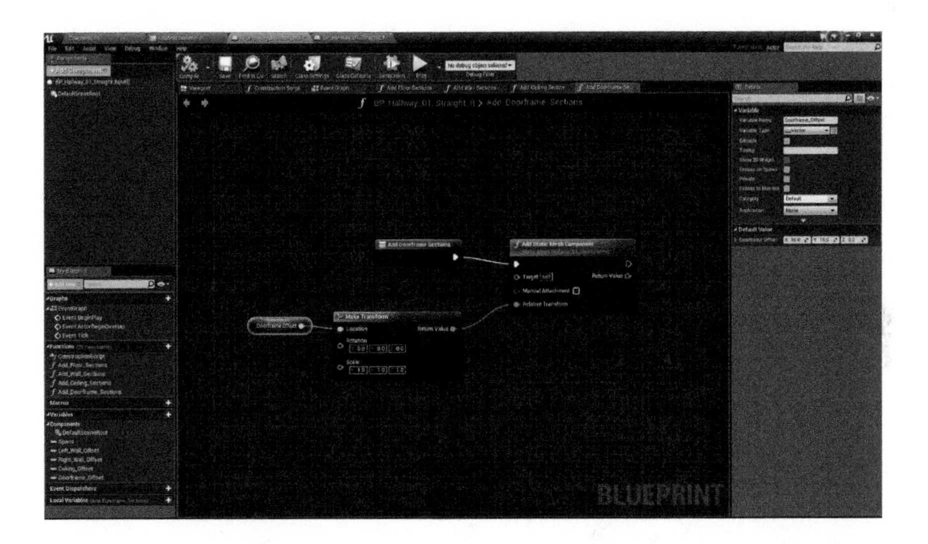

You will again need a vector named *Doorframe_Offset*. Set the default value to

- X—10
- Y—15

Using the same method as before, create the *Make Transform* node and connect it to the Relative Transform input of the *Add Static Mesh Component* node.

Note: If you are wondering where the location data are coming from, you can look at the original BP_Hallway_01_Straight_No_Door blueprint to get the location of the different sections.

In the construction script add the *Add_Doorframe_Sections* node to the end of the chain.

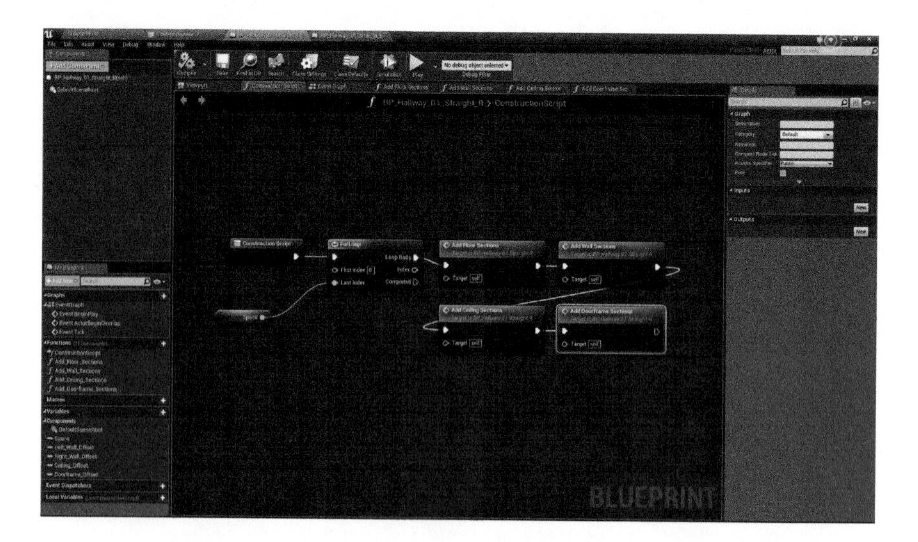

After compiling, a quick look at the viewport should reveal a hallway similar to that in the image below.

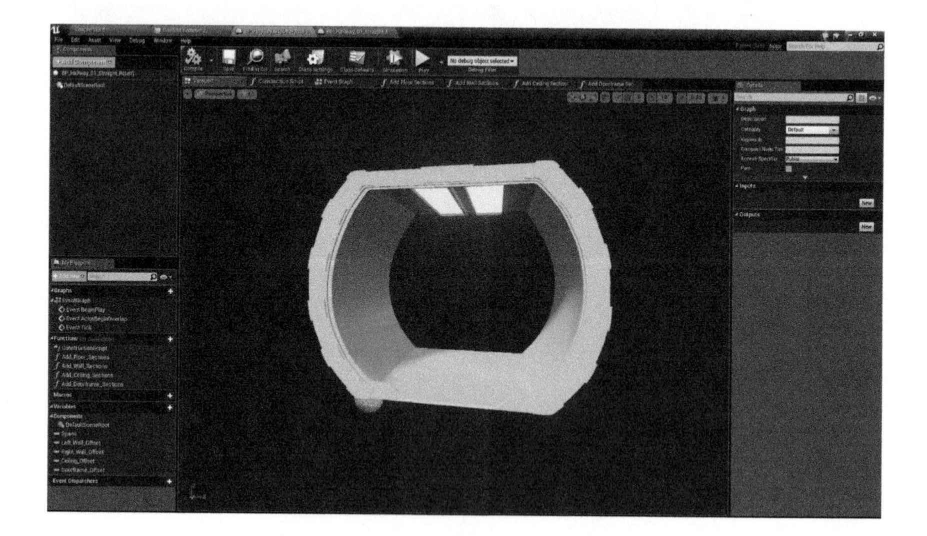

If you were to refer back to the *BP_Hallway_01_Straight_No_Door* blueprint, you would see that there is one last thing you need to add: the light. Adding a light is a little more complex than adding the different sections because you have to adjust a few settings, such as light color, intensity, and attenuation radius, when you add the point light. You will need an offset variable for the light since it will not reside at the origin of the blueprint.

Start by adding a new function called *Add_Lights*. In the *Add_Lights* function graph, add a node named *Add Point Light Component*. Create a vector variable named *Light_Offset*. Add a Get node for the light offset variable. Add a *Make Transform* node and connect it as you have in the past.

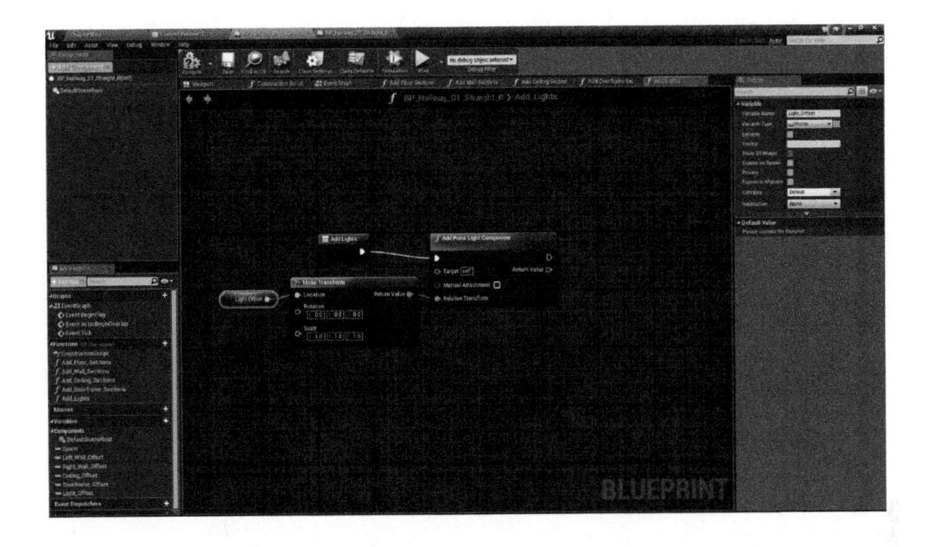

To add the next three nodes, it will be much easier if you use the return value of the *Add Point Light Component* node. Drag off the return value output and search for the *Set Light Color* node. Again, from the return value output, search for *Set Intensity*. One last time, drag off the return value output and find the *Set Attenuation Radius* node. Connect the exec pins as seen in the figure below.

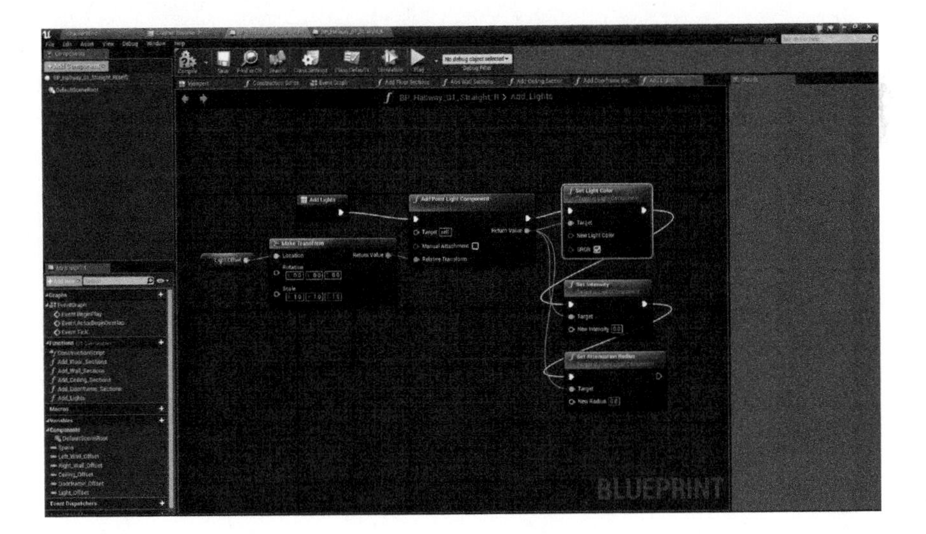

Okay, you are all done, right? Not just yet. Set the New Light Color on the Set Light Color node to a pale blue color. Set the New Intensity of the Set Intensity node to 1000. Finally, set the New Radius on the Set Attenuation Radius node to 500. Next, you need to set the starting value for the *Light_Offset* vector to

- X—165
- Y—(-170)
- Z—300

To finish out this part of the light, you need to add the *Add_Lights* function to the construction script. Compile your blueprint and take a look in the viewport.

You are ready to test your blueprint, so add it to your level now.

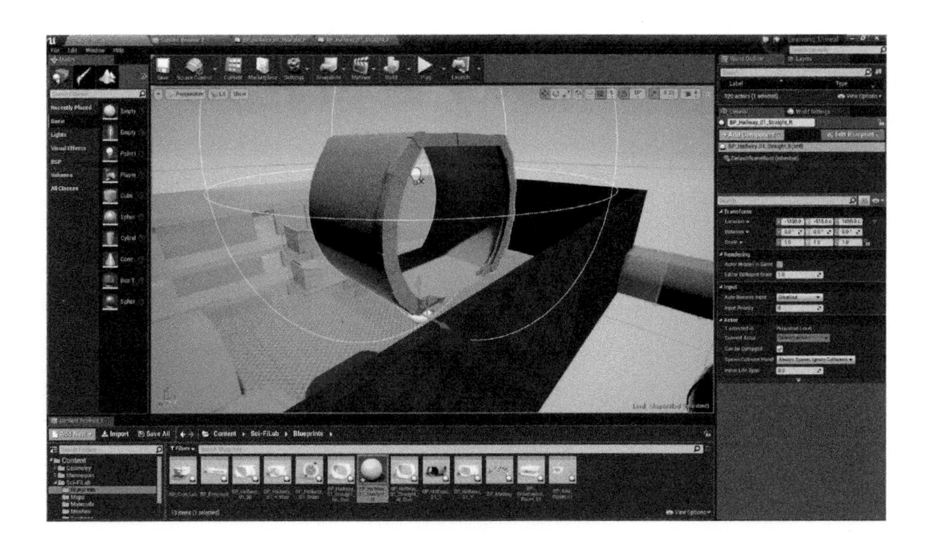

This looks good so far, but you are missing something. Your slider to adjust the length is not visible yet. You need to set the spans variable to Public. Back in the Blueprint Editor, find the spans variable and click on the eye beside it to make the variable public. A public variable can be edited outside the blueprint, but a private variable cannot.

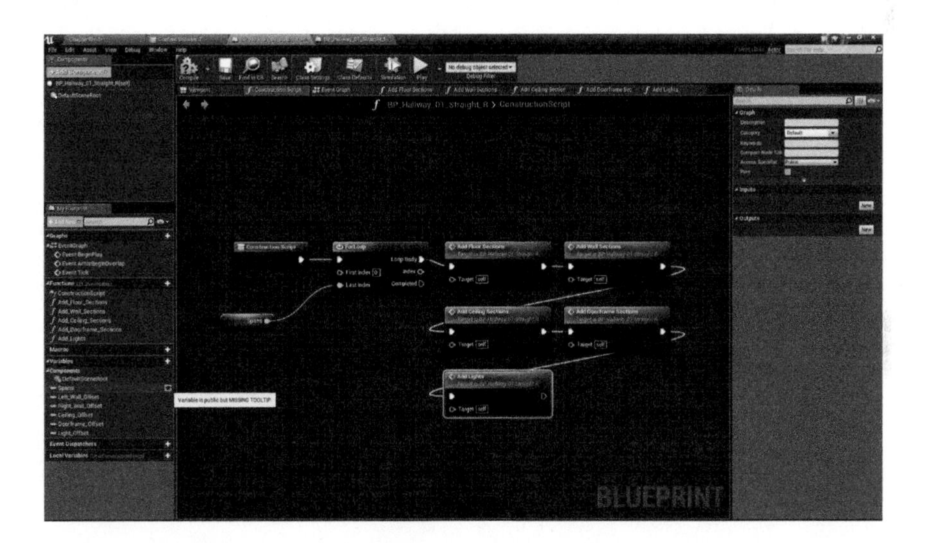

Compile your blueprint and then switch back to the Level Editor. With the blueprint selected, you should now see the Spans variable in the Details tab under the Default section.

Adjusting the slider right now does not seem to have the desired effect. You can tell that something is changing, but it is hard to tell exactly what is happening. As you move the slider up, it is adding the new sections; however, you have not adjusted the location of the offsets to change as you add more sections. You have already made almost all the necessary variables; you just have to add a couple tweaks to make it work correctly.

You will start by correcting the floor. Switch back to your blueprint and open the *Add_Floor_Sections* graph. You need to create an offset variable for the floors. Name your new variable *Floor_Offset*. Since the floor will start out in the location it is already in, you do not need to add a default value. Add a set node for the *Floor_Offset* variable to your graph. You will also need a Get node, so add that now. Add a Make Transform node as you have previously. Connect the exec output from the *Add Static Mesh Component* node to the in-exec of the Set node. The last step for your floor is to add a Vector + Vector node. Drag off the output from the Get node and type +. Find the Vector + Vector node and add it to the graph. In the add node, set the Y value to 320. Finally, connect the output of the add node to the Floor Offset input of the Set node.

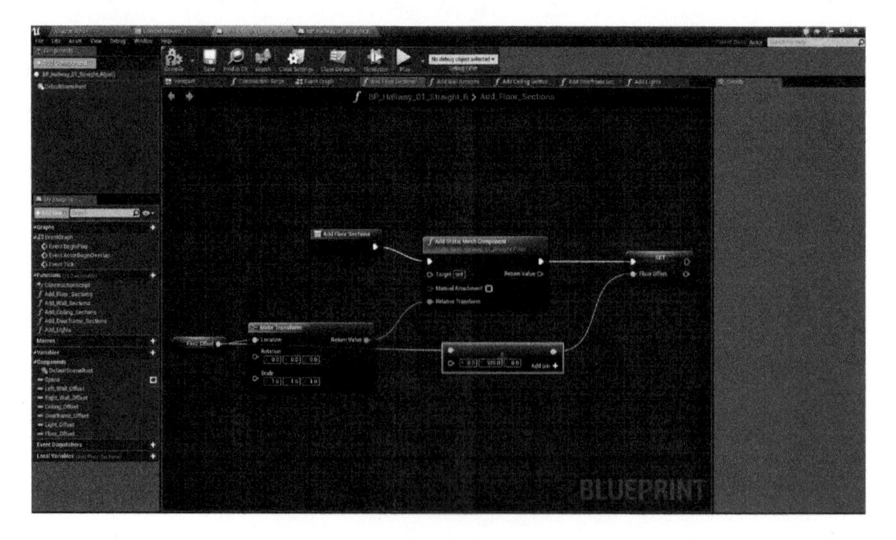

If you compile the blueprint and switch to the Level Editor, you should notice that you have a new issue.

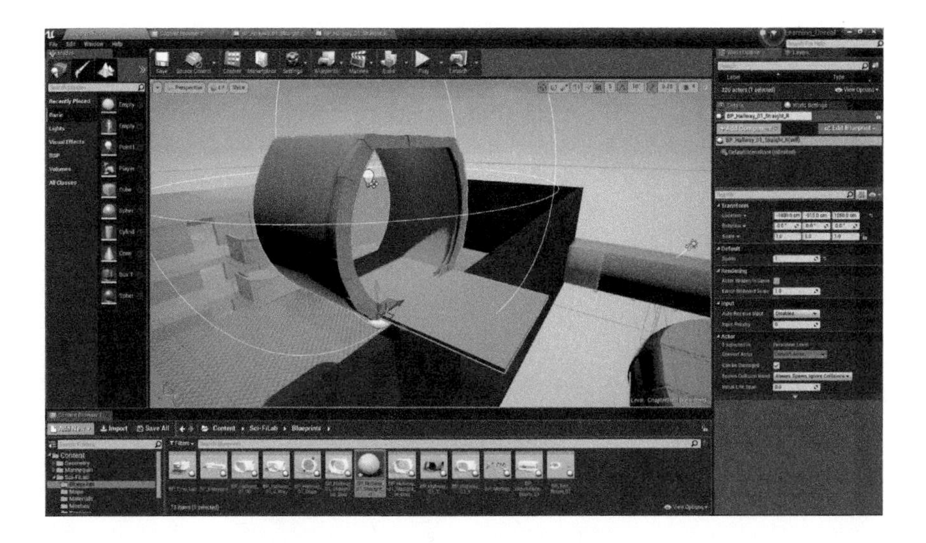

The good news is that if you move the slider, it will add floor sections correctly. The bad news is that you have an extra floor section. The reason for this extra has to do with the *For Loop*. If you remember, the default value of the *Spans* variable is 1. You also set the loop to start at 0. This means that you have a section being built at 0 and 1, which is why you have the extra floor. If you go back to your construction script, you can fix the issue in a couple ways. The easiest way to correct the issue is to set the first index of your *For Loop* to 1. When you compile the blueprint after making the change, you will find that nothing shows up in the viewport anymore. Do not worry, though. A quick look back in the Level Editor shows that the blueprint is intact. There is no extra section now, and your slider works correctly on the floor. Setting the spans slider to 7, you should see something similar to the image below.

Set *Spans* back to 1 and then return to the Blueprint Editor. You need to correct your walls next. Open the *Add_Wall_Sections* graph. Since you already have offsets made for each wall, you do not need to make more. You do, however, need to add a Set node for *Left_Wall_Offset* and *Right_Wall_Offset*. Once you have the set nodes added to the graph, you need to connect them to the exec chain. For clarity, add the Set node for the left wall after the *Add Static Mesh Component* node for the left side. Add the Set node for the right side directly after the right side *Add Static Mesh Component* node. From the Get *Left_Wall_Offset* node, drag off the output and add a Vector + Vector node. Set the Y value to 320 and then connect its output to the Set left wall input. Repeat the process for the right side.

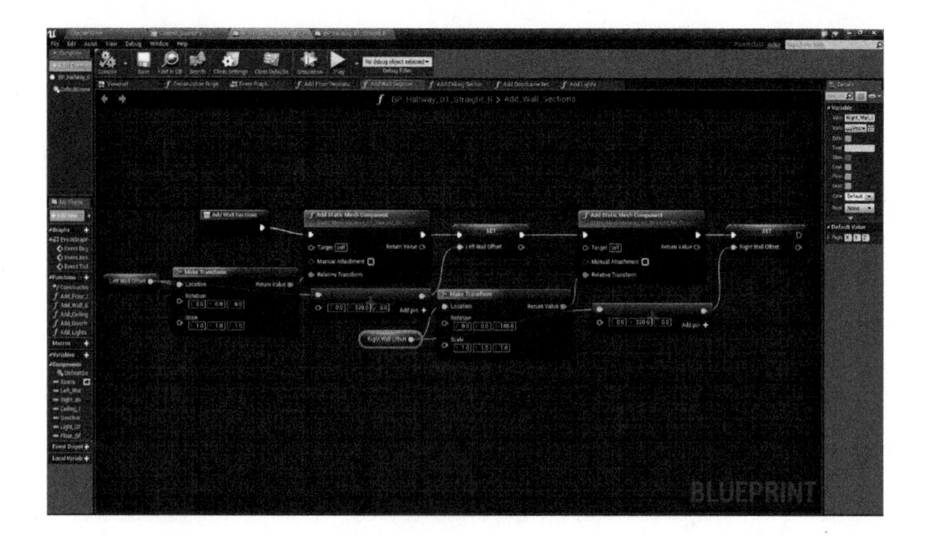

Repeat the process of adding the set and Vector + Vector node to the *Add_Ceiling_Sections* graph, *Add_Doorframe_Sections* graph, and *Add_Lights* graph. Remember to set the Y value to 320 for each graph. Use the next three images as guides.

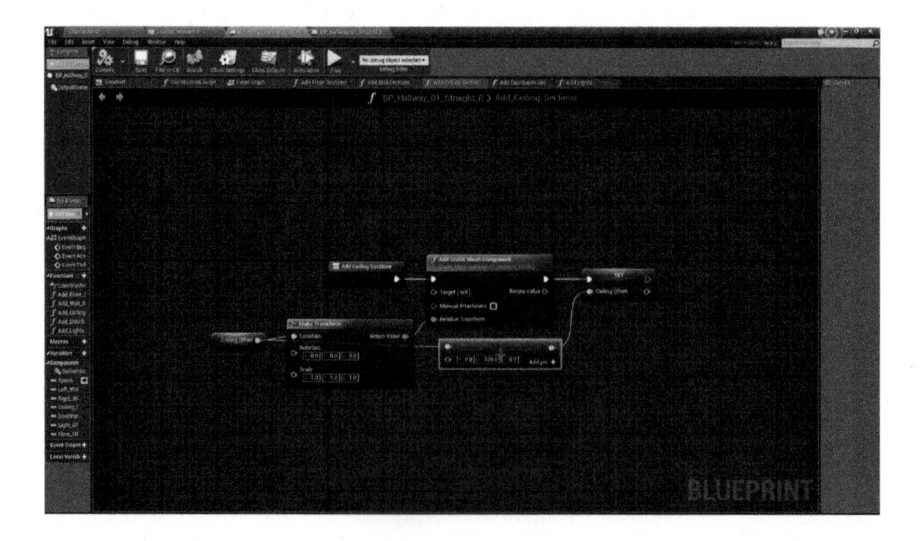

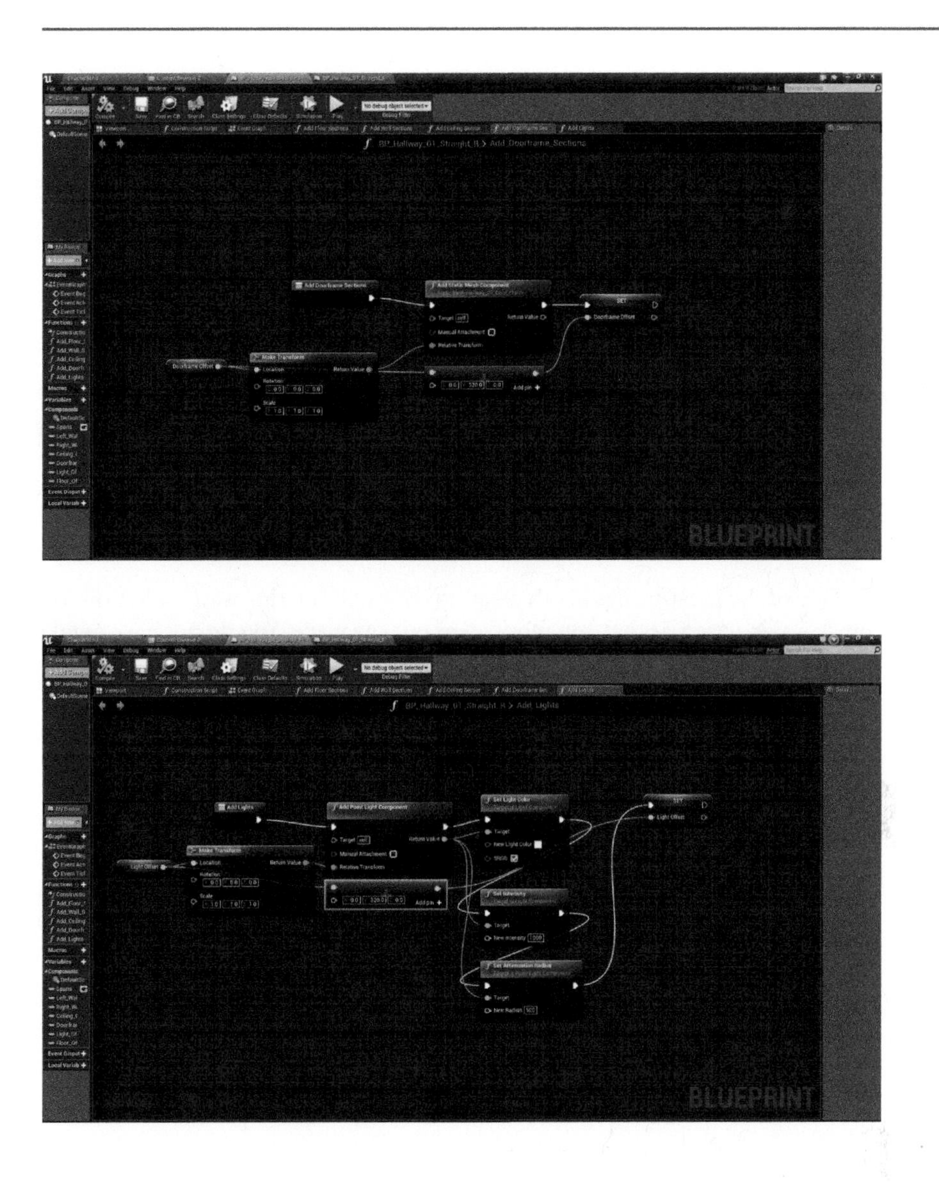

Once you have completed all the set nodes in each of the graphs, compile and save your blueprint. Switch back to the Level Editor and adjust the slider to see your new blueprint in action!

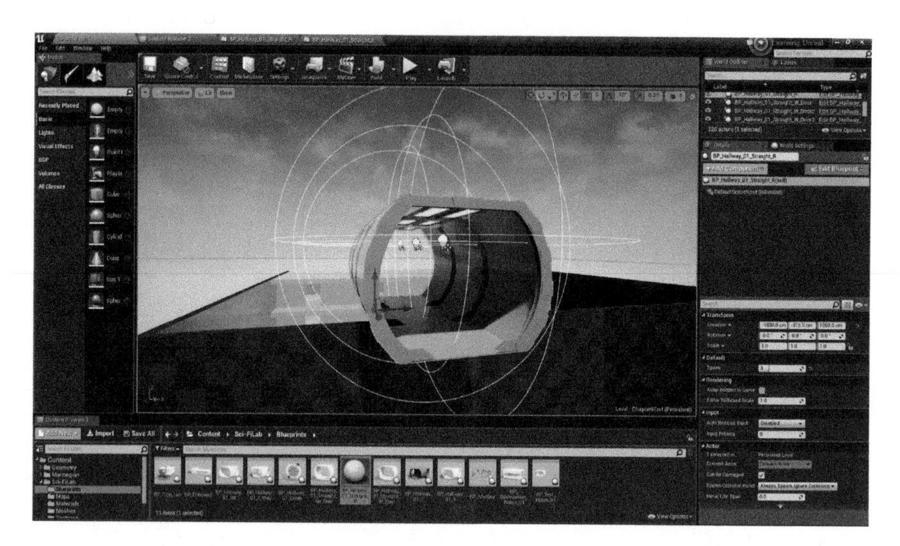

One of the great things about creating your hallway this way, aside from the quick slider action, is that you move all as one big piece. You do not have to take the time to line up each section individually because the graphs are doing that for you. Take a minute to enjoy your creation.

Chapter Challenge

Now that you have an idea of how to create functions and variables, think of exciting ways to expand into other blueprints. While you may not have an opportunity to make another expanding hallway, you could use the same process to add a series of cryo chambers to a room. You could use the Make Transform nodes along with variables to adjust the rotation as well as location of the objects. You could also use the process to create a series of rooms with different components. If you mix and match the Boolean processes you explored earlier (with the branch nodes), you could create a blueprint that only adds objects if you check their associated Boolean variable.

Changing Colors during Runtime

In an earlier chapter you made some automatic doors. For the next two sections of this chapter you will be improving upon that blueprint. The first thing you will cover is how to swap materials during game play. You will change the green glow of your doors to a red glow while the doors are shut.

Before you can start building the blueprint, you need to check a couple of things. The first thing you need to be sure of is that you have the materials you need. You will need a red glow material. You can continue to use the green glow material you have already created. Once you have both materials, open the *Hallway_01_Right_Door* in the Static Mesh Editor. Scroll through the materials of the door and find the green glowing material. Take note of the **Element** number as you will use this to change materials later. Do the same for the *Hallway_01_Left_Door.*

If you want to keep your original doors, you will need to make a duplicate of the blueprint. You *cannot* do this by right-clicking on the blueprint and choosing Duplicate. You will need to rebuild the entire blueprint. Open your blueprint in the Blueprint Editor. The first thing you need to do is to create variables in which to store your material instances. In the Variables section of the My Blueprint tab, add a new variable. Set the variable name to *M_Green_Glow*. Set the variable type to **Material Instance**. Compile the blueprint to gain access to the default value. Set the default to the *M_Hallway_01_Light_Green_Inst* material.

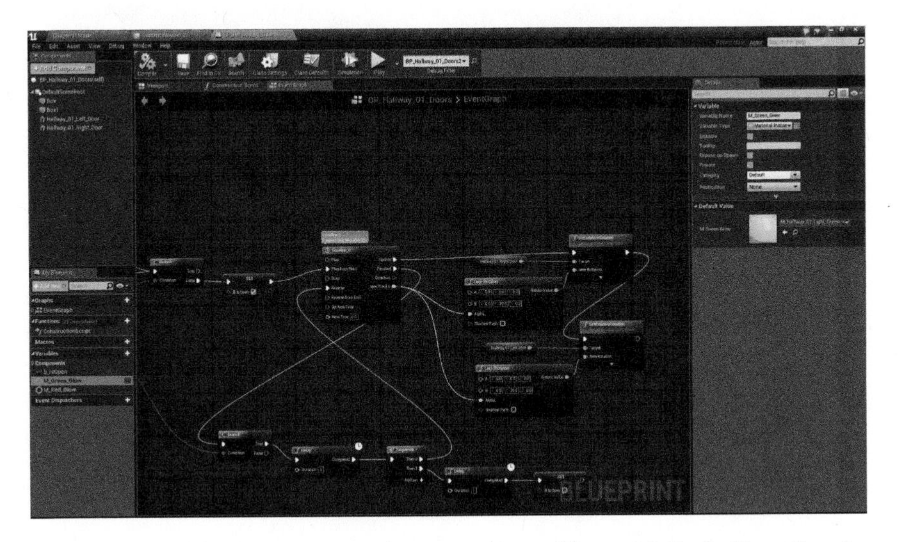

Repeat the process, naming the second variable to *M_Red_Glow*. Set the default material to your red glow material.

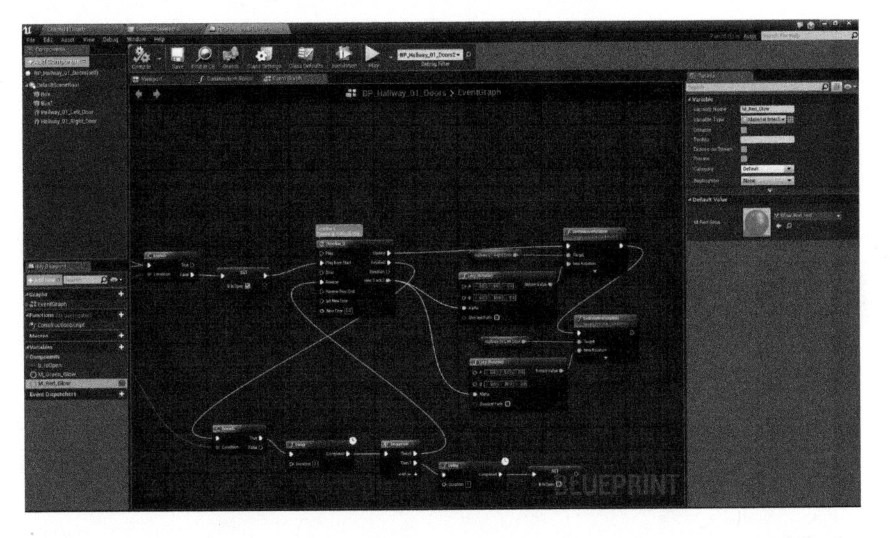

Once the material variables are created and set, you can begin to modify the graph. You can use the two materials in a couple different ways. You can set the starting material to the red glow, indicating that the door is closed, and then switch to the green material when the door opens. Alternately, you can leave the green glow as the starting material to indicate that the door can be opened and then switch to the red glow when you activate the door. The choice is yours. I prefer to have the red glow as the starting material.

You can change the starting material in the Static Mesh Editor if you would like, or it can be changed in the construction script of the blueprint. Either method will have the same overall effect. Because you are learning how to swap materials in the blueprint, that is the method to use.

Open the construction script of the blueprint. Add both of the door variables as Get nodes to the graph.

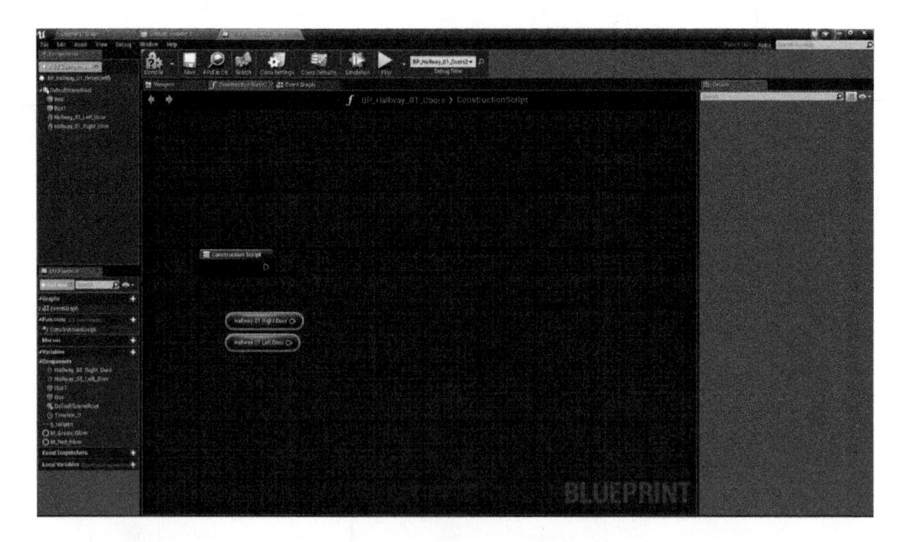

Starting with the right door, drag off of the out-pin and search for material. Select the *Set Material* node from the list to add it to the graph. Add the *M_Red_Glow* variable to the graph and connect it to the Material input on the Set Material node. Set the Element Index to the number of the element you took note of earlier. (This should be the element that has the green glow material in the Static Mesh Editor.) From the left door out-pin, drag and add another *Set Material* node. Connect the *M_Red_Glow* node to the Material input. Set the element to the element you marked for the left door.

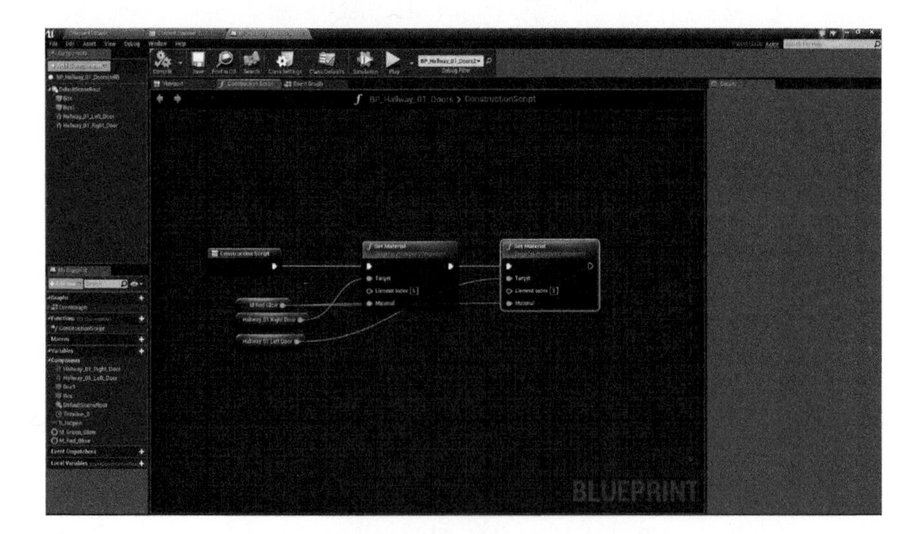

Compile and save the blueprint. If you switch back to the viewport view now, you should notice that the green glow has been replaced with the red glow.

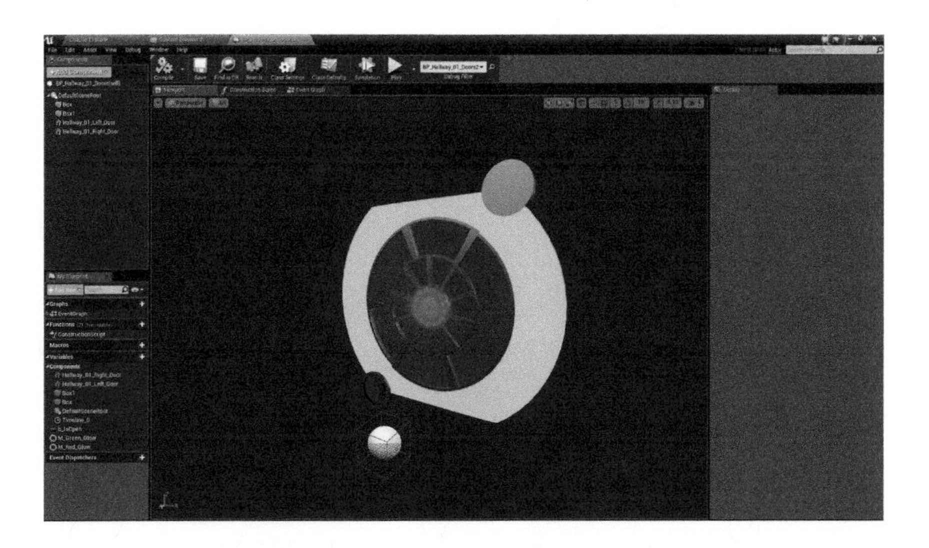

Switch back to the construction script graph. Select all the nodes you added and copy them using Ctrl + C. Switch to the event graph. Paste the nodes you copied using the Ctrl + V method. You will need to add some room between the first branch node and the Set node for the Boolean. Delete the *M_Red_Glow* material and replace it with the *M_Green_Glow* material. Connect the material to the Material input on both Set Material nodes. From the False output of the Branch node, connect to the input exec of the first *Set Material* node. From the second *Set Material* node, connect the out-exec to the in-exec on the Set Boolean node.

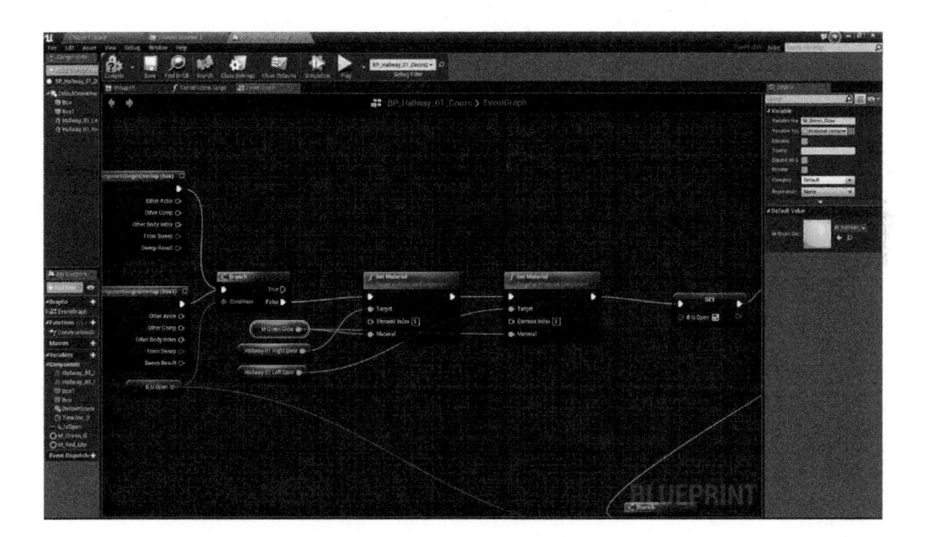

A quick play-test of the level should show that the material does change from red to green when you activate the door. However, the material does not switch back once the door has closed. To correct this issue, copy the nodes in the construction script and paste them at the end of the event graph chain. Connect the output of the Set Boolean to the first Set Material.

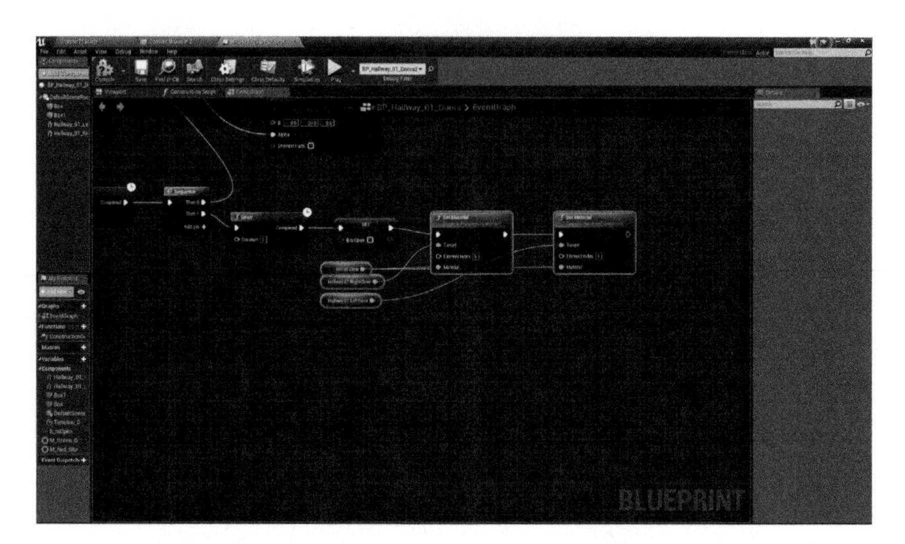

Compile the blueprint and then save it. Play your level now to ensure that the doors work properly. The light should be red until you activate the door, and then it should return to red when it closes.

Interacting with Blueprints

For the final section of this chapter, you will make your doors interactive. Instead of simply walking up to the door to open it, you will have to use a key on the keyboard to activate the door (typically the "E" key). Again, if you want to have both types of doors, you will need to duplicate the blueprint. I also need to point out that there are a number of different ways to accomplish this task. The method that will be used here was created to give the level designer the most control possible while keeping the complexity of the blueprint at a minimum.

You will be adding a few more nodes and two more Boolean variables. Open your blueprint in the Blueprint Editor.

To better understand what you will be doing, we can talk for a moment about how you want the door to work. Since you do not want the door to open if the player is not directly in front of it, you will continue to use your trigger volumes. Instead of having the triggers open the door, you will have them set b_CanActivate to true. While b_CanActivate is true, you will be able to press the "E" key to open the door. That is where the b_OpenPressed variable comes into play. You will need to add two more control nodes for the triggers called OnComponentEndOverlap. These nodes will trigger when the player exits the trigger volume. You will have a delay of a short time that runs upon leaving the volume before it sets the b_CanActivate Boolean back to false. This ensures that while you do have a small window to activate the door even if you step outside the trigger, it will not continue to be active indefinitely.

Now that you have a basic idea of how the triggers and key input will work, you need to do one more thing before the door will actually work. You have to tell the blueprint that it can accept the user's input. This is done with the *Get Player Controller* and *Enable Input* nodes. You will use these two nodes in conjunction with the Event Tick node, which periodically runs. You could in turn attach these nodes to the *Begin Play* node; however, you would run into another issue of when and how pressing the "E" key would affect the door.

In the event graph, disconnect the OnComponentBeginOverlap nodes. Move them to a different location on the graph—out of the way of the rest of the nodes. You now will create your two new Boolean variables. In the Variables section of the My Blueprint tab, add a new Boolean named *b_OpenPressed*. Repeat the process and name the second variable *b_CanActivate*. Add a set *b_CanActivate* node to the graph. Connect the out-exec pins from the *OnComponentBeginOverlap* nodes to the in-exec on the set node. Set the value of the set node to true by checking the box beside the B Can Activate input.

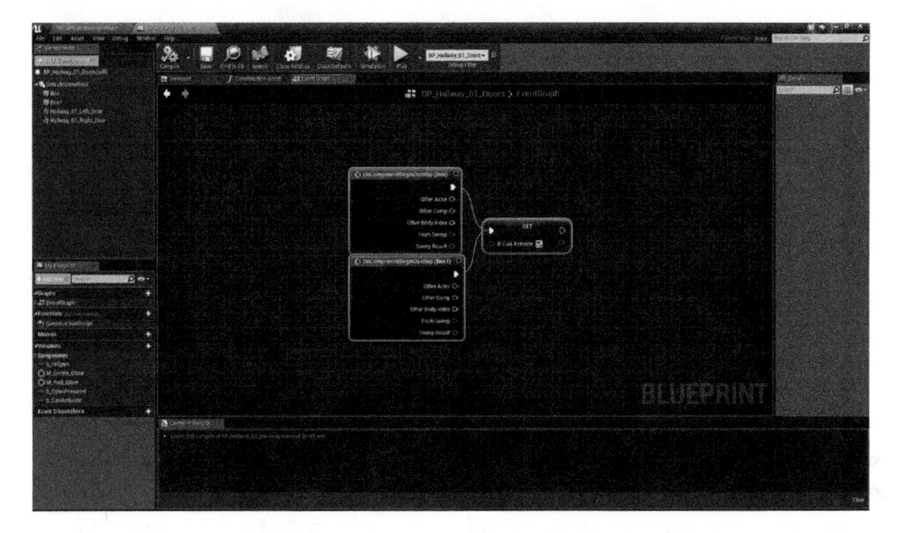

In the Components tab, select Box. In the Details tab scroll down and find the Events section. Add the *OnComponentEndOverlap(Box)*. Repeat the process for Box1. Duplicate the set node for the *b_CanAcivate* Boolean. From the out-exec of one of the *OnComponentEndOverlap*, drag off and add a Delay node. Set the duration to 0.5. Connect the completed output of the delay to the input of the second set Boolean node. Set the value of the set node to false.

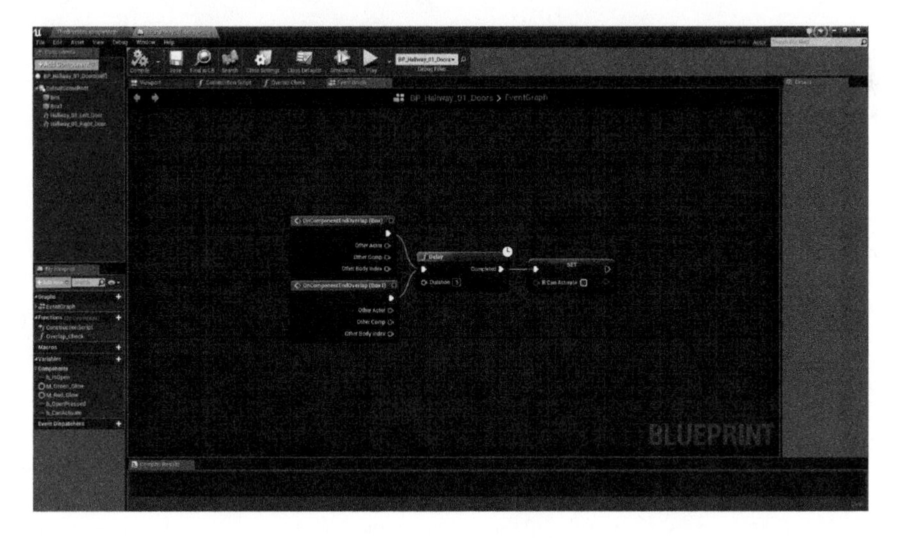

Now, your triggers will not open the door, but they will give you time to press the "E" key to open the door. Keep in mind that as long as you stay on either of the triggers, you will have as much time as you need to activate the doors. The delay to set *b_CanActivate* to false will only trigger once you leave the box.

The next part of the equation is to add the input. Right-click in the graph and expand the input section in the Context menu. Scroll down to the keyboard events section and expand it. Scroll down again to find the "E" event.

Add the "E" event to the graph. Add a Set node for *b_OpenPressed* to the graph also. Connect the Pressed out-pin from the "E" event to the in-exec of the Set node. Set the value of the B Open Pressed input to true. Duplicate the set node. Using the same method, connect it to the Released output of the "E" event and set its value to false.

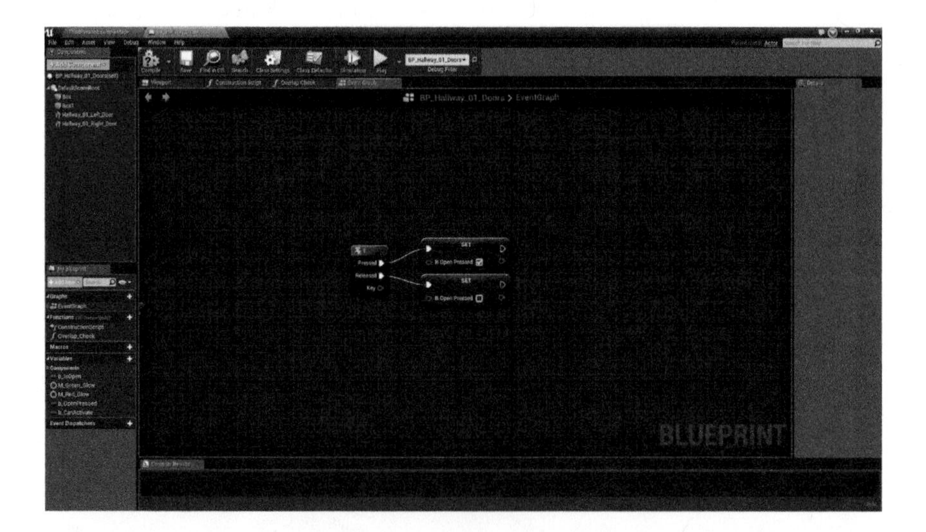

So far so good. The final piece to the puzzle is completed by connecting the *Event Tick* node with the *Get Player Controller* and *Enable Input* nodes. However, as we discussed earlier, you do not want to be able to activate the door from anywhere on the map, so you need to work through a branch node. Move the *Event Tick* node down to the rest of the main portion of the graph. Add a Get *b_CanActivate* node directly below the *Event Tick* node. From out of the Get node, drag off and add a Branch node. Since you only want to continue if the Boolean value is true, you will drag off the true output of the Branch node. Search for the *Enable Input* node and add it to the graph. You need to get the player controller before you can continue. Right-click in the graph and search for *Get Player Controller.* Add the *Get Player Controller* node to the graph. Connect the Return Value to the Player Controller input of the *Enable Input* node.

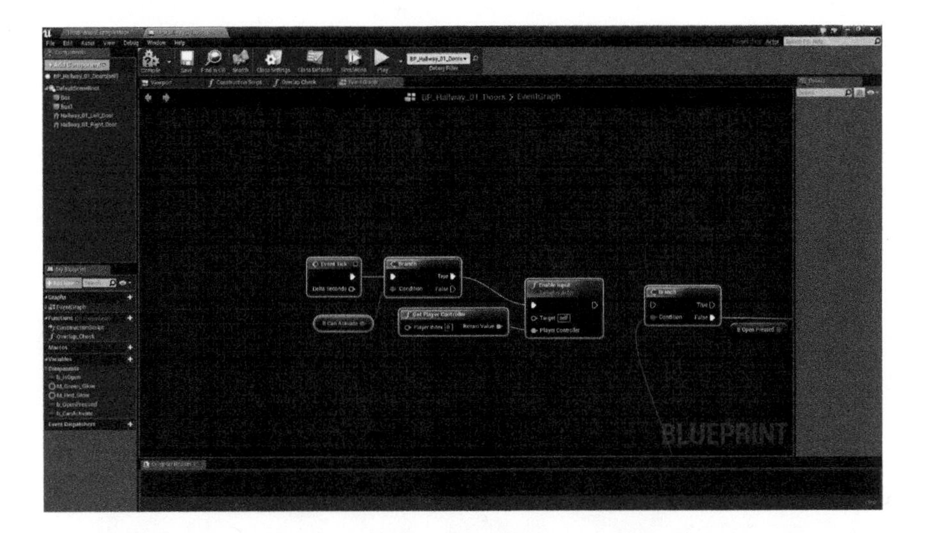

The next thing you want to check is whether the door is open or closed. You can connect the output of the *Enable Input* node to the Branch node connected to the *b_IsOpen* Boolean you added when you first created this blueprint.

While this should open the door, now you are skipping the user input section. To add the input you need to check the value of the *b_OpenPressed* Boolean. Start by adding a Get node for the variable. From the output of the Get node add another Branch node. Connect the false output of the *b_IsOpen* Branch node to the in-exec pin of the newly added Branch node. From the true output of the Branch node connected to the *b_OpenPressed*, connect it to the Set Material exec input.

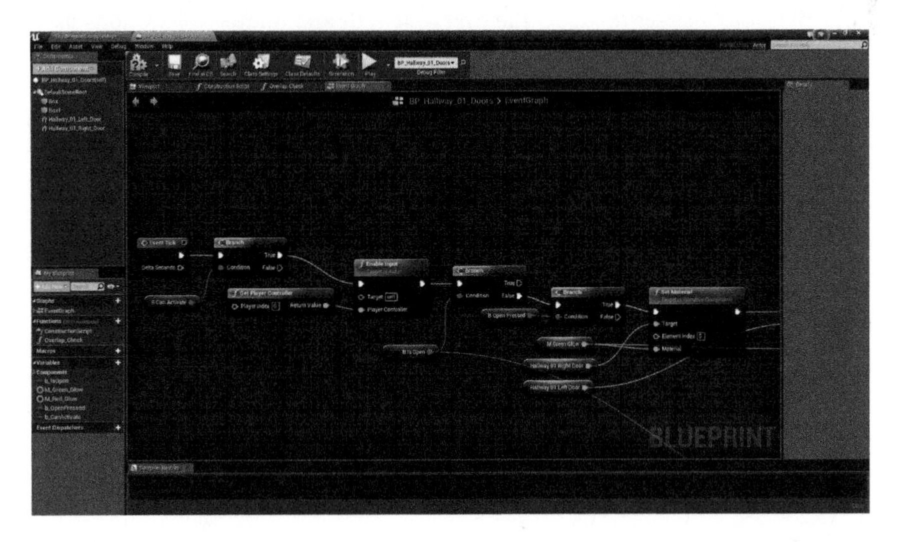

Your doors should now only work when you have entered the trigger *and* pressed the "E" key. Take a moment to test your blueprint out.

Before we close out this section, we will look at a way to clean up the blueprint slightly. Blueprints have a built-in function that allows you to group nodes together called a Comment. **Comments** surround the selected nodes and allow you to move them as a group. You can also type in a name for the comment and set the color as desired. To create a Comment, select the nodes you wish to add and press the "C" key.

Select the nodes for the triggers and "E" input and create a Comment now. Name the comment **Input Nodes.**

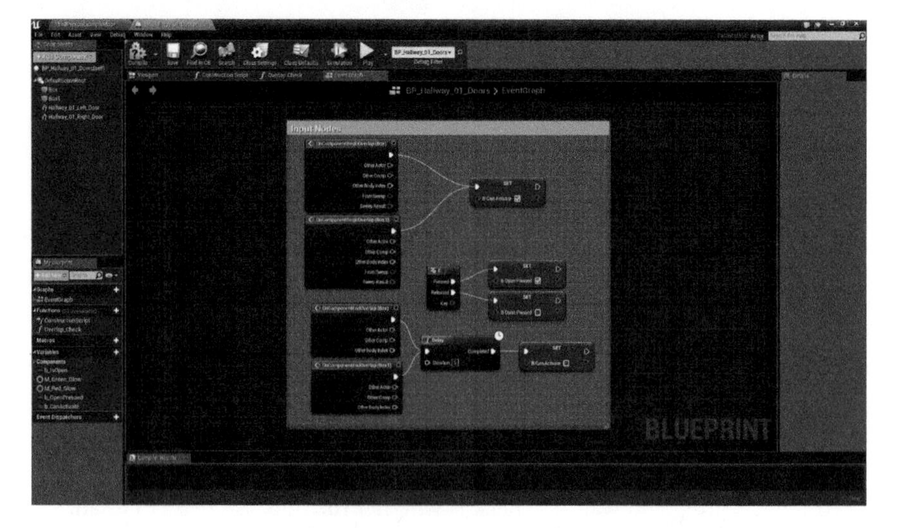

You can now move the whole group by moving the Comment wrapper or the individual nodes by selecting them and moving them. You can add or remove nodes to the Comment by dragging them into or out of the Comment wrapper respectively. Compile and save your blueprint.

Chapter Review

We covered a lot of material in this chapter. First, you created a new, straight hallway that uses a slider to adjust the overall length and number of sections used. You looked at how to add different graphs in the form of functions and also used the graph to set a number of different properties. You set static meshes within the graph, created a light, and set the color, attenuation, and intensity through the graphs. Next, you looked at how you can use a graph to change materials on selected objects. You used material swapping to change the color of the lights on the automatic doors from red to green and back. Finally, you looked at how you could add user inputs to control objects in the level. The new automatic doors now only work when the player is within range of the door *and* uses the "E" key.

While a key mechanic was not specifically covered, you could use the same method to check if a player is carrying a specific object (like a key). If the player has the key, you could then open the door. If the player does not have the key, the door could remain locked. Remember that the concepts that have been reviewed can be used and modified in a lot of different ways to create unique and exciting levels. Take the time to explore some of the different ideas that you may have come up with along the way.

12

Working with Landscapes

Introduction

Our time together is drawing to a close. In this last chapter we will be creating a landscape. Unreal has the ability to create enormous levels (a single level in Unreal Engine 4 can be as large as the entire Skyrim game). While relatively uncommon, these large levels can be great for open world games. There are a few common techniques that you will use to build some simple landscapes while adding both materials and foliage. Let us get going!

Creating and Working with Landscapes

Up to this point, you have been working with BSPs to create the base of your level. You will change gears now to create an expansive outdoor landscape. In order to continue, you will need a new level. Select File→New Level. In the New Level window, choose Default. Before you build your first landscape, remove the default ground.

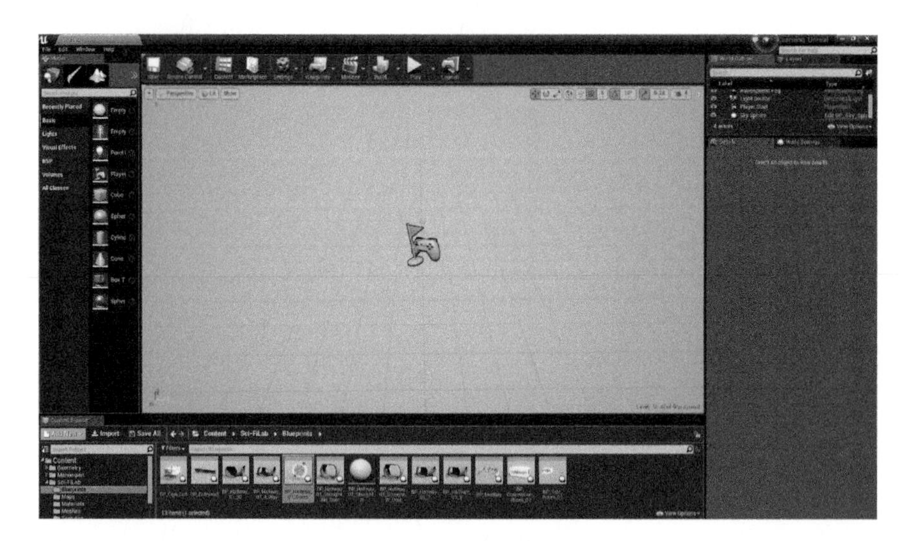

In the Modes tab, switch to the Landscape menu.

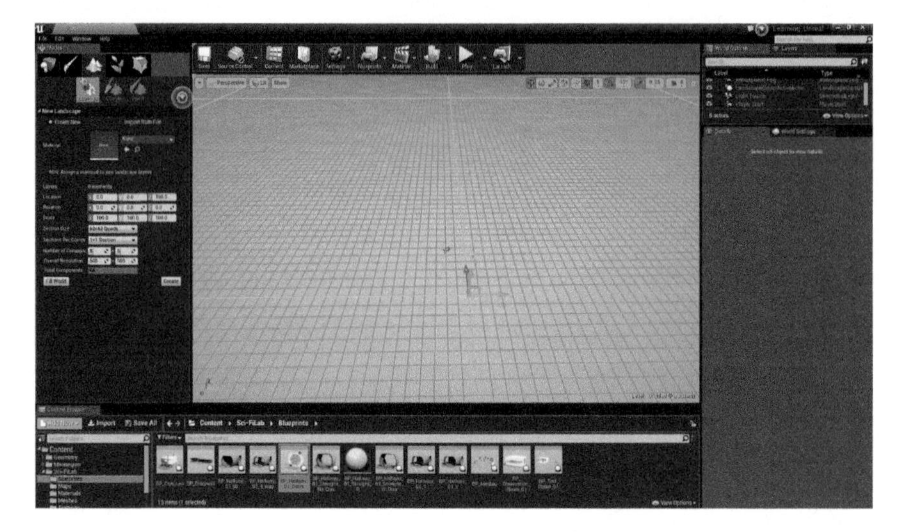

Looking at the Landscape tab, there are a few options that you need to check out. First, you should notice that there are two different options to creating the default landscape. The first one is the Create New option. This is the default option and allows you to build a landscape from scratch. Under the Create New menu, the first option is the material. Landscape materials are typically a little different from the basic materials you have been working with. Landscape materials are usually layered materials that contain different types of ground materials, like snow, grass, mud, or dirt. The landscape layered material will allow you to paint these different materials wherever you would like on the landscape.

Moving down in the Options menu, you have the Layers section. This section is controlled by the material. Next, you have the Transformation inputs. Location, rotation, and scale are all present. Following the transformations, you have the section size. Section size controls the overall detail of the landscape. A lower section size offers lower detail per section, but is much easier on the CPU; higher section sizes offer higher detail and will be harder on the CPU. While the section size will largely depend on the overall size of your level, it is generally advisable to keep the sections lower and have larger levels. If you were to build a huge level with a high number of sections the strain on the computer may be too much.

The next option is the section per component, which is a devisor of the section size. If you have a section per component value of 1 × 1, then each section size would be a single component, while a sections per component value of 2 × 2 would split the sections into 4. Both the section size and section per component will help with the level of detail (LOD) rendering; remember that having higher values will always be harder on the CPU. Number of components works with the section size to create the overall size of the landscape. This value maxes out at 32 × 32 to reduce performance issues. The last two main options are Overall Resolution, which controls the number of vertices being used by the landscape, and Total Components, which contains the total number of components created for the landscape.

Importing Landscapes

The second method of landscape creation is Import From File. Unlike the Create New method, the Import From File method uses a height map to create the basic landscape. A height map is a grayscale image that uses the scale from white to black to create the height of the landscape. When using the height map, white will represent the highest point of the level and black will represent the lowest.

Building a Landscape

You do not have a height map to work with, so you will use the Create New option. Leave the default settings as they are and click the Create button.

Now is the fun part. While sculpting the landscape is time consuming, it can be quite interesting to see the ground come into shape. The first tool you will work with is the Sculpt tool. This is the default tool and once your landscape is created, it should be the tool that is active. In the Modes tab under the Landscape Editor section, make sure that the tool is set to Sculpt. The default settings of the brush should work for your needs. To begin shaping the landscape, you can simply use the left mouse button (LMB), drag the cursor around to add height, and then hold Ctrl + Shift and LMB drag to lower the landscape.

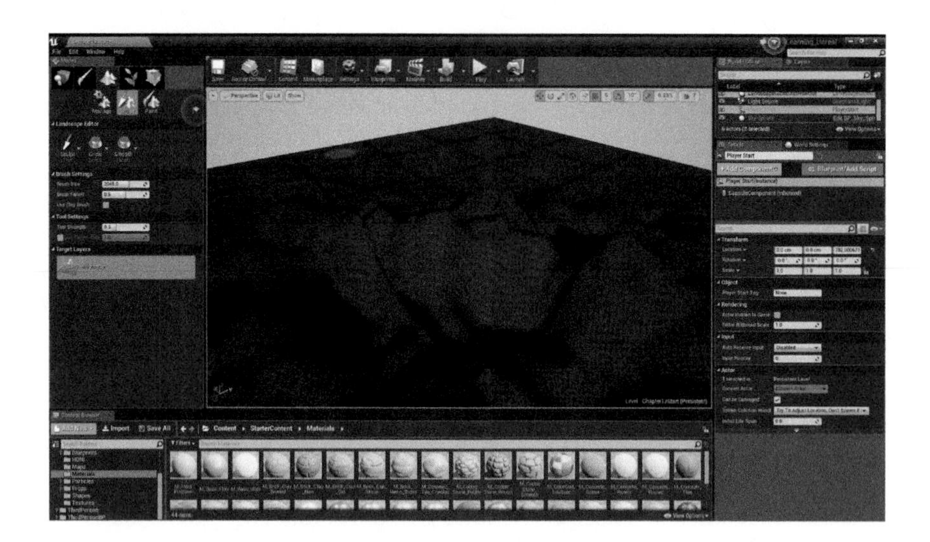

Remember that if your camera movement is slow, you can change the camera speed to a higher value in the upper right corner of the viewport. The next two tools you will look at have a similar effect on the landscape. The Smooth tool will allow you to soften the high and low areas, while the Flatten tool will adjust the landscape to the height the brush is at when it is started.

The Smooth tool results on the rough area should resemble those in the image below, while the Flatten tool results look more like those shown in the top image of the next page.

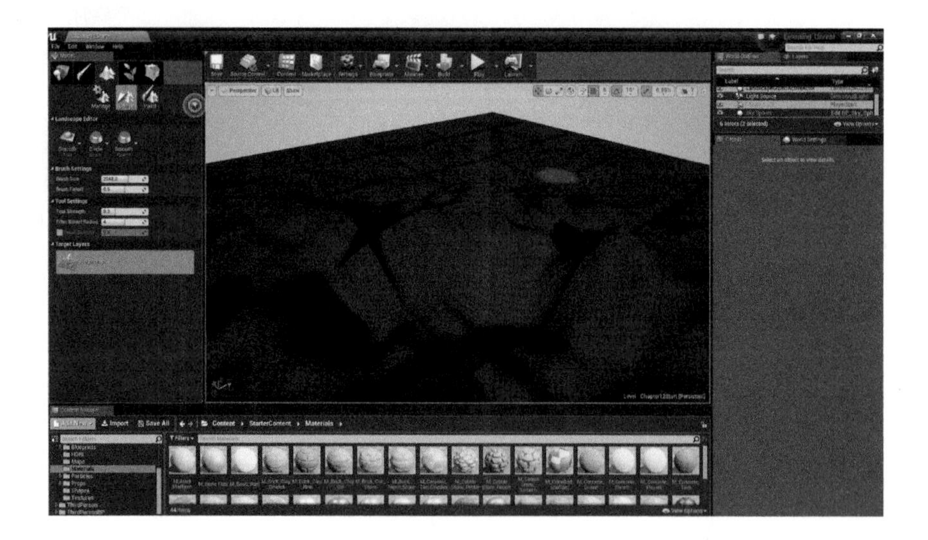

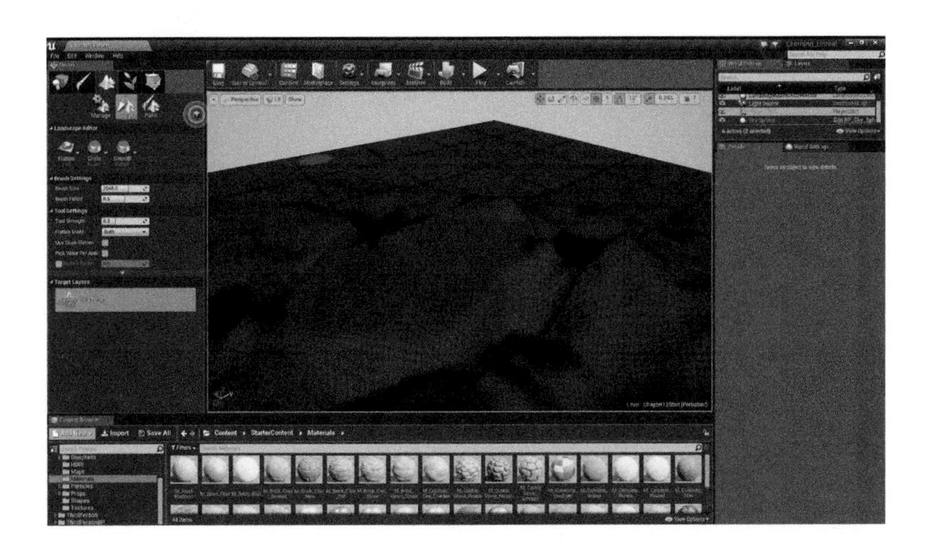

The next two tools you can look at are the Erosion tool and the Hydro-Erosion tool. Again, these two have a similar effect. The Erosion tool simulates erosion from soil moving from high to low, similarly to the image below.

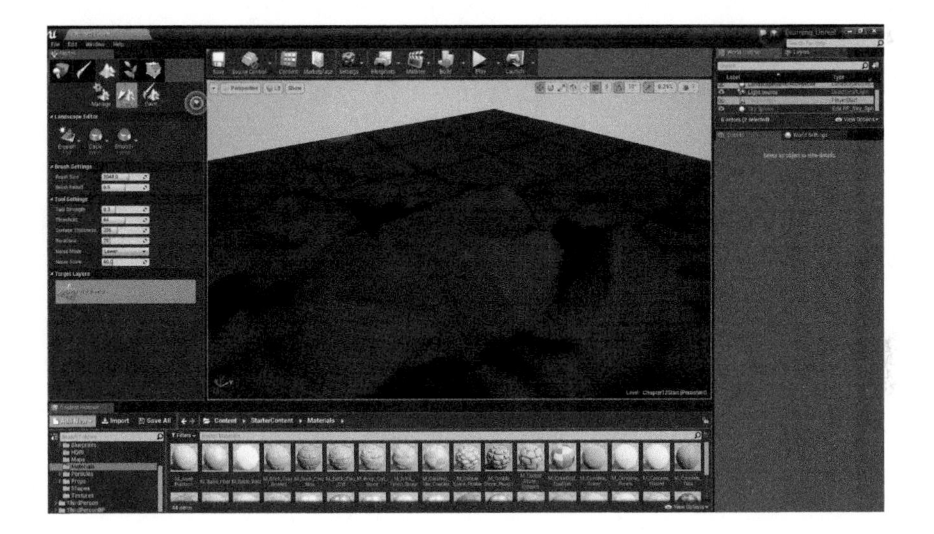

The Hydro-Erosion tool simulates erosion caused by rain.

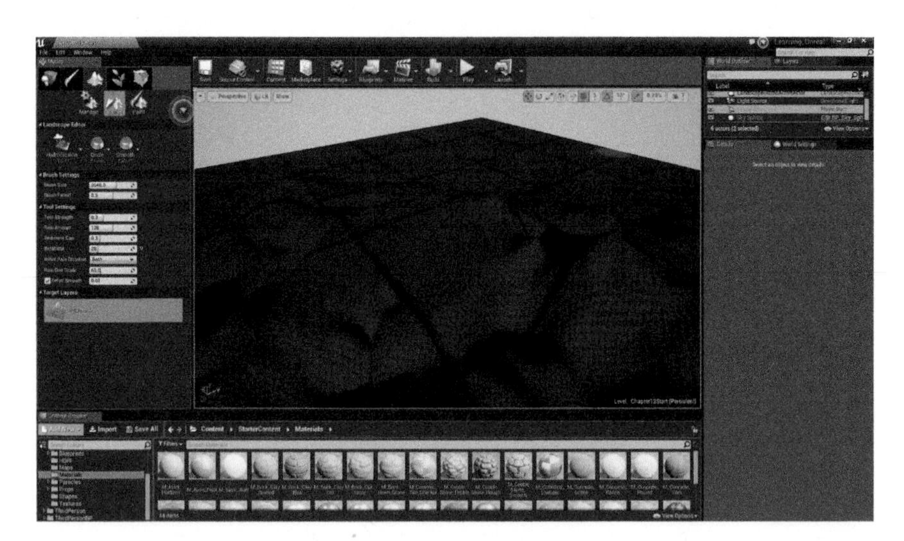

The last sculpting tool you will look at is the Noise tool. As it is referred to here, Noise is a random sculpt of both raising and lowering the landscape noise.

There are a few other tools in the menu, like the Ramp tool and the Retopologize tool. The Ramp tool creates a ramp, while the Retopologize tool recalculates the vertices to even the space between them.

Chapter Challenge

Using the different sculpting tools, try creating some tall mountains. Increase the brush size to create larger mountains and decrease the brush size to create smaller, more detailed areas. Once you have the mountains sculpted, try going into more detail by adding some paths for the player to follow. Remember to play-test the level to help get the scale correct.

Painting on Landscapes

Creating a landscape material is a bit more complex than creating the materials you have made in the past. In order to create a proper landscape material, you have to use layer blending. When using the LandscapeLayerBlend node, you can specify the number of layers, the name of a layer, and the type of blend mode used. You will create a simple landscape material that has two layers. You will use a dirt material and a grass material so that you will have an easily identifiable difference as you paint your landscape.

To begin, create a new material and name it M_Terrain. Open the new material in the Material Editor. You will need a couple textures to complete the material. In the StarterContent folder, browse to the Textures folder. Find the following textures and drag them into the graph:

- T_Ground_Grass_D
- T_Ground_Grass_N
- T_Ground_Gravel_D
- T_Ground_Gravel_N

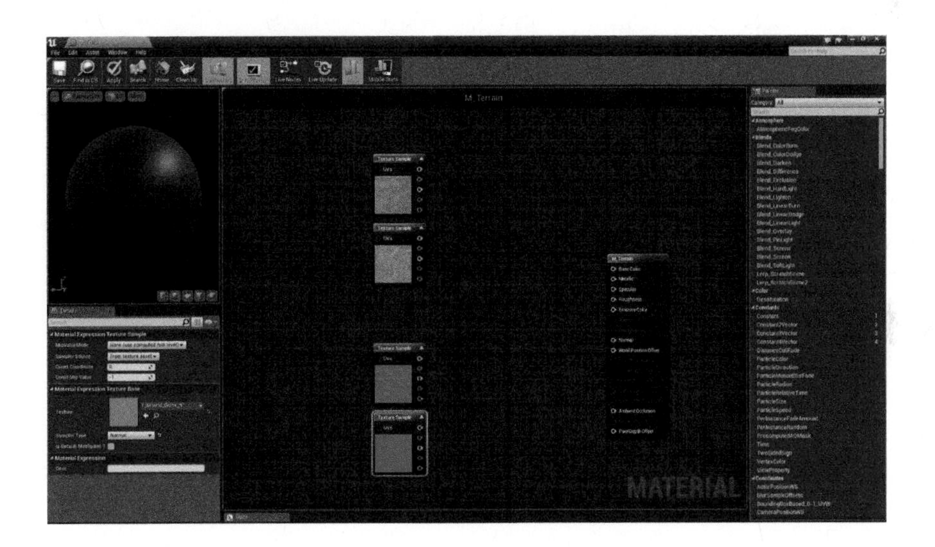

You need to add a new node named LandscapeLayerBlend.

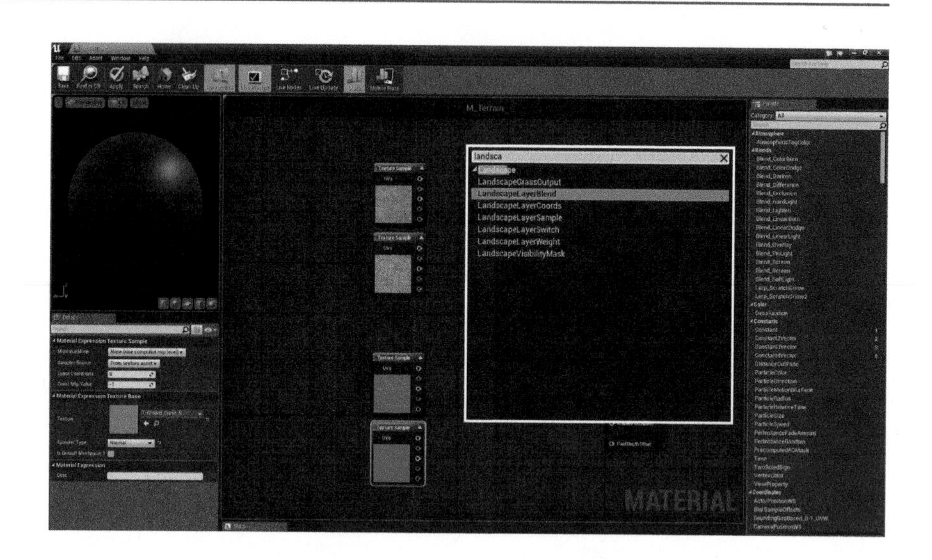

The LandscapeLayerBlend node has no inputs when it is first added to the graph. Make sure it is selected. In the Details tab, click on the + sign next to the Layers property. Name the first layer Dirt. Set the blend type to LB weight blend and the preview weight to 1.

Add a second layer. Name the second layer Grass. Set the blend type to LB height blend.

Notice that, as you add layers in the Details tab, the Layer Blend node in the graph gains inputs that are named similarly to the layer names.

Connect the T_Ground_Gravel_D texture node to the Layer Dirt input. Connect the T_Ground_Grass_D texture to the Layer Grass input. Connect the last input of the grass texture to the Height Grass input. Finally, connect the output from the Layer Blend to the Base Color input of the material.

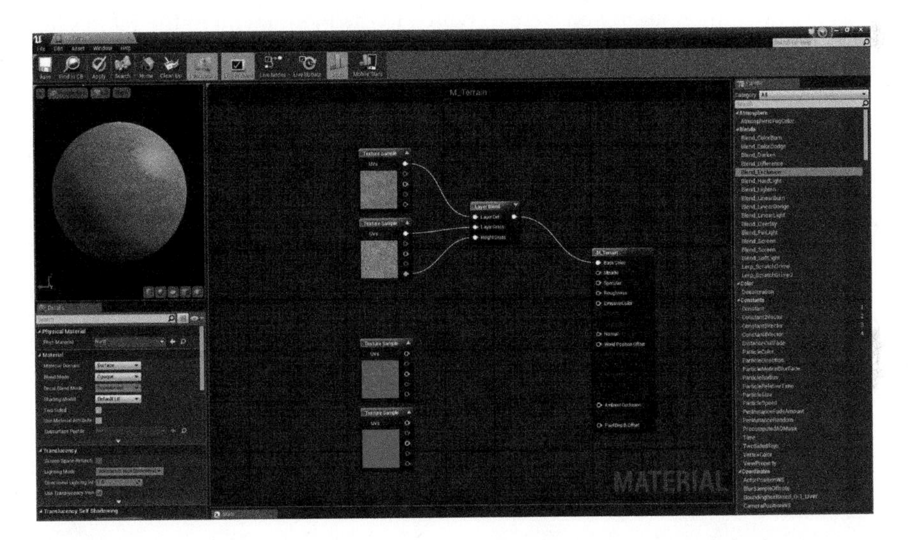

Duplicate the Layer Blend node and connect the normal textures in the same manner. You need to add two Texture Coordinate nodes. Right-click in the graph, type "coord," and then select Texture Coordinate. Duplicate it to create the second node. Connect the first of the Texture Coordinate nodes to the color textures and the second to the normal textures. For now you will leave them at their default settings. Finally, add two constants and connect them to Metallic and Roughness as you have in the past. Set the Roughness constant to 1. You should have a graph similar to that shown in the following figure.

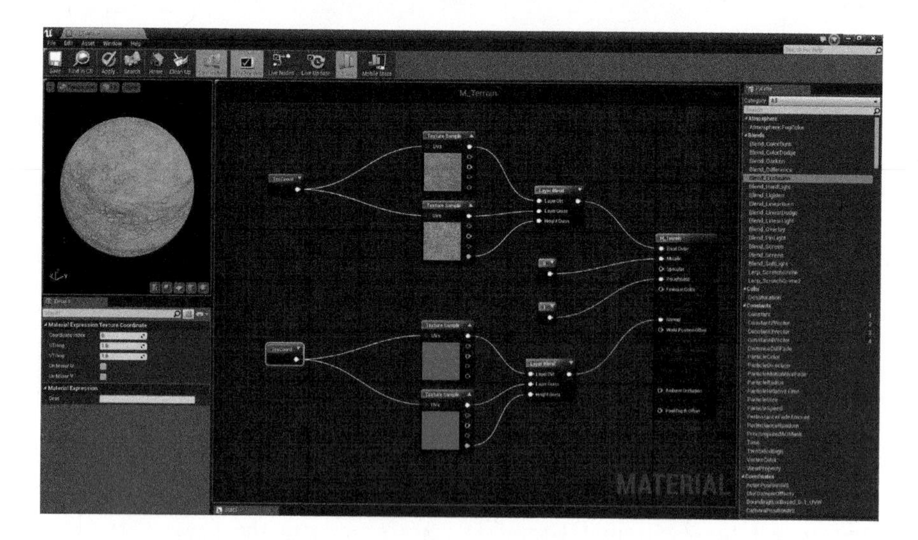

Once you have all the nodes connected, apply the changes and save the material. You can now close the Material Editor.

Since you already have a landscape created, the process of adding the material is a little different. If you were to switch to the Paint menu in the Modes tab, there would be no layer info to work with. The easiest way to add the material is to switch back to the Place mode. Before you add the material, you need to create an instance of it. Once you have switched back to Place mode, select the landscape in the viewport. It may take a moment to compile the material, but once it has completed it should apply to the landscape.

You may notice that there is a large grid that has appeared on the landscape. You do not need to be concerned about this right now, as it will disappear when you build the level. In the Modes tab, switch back to the Landscape menu. Switch to the Paint tool.

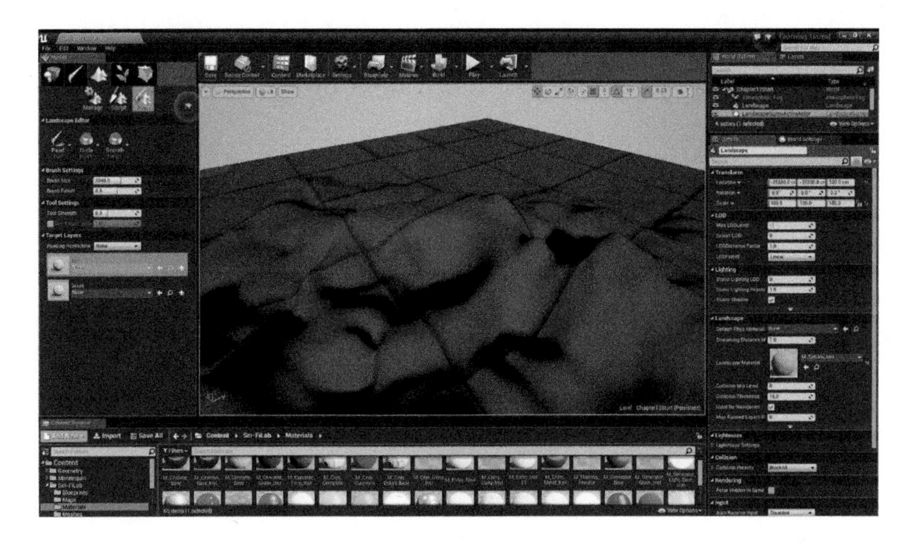

If you were to try to paint the grass texture right now, you would get an error message.

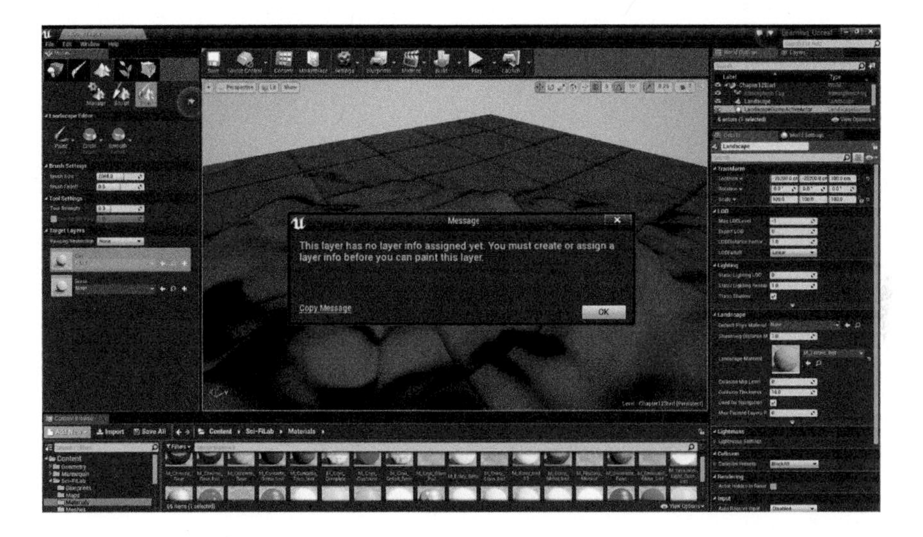

Before you can paint, you need to add the layer information. Click on the "+" beside the grass texture and choose Weight-Blended Layer (Normal). A dialog box will open, asking you for a location to save. By default it will add a new folder. Click OK to continue.

Click on a section of the landscape to add the grass texture. You may notice right away that it will not allow you to paint parts of the landscape, but rather add it to entire sections. This is because there is no layer information for the dirt layer. Click the + beside "Dirt" to add the layer info. Now you can paint either the grass or the dirt. As you paint, you may notice that a new issue arises. Large black areas show up as you paint. To remove the sections, simply paint over them. You should be able to blend the layers now as you see fit.

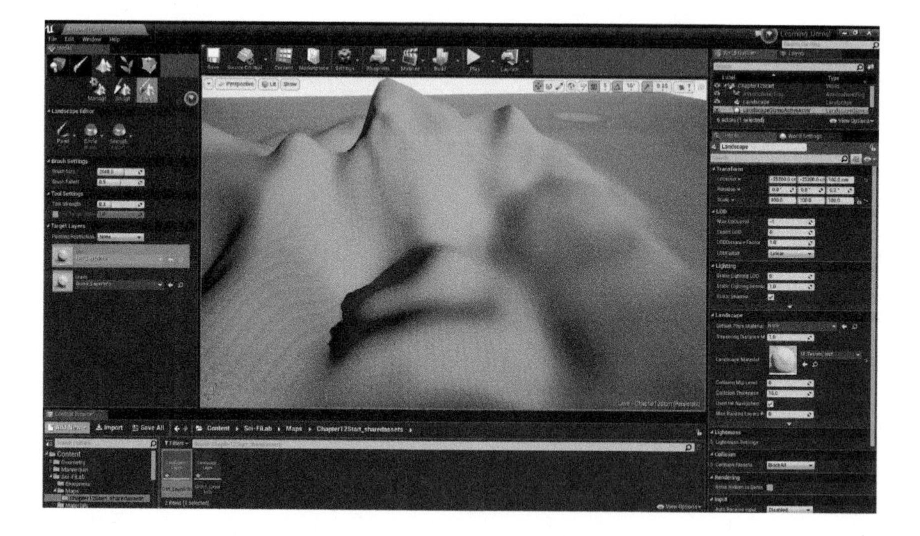

As you continue to paint, you may notice the texture repeats quite often, but does not appear quite right. You can move back to the Material Editor by opening the M_Terrain material. The Texture Coordinate nodes you added earlier control how the tiling of the material appears.

The before-adjustment material appears like that shown in the following image.

By adjusting the TexCoord node connected to the color inputs to 0.25 for both UTiling and VTiling, you should get a much smoother result.

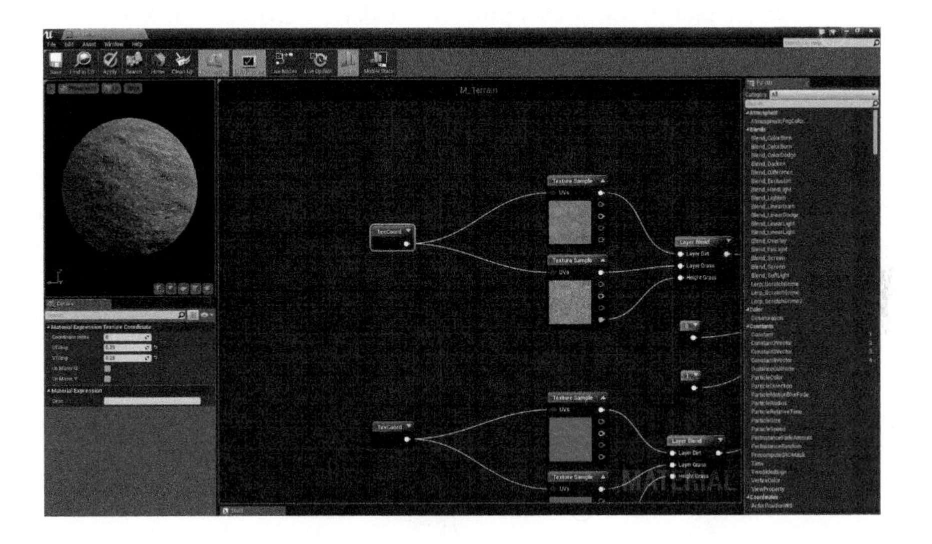

The end result should appear more like that shown in the next image.

You can continue to adjust the TexCoord settings as you see fit. Remember that you should also adjust the TexCoord connected to the normal textures.

Adding Water

Adding water is a relatively simple process. Before you start, we need to talk about some of the limitations. If you are working with a third-person project, you should know that while you can make a water volume that reacts as you would expect (slower movement, color changes), the default character does not have "swimming" animations. This means that, as you enter the water, your character movement will be restricted because of the friction of the water; however, the character animations will still be walking or running.

To begin, you need to sculpt a place for the water to reside. After you have sculpted an area for the water, you need to add a plane to cover the hole. In the content browser, select the Content folder. In the right-hand side next to Filters, type "plane."

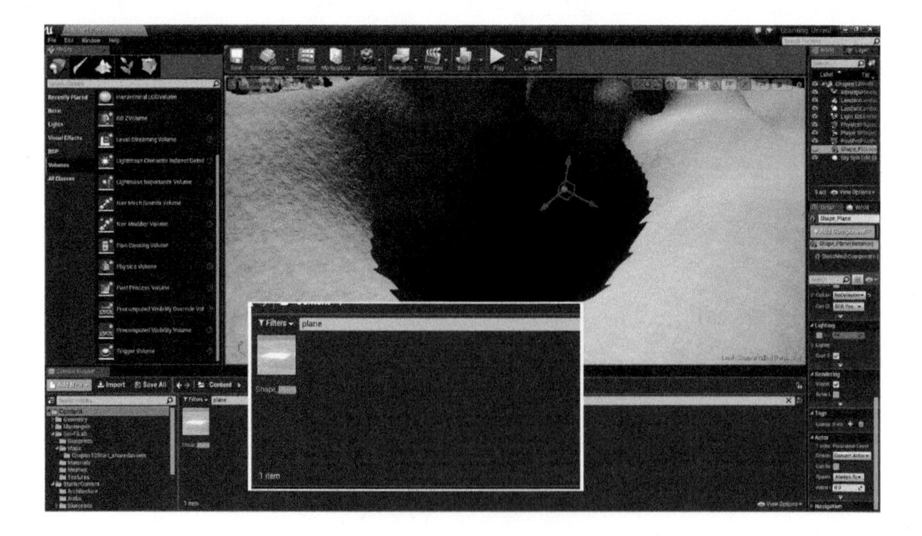

Add the plane to the level and resize it to cover the area you sculpted earlier. Use the search function again to find a water material. There are two in the Starter Content. You can drag either one onto the plane.

The next step is to add a **physics volume**. In the Modes tab under the Place menu, select Volumes. Scroll down to find Physics Volume. Add the volume to the level. Use the Brush settings to resize the brush so that it covers the sculpted area. Be sure that the volume runs from the plane all the way down past the lowest point of the landscape. Once you have the volume in place, scroll down in the Details tab to the Character Movement section. Check the Water Volume checkbox. You can now test your water. You should notice that the character's movement is drastically different inside the water than it is outside the water. However, it does not look like water inside. You can use another volume called a **Post Process Volume**, which has a lot of different uses, but, for your needs, you will use it to change the color while inside. Set the size and location to match your physics volume. With the Post Process Volume still selected, find the post process volume section in the Details tab. Expand the Settings properties. Under Scene Color, check the Scene Color Tint checkbox. Set the color value to a light blue. Build your level. Play-test your level and you should have an effect similar to that in the next image.

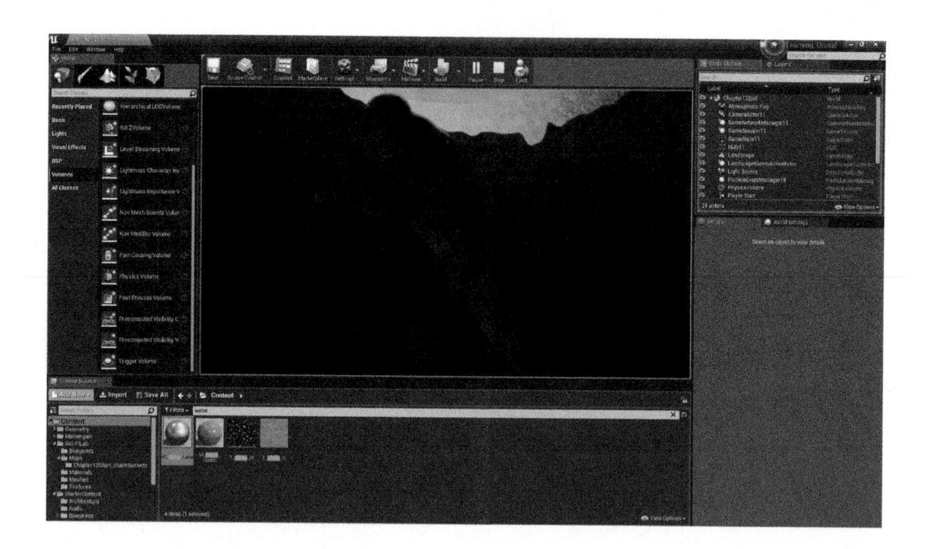

Since you do not have any "swimming" animations, this is about as far as you can get with your water. If you do implement water, be sure that the player can get out of the water by walking up the side. Hopefully, there will be some animations added later.

Adding Foliage

Foliage is another way to help break up the look and feel of a large landscape. The Paint Foliage tool works similarly to the Layer Paint tool. In the Modes tab, switch to the Foliage menu.

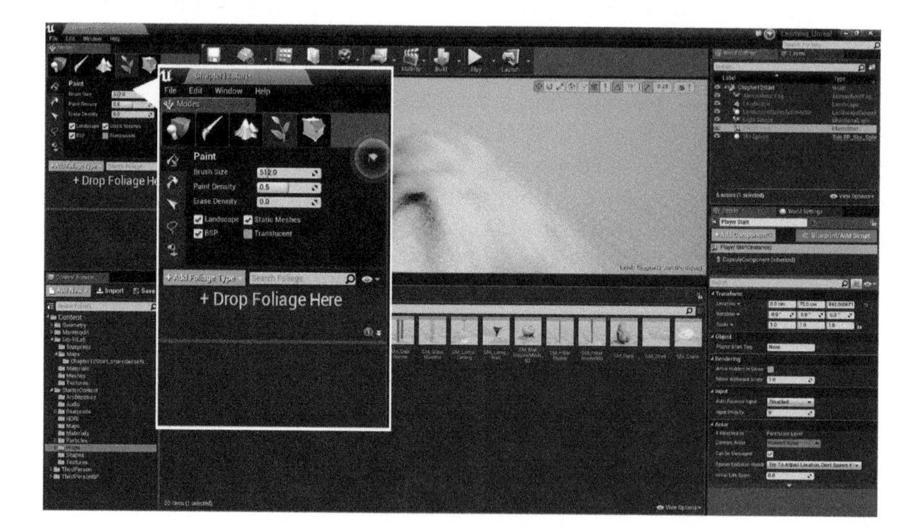

In the content browser, open the Props folder within the StarterContent folder. Find the SM_Bush mesh and drag it to the + Drop Foliage Here section of the Modes tab.

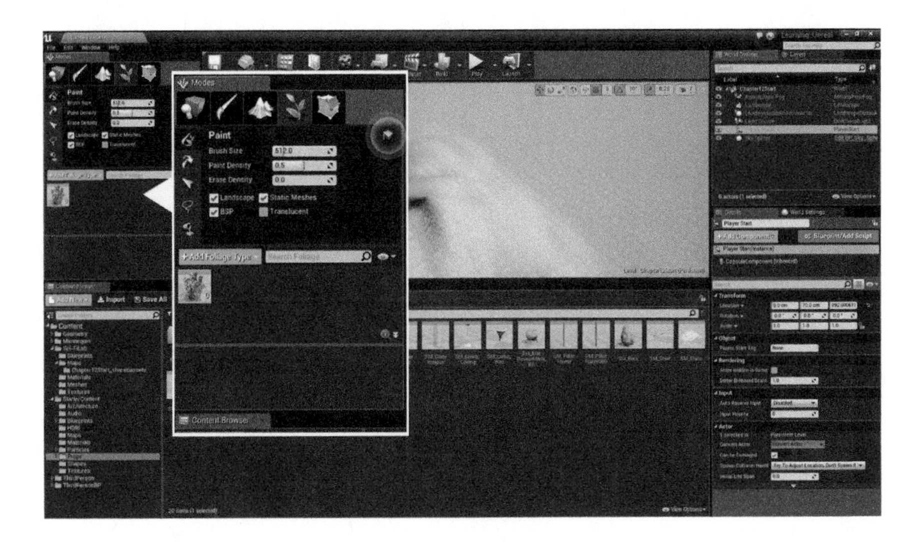

Now you can paint the bushes onto your landscape.

Take your time painting. Use the Brush Size, Paint Density, and Erase Density settings to change how the bushes are painted. Do not forget to play-test your level. In-game appearance will differ from the Editor view slightly.

Before we close out this chapter, there is one final part you can look at. Even though the mode you are currently using is called Foliage Painting, you can actually use nearly any mesh as foliage. For example, you could add SM_Rock to the Foliage types and paint rocks on your landscape.

Chapter Challenge

Try creating a new landscape that uses a combination of all the things learned in this chapter. Use the sculpting tools along with texture and foliage painting to see what different combinations you can create. There are a number of different textures you can add to your terrain material. Add layers using the same method as before.

Chapter Review

In this chapter we took a closer look at creating landscapes. Using the different landscape tools, you sculpted hills and valleys. You also took some time to create a simple terrain material with two layers. You looked at how to paint foliage onto your landscape and, finally, took a quick look at how to add water effects to a level.

You should now have all the tools necessary to create a vast array of levels. From indoor close-quarter designs to expansive landscapes, you have all the knowledge you need. I hope that you have enjoyed this book and feel like you are ready to create levels on your own. While we did not directly cover the combination of landscape and buildings, you have learned how to create each type separately, so you should have no problem combining the two.

Index

2D projects, 3, 4
3D projects, 4, 7–11

A

Accuracy option, 96–98
Actors
  adding, 181–192
  options for, 53–54
  physics for, 189–192
Additive brush, 34–35; *see also* Brush Settings
Additive BSP, 35, 40–41, 80; *see also* Binary space partitions
Animation
  automatic doors, 133–156
  blueprint animation, 133–164
  character animation, 246–247
  matinee options, 156–163
Assets, adding, 11, 33
Assets, importing, 47–50
Atmosphere, creating, 11
Attenuation Radius, 61–62, 68, 216–218
Auto Convex Collision, 94–98, 156, 187, 191
Auto Generate Collision, 48–49
Automatic doors, creating, 133–156

B

Balconies, creating, 30–31, 55–56
Basement
  creating, 40–46
  lighting for, 119–120, 123–124
  stairs and, 40–46
  walls for, 40–46
Binary space partitions (BSPs)
  additive BSP, 35, 40–41, 80
  for blocking, 30–35, 40–43, 48, 53, 56, 59–62
  blocking volumes and, 16, 53–55, 62, 74, 78–81, 88–89
  blueprints and, 74, 78–81, 86–88
  for foundation, 16–20
  Geometry Editing mode for, 24–31
  hierarchal system for, 35
  for landscapes, 233
  for levels, 11, 15–31
  subtractive BSP, 35, 40–41, 80
Blocking process
  finishing blocking, 33–62
  first level blocking, 11–12, 15–31
Blocking volume
  collisions and, 97–99
  converting BSPs into, 16, 53–55, 62, 74, 78–81, 88–89
  explanation of, 11, 16
  swapping process and, 53–55
Blueprint Editor
  for automatic doors, 135
  for blocking levels, 50–51
  for hallways, 205–206
  for modifying blueprints, 91–93
Blueprints
  advanced techniques, 205–232
  animation, 133–164
  binary space partitions, 74, 78–81, 86–88
  components, 51–52
  creating, 50–51, 63–99
  error checking, 88–89
  hallway blueprints, 63–78, 205–224
  interacting with, 228–232
  Level Blueprint, 123–124, 131, 160–164
  modifying, 89–92

options, 51–52
toolbar, 51
viewport, 51
Box collisions, 135–136, 189–191
Boxes, creating, 23–25, 29–30
Brush Settings
additive brush, 34–35
for floors, 20–23
for foundation, 16–17
order options, 35
subtractive brush, 34–35
Build options, 37–38

C

C++ projects, 3
Camera group, 157–158
Camera options, 6, 27, 157–164
Camera speed, 6
Cascade Editor, 194–196, 203
Channels, modifying, 109
Character animation, 246–247
Character layers, 172
Character movement, 246–247
Collision menu, 94–98, 135–136, 189–191
Collision Volume, 94, 183, 190
Collisions, correcting, 92–98
Color nodes, 108, 174–175, 195–196, 217
Color Over Life module, 196, 199–200, 202
Colors
adjusting, 109–110
changing, 224–228
converting, 108
of materials, 103–106, 114, 169–175, 224–228
Particle Color, 195–196
time-based materials, 169–172
Components, adding, 51–52, 68, 135–137, 207–224
Concrete materials, 114
Constant node, 57–58, 103–104, 112
Content browser, 5, 11–12
Content folder, 4–5, 11–12
Convert Actor option, 53–54
Convex Decomposition tab, 96
Corners, correcting, 97–98
Create Material Instance, 59–60
Curve Editor, 157, 202–203

D

Details panel, 5, 16, 57, 61
Details tab, 7, 11, 16, 19
Directional light, 118; *see also* Lighting
Dirt, adding, 234, 239–244
Doorframes, adding, 89–92
Doorways
automatic doors, 133–156
creating, 34–36, 43–44, 78–86, 133–156
doorframes for, 89–92
interactive doors, 228–231

E

Editing mode, 24–31
Editor Preferences, 7
Emitters, 196–202
Entrywall blueprint, 50, 53
Entryway, creating, 36–39, 49–52, 56, 59
Entryway blueprint, 50–52
Erosion tool, 237
Error checking, 88–89
Escalators, creating, 56
Event graph, 138–147, 155, 164, 206, 227–230
Extrude function, 25–26, 82–86

F

First-person projects, 3, 4, 6
Flatten tool, 236
Floors
adding, 206–209, 220–221
Brush Settings, 20–23
creating, 20–22
number of, 23–31
ramps and, 23–32
resizing, 39
stairs and, 22–32
Flying projects, 3
Foliage, adding, 248–250
Foundation, building, 16–20

G

Game types, 3–4
Geometry Editing mode, 24–31, 80–86, 97
Get option, 140–141
Get Player Controller, 160–163, 228–231
Grass, adding, 234, 239–244
Grid toggle, 6, 18, 22
Ground, creating, 15–20, 44; *see also* Floors

H

Hallways
blueprints for, 63–78, 205–224
creating, 38–39, 47–50, 63–78, 205–224

custom lengths, 205–224
lighting for, 119–121, 123–124
materials for, 101–115
modifying, 89–98
Hills, adding, 238–239
Hydro-Erosion tool, 237

I

Import options, 47–50, 90, 165–166
Initial Size module, 196, 198
Initial Velocity module, 196, 199
Input nodes, 228–232
Interactive doors, 228–231

L

Landscapes
binary space partitions, 233
building, 235–239
creating, 233–235, 250
dirt, 234, 239–244
erosion, 237
foliage, 248–250
grass, 234, 239–244
hills, 238–239
importing, 235
layered materials on, 172, 234
mountains, 238–239
painting on, 239–246
rain, 237
sculpting tools for, 235–240, 246–247, 250
terrains, 239–250
valleys, 238–239
water, 246–248
working with, 233–250
Layered materials; *see also* Materials
on characters, 172
creating, 172–180
on landscapes, 172, 234
on textures, 172
Layers tab, 78–84
Level Blueprint, 123–124, 131, 160–164
Levels
adding BSPs to, 11, 15–31
assets for, 11, 33, 47–50
atmosphere for, 11
blocking process, 11–12, 15–31, 33–62
cleaning up, 47–48
concept for, 9–13
creating, 9–13, 15–16, 250
creating landscapes, 233–235
default level, 8, 12–13
design of, 9–13
details for, 11
fine-tuning, 11
floors and, 20–32
lighting for, 11
naming folders, 4–5, 11–12
populating, 165–192
stairs and, 22–32
swapping process and, 52–56
work flow for, 10–11
Lifetime module, 196, 198
Light sources, 18–20, 37–38, 60–61, 117–118
Lighting
for basement, 119–120, 123–124
building, 11, 37–38, 118
directional light, 118
for hallways, 119–121, 123–124
intensity of, 118
lightmass importance volume, 118, 131
for lobby, 118–120
options for, 37–38
point lights, 60–61, 118, 126
reflections, 119–121, 131
sky light, 118
sources of, 18–20, 37–38, 60–61, 117–118
spot light, 118
techniques for, 117–118
toggleable lighting, 122–131
trigger volumes, 122–125, 128–129
turning on and off, 122–123, 128–131
Lighting mode, 55
Lighting options, 37–38
Lighting quality, 38
Lighting techniques, 117–118
Lightmass importance volume, 118, 131
Linear Interpolate node, 107
Linear stair, 22, 31, 40–44; *see also* Stairs
Lobby
blocking, 33
lighting for, 118–120
physics for, 189
resizing, 39

M

Manipulator, 6
Material Attributes, 103, 175–181
Material Editor, 57, 101–115, 169, 173
Material Functions, 173–175, 192
Material Graph, 57

Material Instance, 59–60, 109, 115, 225
Material Palette, 57
Materials
changing, 57–58, 112–113, 224–228
colors of, 103–106, 114, 169–172, 224–228
concrete materials, 114
concrete textures, 114
creating, 56–59
folder for, 57, 102, 110–115, 169–173
for hallways, 101–115
importing, 49
input types, 103
layered materials, 172–180, 234
opacity of, 110–111
options, 102–109
textures, 101–109
time-based materials, 169–172
types of, 101–103
Matinee Editor, 156–159, 164
Matinee options, 156–163
Max Hull Verts option, 96–98
Mesh objects, 47–50; *see also* Static Mesh
Meshes folder, 48–51, 55, 63–64, 90–93, 113, 133, 165
Modes panel, 5, 16, 22–24, 61
Modes tab, 16, 27
Modules, 196–203
Mountains, adding, 238–239
Move gizmo, 6–7, 17, 19, 26
Movement Options, 6–7, 17–18, 22
Multiply node, 114
Music, adding, 11
My Blueprint tab, 51, 140, 206–212, 225, 229

O

Objects, grouping, 50, 78–84, 133
Objects, importing, 47–50, 165–169
Opacity, adjusting, 110–111
Order options, 35

P

Palette, 57
Particle Color, 195–196
Particle systems
Cascade Editor, 194–196, 203
Curve Editor, 202–203
Emitters, 196–202
Particle Color, 195–196
Perspective view, 6, 8, 26–28, 74
Physics, adding, 189–192, 247
Physics Volume, 247
Pick Parent Class, 50
Player Start, 17–18, 49, 88
PlayerCamera, 160–164
Point lights, 60–61, 118, 126; *see also* Lighting
Populating levels, 165–192; *see also* Levels
Post Process Volume, 247
Projects
choosing, 2–4
creating, 2–4, 8, 15–16
naming, 4–5, 11–12
new projects, 2–5, 8–13, 15–16
space requirements, 4
types of, 3–4
Puzzle projects, 3

R

Rain, adding, 237
Ramps, creating, 23–32, 238
Ramps, swapping, 56
Reflection Capture node, 119
Reflection nodes, 119–121, 131
Required module, 196–197
Rolling projects, 3
Roofs, adding, 29, 52
Rotate gizmo, 6–7, 19, 22

S

Scale gizmo, 6–7
Sculpting tools, 235–240, 246–247, 250
Set option, 140–141
Show menu, 6
Side-scroller template, 3
Sky Sphere, 19–20
Smoke, adding, 184, 193–195, 202
Smooth tool, 236
Snapping toggle, 6, 18, 22
Sound, adding, 11
Space modifier, 6
Spawn module, 196, 198
Sphere Reflection Capture node, 119
Stairs
basement and, 40–46
creating, 22–32, 40–46
floors and, 22–32
linear stair, 22, 31, 40–44
swapping, 56
Starter content folder, 4–5, 11–12
Static Mesh
for components, 207–226
for ground, 15–16
for levels, 51–52, 55

Static Mesh Editor
for animation, 134–137
for collisions, 97–99, 156, 189–190
for materials, 113, 224–226
for walls, 92–93
Steam, adding, 193–197, 202–203
Subtractive brush, 34–35; *see also* Brush Settings
Subtractive BSP, 35, 40–41, 80; *see also* Binary space partitions
Swapping process, 52–56
Swarm Agent, 38

T

Tab system, 4–5
Terrains, 239–250; *see also* Landscapes
Textures
adding, 104–109
concrete textures, 114
dirt, 234, 239–244
file types for, 101–102
grass, 234, 239–244
importing, 49, 102
layered materials on, 172
time-based materials, 169–172
types of, 101–103, 112
Third-person projects, 3, 4, 8, 246
Time-based materials, 169–172; *see also* Materials
Timeline, 145–151, 154–160, 164
Toggle Visibility, 126–129
Toggleable lighting, 122–131; *see also* Lighting
Toolbar, 5
Top-down projects, 3
Tracks tab, 157
Trigger Volumes, 122–125, 128–129, 135, 228
Twin stick shooter projects, 3

U

Unreal Editor, 4–8
Unreal Engine
space requirements, 4
user interface, 4–8
versions, 1–2
Unreal Launcher, 1–2, 8
Unreal Project Browser, 2
User Inputs, 228–232
User interface, 4–8

V

Variable Type, 140–141, 161, 206, 210, 225
Vector node, 58, 103, 112, 114
Vehicle projects, 3
View mode, 6
Viewport maneuvers, 7–8
Viewport maximize, 6
Viewport options, 6–8, 51
Viewport restore, 6
Volumes; *see also* Blocking volume
Collision Volume, 94, 97–99, 183, 190
Physics Volume, 247
Post Process Volume, 247
Trigger Volumes, 122–125, 128–129, 135, 228
Water Volume, 246–247

W

Walls
basement walls, 40–46
blocking in, 20–22, 92–97
building, 16–20, 22–32
walking through, 92–97
Water, adding, 246–248
Water Volume, 246–247
World Outliner, 5, 7, 17–19, 60–61, 78–79